Contributions to Economics

The series *Contributions to Economics* provides an outlet for innovative research in all areas of economics. Books published in the series are primarily monographs and multiple author works that present new research results on a clearly defined topic, but contributed volumes and conference proceedings are also considered. All books are published in print and ebook and disseminated and promoted globally.

The series and the volumes published in it are indexed by Scopus and ISI (selected volumes).

More information about this series at https://link.springer.com/bookseries/1262

Linda Glawe • Helmut Wagner

The Economic Rise of East Asia

Development Paths of Japan, South Korea, and China

Springer

Linda Glawe
University of Hagen
Hagen, Germany

Helmut Wagner
University of Hagen
Hagen, Germany

ISSN 1431-1933 ISSN 2197-7178 (electronic)
Contributions to Economics
ISBN 978-3-030-87127-7 ISBN 978-3-030-87128-4 (eBook)
https://doi.org/10.1007/978-3-030-87128-4

This Springer imprint is published by the registered company Springer Nature Switzerland AG
The registered company address is: Gewerbestrasse 11, 6330 Cham, Switzerland

Preface

The East Asian countries can look back on half a century of economic rises or "miracles", during which many have evolved from the status of very poor, backward countries to highly developed prosperous, often even rich, countries. In other words, the post-World War II period evolved into a success story for East Asian countries, which serves as a model for many other developing and emerging economies today. What is behind this success story? This is the question we explore in this book. We look into the driving forces behind this extraordinarily positive story.

In doing so, we use the examples of Japan, South Korea, and China to examine whether there are commonalities that justify the image of an "East Asian development model" or strategy. Also, whether there are common challenges for the (foreseeable) future that generate similar responses in East Asia. At the same time, however, we also elaborate on the differences between the three countries in terms of these strategies and responses.

This book emerged from an intensive study of the relevant literature as well as from on-the-ground observations in East Asia over the past years and decades.

For helpful comments over the years, we thank the participants and discussants at our many presentations on East Asian topics at conferences (among others of the American Economic Association (in Philadelphia), the Econometric Society (in Shanghai, Seoul, and Miri/online), the European Economic Association (in Cologne), the previous World Congresses of the Comparative Economic Association (in Rome and Saint Petersburg)), and at the guest lectures of Helmut Wagner on East Asian, especially Chinese development strategies in recent years at Harvard University (Fairbanks Center), Xiamen University (Xiamen, China), the Bank of International Settlements (in Basel and in Hong Kong), the International Monetary Fund (Asian Department; in Washington, DC), and other places. The experiences (with lectures, discussions, exchange of ideas) of Helmut Wagner's longer stays (visiting professorships) in Japan at the Bank of Japan, at Hitotsubashi University (Tokyo), the EU Studies Institute in Tokyo, and in China at various universities since 1981 should also be mentioned as background for writing this book.

Hagen, Germany
July 2021

Linda Glawe
Helmut Wagner

Contents

1 Introduction

East Asian countries have shown impressive growth and development successes over the last 70 years. This sometimes led to the statement of an "East Asian miracle". Not infrequently, there has even been talked of an imminent (East) Asian century.

These statements are based on the following empirical facts: While, in 1950, all East Asian countries were still underdeveloped (with the exception of Japan, whose level of development, however, had declined sharply after the defeat in World War II), all of them caught up exceptionally fast over time and reached the level of a developed rich (high-income) country (except for China,[1] which started later but is currently on its way).

In the following, we look into several development indicators:

In Table 1.1, we choose GDP/capita as the most common, significant economic measure of development, which measures the average economic wealth of a country.

Table 1.1 shows that all East Asian countries have experienced outstanding GDP per capita growth between 1960 and 2019 (except for Japan which has only grown at best modestly over the past decades but experienced a threefold increase in per capita income between 1960 and 1980). With the exception of China, all East Asian countries listed in our table have already managed to rise to the ranks of high-income countries and have even partly overtaken the UK and the USA (see also Table 6.1 in Chap. 6).

[1] Throughout the book, we use China as an abbreviation for Mainland China.

L. Glawe and H. Wagner, *The Economic Rise of East Asia*,
Contributions to Economics, https://doi.org/10.1007/978-3-030-87128-4_1

Table 1.1 The development process in East Asia (measured by GDP p.c.)

	Japan	South Korea	China	Taiwan	Hong Kong	Singapore*	USA**	UK**
Panel A: GDP p.c. (2010 US$)								
1960	8608	932	192	–	–	3503	17,563	13,934
1980	25,855	3679	347	–	10,727	13,534	28,590	21,865
1990	38,075	8496	729	–	18,250	22,572	36,059	28,695
2000	42,170	15,414	1768	–	23,015	33,851	44,727	35,673
2010	44,508	23,087	4550	–	32,550	47,237	48,468	39,436
2019	49,188	28,675	8242	–	37,928	58,830	55,753	43,511
Panel B: GDP p.c. (PPP)								
1950	2879	–	–	–	–	–	15,734	9967
1960	5821	1225	996	2554	4148	2753	18,901	12,861
1980	21,001	5097	1680	11,443	16,538	12,836	30,788	21,380
1990	28,534	13,168	2478	21,249	26,370	21,527	39,059	25,199
2000	36,830	24,278	4272	35,589	38,861	41,271	50,089	35,660
2010	38,652	35,447	10,127	43,518	53,039	77,815	53,666	40,132
2019	39,637	40,819	13,988	48,896	59,245	88,619	63,393	46,187

Source Panel A: World Bank (2021); Panel B: Penn World Tables Version 10, Feenstra et al. (2015)

Notes "–" indicates missing data. GDP p.c. in PPP is calculated using data from the PWT, Version 10 (expenditure-side real GDP at chained PPPs in 2017 US$ divided by the population). "*" Singapore is here the only Southeast Asian country, which, however, has a high (North) East Asian population share. "**" USA and UK: benchmark countries (have been among the most developed countries, the hegemonic powers of the last three centuries, and among the winners in the World War II, with the difference that parts of the UK were badly destroyed after World War II, while the USA had suffered almost no major damage (relatively speaking))

In Table 1.2, we regard some other, mainly non-economic development indicators. The average years of schooling and the percentage of the population with no schooling can be seen as proxies for the level of human capital of a country, and infant mortality and life expectancy as proxies for the quality of the health sector. Both, the level of human capital and the quality of the health sector are important areas of a country's institutional quality, which, in turn, has a decisive influence on a country's economic prosperity (in terms of GDP per capita or economic growth).

Table 1.2 shows that the improvements regarding education and health were equally remarkable than those with respect to per capita income. Except for Japan, all countries started with relatively low levels of education in 1950. South Korea and Hong Kong reported average years of schooling of only slightly above 4 years, Taiwan and Singapore of around 3 years, and China even below 2 years. By 2010, the situation had changed drastically and except for China, all countries reported mean school years of above 10 (most of these improvements had taken place between 1960 and 1980). While China is still lagging behind with mean school years of "only" 8, it has seen the most drastic improvement (by almost 400% between 1950 and 2010). Over the same period, the percentage of the population

Table 1.2 The development process in East Asia (measured by education/schooling, illiteracy rate, infant mortality, life expectancy, and poverty rate)

	Japan	South Korea	China	Taiwan	Hong Kong	Singapore	USA	UK
Panel A: Average years of schooling								
1950	6.73	4.50	1.61	3.03	4.36	2.71	8.40	6.39
1960	7.76	4.20	2.51	3.71	4.89	3.70	9.17	6.86
1980	9.10	8.13	5.31	6.74	7.97	5.26	12.03	8.41
2000	10.94	11.06	7.38	9.58	9.31	9.15	12.64	9.92
2010	11.60	12.05	7.97	11.09	11.38	10.81	13.18	12.24
Panel B: Percentage of the population with no schooling								
1950	4.66	27.86	70.64	46.51	38.65	61.16	2.22	2.22
1960	2.40	42.60	56.90	33.65	31.70	49.39	1.96	2.07
1980	0.31	13.07	24.75	15.70	16.22	29.82	0.84	3.31
2000	0.17	5.93	10.97	4.86	18.30	19.56	0.43	2.94
2019	0.13	3.44	5.35	2.38	5.38	15.27	0.35	0.15
Panel C: Infant mortality								
1960	3.97	11.14	–	–	–	4.78	3.01	2.66
1980	0.99	3.6	6.23	–	–	1.48	1.5	1.41
2000	0.45	0.75	3.68	–	–	0.39	0.84	0.65
2019	0.26	0.33	0.93	–	–	0.28	0.66	0.43
Panel D: Life expectancy								
1950	61.15	37.57	42.97	55.56	62.14	58.39	68.20	68.71
1960	67.89	55.19	43.73	64.19	67.40	65.48	69.94	70.87
1980	76.25	66.12	66.84	71.48	74.68	71.96	73.91	73.59
2000	81.17	76.05	71.40	76.04	80.76	77.97	76.81	77.76
2019	84.63	83.03	76.91	80.46	84.86	83.62	78.86	81.32

Notes Data on the "average years of schooling" and on the percentage of the "population with no schooling" are obtained from the Barro and Lee (2013) dataset. Data on infant mortality are obtained from the World Bank (child mortality rate is expressed as the probability per 1,000 that a newborn baby will die before reaching age 5, if subject to age-specific mortality rates of the specified year). Data on life expectancy are obtained from Riley (2005), Zijdeman and Ribeira da Silva (2015), and the UN Population Division (2019). See also Notes of Table 1.1

with no schooling had declined considerably. In 2010, the number ranged between 0 and 5.4% (only Singapore recorded a higher value of around 15%), while in 1950, most countries still recorded very high values (for instance, in South Korea 28% of the population had no schooling, in Hong Kong 39%, and in China, the number even stood at above 70%).

Also, the healthcare sector has seen drastic advances since 1950. For instance, by 2019, infant mortality had fallen to below 1% while life expectancy had increased to more than 80 years in most countries (except for China where it was around 77), thus surpassing even that of Western countries such as the UK and the USA. In contrast, the average life expectancy was still only around 53 years in 1950.

As we can see from Tables 1.1 and 1.2, South Korea, China as well as Taiwan were among the poorest (agricultural)[2] countries in the world in 1950.[3] Japan, on the other hand, was already more developed, but after World War II, from which Japan emerged as one of the losers, it had been severely set back (which mainly affected infrastructure and GDP per capita and the poverty rate, less so human capital). In China, in just over 20 years from 1990 to 2011, the poverty headcount ratio fell from 60.73 to 6.26% according to IMF, World Economic Outlook Database, April 2015, and the number of poor at $1.25 a day (on a PPP basis)[4] was reduced from 689 to 84 million during the same period.

What is striking is that the East Asian countries are very heterogeneous in size. While China, Japan, and South Korea tend to be larger countries (China even the largest country in the world by population; see Table 1.3 in the Appendix of this chapter), the other countries such as Taiwan and Hong Kong (as well as Southeast Asian Singapore) tend to be rather small to very small countries (Hong Kong and Singapore are city-states). China is in the meantime also the largest country by GDP (in PPP). Table 1.3 shows that, in 2019, China attained about the same level in PPP as the USA. In the meantime, China even surpassed the USA in this respect. Of course, as China is much larger than the USA by population, its GDP per capita (GDP divided by population) is still much lower; China's share in world GDP is around 18% (IMF, World Economic Outlook April 2021)[5] and its share in world population also around 18% (World Bank 2021). The respective US shares are 16% and 4%, respectively.

Assuming that it tends to be more difficult for larger countries than for very small ones to catch up quickly in the development process (many or most of the richest countries in the world are small, see Alesina 2003: 308),[6] this rapid catch-up success is particularly impressive for the three larger countries Japan, South Korea, and China. Also, the global economic significance of the catch up of these three countries is much larger than that of the small countries (Hong Kong, Singapore, and in principle also Taiwan). Not least for this reason, we limit ourselves in our book to a detailed analysis of the development paths or strategies of Japan, South Korea, and China.

[2] "China was a poor country in 1949 with agriculture's contribution to output value of more than 70 per cent", see Wagner (2021: 5) referring to the data given in Muqiao (1981: 19).

[3] Ravallion (2021) in his study arrived at a poverty rate of 87.5% for China and 73.6% for South Korea and Taiwan (in aggregate; abbreviated as SKT) in 1950. He apparently attributes this difference (the lower rate for South Korea and Taiwan) to benefits from the former Japanese colonial rule. "A notable difference in this context is that mainland China lagged in human development relative to SKT; for example, the Barro-Lee data for 1950 indicate that 55% of those aged 15–64 had completed primary school in South Korea, as compared to 29% in Taiwan and only 7% in mainland China" (Ravallion 2021: 4).

[4] PPP stands for purchasing power parity.

[5] Own calculations based on current GDP in international dollars adjusted by PPP.

[6] Of the 10 richest countries, 6 are very small countries, meaning they have a population of less than 1 million (own calculations based on World Bank (2021) data on population and GDP per capita in constant 2010 US dollars of the year 2005).

The success of East Asian countries is also evident in relative comparison to others. For example, in a very highly regarded joint study by the World Bank and the Development Research of the State Council, P.R. China (2013), it was found that of 101 countries that were middle income in 1960, only 13 had managed to achieve high-income status by 2008. The remaining 88 countries, on the other hand, remained either poor or stuck in middle-income status. Among the successful countries were mostly smaller states (most of which received strong financial and structural development assistance either from the USA or the EU).[7] Only three were larger states (with a population higher than say 30 million), and of which two were East Asian states, namely, Japan and South Korea.[8] The other country is Spain which profited from the EU integration process (cf. Glawe and Wagner 2021; Schönfelder and Wagner 2016).

Among the 13 countries that successfully overcame the middle-income trap, some followed (more or less forced by dependence on the USA or, respectively, the EU) the Western (American/European) model of development, based on the market economy and democracy principles, while the others—partially (like Singapore) or very strongly (like China)—deviated from this model and took their own path. Nevertheless, all of them, even those that took a different path, were eminently successful in catching up. As said above, perhaps most impressive is the success of the three larger East Asian countries that are the subject of our reflections in the further chapters.

In this book, the drivers of the development success of these (three larger) East Asian countries will be elaborated. In doing so, we will see that not only economic factors have played a role but also cultural, institutional, political, and ecological conditions and their interaction with economic factors.

We then ask whether there are strong commonalities that allow us to speak of an "East Asian development model", or even of an "East Asian secret of success". However, we also elaborate on the differences between the three countries and their growth drivers.

Finally, in the book, we look into the challenges for the three countries in the coming decades. These are partly the same/similar; however, there are also country-specific challenges that we analyze. It is always important to keep in mind that the three countries have developed in a staggered manner over time (in a kind of "flying geese" formation, with Japan at the top, followed by South Korea and China, each 20–30 years apart in time). This provided the opportunity for countries to learn from each other (especially from each other's mistakes). Specifically, South Korea could learn from Japan, and China could learn from Japan as well as South Korea.

In the following, we give an **overview** of the content of the individual chapters of this book.

---

[7] These 13 countries were Israel, Japan, Ireland, Spain, Hong Kong, Singapore, Portugal, Taiwan, Mauritius, Equatorial Guinea, South Korea, Greece, and Puerto Rico.

[8] Overall, 5 of the 13 states were from East Asia (including Singapore).

Chapter 2 traces the history of Japan's development from the Middle Ages to modern times. In this way, it attempts to uncover the historical background/determinants and mainly the drivers of the development process in Japan since World War II. These, as well as the associated successes and crises in Japan, also served as an illustrative background for the equally successful, but later developments in South Korea and China, as explained in Chap. 5.

After about two centuries of isolation during the Edo period, Japan was forced by the American forces to open up its economy in 1854. Japan consequently became increasingly exposed to Western ideas and institutions. During the Meiji period, Japan underwent its first Industrial Revolution. An initial state-led big push failed; however, subsequent reforms enabled a successful private sector-led big push. In this context, the zaibatsu conglomerates played an important role since they enabled coordinated big investment across a wide range of industries. It was also during this period that Japan became increasingly internationally competitive in the light industry. After the turn of the century (especially since 1912), Japan then turned more and more toward militarism, and by the middle of the 1930s, it was a de facto military dictatorship. After the country's defeat in World War II, it was occupied by the allied powers (led by the USA), which pushed forward economic demilitarization (among others, the zaibatsu conglomerates were dissolved) as well as democratization measures; in addition, land, labor, and educational reforms were implemented. Since Japan's infrastructure and industrial plants had been heavily destroyed during the wartime period, major investments were undertaken to finance the necessary economic reconstruction measures. Japan also profited from "favorable" circumstances including the Korean War, which considerably raised the demand for Japanese manufactured goods (it was also thanks to this demand increase that the "Dodge line" monetary retrenchment measures to fight inflation did not result in a long-term recession).

Between the mid-1950s and 1973, Japan experienced its high growth period and managed to rise to the ranks of advanced countries. It was a mix of high savings and investment rates, vast exports, imported foreign technologies, and related productivity increases (through reverse engineering), as well as a domestic consumption boom that enabled the Japanese growth miracle. Also, industrial policy very likely played a role (even though there are opposing views on the role of such policies). Among others, the emergence of the so-called keiretsu conglomerates (the successors of the zaibatsu) was supported by the Ministry of International Trade and Industry (MITI). In 1960, Prime Minister Hayato Ikeda, pursuing a heavy industrialization policy, introduced the Income Doubling Plan which—as implied by the name—aimed at doubling Japan's income within 10 years, a goal that was even surpassed. Also, trade liberalization was pushed forward by the Ikeda administration. Over the subsequent two decades (that is, in the 1970s and 1980s), economic growth then slowed down. Various factors contributed to this slowdown, among others, several external shocks (in particular, the Nixon shocks leading to an appreciation of the yen, and the two oil shocks), macroeconomic policies conducted by the Japanese government, delayed structural reforms, and a natural growth slowdown (since Japan had already become an advanced country). Still, the growth rate was on average around 4%, leading to the name "period of stable growth".

However, since the middle of the 1980s, an asset price bubble was forming. The bubble eventually burst in the early 1990s, marking the beginning of the "Lost Two Decades" lasting from 1992 to 2012, which were characterized by economic stagnation and deflation. The recovery of the Japanese economy was repeatedly thrown back by external crises such as the Asian financial crisis (1997–98), the dot-com bubble (2000), and the global financial crisis (2007/8). Only after Shinzo Abe became (for the second time) Prime Minister in 2012, the economy started to recover under his Abenomics program. Abenomics was based on three arrows, namely, fiscal stimulus, monetary easing, and structural reforms. However, even though the expansionary macroeconomic policies enabled (at least temporarily) an economic recovery and slightly increasing inflation rates, the latter remained mostly significantly below the target of 2%. Moreover, up to the present day, Japan has still not sufficiently addressed the structural problems it is facing. Two key problems are the demographic change (with a shrinking working-age population) and lacking innovation.

Chapter 3 details South Korea's success story since the 1950s.

After South Korea's independence from the Japanese colonial rule and the subsequent devastating Korean War, the country was completely destroyed and impoverished. During the 1950s, South Korea was heavily dependent on US' foreign aid and plagued by political volatility, crony capitalism, economic stagnation, and inflation. The government followed an import substitution industrialization policy, which negatively affected exports. However, the educational and land reforms implemented during this period were decisive for the later industrialization process. In the 1960s, the "Miracle on the Han River" began under Park Chun-hee's military government. Among others, 5-year economic development plans were established, and the government gained control over credit allocation. South Korea switched to an export promotion industrialization strategy and focused particularly on light manufacturing in which it had a comparative advantage due to its abundant (and therefore cheap), well-educated labor force.

As wages started rising in the 1970s, South Korea focused more on capital-intensive industries and started its heavy and chemical industry (HCI) drive (with a focus on steel, machinery, chemicals, metals, shipbuilding, and electronics). It was during this period that the chaebol conglomerates became increasingly powerful, partly because they were heavily supported by the government. (Similar to Japan, the role of industrial policy is also subject to controversies in the South Korean case.) While the HCI drive was successful in continuing economic growth, it came at the cost of severe imbalances (including high foreign debt levels, non-performing loans, excess capacity, and soaring inflation) that could no longer be ignored in the 1980s: the growth first policy had to be abandoned in favor of macroeconomic stabilization. Among others, the government pursued a tight macroeconomic policy, restructured the HCI sectors, and reduced government intervention. Thanks to these reforms, South Korea was able to get back on its high-growth path.

The 1990s were then dedicated to further financial liberalization and an accelerated opening up of South Korea's capital markets. Various chaebols took the opportunity and gained control of the still rather inexperienced newly formed non-bank financial institutions. This enabled them easy access to foreign capital without bothersome state supervision, leading to an investment boom but also high debt-to-equity ratios of many conglomerates. The problems of the corporate and financial sector (in particular very high levels of short-term foreign debt) eventually came to light when South Korea was confronted with very unfavorable conditions in the mid-1990s, including a rise in the oil price, the depreciation of the yen, and declining semiconductor prices. Moreover, South Korea was hit hard by the Asian Financial Crisis and had to apply for an IMF bailout at the end of 1998. South Korea had to install various monetary and fiscal retrenchment measures, accompanied by a comprehensive structural reform program encompassing the corporate, financial, public, and labor sector. Among others, the large conglomerates sold off inefficient areas and began to concentrate on their respective core areas. The drastic reforms were successful and growth resumed (even though at a lower rate during the early 2000s). When South Korea was hit by the Global Financial Crisis in 2007/8, it was, however, again its heavy reliance on a short-term foreign debt that made the country very vulnerable to the global credit crunch. In addition, exports dropped considerably in 2009. Thanks to expansionary monetary and fiscal policy measures and the bank recapitalization strategy, South Korea managed to recover relatively fast from the crisis, also when compared with other OECD countries.

Chapter 4 shows how China has developed, starting from the Middle Ages to the present. In particular, however, the upheavals in the second half of the last century and in the first two decades of this century are examined and analyzed in more detail (on the basis of this historical background).

China had once been one of the technologically and culturally most advanced countries in the world (particularly during the Tang and Song dynasties); however, it was outpaced by advanced Western countries such as Britain during the Qing dynasty (there is disagreement regarding the exact timing, but it was at the latest since the beginning of the Industrial Revolution). The next decades were characterized by political instability during the Warlord era in the 1910s, the unification of China under the Nanjing government in 1927, and the Civil War between nationalists and communists. In 1949, the Communist Party of China (CPC) came to power and the People's Republic of China (PRC) was established. Under the CPC's Chairman Mao Zedong, China turned toward a planned economic system based on the Soviet model. To push forward economic development and socialism, Mao relied on mass campaigns such as the Great Leap Forward (1958–1962) (contributing to the Great Famine, 1959–1961) and the Cultural Revolution (1966–1976), which set the country back many years. After Mao's death in 1976, Hua Guofeng became his successor and ended the Cultural Revolution. Two years later, Deng Xiaoping became the paramount leader of China. Deng started a new era of "Reform and Opening up".

The Chinese reforms under Deng have followed a rather gradual, evolutionary, and experimental approach, which is often described as a trial and error process ("crossing the river by feeling the stones"). Economic development became a top priority since it was regarded as essential for the survival of the political regime. The reforms started in the agricultural sector. In particular, the state procurement prices for agricultural commodities were raised, agriculture was decollectivized through the household responsibility (HRS) system, and free markets for agricultural commodities were expanded. The reforms incentivized farmers to work more efficiently and increased rural incomes and productivity. In the middle of the 1980s, the focus of reforms shifted to the industrial sector. The so-called Township and Village Enterprises (TVEs) were the major growth engine during this second reform phase and pushed forward the transformation toward a market economy.[9] During the late 1970s and 1980s, also the first opening-up policies and laws were passed. Among others, the special economic zones (which provided preferential tax treatment to foreign investors) were established and gradually expanded to encompass the entire coastal area by 1988. However, it was not until Deng Xiaoping's southern tour and his (re-)commitment to the open-door policy in 1992 that China intensified its liberalization reform efforts and also followed a nationwide implementation of foreign direct investment (FDI) enhancing policies. In 1993, the 3rd Plenum of the 14th National Congress of the CPC decided to establish a "socialist market economy", paving the way for fiscal, financial, and state-owned enterprise (SOE) reforms, which had so far been neglected. Also, the share of private firms in industrial production increased considerably in the 1990s.

In 2001, China finally entered the World Trade Organization (WTO), which also led to greater competition on the Chinese goods market (moreover, in anticipation of the WTO accession, China had intensified its trade liberalization efforts). However, economic reform efforts slowed down significantly after 2003 (under the Hu Jintao-Wen Jiabao administration), even though this change was not immediately noticeable since GDP growth remained relatively high. One of the various reasons for the change in the reform course can be attributed to the fact that the policy measures during the 1990s had created a group of "reform losers" (especially SOE workers). Since it was feared that social conflicts could lead to instability, the subsequent reforms focused on tackling social problems (e.g. through reforms of the social security and pension systems as well as the health sector). The 2000s have also seen a resurgence of "techno-industrial policy". The Global Financial Crisis finally revealed the vulnerability of the Chinese development model, which relied heavily on export and investment, causing severe imbalances (including overcapacities and rising debt levels). An expansive macroeconomic policy program absorbed the subsequent severe slowdown in growth. Still, there were rising concerns that China could become stuck in a middle-income trap. At around 2012, the new paramount leader Xi Jinping introduced the strategy of "rebalancing", which is, among others, characterized by recentralization and authoritarianism as well as stronger controls and the transition toward a more consumption- and

[9] TVEs were collectively owned by a village or township, which made them ideologically much safer than normal private enterprises; at the same time, they faced a harder budget constraint than state firms, which made them much more productive than state firms.

service-led growth strategy. In the 2010s under Xi Jinping, China has strengthened its ambitions for global political and technological leadership, supported by projects such as the One Belt One Road initiative with which China is currently extending its influence in Africa, Asia, and Southeastern Europe.

Chapter 5 then compares the development processes in Japan, South Korea, and China presented in detail in the previous chapters. We first try to identify the commonalities in the development of the three countries and then ask ourselves whether these commonalities justify speaking of a special "East Asian path/development model" or an "East Asian secret of success" that has made East Asia so extremely successful in the post-World War II period and might even (as occasionally claimed) establish a new imminent East Asian dominance. Before we can come to a balanced judgment on this, however, we will then also work out in detail the manifold differences between the three countries and their development strategies. Here we look, in particular, into the different starting levels at the beginning of reforms after the World War II, the varying driving forces of development, the different political systems (and the rise of democracy), the different economic systems, the different development strategies (especially with respect to the adoption of foreign technologies), as well as the differences in the culture, size, geography, institutions, economic/industrial policies, breaks in the development processes, and inequality.

One similarity of the three countries is that they all experienced extraordinary GDP growth rates over decades, which enabled them to join the group of high-income countries (in the case of Japan and South Korea) or respectively to attain middle-income status (in the case of China) in a rather short amount of time. They all followed an export-oriented development model and recorded high savings and investment rates. Furthermore, all three countries shared similar institutional-cultural characteristics (at least in comparison to Western countries)[10] and had relatively homogeneous populations. In addition, they all had (and partly still have) rather authoritarian governments.

Besides these similarities, there are several differences between Japan, South Korea, and China. Here, we only touch upon some of them. The initial development levels of the three East Asian countries (after World War II) differed considerably. In particular, Japan was much more developed than South Korea and China; not only with respect to per capita income but also with respect to the initial human capital endowment and the structural transformation process. This was partly due to the fact that Japan had already undergone the first wave of industrialization during the Meiji period. One of the most obvious differences is probably the varying sizes of the three countries. While South Korea is a rather small state (in terms of population and area), China is one of the largest countries (the largest by population) in the world. As we will discuss, this has important implications for the growth strategy (for instance, China has more bargaining power vis-à-vis foreign investors due to its large domestic market). The varying political systems present another apparent difference: Japan and South Korea have both been democracies for quite

[10] There do, however, exist differences among the three East Asian countries.

some time while China still has an authoritarian political system controlled by the CPC. However, there have also been differences between Japan and South Korea, for instance regarding the democratization process (top-down versus bottom-up), government-opposition power shifts, and the timing of democratization (prior versus after the economic take-off). With regard to the economic/industrial structures, South Korea and Japan both relied on conglomerates to achieve the coordinated development of firms in diverse industries (also with the help of industrial policy), while no such business groups existed in China (however, the institutional legacy of the TVEs enabled clusters of abundant small private firms managed by Township governments, which somehow resemble the conglomerate structures). Moreover, even though also China's development strategy involved industrial planning, it was usually formulated less concretely compared with that of Japan and South Korea. The three countries also differed with respect to the adoption of foreign technologies. While Japan and also South Korea relied primarily on reverse engineering, China primarily focused on fostering FDI in order to generate knowledge spillovers.

Chapter 6 then focuses on the challenges that the three countries are currently facing and will face in the next two to three decades. After a brief look into where East Asia stands today and the recent policy course in Japan, South Korea, and China, we first address the general challenges that affect all countries globally, including East Asia, such as demographic change, climate change, digital change, cultural change, international integration (globalization), sectoral structural change, and their interdependencies. We then look into key challenges facing the East Asian countries, which or their consequences are also likely to be relevant for the other Asian and non-Asian countries. These include, but are not limited to, the debt dynamics in the East Asian countries, which is currently particularly visible in Japan and China. In addition, there is the danger posed by the increasing importance of shadow banks (and fintechs in particular) and the booming housing sector in China. Furthermore, and in particular, the "system competition" and the struggle for economic and technological supremacy between the US and China threatens to become increasingly dangerous in the coming decades, and thus to cause ever greater political tensions not only between these two countries but also between the respective allies of the two, which also include East Asian countries represented on both sides. In this context, (too high) expectations could also be aroused on both sides, which will ultimately have to be disappointed (at least in part), with uncertain domestic political consequences. Finally, there is also the threat of ever greater income and wealth inequalities and the associated increase in social tensions, especially in China.

Finally, we address some other specific challenges in individual East Asian countries, such as how to overcome or avoid an impending middle-income trap (related to China) or a high-income trap (related to Japan and South Korea). Furthermore, we analyze challenges related to the productivity and human capital weaknesses, and resource scarcities, found in East Asian countries.

At the very end of this chapter, we also briefly address the question of which country in Asia could perhaps become the next China or model of success, taking a closer look into India and Vietnam.

Chapter 7 summarizes the arguments of the book and draws some further conclusions.

Appendix

See Table 1.3.

Table 1.3 The development of the economic power and population in East Asia

	Japan	South Korea	China	Taiwan	Hong Kong	Singapore	USA	UK
Panel A: GDP (PPP, in billions)								
1960	550.8	30.3	653.8	27.2	12.4	4.5	3489.1	672.9
2019	5028.3	2090.9	**20056.1**	1153.8	440.6	514.4	**20860.5**	3119.0
Panel B: Population (in millions)								
1960	94.6	24.7	656.4	10.7	3.0	1.6	184.6	52.3
2019	126.9	51.2	**1433.8**	23.6	7.4	5.8	**329.1**	67.5

Source Penn World Tables Version 10, Feenstra et al. (2015)
Notes Expenditure-side real GDP at chained PPPs in 2017 US$

References

Alesina A (2003) The size of countries: does it matter? J Eur Econ Assoc 1(2–3):301–316

Barro R, Lee J-W (2013) A new data set of educational attainment in the world, 1950–2010. J Dev Econ 104:184–198

Feenstra RC, Inklaar R, Timmer MP (2015) The next generation of the Penn World table. Am Econ Rev 105(10):3150–3182. Available for download at www.ggdc.net/pwt

Glawe L, Wagner H (2021) Divergence tendencies in the European integration process: a danger for the sustainability of the E(M)U? J Risk Finan Manage 14(104):1–22

IMF (2021) World Economic Outlook database: April 2021. International Monetary Fund, Washington DC

Muqiao X (1981) China's socialist economy. Foreign Language Press, Beijing

Ravallion M (2021) Poverty in China since 1950: a counterfactual perspective. NBER working paper no. 28370

Riley JC (2005) Estimates of regional and global life expectancy, 1800–2001. Popul Dev Rev 31 (3):537–543

Schönfelder N, Wagner H (2016) Impact of European integration on institutional development. J Econ Integr 31:472–530

UN Population Division (2019) World population prospects 2019. https://population.un.org/wpp/DataQuery/

Wagner H (2021) China's "political-economy trilemma": (how) can it be solved? Chin Econ 54 (5):311–329. https://doi.org/10.1080/10971475.2021.1875158

World Bank (2021) World development indicators. The World Bank, Washington, DC

World Bank and Development Research Center of the State Council (PRC) (2013) China 2030: building a modern, harmonious and creative high-income society. The World Bank, Washington, DC

Zijdeman R, Ribeira da Silva F (2015) Life expectancy at birth (total). https://hdl.handle.net/10622/LKYT53. IISH Data Collection, V1

2 Japan's Catching-Up Process

Abbreviations

AA goods	Automatic Approval System goods
ADB	Asian Development Bank
AFA goods	Automatic Foreign Exchange Allocation goods
BOJ	Bank of Japan
CAB	Current Account Balances
CBPP	Covered Bond Purchase Program
CPI	Consumer Price Index
DPJ	Democratic Party of Japan
ECB	European Central Bank
ETF	Exchange Traded Fund
FA goods	Foreign Exchange Allocation System goods
FEB	Foreign Exchange Budget
FED	Federal Reserve
FEFTCL	Foreign Exchange and Foreign Trade Control Law
FI	Financial Institution
FRC	Financial Reconstruction Commission
FSA	Financial Supervisory Agency
GATT	General Agreement on Tariffs and Trade
GHQ	General Headquarter
GNP	Gross National Product
IMF	International Monetary Fund
IPSS	National Institute of Population and Social Security Research in Japan
JGB	Japanese Government Bond

L. Glawe and H. Wagner, *The Economic Rise of East Asia*,
Contributions to Economics, https://doi.org/10.1007/978-3-030-87128-4_2

J-REIT	Japan Real Estate Investment Trust
LDP	Liberal Democratic Party
LTCB	Long-Term Credit Bank
MBS	Mortgage-backed securities
MHLW	Ministry of Health, Labor, and Welfare
MITI	Ministry of International Trade and Industry
MOF	Ministry of Finance
NCB	Nippon Credit Bank
NGB	National Government Budget
NIRP	Negative Interest Rate Policy
NPL	Non-performing Loan
OECD	Organisation for Economic Co-operation and Development
OPEC	Organization of the Petroleum Exporting Countries
PCB	Project Cost Basis
PKO	Price-Keeping Operations
QE	Quantitative Easing
QQE1	First round of "Quantitative and Qualitative Easing"
QQE2	Second round of "Quantitative and Qualitative Easing"
R&D	Research and Development
SCAP	Supreme Commander of Allied Powers
SOE	State Owned Enterprises
TFP	Total Factor Productivity
UK	United Kingdom
UN	United Nations
USA	United States of America
VAR	Vector Autoregression
ZIRP	Zero Interest Rate Policy

2.1 Introduction

Among the East Asian countries, Japan was the first to succeed in joining the club of high-income economies in the 1970s. As we will discuss in subsequent chapters of this book, the Japanese development strategy also provided important guidance for the South Korean and Chinese economic model. Even though the idea of a "flying geese pattern", with the East Asian economies aligning behind Japan at the top is no longer up-to-date since the Asian economic landscape resembles rather a network (cf. ADB 2020), the Japanese development strategy is still a role model for developing countries today. Even the country's (partly painful) experiences during the Lost Two Decades offer important insights for developed countries with respect to crisis management and the use of unconventional monetary policy.

Eight phases of economic development

The Japanese economic development can be subdivided into various phases, the historical roots, in particular, the Edo period (1603–1868) and the Meiji period (1868–1912), a period of increasing militarism (1912–1945), the phase of American occupation (1945–1952), the period of high growth (mid-1950s–1973), the period of stable growth (1973–1992), the period of the Lost Two Decades (1992–2012), and finally the time of Abenomics (2012–present). Each of these phases and the corresponding reforms will be discussed in Sects. 2.2–2.8. The main focus will be on the post-war period. Still, we think that it is necessary to also briefly outline the time prior to 1945 in order to understand not only how the institutional design changes over time but also how this period partly influenced more recent development (e.g. the keiretsu as a revival of the zaibatsu).

Interpretation of reforms

The impact of economic reforms can be analyzed from different perspectives. Researchers of different schools of economic thought (e.g. Neoclassic versus Keynesian economics) will most likely evaluate the reform measures differently.[1] In the case of the Japanese economic development process, there are for instance opposing views regarding the effectiveness of industrial policy and, in this context, the role that kereitsu conglomerates played for Japan's post-war economic development. Moreover, the importance of the New Deal economist-style structural reforms under American occupation for creating the base for the subsequent rapid economic development is controversial. The literature has also not yet reached consensus regarding the question of whether the Lost Two Decades were caused primarily by demand-side or rather supply-side factors. We try to provide a comprehensive overview of the Japanese economic reforms and take into account various views and interpretations; however, we have to acknowledge that it is a difficult task to do justice to every point of view.

[1] It can also be distinguished between the view of Western scholars ("foreign view") and of Japanese scholars.

A very brief first overview

Our analysis of the Japanese development process starts around **1603**; that is, at the beginning of the **Edo period** that lasted until **1868**. This period was characterized by an unprecedented stability, which was ensured via various institutional control systems installed by the military government (Tokugawa shogunate), for instance, the seclusion policy sakoku. However, with the arrival of Admiral Perry around 1854, Japan was forced to end more than two centuries of isolation and was exposed to Western institutions. After the Tokugawa shogun was replaced by the Meiji emperor in 1868, Japan was rapidly transformed into a modern Western-style state with Japanese institutions being designed according to Western best practices. The so-called **Meiji period** also marks the start of the first Japanese Industrial Revolution. Even though an initial state-led big push failed, subsequent reforms enabled the successful private sector big push and Japan became increasingly internationally competitive in the light industry. The zaibatsu conglomerates played a central role in the industrialization process and dominated the Japanese economy. Since the beginning of the twentieth century, especially after **1912**, Japan turned increasingly to militarism and followed an aggressive expansionism in Asia; at the middle of the 1930s, it was a de facto **military dictatorship.** After having been eventually defeated in World War II in **1945**, Japan was heavily damaged and **occupied by the allied powers**, which established economic demilitarization and introduced various reform measures in order to democratize Japan. When the Cold War started around 1947, the USA allowed a more comprehensive rebuilding of the heavy industry since Japan was a potential ally and strategic base location. This enabled the Japanese economy to address current macroeconomic problems, namely, low productive capacity and rampant inflation. Even though Japanese government managed to increase production, it was not until the implementation of the Dodge Plan in 1949 that inflation was brought under control; however, at the cost of a beginning recession which could only be avoided due to the start of the Korean War which increased the demand for Japanese manufactured goods sharply.

The period between the **mid-1950s and 1973** is often referred to as the "**period of high economic growth**" during which Japan managed to join the club of high-income countries. Often cited success factors include high saving and investment rates, increasing exports, capital accumulation, and productivity increases thanks to imported foreign technologies. Between **1973 and 1992**, the growth slowed down but still contributed to about 4%. Therefore, this period is often referred to as the "**period of stable growth**".

However, since 1985, an asset price bubble was forming, eventually bursting in the early 1990s and leading into a period of economic stagnation lasting from 1992 to 2012, which is often referred to as the **Lost Two Decades.** The Lost Two Decades themselves can be subdivided into multiple phases, the phase of the bubble burst and "normal recession" (1992–1997), the phase of the banking crisis (1997–2003), the short recovery phase under Prime Minister Koizumi (2003–2007), and the recession after the Global Financial Crisis, combined with political chaos (2007–2012). The period after 2012 is often referred to as the period of **Abenomics** (in reference to the economic reforms under the Prime Minister Shinzo Abe) during which the economy started to recover and deflation came to an end (even though only temporarily). However, it is yet to be proven that Japan will be able to successfully overcome the rather structural, supply-side problems such as population aging.

2.2 Historical Roots: Edo Period (1603–1868) and Meiji Period (1868–1912)

Edo Period (1603–1868)

The Edo period that lasted from 1603 to 1868 unified the country and ended the 300 years of civil wars. After its victory in the battle of Sekigahara, Tokugawa Ieyasu founded the feudal military government, **Tokugawa shogunate** or **bakufu** and became the first shogun. The Tokugawa clan governed Japan along with 300 regional **daimyo** lords who each had their own territory (**han**; local government). Therefore, the political system is often referred to as **baku-han**. Ohno (2017) argues that even though Japan was politically centralized (the bakufu operating from Edo had absolute political power over the local governments), it was rather decentralized economically since each *han* could pursue its own administrative, educational, and regulative policies (as long as it was not generally forbidden by the shogunate).

The Edo period was characterized by an unprecedented **stability**, which was ensured via various **institutional control systems** installed, namely, the caste system (shi-no-ko-sho), the concept of alternate attendance of the daimyo (sankin kotai), the (honbyakusho) tax system, as well as isolationist foreign policies (sakoku). Each of these aspects will be briefly discussed in the following.

The **shi-no-ko-sho class system** was based on the ideas of Confucianism and divided the society into four classes, the samurai warriors (shi), the peasants (no), artisans (ko), and merchants (sho) (cf. Fig. 2.1). The total population was around 30,000,000 with peasants constituting the largest class (around 80%, cf. Miyamato et al. 1965). On top of that were the emperor and the court nobility which, however, had no actual but only formal power. Class affiliation was according to birth and could not be changed by marriage. While this strict social order was able to ensure stability, it also limited the exploitation of comparative advantage in the choice of occupation. The smallest unit of social organization was the *ie*, that is, the house, and not the individual person.

The daimyo and samurai had become "warriors with no wars to fight" (cf. Flath 2014: 42) and thus assumed responsibility for civil bureaucracy tasks (see also Fulcher 1988). The daimyo had the power to collect the tax from the peasants within his *han*. The **tax system (honbyakusho**, lit. independent farmers) was a special feature of the Japanese economy. The arable lands and the respective responsible head of each *ie* were recorded (via official land surveys, *kenchi*), and

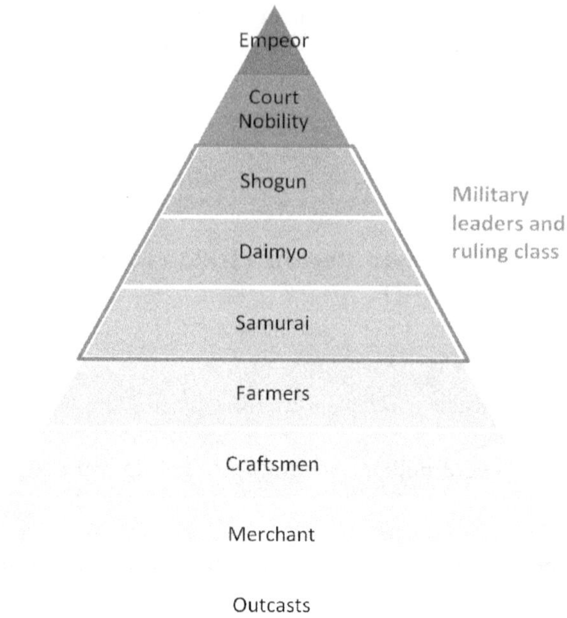

Fig. 2.1 Shi-no-ko-sho class system

internal control systems (a) within **family units** of five people, as well as (b) within the **village** via the official tax collector that intermediated between the samurai and all village people, ensured the tax payments which were based on the rice output and amounted to around 40% of it (cf. Flath 2014).[2] Due to this "lowest-level tax administration", tax revenues could be raised with only little administrative cost (cf. Ohno 2017). Peasants were not allowed to move and were thus tied to the land. In order to widen the tax base, the daimyo proceeded to increase the amount of cultivated land (cf. Hanley and Yamamura 1977) and installed irrigation infrastructure projects (Ohno 2017). However, particularly since the eighteenth century, the expansion of cultivated land slowed down considerably (also partly due the natural limitations, e.g. due to the mountainous geography of the country). Productivity increases, particularly in the southwestern regions—thanks to improved farming tools, fertilizers (such as dried fish), new rice species, and double cropping (cf. Ohno 2017)—allowed a continuously rising rice output. This also enabled farmers to sell their surplus rice in the Osaka Rice Exchange market, even though they faced a relatively high tax burden.

The concept of alternate attendance (**sankin kotai**) required that the daimyo lords alternated their residence between their *han* and the capital Edo, and the daimyo families had to stay in Edo all the time. This allowed the shogun to

[2] Even though this rate could vary from *han* to *han*.

carefully monitor and control the activities of the daimyo and counteract potential offensive activities (cf. Ito and Hoshi 2020).

The **seclusion policy sakoku** was enacted by various addicts and policies over the period 1633–1639 (an extensive overview on the various edicts can be found in Laver 2011). Under the sakoku system, trade and contact with foreigners were almost completely prohibited. The only exception was tightly controlled and very limited trade with Dutch and Chinese traders in Nagasaki, in particular, the island of Dejima (cf. also Kazui and Videen 1982). The sakoku policy had various reasons: first, the government aimed at removing the colonial and religious influence of Spain and Portugal and suppress Christianity; second, the Tokugawa shogunate wanted to prevent military alliances between daimyo and Europeans, as experienced previously (cf. Flath 2014). Even though the sakoku system stabilized the country, the self-isolation also had disadvantages: for instance, it separated Japan from the technological advancements of the industrial revolution that took place in Europe at the same time. The only contact with Western science and techniques was via information and books received from Dutch traders in Dejima (referred to as "Dutch studies" or rangaku) (cf. Morck and Yeung 2017).

Bakumatsu (1854–1868)

The **bakumatsu** can be regarded as a short interim period between the Edo and the Meiji period that started in 1854. It was marked by political chaos. During the bakumatsu, the seclusion policies and the rule of the Tokugawa shogunate eventually came to an end.

In 1854, Admiral Perry forced Japan to sign the Convention of Kanagawa and thus, to open the ports of Shimoda and Hakodate to serve as supply bases for US ships. Probably even more important was the subsequent Harris Treaty of 1858, which resulted in the opening up of the ports of Edo, Kobe, Nagasaki, Niigata, and Yokohama for trade with the USA and which granted extraterritoriality to US citizens. Between 1854 and 1858, other foreign countries negotiated similar treaties with Japan (e.g. England in 1854, Russia in 1855, and France in 1858). After two centuries, Japan's isolation eventually came to an (involuntary) end. Since the trade agreements were disadvantageous to Japan by enabling unfair arbitrage to the USA and the other foreign countries (e.g. by cutting tariffs to low levels and creating foreign concessions in Japan without any Japanese counterparts), these treaties were called "Unequal Treaties". As noted by Morck and Yeung (2017), this was Japan's first exposure to Western institutions.

Due to the unfair treatment, there was a growing anti-Western sentiment among some parts of the population ("expel the barbarians", *joi*); however, there was also an increasing part of the population who favored an opening of the country (*kaikoku*). After some futile efforts of resistance, also the *joi*-advocates realized that the opening of the country was inevitable. Therefore, the second major conflict between daimyos who wanted to "revere the emperor" (*sonno*) and those who still "supported the shogunate" (*sabaku*) came to the fore (cf. Ito and Hoshi 2020). In 1868, the Tokugawa shogun was finally replaced by the Meiji Emperor.

Meiji period (1868–1912)

During the Meiji period (1868–1912), Japan was rapidly transformed into a modern Western-style state, and the **Japanese institutions were designed according to Western best practices,** for instance, they were inspired by the German legal code as well as the British Westminster system (cf. Morck and Yeung 2017); in that way, Japanese leaders created a new form of government that consisted of various Western ideas and also of their own tradition. Another important landmark of the Meiji period was the **start of Japan's Industrial Revolution in 1870**. Similar to the UK, Japan's Industrial Revolution first appeared in textiles, particularly the silk and cotton spinning industries.

The main policies of the Meiji government included the **abolishment of the social caste system** in 1869, which led to rising labor mobility, the introduction of **compulsory education** in 1879, which enabled the building up of a human capital base, an **expansion of infrastructure**, including road networks and irrigation systems (partly building on the already existing infrastructure developed during the Edo period, see also above), and a **land tax reform** in 1873, which improved the incentive structure for landlords, enabling productivity increases, and also reduced the volatility of government tax revenue since taxes were paid no longer in land production such as rice. These earnings were partly used to finance Japan's big push. Moreover, after the **Iwakura mission** (1871–1872) revealed the true extent of Japan's backwardness, the introduction of foreign technology was encouraged by industrial policy. However, the initial **state-led big push** that manifested itself in the establishment of state-owned enterprises (SOEs) in essential industries using imported foreign machinery (so-called "model factories") eventually turned out to be a failure. The original idea that the state-owned mining firms and the increased and stabilized tax revenue would compensate the costs of this rapid industrialization did not realize in the expected way. One of the main reasons was the **soft budget constraint** that **SOEs** faced (some individual SOEs literally had no budget constraint at all). Moreover, the newly adopted Western-style **technologies** were **highly capital-intensive** and thus did not fit the Japanese conditions (Ito and Hoshi 2020). In addition, the suppression of the last major civil war initiated by samurai traditionalists in 1877 (the so-called "**Satsuma rebellion**" or "Seinan War") worsened the government's fiscal situation. These developments led to a **financial crisis in 1879** marked by rising inflation and a collapse of the currency. In order to restore the fiscal balance and fight inflation, finance minister Matsukata installed various **reforms**. Among others, he initiated a **monetary reform** that unified the currency, **created the Bank of Japan (BOJ)**, and **cut subsidies to SOEs** and successfully imposed a **hard budget constraint**. The government realized that liberalization and free markets were the only options to restore the country. Through the consequently following **mass privatization**, Japan—after its failed state-led big push—was eventually able to initiate a **private sector-led big push** (Morck and Yeung 2017: 12). Imported foreign technologies were now often adapted to the structure of the Japanese economy (capital scarcity and labor abundance) (Ito and Hoshi 2020; Ohno 2017). The transfer of Western technology was accomplished via three main channels: the hiring of foreign advisors, the training of Japanese engineers abroad and domestically at the Institute of Technology (*Kobu Daigakko*), as well as copying (reverse engineering), licensing, and technical cooperation (cf. Ohno 2017).

The **spirit of monozukuri** (literally: making things) might have been another rather cultural success factor for the rapid industrialization catching up in Japan. This philosophy brings the historical value of craftsmanship into modern manufacturing and includes the pride and dedication toward production. It significantly improved the image of industrial production jobs since factory work was previously considered as "dangerous, difficult, and dirty" (kiken, kitsui, kitanai). Thus, engineer became a more popular profession than lawyer or businessman at the time in Japan, which was different from many European countries (Ohno 2017).

The so-called **zaibatsu**—family-owned and -controlled, vertically integrated industry and financial conglomerates with a bank at their core (financing the subsidiaries) which operated in nearly all important areas such as steel, international trading, machinery, chemicals, etc.—had a central role in Japan's industrialization process including the borrowing of foreign technology, and thus dominated the Japanese economy (Morck and Yeung 2017; Ito and Hoshi 2020; Goto 1982; Ohkawa and Rosovsky 1973). For example, according to Perkins (2013: 67), they produced more than 50% of Japan's industrial output. The most important zaibatsus (the so-called **Big Four**) were Mitsubishi, Mitsui, Sumitomo, and Yasuda. While Sumitomo and Mitsui had roots in the Edo period, Mitsubishi and Yasuda emerged during the Meiji period.

According to Morck and Nakamura (2007), the conglomerates enabled Japan to overcome the problem of lacking coordinated big investment that—according to **Rosenstein-Rodan** (1943)—prevents developing countries from establishing a complex network of interdependent firms operating in multiple sectors, and which, in turn, was assumed to be crucial for a fast economic catching up with. This was possible due to the special characteristics of the zaibatsus: the high degree of diversification of each zaibatsu ensured that subsidiaries were independent of non-member firms and thus protected them from potential opportunistic behavior. Moreover, the zaibatsus were able to shift money from lucrative firms to unviable but necessary firms. The earnings of profitable firms could also be used to finance investments in new technologies and businesses (cf. Almeida and Wolfenzon 2006). Thus, the zaibatsus presented a private sector mechanism that replaced the state-led coordination, which was later considered as inevitable by Rosenstein-Rodan (1943).

Around 1890, the light industry became increasingly internationally competitive and exports increased continuously. This successful development enabled Japan to accumulate the necessary capital in order to intensify the development of the heavy industry. In 1877, the light industry accounted to 69% of total manufacturing output, while the heavy industry accounted for only 14%. By 1938 (driven by the war economy), however, the heavy industry's share in manufacturing output rose to 51% while that of the light industry fell to 38% (cf. Minami 1994).

Box 2.1 Evolution of Democracy in Japan (I)
During the Meiji period, Japan transformed into a modern Western-style state, and a comprehensive modernization program was installed. The exposure to Western ideas was of course not limited to economic reforms and it proved in fact rather difficult to separate Western industrialization from Western liberal norms (Kennon 2012). There was growing pressure from the Japanese citizens who demanded a more active role in the government. The main political objective was the establishment of a constitutional political structure. In 1889, this so-called "Freedom and People's Rights Movement" eventually forced the Emperor to enact the Meiji Constitution, which had been drafted by Ito Hirobumi and was inspired by Western constitutions. Even though the Emperor still retained the highest authority, a legislative parliament consisting of two houses was created. The representatives of the lower house were elected by popular vote; however, only a small subset of the population was eligible to participate in these elections. According to Kennon (2012: 19), Japan at that time can be described as being "neither fully authoritarian nor democratic, but [...] relatively stable".

2.3 Increasing Militarization and Aggressive Expansionism (1912–1945)

After the death of Emperor Meiji in July 1912, his successor Yoshihito (1879–1926) succeeded the throne and announced the **Taisho era (1912–1925)** during which democratic trends were promoted in Japan ("Taisho democracy"; see also Box 2.2). However, during the subsequent **Showa period (1926–1945)**, the militarization tendencies further intensified.

Box 2.2 Evolution of Democracy in Japan (II)
During the Taisho era, the wish for political liberalism intensified and there were mass (labor) movements asking for political change. Important objectives of the Taisho democracy included the establishment of the parliamentary principle and freedom of speech. In general, imperialistic power policies were rejected. Besides that, the exploitative relations between capitalists and workers, on the one hand, and landowners and peasants, on the other hand, should be improved.

Compared with the Meiji democracy movement, driving force of the Taisho democracy was not any longer the upper-class farmers and ex-samurai intellectuals but rather the newly formed middle class of the city (due to the economic progress). In addition, the movement as such was less coherent and driven by many different groups including labor unions, university professors, and journalists. In contrast, the Meiji era movement had centered strongly around one person, Itgaki Taisuke, and was driven by political organizations (for a more detailed discussion see Takayoshi 1956).

There is no consensus regarding the beginning and end of the Taisho democracy; however, very often the end of the Russian Japanese war in 1905 is regarded as the starting point (some argue that it was the World War I). The end is usually dated somewhere between 1925 and 1932. Key events were the rice riots of 1918 and the subsequent universal suffrage movement. In the second half of the 1920s, popular elections based on universal male suffrage were eventually introduced (Ryota 2014). However, at the same time also, the Peace Preservation Law was enacted. Its main goal was to eradicate any public dissent and it significantly restricted individual freedom in Japan. Among others, political groups that aimed to change Japan's imperial system were made illegal. The Great Depression of 1929 shattered the democratic movement, and during the 1930s, the military gained increasing power and control over the government. Japan turned into a de facto military dictatorship.

Japan's expansionism and militarization

The institutional reforms during the Meiji period were not only designed to overcome Japan's backwardness but also its inferiority as expressed by the second slogan "rich country with a strong army". Initially, the militarization of Japan was aimed at protecting Japan from Western powers and avoiding the potential colonization. However, this soon turned into a rather aggressive **expansionism in Asia**, including Japan's victory in the first Sino-Japanese war and the subsequent colonization of Taiwan, the victory in the Russian-Japanese War 1905, as well as the annexation of Korea in 1910. During the World War I, the Japanese economy experienced an enormous **export-led boom,** which fueled the development of the **heavy industry**. Japan increasingly turned to militarism during the Showa period, and since the middle of the 1930s, Japan was a de facto military dictatorship including **wartime economic planning**. During this period, Japan further shifted the industrial structure from light industries to heavy and chemical industries.

2.4 Post-war Period: Reforms Under American Occupation (1945–1952)

Structural reforms under American occupation (ca. 1945–1947)

After its defeat in the World War II in 1945, Japan was heavily damaged and occupied by the Allied powers (primarily by the American military government under General MacArthur) until 1952. The occupation administration (also referred to as General Headquarters, GHQ, or the Supreme Commander of Allied Powers, SCAP) established **economic demilitarization** and introduced various reform measures in order to **democratize** Japan, including the dissolution of zaibatsu conglomerates accompanied by the installation of fair market rules, a land reform, a labor market reform, as well as reforms of the educational and political system. The promotion of economic recovery, however, was not the SCAP's main goal in the beginning. This attitude changed 2 years later when the Cold War deepened and the Bamboo Curtain[3] emerged, and the occupation administration supported the economic reconstruction and industrialization (of the heavy and chemical industry) (cf. Hamada and Kasuya 1992). We will return to this change in the policy line later.

The economic policy reforms under MacArthur were designed following the **New Deal economists** in the USA (cf. Morck and Yeung 2017: 17) and were of a rather structural nature (Ito and Hoshi 2020). According to Hamada and Kasuya (1992), the SCAP utilized the Japanese political system to implement the occupational reform policies, by delegating them to the Japanese government. This **indirect governance** in Japan together with the preservation of the Emperor who received a symbolic function as well as the support and sympathy of the Japanese for the idealism of the reforms (cf. Hamada and Kasuya 1992) ensured the acceptance of the reform program by the Japanese population. The main occupational reforms are briefly outlined in the following.

The first reform was the **dissolution of zaibatsus** in 1946/47, which (a) contributed to the lasting destruction of Japan's military power (since the zaibatsus were responsible for the production of military equipment during the war) and (b) prevented the concentration of economic power in a limited number of companies, which previously had hindered the formation of labor unions as well as the emergence of new small firms, and thus, in turn, had impeded the creation of a middle class. The breakup of zaibatsus was accompanied by the introduction of **fair market rules**, in particular, the **Anti-Monopoly Act**, prohibiting all cartel activities, as well as **the Law for Elimination of Excessive Concentrations of Economic Power** in 1947, which both further helped to secure market competition (Nakamura and Odaka 2003; Yamamura 1967).

[3] The Bamboo Curtain refers to the political demarcation between the capitalist, non-communist countries in East Asia, South East Asia, and South Asia (e.g. Japan, Indonesia, and India) and communist countries in East Asia (e.g. China). The name is related to the Iron Curtain.

The second reform was an **agrarian reform** imposed over the period between 1946 and 1950. At its core was a restructuring of the formerly feudally organized rural society. The land ownership was transferred from landlords to small tenant cultivators, which became owner-farmers. The land reform enabled a rise in the agricultural productivity, ensured the stability of farmers' household income, and decreased income inequality. It thus also helped to create a stable middle class, ensured an increasing support for the Liberal Democratic Party (LDP), and created more political stability. However, since the maximum lot size was only around 1 ha, the reform prevented potential economies of scale (Ouchi 1966; Kawagoe 1999; Grad 1948; Takigawa 1972; Ito and Hoshi 2020; Iyoda 2010).

The **labor market** was the target of the third bundle of reform measures. It included three important laws that were enacted between 1946 and 1947, namely, the **Labor Union Law**, the **Labor Relations Adjustment Law**, and the **Labor Standards Law**. These laws gave workers the right to organize in unions and to engage in collective bargaining. Moreover, they set standards for the working environment, which eventually paved the way for the special characteristic of the Japanese labor management including lifetime employment, the seniority wage system, and enterprise unions (cf. Iyoda 2010: 30). Between 1945 and 1948/49, the share of workers organized into labor unions increased from 0 to almost 60%. Labor democratization, in particular the formation of labor unions, significantly improved working conditions and higher wages, which, in turn, increased domestic consumption (Hamada and Kasuya 1992; Nakamura 1981).

Besides the three major reforms discussed above, the occupational administration also reformed the educational and political system.

In the course of the **educational reform**, the pre-war dual system (distinction between upper-class education and general public education) was replaced by the American style 6-3-3-4 system and compulsory education was extended from 6 to 9 years. On the one hand, the reform of the school system established a greater equality of educational opportunities, but on the other hand, it has also been responsible for the highly competitive entrance exams (cf. Iyoda 2010: 31).

The **reform of the political system** resulted in the establishment of a constitutional monarchy inspired by the British system. The new Constitution was implemented in May 1947. Important features, especially if compared with the Meiji Constitution, include the guarantee of basic human rights, power separation in legislative, administrative, and judicial branches with the Emperor only having a symbolic function, and that the sovereignty rests with the people. Moreover, according to Article 9 of the Constitution, Japan was not allowed to possess any armed forces (cf. Ohno 2017).

Regarding the importance of the New Deal style reforms under the American military forces for Japan's economic miracle in the 1960s and 70s, researchers have opposing views. While some argue that the labor and land reforms were instrumental in creating mass consumer markets of the 1960s, other scholars do not even mention the reforms introduced by MacArthur (cf. Hadley 1988: 482–3).

Box 2.3 Evolution of Democracy in Japan (III)

After Japan's defeat in World War II in 1945, it was occupied by the allied powers, which introduced various reform measures in order to democratize Japan, including the dissolution of zaibatsu conglomerates. In 1947, Japan eventually made the transition to a full democracy ("at least on paper", cf. Kennon 2012) by adopting a new constitution. Most importantly, it declared that sovereignty resides with the people, the establishment of a parliamentary system in which both chambers were directly elected, freedom of speech, the permission for women to vote, and the abolishment of military forces. However, a large number of the American "Japan experts" somehow ignored that Japan had already prior experience with democracy (cf. Kennon 2012). The democratization process in Japan (after 1945) was rather top-down and imposed by the American occupational forces.

Since its foundation in 1955, the conservative Liberal Democratic Party (LDP) of Japan has been almost continuously in power (the only exception being the years 1993–1994 and 2009–2012)—either on its own or as the dominating coalition party. In the short period during which the Democratic Party of Japan (DPJ) was in power, it was heavily criticized because of its inexperience. Until today, Japan has not managed to accomplish the transition toward a stable two-party system (Fukuyama 2012). However, while lacking alternations between government and opposition can mitigate the inappropriate use of economic policy instruments aiming at the short-term goal of re-election (cf. also public choice theory and new political economy) and can be positive with respect to long-term planning, it may give rise to corruption and complacency (cf. also Stockwin 2018).

Policy change and macroeconomic problems (1947–1949)

As the Cold War started around 1947, the position of the USA regarding the primary objectives of economic reforms in Japan, namely, democratization and demilitarization, started to change. On the one hand, Japan was a potential ally and strategic base location; on the other hand, Japan should start to become independent of economic aid financed by US taxpayers. As a consequence, the American military government allowed the more comprehensive rebuilding of the heavy industry. Therefore, the Japanese government, still operating through command economy in the first years after World War II, was able to undertake various measures in order to address current macroeconomic problems that were plaguing Japan, namely, a **low productive capacity** and **rampant inflation** (Ito and Hoshi 2020). These issues had not been the focus of the international reform measures introduced by the SCAP, which were of a rather structural nature. At least regarding increasing the productive capacities, the actions of the Japanese government were quite successful (however, at the cost of even higher inflation). Under the **keisha seisan hoshiki**, that is, the priority production system, the top priority was to increase the coal production since it was Japan's main energy source. A special linkage between the coal and steel industry was established in the sense that the domestically produced as well as the imported coal and oil were allocated to the steel industry; the domestically produced steel, in turn, would be used to build coal mines (Woronoff 1992: 98; Ito 1998: 29). Moreover, steel products were directed into the shipbuilding as well as the electricity industry. The priority production system was supported by **price subsidies to key industries** and **preferential lending** by the 1947 established **Reconstruction Bank**. As a result, the industrial production increased rapidly in 1947 and 1948 (by 26% and 32%, respectively) and thus was able to recover to about half of the pre-war peak 3 years after the defeat of Japan (Horiuchi and Otaki 2017: 14–15). However, according to Ito and Hoshi (2020: 52), the subsidized lending was equivalent to seniorage financing and worsened the inflation problem since the low production capacity (and not a demand shortage) was responsible for the low production. Overall, the Japanese government managed to increase production; however, at the same time, it was not able to manage the skyrocketing inflation.

The Dodge Plan and the outbreak of the Korean War (1949–1952)

Partly due to the inability of the Japanese government to tackle the inflation problem, a major change in the policy line occurred in 1949, when Joseph Dodge was sent to Tokyo in order to fight the massive inflation and stabilize the economy by introducing an austerity plan (later called **Dodge Plan**) which consisted of four main measures, namely (1) a balanced budget on a consolidated basis, (2) the reduction and abolishment of subsidies, (3) the suspension of new loans from the reconstruction bank, (4) the unification of the yen exchange rates to 360 yen/US dollar.

Even though the Dodge Plan reforms managed to **bring inflation under control** and managed to reduce market barriers, the extreme tightening of the fiscal budget led to a **recession**. Therefore, this shock therapy approach was also criticized; in particular, it was argued that it came too early. However, favorable external conditions most probably prevented the worst: in 1950, the **Korean War** started and Japan became a supply base of the USA. As a consequence, the demand for Japanese manufactured goods increased sharply. The increasing exports in combination with lower imports improved Japan's balance of international payments. While Japan still had an import surplus accounting to US$162 million in the first half of the year 1950, this changed to an export surplus of US$24 million in the latter half of 1950 (Okita 1951: 142). This development allowed Japan to avoid a severe recession and enabled a fast recovery of the economy (Ito and Hoshi 2020; Ohno 2017). However, also the inflation rate rose again. For a more critical evaluation of the impact of the Korean War on Japan's development, see Dingman (1993).

2.5 The Period of High Economic Growth: Mid-1950s–1973

Between the mid-1950s and 1973, the Japanese economy grew at an average rate of roughly 10% per year. According to Hamada (1996), the 1950s can be understood as a period of preparation and transition to the 1960s, the so-called "golden era of high speed growth". By 1970, Japan overtook West Germany in economic size and became the second-largest economy (after the USA). This was Japan's second rise from the bottom to the top, however, at a much faster speed: while the Industrial Revolution during the Meiji period took about 50 years, Japan managed to rise again from a destroyed country to the group of the leading economies in only two decades (Ohno 2017).

2.5.1 The 1950s Booms and the Income Doubling Plan

The second half of the 1950s was characterized by a succession of booms and recessionary balance of payments adjustments. In particular, an excessive expansion of the domestic economy was followed by a balance of payments deficit, which was fought with anti-inflationary monetary policy. The year 1955 had seen the highest post-war growth rate, which surpassed 10%, accompanied by price stability and a balance of payments surplus.[4,5] However, this initial "boom in volume" (also referred to as a "quantitative boom" by Kosai 1986) was intermitted by a balance of payments deficit in 1956. The Jimmu Boom[6] (1956–57) and Iwato Boom[7] (1956–61) followed, again with an adjustment of the balance of payment interim period in 1958 (cf. Hamada and Kasuya 1992).[8] According to Kosai (1986), it was this alternation of booms and adjustments of the balance of payments that gradually established the prerequisites for the high growth during the 1960s.

In July 1960, Hayota Ikeda became Prime Minister. He pursued a heavy industrialization policy with a focus on machinery, petrochemicals, automobiles, and tires. In December 1960, he launched the so-called "**Income Doubling Plan**", which

[4] Important events of 1955 include the creation of the Liberal Democratic Party (LDP) as a merger of the Japan Democratic Party and the Liberal Party, as well as the new system of wage bargaining between unions and employers called "Shunto" (Spring Offensive), which took place every year in spring.

[5] In 1956, the Economic Whitepaper of the Economic Stability Board also officially announced that Japan was "no longer in a postwar reconstruction period" (cf. Hamada and Kasuy 1992).

[6] Named after Japan's legendary first emperor.

[7] In Japanese mythology, Iwato is a cave in which the Sun Goddess Amaterasu hid herself (thus depriving the world of light) until a group of deities lured her out of her seclusion (Kosai 1986).

[8] Kosai (1986) argues that the Iwato boom was much more durable than the Jimmu boom since during the latter, the production capacity could not keep pace with the demand effects of plant and equipment investments. In contrast, during the Iwato boom, demand and supply were much more in equilibrium and the government used prudent monetary policy that eventually allowed the prolongation of the economic expansion.

aimed at doubling the size of Japan's income within 10 years and to catch up to the West (Fujioka 1963). To achieve this ambitious goal, the estimated necessary annual average growth rate amounted to 9% for the first 3 years and 7.2% for the remaining years (cf. Kogiku 1977).[9] The Income Doubling Plan should also help to shift the focus away from the massive protests against the renewal of the 1951 US–Japan Security Treaty (which granted the USA the right to station troops in Japan) toward economic growth. Important policy measures of the plan included a reduction of interest rates and tax cuts to motivate spending, the expansion of the social safety nets as well as targeted investment in infrastructure, communications, and technological innovation. In addition, Ikeda wanted to push forward trade liberalization (see also below). Even though the plan was regarded as overambitious, Japan was even able to exceed the goals set in the Income Doubling Plan (see also Kosai 1986). It had already doubled its national income by 1967 with an average growth rate of around 10%; by 1973, it had even tripled (Hamada 1985).[10] This had not been anticipated by the public which initially doubted that the plan could be realized.

2.5.2 Factors Driving Economic Growth

What is the secret of this rapid economic growth (*Kodo seicho*)? The next paragraphs discuss some of the factors that enabled the Japanese growth miracle.

In general, sources of economic growth can be analyzed from either demand-side or supply-side perspective.

With respect to the **demand-side**, important growth factors included **investment and consumer demand** as well as **exports**. Between 1955 and the beginning of the 1970s, the ratio of private non-residential fixed investment to GNP rose from 10% to almost 25%. According to IFO Institute for Economic Research and Sakura Institute of Research (1997: 83), abundant household savings were the main sources of the continuous upward trend in capital **investment** in Japan. High investment growth enabled the building up of the capital stock, which, in turn, introduced new investment, creating an induced investment cycle. The share of real private plant and equipment investment in real GNP increased from 7.7% in 1955 to 14% in 1960 (Kosai 1986: 115).

The ratio of **exports** to GNP stayed relatively stable during the 1950s and 1960s; however, it started to increase continuously since the second half of the 1960s. Because of the undervalued exchange rate and increasing product quality (thanks to imported technology), Japanese goods became increasingly internationally competitive, and there was a rising demand for Japanese exports.

Another factor that was very likely also partly responsible for the sustained growth in the late 1950s and 1960s is strong **consumption**. In particular, the

[9] It has to be noted that the Income Doubling Plan was more like a blueprint that did not specify instruments to achieve it (Hamada 1996).

[10] The period between 1966 and 1969 is sometimes also referred to as the Izanami period (in the sense that it was "the best period since Izanami" which was the goddess that according to Japanese mythology together with Izanagi created the Japanese archipelago (Hamada 1996).

consumption structure changed considerably during the high growth period, away from daily necessities such as clothing toward washing machines, black-and-white television, and refrigerators (the so-called "three divine devices") in the second half of the 1950s and subsequently toward color television, automobiles, and air-conditioning during the 1960s (cf. Ohno 2017).[11] According to Horioka (1994), per capita private final consumption expenditures grew at an average annual rate of 6.56%, leading to a 2.6-fold increase between 1960 and 1975.

With respect to the **supply side** growth sources, we can identify input factors such as **capital** and **labor** as well as **technology/productivity**.

During the high growth period, the working-age population grew considerably; in addition, there was a non-negligible rural-to-urban migration (especially of younger people). Moreover, educational attainment increased: between 1950 and 1970, the average years of schooling increased from 6.7 to 7.8 years, and the population with higher education rose from 4.5 to 7.6% (Barro and Lee 2013). In addition, Japan could exploit the "latecomer advantages" by importing foreign technology (see also below). Since Japan increasingly engaged in export activities (see the demand-side factors above), the related exposure of Japanese products to competition in foreign markets had positive impacts on productivity and product quality.

According to various empirical studies, Japan's high average annual growth in the 1950s and 1960s can be attributed to both, (capital and labor) input growth as well as productivity growth.

For instance, Denison and Chung (1976: 98–9) find that the Japanese economy reported an average growth rate of 8.81% over the period 1953–1971; the growth of inputs (that is labor and capital accumulation) accounted for 45% of total growth, and productivity accounted for 55%. Similar results are reported by Maddison (1998) and Hayami and Ogasawara (1999). Nishimizu and Hulten (1978) find a somewhat smaller contribution of TFP (ranging from 25 to 32%) whereas capital accumulation accounts between 52 and 58%. However, as noted by the authors themselves they do not take into account that part of the observed growth rates of produced input was a result of productivity change, which can lead to a significant understatement of the importance of technological change (cf. Nishimizu and Hulten 1978: 351).

Hayami and Ogasawara (1999) argue that while both, high capital input growth and high productivity growth (53%), were the drivers of Japan's economic growth in the 1950s and 1960s, the US growth was mainly driven by technological progress (contributing 80% to overall growth) when it found itself at a comparable development stage than Japan. This is also in line with the observations of Gerschenkron (1962) that industrialization latecomers can rely more heavily on the imitation of technology developed by countries that have already undergone industrialization (for an extensive discussion in the Japanese context see Whalley and Zhou 2011). Also, Japan relied on the imitation of foreign technologies (through reverse engineering). Since the Japanese engineers and technical workers

[11] Between 1956 and 1958, the output of black-and-white television sets increased by more than 333% to one million. Also, washing machines reached the one million mark in 1958 (cf. Kosai 1986).

had accumulated sufficient knowledge and skills, this facilitated the utilization (and also the subsequent improvement) of foreign technologies considerably (see also Chap. 5 below). In general, policies concerning science and technology rather supported the diffusion and dissemination of existing discoveries instead of the promotion of new ones. For instance, the Japanese patent system only gives patent holders limited rights of exclusivity (Flath 2014: 377ff).

There is no consensus regarding the question of which factor was most important for enabling Japan's high-growth period. In our view, the **combination** of the factors mentioned above was decisive for Japan's economic success. For instance, the consumption boom incentivized production and facilitated the exploitation of scale economies, leading to cost reductions. In addition, the increased production opened employment opportunities, building an affluent "white-collar middle-class" (Ohno 2017). Moreover, the increased international competition due to the promotion of exports had a positive effect on productivity.

2.5.3 Industrial Policy

There are opposing views regarding the role that industrial policy (**sangyo seisaku**) conducted by the Ministry of International Trade and Industry (MITI) played in Japan's high growth. Industrial policy measures included subsidies, preferential taxes, entry restriction, R&D assistance, low interest policy loans, and (probably most important) the protection of infant industries (Ohno 2017: 171). The advocates of industrial policy argue that it allows rapid reallocation of resources from declining industries to sectors characterized by high growth and high productivity (Dosi et al. 1989). However, Beason and Weinstein (1996) and Okubo and Tomiura (2012) find no positive impact of industrial policies on growth and productivity.

Box 2.4 Industrial Policy in Post-war Japan

Over the course of time, the focus of industrial policy changed (cf. Komiya et al. 1988). In the early post-war period, industrial policy focused particularly on the coal industry and encompassed rather socialist economic planning-type measures such as a preferential production plan. The focus of the industrial policies subsequently switched to the financing of machines and production plants in the 1950s with the rationalization (gorika; in the sense of using labor-saving technology) plans becoming the core element of industrial policy. Since the Japanese economy has transited from planning to market economy, this change was also reflected in the reforms. The rationalization was enabled via special tax provision (Enterprise Regionalization Promotion Law in 1952) as well as the fiscal investment and loan program, which loaned funds to the private sector via the Export Bank of Japan and the Japan Development Bank at low interest rates. In the course of Japan's increasing integration into the global economy in the 1960s, strengthening the industrial competitiveness became the main focus of industrial policy, and in the 1970s, the industrial policy also took increasingly into account environmental issues and the application of antitrust policies.

Also the role of **keiretsu** for the fast development of the Japanese economy is controversial. When the attitude of the USA regarding the development of the heavy and chemical industries in Japan against the background of the Korean War changed, also the Antimonopoly Act restrictions were relaxed continuously (in 1949, 1953, and 1977) and the Japanese government eventually allowed the re-introduction of the old zaibatsu names and the MITI supported the emergence of the keiretsu (Tipton 2008).

It can be distinguished between **horizontal keiretsu** and **vertical keiretsu**. Group members of the horizontal keiretsu are linked via cross-shareholding and can lend from a group bank. They followed the one set principal (*wan setto shugi*), meaning that each keiretsu tried to have one company in any major industry. The six largest keiretsus, also referred to as the **Big Six**, were Mitsui, Mitsubishi, Sumitomo, Fuyo, Sanwa, and Ichikan, the first three being former zaibatsu conglomerates. In contrast, vertical keiretsu describe vertical networks of connected firms (production keiretsu, distribution keiretsu, and capital keiretsu) (Ito and Hoshi 2020: 293, 295, 300).

According to some researchers, cross-shareholding, in particular, the special relationships between member firms and the group bank, mitigates the problem of imperfect information and provides a form of insurance against financial distress problems (see Aoki 1988, 1990, for a rather theoretical discussion). Empirical evidence is provided by Nakatani (1984), Hoshi et al. (1990a, b), Teranishi (1994). However, there is disagreement on the profitability of keiretsu firms compared with non-keiretsu companies. The studies of Caves and Uekusa (1976) and Nakatani (1984) do not find evidence that the keiretsu firms have been more profitable than non-keiretsu companies. Nakatani (1984) also argues that this may be due to the focus on the interests of the employees rather than on those of the shareholders.

Some researchers also argue that keiretsu are collusive institutions. In their view, inter-firm relationships and collusion among the keiretsu groups prevent the entry of foreign firms (Fung 1991; Lawrence 1991; Prestowitz 1988). Weinstein and Yafeh (1995), however, reject this hypothesis. They find that it is rather the fierce competition among group-affiliated firms than collusion that reduces foreign and domestic entry into sectors where keiretsu groups are strong.

According to Noguchi (1998), the **cultural and institutional roots** of the structure of the Japanese corporations lie in the wartime era, including limitations on dividends and shareholder rights, and the focus on the collective interest of employees. This helps to explain why empirical studies find that the main benefits of keiretsu are rather stability than profitability. In the era prior to the war, corporations rather had the goal of profit maximization and were more focused on the shareholders. Thus, the Japanese corporations during this time followed a rather similar spirit than corporations in other capitalist countries.

2.5.4 Monetary Policy

Until August 1971, Japan was part of the so-called Bretton Woods system[12] and kept its exchange rate constant at 360 yen/dollar. Monetary policy in Japan reacted to the current account and followed a stop-and-go policy that enabled a relatively stable path of the price level (cf. Kaizuka 1967). In particular, a contractionary (expansionary) monetary policy was adopted as soon as the current account turned into deficit (surplus) (Hamada and Hayashi 1985; Hamada 1985). As a consequence of the fixed exchange rate regime, the price level of traded goods at home was linked to that in foreign countries. However, thanks to the fact that the USA and other major industrial countries managed to contain price inflation within a low range, the Japanese wholesale price index remained relatively stable during the 1950s and 1960s. Over the same period, the CPI rate increased gradually (because of the varying technological progress rates of the manufacturing and consumer goods sectors, cf. Hamada 1985). After 1968, the situation changed: the US' Johnson administration followed an active expenditure policy, leading to substantial price increases. In order to keep the domestic price level stable without changing the exchange rate parity, Japan could either accept the accumulation of a large surplus in its international balance of payments or, alternatively, inflate the economy in line with world inflation. Until the adoption of Nixon's New Economic Policy in 1971, Japan followed the former strategy.

2.5.5 Trade Liberalization

It was also during the high growth period that Japan re-integrated itself into the global economy. After having already joined the IMF and World Bank in 1952, it also became a member of the GATT in 1955, and 1 year later, it joined the United Nations. In the middle of the 1960s, Japan then became a member of the OECD. It was also during the 1960s that trade was (even though gradually) liberalized. According to Ohno (2017), important features of the trade liberalization during the 1960s included the close link between tariff reduction and industrial promotion measures to improve competitiveness. Moreover, the Japanese government removed import barriers in close consultation with businesses.

The timetable for trade liberalization was pre-committed and regarded as being not negotiable. Consequently, producer focused on efficiency improvements instead

[12] When Japan joined the IMF and the World Bank in 1952, Japan also had to enter the so-called Bretton Woods system, which meant that the exchange rate had to be kept largely constant to the US dollar (with only minor adjustment options).

of finding ways to prolong protection measures. However, as argued by Ohno (2017), such an ambitious strategy is only possible if the country exhibits an adequate institutional capacity (see also Okazaki 2019).

In the following, we briefly describe some of the trade liberalization measures undertaken by the Japanese government.

The **Foreign Exchange and Foreign Trade Control Law (FEFTCL)** that had been enacted at the end of 1949 was the legal framework for private international trade between 1950 and 1964. Unless explicitly authorized, external transactions were proscribed. The central tool of the FEFTCL was the **Foreign Exchange Budget (FEB) System** (*gaikoku kawase yosan seido*) which stated the maximum amounts for overall as well as individual imports (Takagi 1997). Almost all imported goods had to be licensed and were planned in the foreign exchange budget for import goods, which, in turn, consisted of the budget for foreign exchange allocation system goods (**FA goods**) and the budget for automatic approval system goods (**AA goods**) as well as a reserve budget (Okazaki and Korenaga 1999). Import of AA goods was de facto free within the total limit (as long as budget for AA goods was not fully used, import was automatically approved), whereas the MITI could impose de facto import quotas on FA goods (unlike for the AA goods, the budget for the FA goods was allocated to each good individually and not in a lump sum form) (Okazaki and Korenaga 1999). Between 1952 and 1959, the FA budget accounted for an average of 74% of the total foreign exchange budget (cf. also Fig. 2.2).

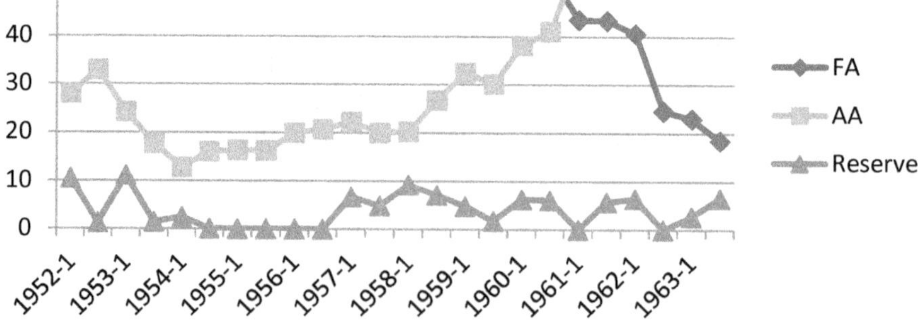

Fig. 2.2 Composition of the foreign exchange budget in percent. *Source* Okazaki and Korenaga (1999), own calculations. *Note* "automatic foreign exchange allocation" (AFA) goods are not taken into account

In the late 1950s, Japan faced increasingly external pressure (among others from the IMF) to push forward trade liberalization (Takagi 1997). The "automatic foreign exchange allocation" (AFA) goods category was introduced. Under this system, the allocation of foreign exchange for the import of goods in this category was automatically made on application to the MITI (Kiyota and Okazaki 2013; Takagi 1997). In June 1960, the Japanese government approved the **Plan for Trade and Exchange Liberalization** (boeki kawase jiyuka keikaku taiko) and announced that the liberalization rate (defined as the ratio of AA and AFA goods in total imports) should be raised to around 80% until June 1963. In July 1960, the yen gained partial external convertibility (in the context of introducing non-resident free yen accounts, cf. Fukao 2003). In the following years, many FA goods were reclassified into AA and AFA goods and the AA ratio indeed increased sharply (cf. Fig. 2.2, note that the numbers in Fig. 2.2 do not take into account AFA goods). In October 1962, the foreign exchange liberalization rate (defined as the AA and AFA goods in total imports) already accounted 88% (see Fig. 2.3). In 1964, Japan achieved the status of an **IMF Article VIII nation** and **abolished the foreign exchange budget** (Takagi 1997; Okazaki 2019); an import quota system was introduced for the remaining FA commodities (cf. Kiyota and Okazaki 2013). The foreign exchange liberalization rate amounted to 93% in 1964, where it stayed until the end of the decade (cf. Fig. 2.3).

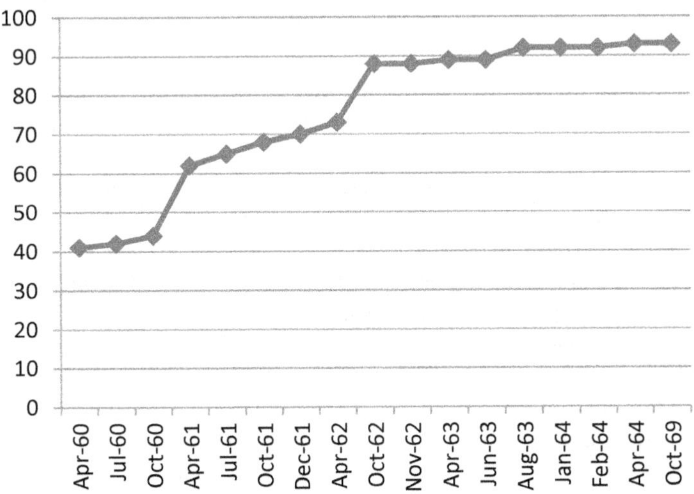

Fig. 2.3 Foreign exchange liberalization rate. *Source* Kiyota and Okazaki (2016), Table 1. *Note* Between April 1964 and October 1969, the liberalization rate stayed at 93%, therefore, we do not list the in-between data points for this period

2.6 Beginning Growth Slowdown in the 1970s

As outlined above, as a consequence of the high growth period, Japan managed to rise up in the rankings and became one of the biggest economies by the beginning of the 1970s. Japan's growth subsequently slowed down in the 1970s and 1980s; however, the Japanese economy still grew at an average annual rate of about 4%. This period is, therefore, sometimes also referred to as a "period of stable growth".

2.6.1 Major Determinants of the Growth Slowdown

Why did Japan's extremely high growth not continue but fell to more moderate levels? In this section, we will discuss four underlying reasons.

First, according to **neoclassical growth theory**, a growth slowdown is only natural and inevitable as an economy approaches the world economic frontier. More precisely, the latecomer advantages such as the possibility to import foreign technologies and productivity increases due to structural change (in particular, shifting workers from the agricultural to the more productive manufacturing sector) become exhausted and cannot be further used to generate the previously experienced high-speed growth (Lewis 1954; Barro and Sala-i-Martin 1997; Glawe and Wagner 2016).

Second, there were **two major external shocks** that hit the Japanese economy: the oil shocks that led to a quadrupling of the export price of oil as well as the Nixon shocks and the subsequent appreciation of the yen against the US dollar.

The **Nixon shocks** refer to various economic and political measures undertaken by the USA in the summer of 1971, namely, the resumption of diplomatic relations with China as well at the announcement of the New Economic Program, including the 90-day freeze on wages and prices, a 10% surcharge on imports, and the abandonment of the gold standard that led to an **appreciation of the yen**. The USA undertook these measures mainly in order to fight domestic inflation and in order to reduce the balance of payments deficit, at least that part of it that was caused by the trade with Japan. Expansionary monetary policy of the Bank of Japan should provide stimulus to the economy in order to mitigate the anticipated adverse effects (cf. Ito and Hoshi 2020; see also below, reason three). As part of the Smithsonian Agreement, the yen-dollar exchange rate was set at 308. In 1973, Japan, together with other industrialized countries, then adopted a system of flexible exchange rates, and thus monetary policy became more autonomous (Hamada 1985).

The first **oil crisis** hit Japan in 1973. The oil price increased from $3 to $13 per barrel. The second oil crisis around 1978/1979 led to a further increase in the oil price up to almost $40 per barrel. The steep increase in oil prices also adversely affected production costs (e.g. via rising energy prices) and forced Japan to switch to a production model less dependent on oil consumption. However, it took various years until the reallocation of resources from the primarily growth-oriented and energy-intensive industries to more sustainable and environmentally friendly ones was accomplished successfully. Especially the period after the first oil shock was also characterized by rampant inflation, which, combined with the wage increase, resulted in a price-wage spiral (Ito and Hoshi 2020). People started hoarding daily goods such as toilet paper; the consequently empty supermarket shelves resulted in even greater panic (Ohno 2017). Also, industrial goods were affected. This period is sometimes also referred to as the period of "crazy prices" (kyoran bukka) (cf. also Kosai 1998).

However, the inflationary pressure was also partly due to political measures undertaken by the Japanese government, which mostly followed an expansionary monetary policy between 1965 and 1973. Thus, the **third** reason for moderate growth can be ascribed to the **Japanese government and its policies**. Between 1970 and 1973, the money supply increased by 20% per annum (Kosai 1988: 537). The main reasons for this expansionary policy course of the Bank of Japan were the Nixon shocks (see also above) and the support of the "Japanese Archipelago Rebuilding Plan" suggested by Prime Minister Kakuei Tanaka.

The "Japanese Archipelago Rebuilding Plan" was presented by Tanaka in 1972 (cf. Tsuzuki 2000: 424). The plan was aimed at continuing the high growth of the post-war era and underlined the importance of increasing investment expenditure, including the establishment of an extensive road and railroad infrastructure in order to connect rural and urban areas (Ohno 2017; Ito and Hoshi 2020; Cargill and Royama 1988: 110). The announcement of the plan fostered land speculation and initiated an increase in land prices, soon followed by increasing commodity prices giving rise to land speculation (Kosai 1988).

Fearing the negative impact of the yen appreciation in the course of the Bretton Woods system (e.g. on the Japanese export performance), the early 1970s were characterized by a lax monetary policy. The Japanese government explicitly approved inflation to avoid appreciation (so-called adjustment inflation) and exerted pressure on the BOJ, which was not legally independent from the government at this time (Ito and Hoshi 2020). Only in April 1973, the official discount rate was eventually raised, followed by four more increases over the next 9 months (Ito and Hoshi 2020). Already prior to the first oil shock, the inflation rate stood at 10%. The tight monetary policy measures eventually succeeded in decreasing the inflation rate at the end of 1974; however, it also resulted in an economic contraction (Ito 2013). The first oil crisis taught the Bank of Japan an important lesson: Sacrificing the objective of price stability to maintain a stable parity of the yen can be dangerous. Consequently, the BOJ acted in a timelier manner in 1979 when oil prices were again raised by OPEC and quickly adopted monetary retrenchment measures (Hamada 1985). Also, labor union leaders learned the hard way that considerable wage rate increases (26.2% in the course of the spring labor offensive in 1974) could come at the expense of potential job losses (Hamada 1985).

Fourth, many institutional features of the Japanese economy (such as lifetime employment, the main bank system, as well as administrative guidance) that turned out to be appropriate for the reconstruction of the war-devastated Japan and, among other factors, enabled the high growth rate in the 1950s and 1960s (cf. Morck and Yeung 2017), became problematic after Japan had become a high-income country that had to rely on total factor productivity in order to sustain growth. However, due to the external shocks during the 1970s (see reason two), policymakers had to focus on coping with the related problems (see reason three), and thus the **systematic, structural reforms of the economy, and its institutions were delayed** (Ohno 2017).

2.6.2 Macroeconomic Policy Patterns and Performance

In the 1980s, austerity policies dominated the economic policy landscape worldwide. Fighting inflation became the top economic policy objective after the shocks of the two oil crises in the 1970s and the inflation that subsequently built-up (driven also by expansionary monetary and fiscal policies to fight the recessions and stagnations of the 1970s, all also accompanied by the aftermath of the collapse of the Bretton Woods system in the wake of the inflationary Vietnam War funding by the Johnson and Nixon administrations). If we look into two countries that have much in common although they come from different cultural backgrounds (the development process/success of the two countries in the 1950s and 1960s is commonly referred to as the two "economic miracles" of the post-war period), namely, Japan and West Germany, we can note the following differences in economic policy and macroeconomic performance in the 1970s and 1980s (see Wagner 1989).

While the macroeconomic patterns in the two countries were not so different, a difference in the timing of disinflation policies was visible. The Bank of Japan reacted relatively late to the inflationary tendencies after the first oil crisis, whereas the Bundesbank started relatively late to fight inflation in/after the second oil crisis. In any case, inflation aversion in Japan was always lower and less significant for economic policy than in West Germany. However, this only led to different macroeconomic outcomes because the labor market flexibility conditions were also different in the two countries. By labor market flexibility, we mean here not only wage flexibility but also the flexibility of supply and demand structures more broadly. Labor supply flexibility consists of mobility of workers and flexibility of working hours (wage contracts in Japan are rather short). Labor demand flexibility, on the other hand, is based on employers' (expected) ability to transfer or lay off "surplus" workers and reduce wage costs in adverse economic situations. In terms of all these categories, Japan has shown higher flexibility than West Germany (Wagner 1989: 61–72).

Japan was then (and still is) a country where traditionally, compared to West Germany, labor relations were (are) more harmonious, people were (are) less individualistic, had higher work preferences (depending, among other things, on housing and leisure opportunities) and were more open to new developments or technologies. This made it easier to absorb shocks at the time. Consequently, Japan disinflated faster after the second oil crisis and produced much less unemployment.

Table 2.1 Macroeconomic trends in Japan and West Germany, 1960–1987

		Real GNP growth		Inflation		Unemployment	
		Japan	West Germany	Japan	West Germany	Japan	West Germany
1960–87*	Mean	6.6	3.1	6.1	3.6	1.8	3.8
1960–69		10.5	4.5	5.6	2.6	1.3	1
1970–79	Mean	5.4	3.1	9.1	4.9	1.7	2.9
1980–87		3.9	1.5	2.7	3.1	2.6	7.8
1960–87*	S.D.	4	2.6	4.8	1.9	0.6	3.2
1960–69		2.8	2.8	1.8	0.8	0.1	0.5
1970–79	S.D.	3.6	2.4	6.1	1.5	0.4	1.7
1980–87		1	1.7	2.6	2.4	0.3	2

Source Wagner (1989)
Notes "*" Real GNP growth and inflation data only available since 1961. S.D. stands for standard deviation

In particular, the lower pressure of labor supply from young people, female workers, and foreign workers, as well as the higher share of temporary workers and self-employed in Japan, also contributed to the fact that unemployment there was lower then and still is. Moreover, Japan followed an implicit concept of wage indexation to firms' profits (as in bonus payments) and to nominal GNP (as in base wage payments), but with low index factors (cf. Wagner 1989: 76ff.). This indexation scheme compensates for the risk that companies are unable to get rid of "surplus" workers without high economic or social costs ("Surplus" here means "in excess" at the going real wage level.). In Japan, these workers, therefore, were not really "surplus" or only for a short time because real-wage incomes then adjusted (via the indexation scheme) so that the new equilibrium real wage at the stable employment level was soon reached again. This kept employment stable and real growth high in Japan (Wagner 1989: 68).

All this paid off in that in Japan, unemployment was much lower and more stable (at least from the 1970s on), and real GNP growth was higher, but also more unstable (compared with West Germany). Inflation, on the other hand, was much higher and more unstable (at least in the 1970s) (Table 2.1).

To cope with the prolonged stagflation after the first oil crisis, the Japanese government then aggressively expanded fiscal spending even though tax revenues were stagnating, so that government debt began to rise (Part of the expansion of public expenditures in the second half of the 1970s was based on the large expansion of welfare programs that had already taken place in 1973.). Compared with West Germany, Japanese fiscal policy in the 1970s and 1980s was always more "activist" (with the exception of the 1982–1984 period; see Fig. 7 in Wagner 1989: 58).

This is somewhat surprising in that governments in Japan had not relied on deficit-financed spending to any great extent before the first oil crisis. Before 1965, the individual income tax schedule had regularly been adjusted to keep public spending within one-fifth of GNP (Hamada 1985: 191). The issuance of government bonds to finance current expenditure had been prohibited by the Government Budget Law (Zaiseiho). Only when a recession hit the Japanese economy in 1965 did the government introduce a special law allowing it to issue long-term bonds. But it was not until the 1976 fiscal year that public bonds were issued on a larger scale.

In the second half of the 1970s, in connection with aggressive deficit-financed spending, public debt in Japan began to rise (see Table 1 in Wagner 1989: 57). In the first half of the 1980s, as the public debt problem intensified, the government pursued a policy of fiscal austerity and significantly curbed the growth rate of public investment along with the growth of current expenditure. This policy line proved successful in that it alleviated the problem of the budget deficit in the mid-1980s. In the second half of the 1980s, however, Japan turned again to a more expansionary fiscal and monetary policy (in October 1985 the federal government decided on 3100 billion yen in additional spending, in September 1986 3600 billion yen and in May 1987 5000 billion yen, as well as tax cuts; see Wagner 1989: 59).

Taken together, Japan still performed disproportionately well in a global comparison of industrialized countries in the 1980s, catching up more and more with the USA (see also Table 6.1 in Chap. 6 below). In the second half of the 1980s, this even led there to fears that Japan could not only overtake the USA (economically and technologically), but that a new "Japanese century" was dawning with Japanese economic and technological dominance. The financial crisis in Japan in the early 1990s put an end to this, and Japan's temporary(?) "decline" began ("Lost Two Decades"; see in the following).

2.7 Japan's Lost Two Decades

The period between 1992 and 2012 is often referred to as the Lost Two Decades and was characterized by very low economic growth and since the end of the 1990s additionally by deflation. There are competing views of whether supply-side or demand-side factors are the main causes of prolonged stagnation. According to the demand-side view, the bursting of the asset price bubble in combination with the following macroeconomic policy mistakes induced a demand shortage (partly based on the reverse wealth effect on consumption (induced by the decline in asset and house prices) and pessimistic future expectations of households and firms, cf. Asako and Ochiai 2010). The existence of deflation over the second half of the Lost Two Decades supports this view. In such a case, adequate measures include expansionary monetary and fiscal policies. On the other hand, proponents of the supply-side view argue that structural factors such as population aging as well as the absence of adequate institutions for promoting innovation are the main culprits of the Lost Two Decades. It is indeed plausible that such a long-lasting economic stagnation is probably also related to underlying structural problems, which have to be addressed with adequate long-term restructuring reforms. While the literature has not yet reached consensus regarding the question of which hypothesis is more convincing, we argue that both views are not mutually exclusive and that different effects most likely interacted with and negatively reinforced each other, thus magnifying the negative impact on the overall economic performance. Moreover, while the bursting of the bubble and inadequate policy responses most probably initiated the Lost Two Decades, supply-side factors became increasingly important in the second half of the Lost Two Decades.

In the following, we briefly outline the crisis timeline, describe the key indicators, and elaborate on the undertaken policy measures.

As suggested by Ito and Hoshi (2020), the Lost Two Decades can be subdivided into four time periods, (1) the bursting bubble and the start of the recession (1992–1997), (2) the banking crisis during which the recession turned into a chronic stagnation (1997–2003), (3) the short recovery period under Prime Minister Koizumi (2003–2007), (4) the Global Financial Crisis and political instability (2007–2012).

Bubble economy and First Phase

In the period **prior** to the Lost Two Decades an asset price bubble was forming. From 1983 to 1989, the stock price index and the land price index quadrupled (Ito and Hoshi 2020). Proponents of the demand-side view argue that this steep increase was mainly caused by a too lax monetary policy that was installed in order to offset the adverse economic effects of the yen appreciation (among others because of the Plaza Accord in 1985) (Yoshino and Taghizadeh-Hesary 2015). This was in line with the BOJ policy reaction function, which recommended expansionary monetary policy in order to address an appreciation of the yen or a recession (cf. Ohno 2017).

There are two opposing views regarding how monetary policy should be conducted in the event of a potential asset price bubble (the so-called "clean versus lean debate"): researchers and policymakers following the **cleansing view** (also referred to as **benign neglect**) argue that monetary policy should ignore fluctuations in asset prices and potential bubbles (since such intervention might be associated with considerable costs) and rather "clean up" after the bubble has burst (see e.g. Bernanke and Gertler 1999, 2001; Greenspan 2002). In contrast, proponents of the **leaning view** believe that central banks should "lean against the wind". In particular, monetary policy should react to asset price misalignments to prevent or control asset price bubbles (see e.g. Cecchetti et al. 2003; Borio and White 2004).[13]

The Bank of Japan only started to tighten the monetary policy in 1989 in order to calm down the demand for real estate and equity. In only 1 year, the policy rate was increased from 2.5 to 4.25% and finally to 6% in 1990 (Himino 2021). In addition to the monetary tightening, various other (credit, fiscal, and tax) policy measures were installed to slow down the rise in land prices: among others, the Ministry of Finance (MOF) limited lending to the real estate sector and introduced a new national land tax as well as the short-term capital gains tax (cf. Yokoi-Arai 2002:

[13] See also Wagner (2010).

Table 2.2 Fiscal stimulus packages (1992–1995)

	Amount (in trillions of yen)	% of GDP
August 1992	10.7	2.3
April 1993	13.2	2.8
September 1993	6.0	1.3
February 1994	15.3	3.2
September 1995	14.2	3.0
Total	59.4	2.52 (avg.)

Source Suzuki (2000)

302; Huang and Armstrong 2014).[14] These rather macro-prudentially spirited policies in combination with the monetary tightening eventually caused the bursting of the bubble at the beginning of the 1990s.

In the view of Okina et al. (2001), tightening measures should (if it all) have started earlier. Hamada et al. (2011) argue that the negative wealth effects of the collapse of the bubble and the associated consumption decline were underestimated by the policymakers, who responded only slowly with expansionary fiscal policies (Hamada et al. 2011). In the view of Ahearne et al. (2002), more aggressive easing after the collapse could have contained deflation.

Starting in August 1992, various economic stimulus packages were introduced, which enabled a (short) economic recovery in 1996. An overview of the fiscal stimulus packages is provided in Table 2.2.

¥2.8 trillion of the first fiscal stimulus package was explicitly earmarked for price-keeping operations (PKO),[15] in the course of which public funds were injected into the stock market in order to prevent stock prices from further falling. Controversial is the success of the PKO: even though the Nikkei 225 stabilized for some time (between around ¥16,000 and ¥20,000), opponents of the PKO argue that it only "prolonged" the pain and was not able to mitigate the difficulties in the financial sector (Lipscy and Takinami 2013; Katz 2003).

Second Phase

The short economic rebound with growth rates rising above 3% around 1996 was only short-lived, and in 1997 and 1998, a banking crisis hit the country. This also marked the beginning of the second phase of the Lost Two Decades during which the recession turned into a chronic stagnation and the inflation rate dipped into negative territory.

Many causes that led to the erosion of the financial system can be traced back to the period of the bubble economy as well as to the first phase of the Lost Two Decades. While the bursting of the bubble probably triggered the financial crisis,

[14] For an overview of the land tax reform in Japan, see also Ishi (1991).

[15] A wordplay, making reference to the UN "peace-keeping operations" (cf. Grimes 2018: 153).

the deeper underlying structural problems intensified the adverse effects (Görger 2001).

During the first phase of the Lost Two Decades, government and financial regulators underestimated the problem of non-performing loans (NPLs) and delayed serious banking reforms and restructuring measures. There was a concentration of loan portfolios in property-related businesses including real estate and construction; however, the quality of these loans was increasingly eroded once asset prices started falling. The loan losses depleted the capital base of banks; however, the government and financial regulators still believed that in the future, real estate prices would recover and the NPL problem thus be eliminated ("wait-and-see" policy, cf. Nakaso 2001). Therefore, Japanese banks continued to lend to otherwise insolvent firms (so-called "**zombies**") so that they could meet their expenses to avoid default. This practice of **evergreening** loans led to a distorted competition, in particular, it depressed the prices for zombie firm's products and raised their wages, and thus reduced profits of new, more productive firms that were discouraged from market entry and investments (cf. Caballero et al. 2008). In March 1998, the NPLs accounted for 5.5% of loan supplied by domestically licensed banks (Watanabe 2007) and amounted to approximately 7% of GDP (cf. Hoshi and Kashyap 2000a, b). The increasing number of NPLs since the bursting of the bubble led to a growing mistrust between the financial institutions, and the shrinking net worth of the banks increasingly impeded their lending abilities. The full extent of the problem eventually became apparent when the Asian Financial Crisis deteriorated the external environment, a wave of large-scale failures in the financial sector, and a subsequent liquidity crisis ("credit crunch") followed (Görger 2001). In November 1997, three major financial institutions failed: Sanyo Securities, the Hokkaido Takushoku Bank, and Yamaichi Securities (Nakano 2016).

An additional demand-side factor most likely exacerbated the slump in the growth rate. In April 1997, the consumption tax rate was increased from 3 to 5% in order to restore the fiscal balance. This policy measure was accompanied by the phasing-out of temporary income tax cuts and a rise in the Social Security contributions (IMF 1999). There was criticism that these measures in combination imposed a heavy burden on households' disposable real income and significantly reduced consumption expenditures (Ito and Hoshi 2020), which, in turn, hampered economic activity.

At the end of November 1997, the fourth collapse of the Tokuyo City Bank led to rumors and speculations over other bank failures. Western financial institutions started demanding a higher Japan premium for funding, which further increased the stress on the Japanese banking system (Okubo 2003). To cope with these problems, two major institutional and legal reforms were initiated: (1) the creation of a more independent financial supervision agency (the Financial Supervisory Agency, FSA) that took over the functions of the Ministry of Finance (MOF) and (2) The Financial Function Stabilization Act that enabled the government to induce capital injections amounting to ¥30 trillion of public funds (¥13 trillion for the recapitalization of major banks and ¥17 trillion to protect depositors from failed financial institutions) and to temporarily nationalize banks (Hoshi and Kashyap 2010). In March 1998, ¥1.8 trillion were injected to 21 major banks, however, they were considered as too small to substantially recapitalize the banking system and stabilize the market and were also criticized for not adequately addressing the NPL problem (Nakaso 2001; Fuji and Kawai 2010). At the end of 1998, the Long-Term Credit Bank (LTCB) and the Nippon Credit Bank (NCB) still had to be temporarily nationalized in October and November, respectively. It was not until March 1999, when a second, much bigger capital injection into 15 banks amounting to ¥7.5 trillion followed, so that the stability of the banking sector could be restored, markets calmed, and the Japan premium started to decline. This was partly achieved by an improved implementation design, including rising standards for securing public funding, a stricter definition of net worth, higher standards regarding the classification of loans into performing and non-performing categories, the obligation to submit detailed restructuring plans (so-called management improvement plans) to the Financial Reconstruction Commission (FRC, founded in 1998), and the encouragement of private sector-driven capitalization (Fuji and Kawai 2010; Nakaso 2001; Cargill 2003; Hoshi and Patrick 2000). Between 1998 and 2001, a new financial supervision framework was established (Table 2.3).

Zero Interest Rate Policy and Quantitative Easing

In order to address the low growth around 1997/98, the BOJ adopted a zero interest rate policy (ZIRP) between early 1999 and August 2000. In April 1999, the BOJ announced to maintain zero interest rates "until deflationary concerns are dispelled" (Baba et al. 2004). Growth recovered shortly in 2000; however, the inflation rate

Table 2.3 Overview of the financial supervision framework

Pre 1998	1998	2000	2001
Ministry of Finance (MOF)	**MOF: Financial System Planning Bureau (FSPB of MOF)**	**Financial Services Agency (FSA 2)** (July 2000)	**Financial Services Agency (FSA 2)** (January 2001)
	Financial planning responsibility		
	Financial Supervisory Agency (FSA 1) (June 1998)		
	Inspection, licensing, and supervision of the financial system		
	Financial Reconstruction Commission (FRC) (Dec 1998)	**Financial Reconstruction Commission (FRC)** (Dec 1998)	
	Financial crisis management, parent body of the FSA	Financial crisis management, parent body of the FSA	

was still in negative territory. As growth decreased again at the end of 2000, the BOJ adopted an unconventional monetary policy measure, the so-called quantitative easing (QE), hoping that this policy could stop the continuous price decline and also form the basis for future sustainable economic growth. Japan was the first country ever to use QE (later followed by many other central banks). Under the QE policy, the Bank of Japan increased its target for current account balances (CAB) of financial institutions at the BOJ far in excess of their required reserve levels, thereby reducing the already low overnight call rate (around 0.02–0.03% during the ZIRP) to 0.001% (cf. Ugai 2007). Moreover, the BOJ committed to maintain the QE policy until inflation registered stably at 0% or reached a positive increase year on year (cf. Berkmen 2012; Spiegel 2006). The CAB target was initially increased from ¥1 trillion to ¥5 trillion in 2001 and, until the end of 2004, it was raised 9 more times until it eventually reached ¥35 trillion (cf. Spiegel 2006). In order to meet the increasing CAB target, the Bank of Japan purchased Japanese government bonds (JGB) in open market operations. The literature has identified three main transmission channels, namely, the commitment effect (also referred to as the policy duration effect), the portfolio rebalancing effect, and the signaling effect.

The policy duration effect has clearly been confirmed in various empirical studies (cf. Baba et al. 2006; Okina and Shiratsuka 2004). By committing to maintain the quantitative easing policy, the BOJ fostered the private sector's expectation that the zero short-term interest rate would be maintained until the conditions of the commitment were met, thereby lowering the yield curve centering on the short- to medium-term range (cf. Ugai 2007).

There is less clear empirical evidence regarding the latter two effects, that is, the portfolio rebalancing effect and the signaling effect (cf. empirical studies of Oda and Ueda 2005; Kimura and Small 2006).

Regarding the overall effect of quantitative easing on economic activity as well as on inflation, most empirical studies report only a limited effect (cf. Berkmen 2012; Ugai 2007; Ito and Hoshi 2020). Moreover, Spiegel (2006) claims quantitative easing might have delayed structural reforms by strengthening the performance of the weakest banks. In addition, Ito and Hoshi (2020) claim that the communication regarding both, the ZIRP and QE, was vague and there was no well-defined exit from QE.

Third Phase

The third phase of the Lost Two Decades lasted from 2001 to 2007. During this time, Prime Minister Junichiro Koizumi undertook various reform measures in order to revive the economy. The reforms focused on the banking sector, with the main aim to further reduce the NPLs, as well as on budget reconsolidation by reducing public works (e.g. infrastructure projects). Moreover, he delegated authority from the public to the private sector, e.g. by privatizing the postal system. Koizumi also started to reform the financial system, in particular, he promoted decentralization. In the course of the so-called trinity reform, functions and budgetary resources were shifted from the central to the local governments, providing the latter more autonomy. The impact of the reforms is disputed. While some argue

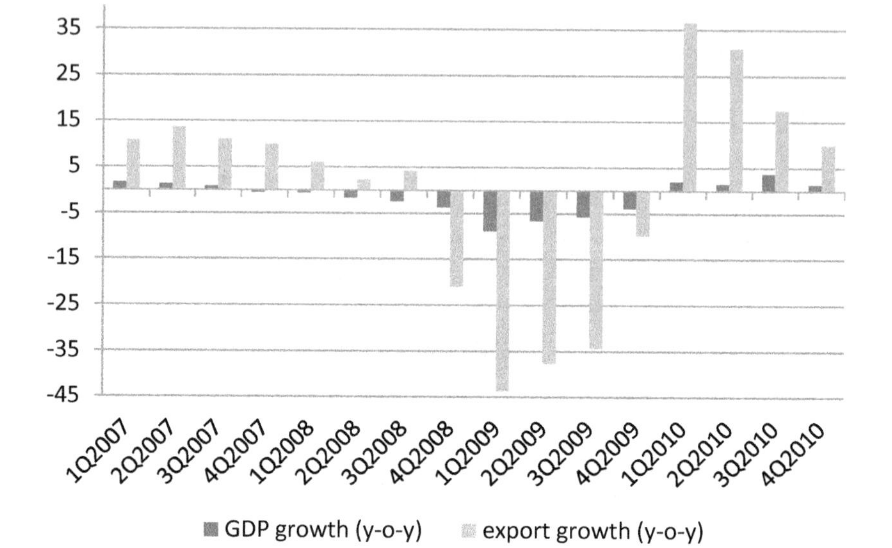

Fig. 2.4 Quarterly GDP and export growth (year-over-year), 1Q2007-4Q2010. *Source* Statistics Bureau of Japan (2021). *Note* Nominal; year-over-year percentage change

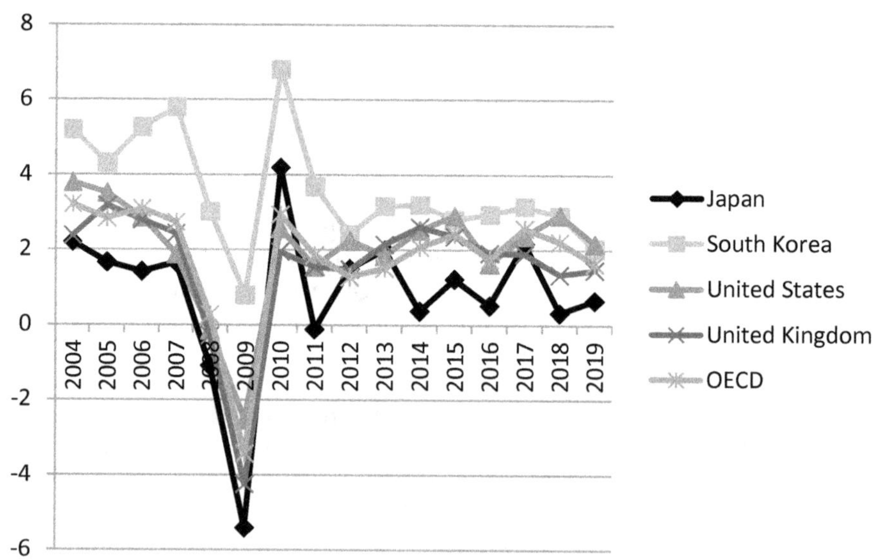

Fig. 2.5 GDP growth rates, 2004–2019. *Source* World Bank (2021)

that the reforms were rather slowly implemented and less complete than previously expected (cf. Callen and Ostry 2003), it is also true that Koizumi still managed to restore growth to almost 2%. However, just as there were slight signs of an economic recovery around 2007, the Global Financial Crisis hit the country.

Fourth Phase

In 2007, the Global Financial Crisis hit the world economy. Japan was no exception and suffered heavily under the crisis. As depicted in Fig. 2.4, the year-over-year quarterly GDP growth turned negative in the fourth quarter of 2007 and stayed in negative territory until the first quarter of 2010. In the first quarter of 2009, the growth rate then reached its low at −8.8% (cf. Statistics Bureau of Japan 2021); the corresponding quarter-over-quarter growth rate fell to −4.7% (cf. Fig. 2.6).

As shown in Fig. 2.5, Japan was most severely hit among the developed countries with its annual growth rate declining to −5.4% in 2009, while the growth rate of the USA, the epicenter of the crisis, only shrank by −2.4% (the average growth rate of the OECD countries was −3.4%). At least at first glance, this appears counterintuitive since Japan's financial system was quite resilient, and thanks to their minimal involvement in the subprime loan problem, Japan's domestic financial institutions (FIs) were not seriously affected (Kawai and Takagi 2009; Asako and Ochiai 2010). For instance, the subprime-related losses of Japanese banks amounted to only slightly above ¥1000 billion by September 2010, which was less than 2.2% of the Tier-1-capital; these losses were for the most part absorbed by capital buffers (Vollmer and Bebenroth 2012). However, as a result of **international capital movements** after the failure of Lehman Brothers in the second half of 2008, Japan's capital and financial account deficit increased considerably (among others driven by short-term portfolio investments), namely, from ¥12,296 billion in 2006 to ¥22,538 billion in 2007. The Japanese interbank markets shrank drastically since (especially foreign) banks lowered their supply of funds considerably (Vollmer and Bebenroth 2012). Between July 2007 and March 2009, the Nikkei stock index fell by almost 40% from 18,000 to 7000. The slump in stock prices adversely affected the capital base of banks since around one-third of the Tier-1-capital was held in stocks.

Japanese firms were also noticeably negatively affected by the crisis through the trade channel (Hosono et al. 2016). Because of the recession of the US economy (and also the slowdown in other countries including China), the **demand for Japanese exports declined** considerably. This is also reflected in the sharply decreasing year-over-year quarterly export growth rate in Fig. 2.4, reaching a low point of ca. −44% in the first quarter of 2009. Accordingly, also Japanese companies producing durable export goods had a declining demand for intermediate goods, and firms, therefore, cut operations. Consequently, unemployment increased and the deflation problem worsened (Ito and Hoshi 2020).

The **frequent government changes** between 2006 and 2012 and the political chaos of the divided parliament after the LDP lost the House of Councilors' elections in 2007 represented another factor that aggravated the overall situation (Ito and Hoshi 2020).

Finally, the Bank of Japan adopted a rather **conservative monetary policy**. The target rate for the uncollateralized overnight call rate was first lowered from 0.5% to 0.3% in October 2008 and subsequently to 0.1% in December (cf. Montgomery and Volz 2021).[16] Over the same period, the basic loan rate was reduced from 0.75% to 0.5% and then to 0.3%. In addition, the BOJ established a Complementarity Deposit Facility (equivalent to the "Deposit Facility" of the Euro system that had existed since the late 1990s, cf. Vollmer and Bebenroth 2012) that allowed banks to deposit excess reserves with a fixed interest rate of 0.1%. At the same time, the FED and central banks of other Western countries such as the Bank of England engaged heavily in monetary easing. In November 2008, the FED announced to buy up to $600 billion in mortgage-backed securities (MBSs). The program (later called "QE1") officially started in December of the same year and was expanded in March 2009. It involved total purchases of $1.75 trillion in Treasury securities, MBSs, and federal agency debt (Bauer 2012). The Bank of England conducted quantitative easing starting from March 2009. Two months later, the ECB announced the Covered Bond Purchase Programme (CBPP), and in May 2010, it started its Securities Markets Program in the course of which it bought securities of more than 200 billion euros (Kenourgios and Ntaikou 2021). The decision of the BOJ not to adopt unconventional monetary policy measures in a timely manner was partly due to the fact that the Japanese financial system was regarded as being relatively resilient (see also above) and also because the BOJ evaluated monetary policy as being already too easy-going. This miscalculation led to a significant **appreciation of the yen**. The average monthly US dollar-yen exchange rate decreased from slightly above 120 in July 2007 to around 100 in October 2008 and then further to around 90 in October 2009 (in July 2011, it even fell temporarily below 80; cf. Bank of Japan; see also Fig. 2.8).[17]

While Japan's response to the Global Financial Crisis with respect to monetary policy was modest, its fiscal policy reaction was rather strong, also in international comparison. Table 2.4 provides an overview of the various policy packages passed between August 2008 and December 2009.

Alone in 2008, three policy packages were launched that together accounted for around ¥75 trillion of which ¥12 trillion was supported by the national government expenditure (around 2% of GDP) (cf. Asako and Ochiai 2010). The first policy package was launched under the Fukuda government whereas the latter two under the Aso government. In April 2009, the Aso government announced the fourth package labeled "Policy Package to Address the Economic Crisis", which amounted to ¥72.2 trillion (of which 21% was supported by national government expenditure, cf. Asako and Ochiai 2010). This policy package aimed at overcoming

[16] See also the Bank of Japan's homepage for an overview (BOJ, https://www.boj.or.jp/en/mopo/outline/cfc.htm/). The uncollateralized overnight call rate was the Bank of Japan's main policy target after the temporary end of the quantitative easing policy in the 2000s (cf. Vollmer and Bebenroth 2012).

[17] Time series FM08'FXERM09 US.Dollar/Yen Central Rate, Average in the Month, Tokyo Market.

Table 2.4 Overview of policy packages in Japan, August 2008–December 2012

Date	Government	Name Policy Package	Program aims/description
29 August 2008	Fukuda	Comprehensive Immediate Policy Package	¥13.7tn (¥2tn NGB; ¥11.7tn PCB)
30 October 2008	Aso	Economic Policy Packages: Measures to Support People's Daily Lives	¥26.9 trillion
19 December 2008	Aso	Immediate Policy Package to Safeguard People's Daily Lives	¥43tn (¥10tn NGB (fiscal measures); ¥33tn PCB (financial measures))
10 April 2009	Aso	Policy Package to Address the Economic Crisis	¥72.2tn (¥15.4tn NGB; ¥56.8tn PCB)
08 December 2009	Hatoyamo	Emergency Economic Countermeasures for Future Growth and Security	¥31.6tn (¥7.2tn NGB; ¥24.4tn PCB)

Source Information obtained from Asako and Ochiai (2010)
Note "NGB" stands for national government budgets, "PCB" for on a project cost basis

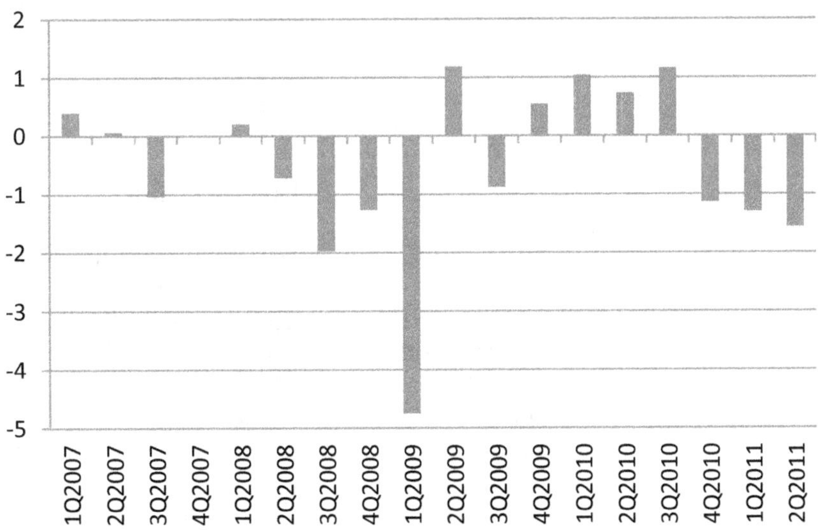

Fig. 2.6 GDP growth rate, quarter-over-quarter 1Q2007-04Q2010. *Source* Economic Research Division, Federal Reserve Bank of St. Louis (https://fred.stlouisfed.org), accessed 21 May 2021

the so-called twin crisis, the short-term crisis on the one hand and the structural crisis on the other hand. With respect to the former, the government feared a negative spiral. In particular, the government was worried that the Japanese economy would be "facing a rapid contraction of exports and the severe financial environment" amid the deepening Global Financial Crisis and the Great

Recession.[18] In December 2009, the newly formed Hatoyama Cabinet launched a new policy package, which amounted to ¥31.6 trillion of which almost 22% were supported by national government expenditures. The policy package focused primarily on the structural crisis. The Hatoyama administration had rather long-term oriented policy targets, for instance children and educational support as well as the promotion of science and technology (Iwaisako 2010). Moreover, a public viewer's budget screening operation was introduced in order to improve the transparency of the budgeting process (Iwaisako 2010).

As shown in Fig. 2.6, the quarter-over-quarter GDP growth rate again turned positive during 2009, but then dipped into negative territory at the end of 2010.

In October 2010, the **first phase of unconventional monetary policy ("Comprehensive Monetary Easing")** began. The target level for the short-term interest rate was reduced from 0.1% to a range between 0 and 0.1% (Kuttner 2014; Montgomery and Volz 2021).[19] The Bank of Japan announced that the zero interest rate policy would remain in place until "price stability is in sight" (conditional that no major (financial) risk occurred, cf. Filardo and Hofmann 2014). In addition, the asset purchase program was introduced and the BOJ announced to purchase ¥5 trillion assets. This amount was later increased to ¥20 trillion, which corresponded to 4% of GDP (cf. Dell'Ariccia et al. 2018). In February 2012, the Bank of Japan confirmed its intention to maintain the zero interest rate policy and to use asset purchases until the 1% inflation goal would be in sight (again conditional on the absence of significant risks). The asset purchases were increased by ¥10 trillion (Dell'Ariccia et al. 2018).

The effects of the first phase of unconventional monetary policy measures were rather modest. The announcement of the asset purchase program in 2010 and the commitment to the zero interest rate policy resulted in a 10 basis points reduction in government bond yields (at the 10-year maturity) according to the event studies of Lam (2011) and Ueda (2012). However, the inflation expectations barely changed and there was still mild deflation (see also Fig. 2.7). According to Dell'Ariccia et al. (2018), this can partly be attributed to the BOJ's limited credibility to fight deflation in the past as well as the rather small quantity of asset purchases (see also Kuttner 2014). Only after the election of Abe in 2012, the monetary policy reaction of the BOJ became stronger. The corresponding unconventional monetary policy measures will be discussed in the next section.

Besides the problems outlined above, Japan also faced **structural, supply-side problems** which have already partly been mentioned in previous sections. First, Japan was confronted with a **declining working-age population** due to demographic change. Second, Japanese firms increasingly **offshored business activities abroad** because of the rising production costs in Japan (aggravated by the yen appreciation). Third, Japan experienced a **slowdown in technological progress**. According to Ito and Hoshi (2020), this was partly because of the slow adoption of

[18] Homepage of the Prime Minister of Japan and His Cabinet, online available at: http://japan.kantei.go.jp/keizai/index_e.html.

[19] The BOJ reverted to the medium- to long-term price stability which (since March 2006) was defined as a positive range of 2% or lower with a midpoint of around 1% (Shirai 2013; Montgomery and Volz 2021).

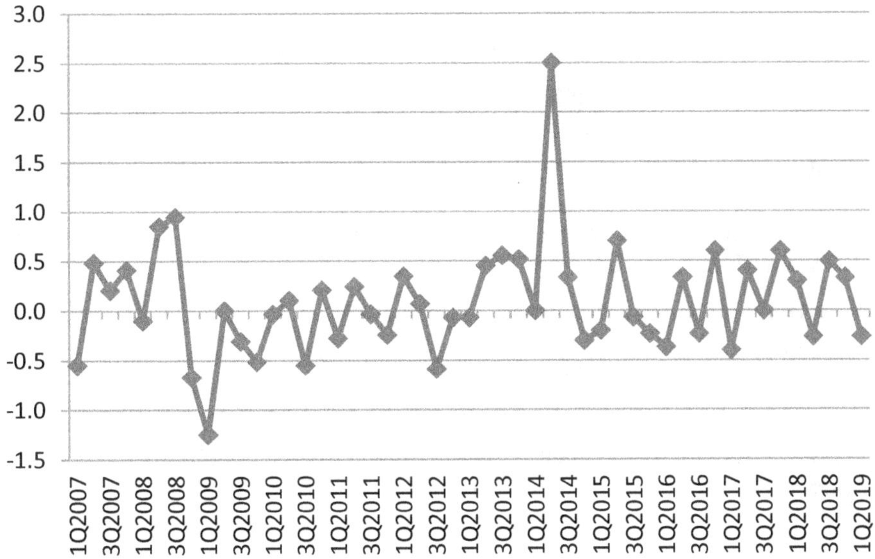

Fig. 2.7 Quarter-over-quarter inflation rate (in %). *Source* OECD (2010), "Main Economic Indicators—complete database", Main Economic Indicators (database), https://doi.org/10.1787/data-00052-en. *Notes* Growth rate of the consumer price index of all items in Japan, index 2015 = 100, quarterly, not seasonally adjusted

information technologies (particularly in the service sector and in SMEs), especially compared with Western advanced economies (but also compared with China). This, in turn, was a result of the protection of incumbent firms (conglomerates), which consequently did not need to improve their productivity to keep pace with new innovative start-ups. Overall, this led to a slowdown of the process of creative destruction (cf. also Aghion et al. 2021). The "Abenomics" policy program described below also tried to tackle these (long-term) structural supply-side problems (in addition to the (short-term) demand-side problems).

2.8 Abenomics (2013–2020)

Shinzo Abe assumed the Prime Minister post in December 2012 for a second time and stayed in office until September 2020. He introduced a comprehensive set of economic reforms labeled **"Abenomics"** in order to end the decades-long deflationary slump (Xu 2014). Abenomics is based upon **"three arrows"**, namely **(1) fiscal stimulus** through government spending, **(2) monetary easing**, and **(3) structural reforms** (McBride and Xu 2018; Ito and Hoshi 2020). The three arrows are a reference to the Japanese legend, which teaches that one arrow can easily be broken, but three arrows together are much harder to break. The immediate goal of the expansionary macroeconomic policy was to boost domestic demand and GDP growth as well as to raise inflation to 2% and thus buy time to implement the crucial structural reforms. The structural policies aimed particularly at improving Japan's competitiveness in international comparison. In the following, we will briefly present the reform measures of each "arrow" and subsequently evaluate the effectiveness of these policies. The first two arrows, the fiscal stimulus and the monetary easing were immediately implemented after Abe began his second term in office.

Arrow 1: Expansionary/flexible fiscal policy

In 2013, Abe announced a ¥22.2 trillion stimulus package (US$210 billion), ¥10.3 trillion (US$116 billion) from direct government spending (Xu 2014). The focus of this stimulus package was on infrastructure projects (especially on building bridges, tunnels, and earthquake-resistant roads). In April 2014, an additional ¥5.5 trillion package followed, and 8 months later another ¥3.5 trillion package was passed since there were again growing concerns about deflation and an economic downturn (McBride and Xu 2018).

In order to finance the fiscal stimulus programs, the consumption tax was raised from 5 to 8% in April 2014; however, this further depressed consumption spending. In fact, the tax rate subsequently was to be increased to 10%; however, this increase had been postponed various times (until the consumption tax was eventually raised in October 2019). Because of the COVID-19 pandemic, even a temporary reduction of the "reduced consumption tax" from currently 8–5% until the end of 2022 was being discussed.

Arrow 2: Expansionary monetary policy

Besides the enormous fiscal stimulus program, the Abe administration also pursued an aggressive monetary policy. The Bank of Japan introduced an explicit 2% inflation target and announced that it would use asset purchases to keep interest rates low in order to "achieve this target at the earliest possible time" (Dell'Ariccia et al. 2018). In April 2013 (under its new Governor Haruhiko Kurada), the BOJ announced its first round of "quantitative and qualitative easing" (**QQE1**) that doubled the BOJ's balance sheet (McBride and Beina 2018). The program comprised open-ended purchases of ¥50 trillion Japanese government bonds (JGBs) per year as well as the expansion of purchases of risk assets including exchange-traded funds (ETFs) (by ¥1 trillion) and Japan real estate investment trusts (J-REITs) (by ¥30 billion) (Montgomery and Volz 2021). In October 2014, a second round of "quantitative and qualitative easing" was launched (**QQE2**). The asset purchasing program was increased up to ¥80 trillion JGBs per year, and the ETFs and J-REITs purchases were increased by ¥3 trillion and ¥90 billion, respectively (Dell'Ariccia et al. 2018). The above-described measures constituted the **second phase of unconventional monetary policy** in the aftermath of the Global Financial Crisis (for an overview on the first phase, cf. Sect. 2.7 "Fourth phase").

Empirical studies indicate that the announcement of the QQE1 program resulted in a reduction in long-term yields. For instance, Arai (2017) reports an 11 basis point decrease; Hausman and Wieland's (2014) VAR analysis indicates a 14 basis point reduction. In addition, de Michelis and Iacoviello (2016) show (by using VAR analysis) that the announcement of the 2% inflation target had a significant effect on inflation. It is in general difficult to evaluate the actual effect of QQE1 since it was accompanied by the huge fiscal stimulus program outlined above. In general, empirical studies only report a moderate positive impact on inflation and output (see e.g. Kan et al. 2016; Michaelis and Watzka 2017).

The impact on the exchange rate was minuscule (cf. also Fig. 2.8). According to Dell'Ariccia et al. (2018), this is partly due to the fact that the exchange rate had already depreciated previously (during Abe's electoral campaign). As indicated by Fig. 2.7, inflation decreased again in the second half of 2014 and fluctuated around zero since then, being far away from reaching the 2% target. Thus, the QQE programs under Abe did not succeed to have a lasting effect on inflation.

The **third phase of unconventional monetary policy** started with the announcement that the BOJ would introduce a negative interest rate of −0.1% on new excess reserve deposits that FIs held at the BOJ (Montgomery and Volz 2021). The negative interest rate policy (NIRP) should supplement the QQE programs. In addition, in September 2016, the **yield curve control** framework was introduced in order to affect the long-term interest rates. In particular, the BOJ announced that it would keep the short-term policy interest rate at −0.1% and that it would continue

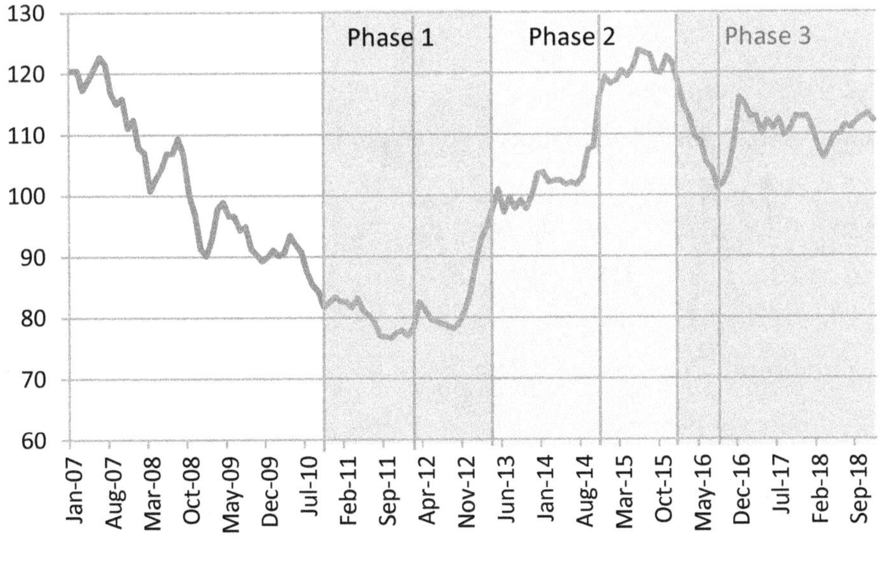

Fig. 2.8 Monthly Yen-US dollar exchange rate. *Source* Board of Governors of the Federal Reserve System (US). *Note* The vertical lines indicate the main unconventional monetary policy measures. The shaded areas mark the three different phases of unorthodox monetary policy

purchasing JGBs to keep the target level of the 10-year JGB yield at around 0%. Moreover, the **inflation overshooting commitment** was introduced. The BOJ committed itself to expand the monetary base until inflation would exceed 2%. By doing so, the BOJ aimed at increasing the credibility of achieving the 2% price stability target (cf. BOJ 2016; Dell'Ariccia et al. 2018).

According to the IMF (2017), the NIRP led to a downward shift in the yields curve (in particular, the 10-year yields fell below zero). Moreover, the lending and deposit rates declined and FIs accelerated their portfolio rebalancing. Still, any positive effects on inflation and growth remained at best modest (cf. also Figs. 2.7 and 2.9).

In addition, there were concerns about the impact of the NIRP on bank profitability (for further discussion see IMF 2017). Moreover, it was feared that a prolonged use of NIRPs and monetary easing could damage the banking system and cause speculative bubbles. The rising debt levels were also criticized by the IMF (cf. IMF 2016).

Arrow 3: Structural reforms ("growth strategy")

The expansionary macroeconomic policies were accompanied by structural reforms in order to increase Japan's competitiveness. Besides the external and domestic shocks (the Global Financial Crisis and the catastrophic earthquake and tsunami in 2011, respectively), Japan also faced considerable structural problems including population aging (cf. Grabowiecki 2019; see also Chap. 6). The reform package included the lowering of business regulations (especially for the energy,

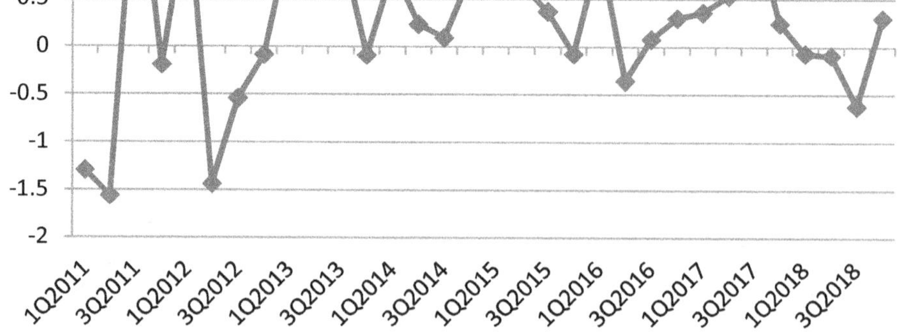

Fig. 2.9 GDP quarter-over-quarter growth, 2011–2018. *Source* Economic Research Division, Federal Reserve Bank of St. Louis (https://fred.stlouisfed.org), accessed 21 May 2021

environmental, and healthcare sectors), a labor market reform, the empowerment of women ("womenomics"), and the liberalization of agriculture (McBride and Xu 2018).

Reforms to combat population aging

The size of the working-age population (as of percentage of total population) had decreased from around 70% in the early 1990s to around 64% in the early 2010s. By 2019, it had fallen below 60% and according to projections of the National Institute of Population and Social Security Research in Japan (IPSS) (2017), it will further decline to below 52% by 2049. In order to counteract this trend, Finance Minister Taro Aso proposed (a) to raise the female labor force participation (among others by improving childcare facilities; see also the discussion of "womenomics" below) and (b) to encourage retired people to continue working (cf. Yoshino and Taghizadeh-Hesary 2014). Prime Minister Abe also introduced the "Abenomics 2.0" platform with a focus on raising birth rates and the expansion of social security in September 2015 and established a new cabinet position with the task of reversing the demographic decline in Japan (McBride and Xu 2018). However, it is questionable whether these reform measures will be enough to cope with the demographic change Japan is facing.

Womenomics

In 2013, Abe also introduced several reforms labeled "womenomics", building upon the ideas of Kathy Matsui, who had already applied the term in 1999 in a group of investment strategists at Goldman Sachs. During Abe's speech at the United Nations General Assembly on 26 September 2013, he underlined that "creating an environment in which women find it comfortable to work… is no longer a matter of choice for Japan. It is instead a matter of the greatest urgency". The Abe government formulated two main policy targets with respect to female employment (Song 2015). First, the labor force participation of women should be increased (from 68 to 73% by 2020, cf. Okada 2014; see also above). As already argued above, this was decisive against the background of the deteriorating demographic situation and the related declining working-age population in Japan. Second, a higher share of women in leading positions such as managers and executives should be promoted (the numerical target was 30%). Even though the first goal has been quantitatively more or less accomplished—according to OECD data, the female labor force participation rate stood at 72.6% in 2019, above the OECD average of only around 65.1%—these numbers do not reflect that the actual problem is not so much the quantity of jobs female workers hold but rather the **quality** of these jobs. More than 50% of female workers are engaged in non-regular employment (that is, part-time, temporary, and contract work) while the rate for men is only slightly above 20%.[20] Cultural aspects (e.g. the still persisting view that women are responsible for housework) are at least to some extent the cause of the problem. According to the OECD (2018), in 2016 women spent around 148 h per

[20] Cf. the Statistics Bureau of Japan, https://www.stat.go.jp/english/data/shugyou/index.html.

week for routine housework, whereas men only spent 14 h. While the overall time spent on housework in Japan is still low compared with the OECD average, the gap between women and men is one of the widest (together with South Korea and India). The design of the Japanese tax code, especially the tax deduction for spouses might also play a role. In particular, in Japan, one partner can claim a tax-free income of 1.5 million yen, which discourages many women from working more after having reached this threshold.

In addition, there is still considerable room for improvement regarding the participation of women in corporate management and also in politics. Between 2012 and 2019, the number of female executive officers had increased by 3.4 times but the percentage is still rather slow (only 5.2% in 2019, cf. Gender Equality Bureau Cabinet Office 2020). The same applies to the share of women holding manager positions: only 6.7% of senior manager positions and 9.3% of middle manager positions were held by women in the fiscal year 2018 (cf. Ministry of Health, Labour, and Welfare (MHLW) 2019); a more detailed analysis can be found in Nakamura and Horimoto (2021).[21] Overall, there is still significant room for improvement with respect to female empowerment in Japan.

Overall, the Abenomics policy bundle appears to have worked to some extent. At least temporarily, the expansionary monetary and fiscal policy measures helped to foster economic growth (even though only modestly). Also, inflation increased temporarily; however, it is still far away from reaching the 2% target. The current COVID-19 pandemic further aggravated the situation. It has to be noted that the enormous expansionary macroeconomic policy measures ("Arrow 1" and "Arrow 2") came at a high cost, namely, rising debt levels which are judged as being unsustainable by the IMF (see also Sect. 6.3.2.1). With respect to the third arrow, that is, the structural reforms, some progress has been made (for instance, the female labor market participation has increased over the past years). However, as outlined above, these achievements are far too little to successfully cope with the even worsening demographic situation Japan will be confronted with in the next decades. Some of these (and other) future challenges Japan is going to face will also be discussed in Chap. 6.

References

Aghion P, Antonin C, Bunel S (2021) The power of creative destruction: economic upheaval and the wealth of nations. The Belknap Press of Harvard University Press, Cambridge, MA

Ahearne A, Gagnon J, Haltmaier J, Kamin S (2002) Preventing deflation: lessons from Japan's experience in the 1990s. International Finance Discussion Papers 729, Board of Governors of the Federal Reserve System

[21] Moreover, only around 10% of seats in the House of Representatives are filled by women. Shortly after it was announced that of the 21 members of the new Suga Cabinet, only 2 were women, Tomomi Inada described the Japanese politics as a "democracy without women" (see McCurry 2020).

Almeida H, Wolfenzon D (2006) A theory of pyramidal ownership and family business groups. Journal of Finance 61(6):2637–2680
Aoki M (1988) Information, incentives and bargaining in the Japanese economy. Cambridge University Press, Cambridge
Aoki M (1990) Toward an economic model of the Japanese firms. J Econ Lit 28:1–27
Arai N (2017) The effects of monetary policy announcements at the zero lower bound. Int J Cent Bank 13(2):159–196
Asako K, Ochiai K (2010) Macroeconomic adjustments to the Lehman shock in Japan. J East Asian Econ Integr 114(1):3–46
Asian Development Bank (ADB) (2020) Asia's journey to prosperity: policy, market, and technology over 50 years. Asian Development Bank, Manila
Baba N, N Nishioka S, Oda N, Shirakawa M, Ueda K, Ugai H (2004) Japan's deflation, problems in the financial system and monetary policy. Bank of Japan, July 2004
Baba N, Nakashima M, Shigemi Y, Ueda K (2006) The Bank of Japan's monetary policy and bank risk premiums in the money market. International Journal of Central Banking, 2(1):105–135
Bank of Japan (BOJ) (2016) New framework for strengthening monetary easing: "quantitative and qualitative monetary easing with yield curve control". Bank of Japan, Tokyo
Barro R, Lee J-W (2013) A new data set of educational attainment in the world, 1950–2010. J Dev Econ 104:184–198
Barro RJ, Sala-i-Martin X (1997) Technological diffusion, convergence, and growth. J Econ Growth 2(1):1–26
Bauer MD (2012) Fed assets buying and private borrowing rates. FRBSF Economic Letter May 21, 2012–16
Beason R, Weinstein D (1996) Growth, economies of scale, and targeting in Japan (1955–1990). Rev Econ Stat 78(2):286–295
Berkmen SP (2012) Bank of Japan's quantitative and credit easing: are they now more effective? IMF Working Paper 12/2, International Monetary Fund, Washington DC
Bernanke B, Gertler M (1999) Monetary policy and asset price volatility. Econ Rev (Federal Reserve Bank of Kansas City) 84(Q IV):17–51
Bernanke B, Gertler M (2001) Should central banks respond to movements in asset prices? Am Econ Rev 91(2):253–257
BOJ (noyear) The Bank of Japan's policy measures during the financial crisis. https://www.boj.or.jp/en/mopo/outline/cfc.htm/
Borio CEV, White WR (2004) Whither monetary and financial stability? The implications of evolving policy regimes. BIS Working Paper No 147, Bank of International Settlements, Basel
Caballero RJ, Hoshi T, Kashyp AK (2008) Zombie lending and depressed restructuring in Japan. Am Econ Rev 95(5):1943–1977. https://doi.org/10.1257/aer.98.5.1943
Callen T, Ostry JD (2003) Japan's lost decade: policies for economic revival. International Monetary Fund, Washington DC
Cargill TF (2003) Central banking and financial institutions. In: Blomström M, Gangnes B, La Croix S (eds) Japan's new economy: continuity and change in the twenty-first century. Oxford University Press, Oxford
Cargill TF, Royama S (1988) The transition of finance in Japan and the United States: a comparative perspective. Hoover Institution Press, Stanford, California
Caves RE, Uekusa M (1976) Industrial organization in Japan. The Brookings Institution, Washington DC
Cecchetti S, Genberg H, Wadhwani S (2003) Asset prices in a flexible inflation targeting framework. In: Hunter W, Kaufmann GG, Pomerleano M (eds) Asset price bubbles: the implications for monetary, regulatory, and international policies. MIT Press, Cambridge MA
De Michelis A, Iacoviello M (2016) Raising an inflation target: the Japanese experience with Abenomics. Eur Econ Rev 88:67–87
Dell'Ariccia G, Rabanal P, Sandri D (2018) unconventional monetary policies and the Euro Area, Japan, and the United Kingdom. J Econ Perspect 32(4):147–172

Denison EF, Chung WK (1976) How Japan's economy grew so fast, the sources of postwar expansion. The Brookings Institution, Washington DC
Dingman R (1993) The dagger and the gift: the impact of the Korean war on Japan. Am-East Asian Relat 2(1):29–55
Dosi G, Tyson LD, Zysman J (1989) Trade, technologies and development: a framework for discussing Japan. In: Johnson C, Tyson LD, Zysman J (eds) Politics and productivity: the real story of why Japan works. Ballinger, Cambridge, MA
Filardo A, Hofmann B (2014) Forward guidance at the zero lower bound. BIS Q Rev 1403f. http://www.bis.org/publ/qtrpdf/r_qt1403f.htm
Flath D (2014) The Japanese Economy. Oxford University Press, Oxford
Fuji M, Kawai M (2010) Lessons from Japan's banking crisis, 1991–2005. ADBI Working Paper 222, Asian Development Bank Institute, Tokyo
Fujioka M (1963) Appraisal of Japan's plan to double income. International Monetary Fund, Washington DC. https://www.elibrary.imf.org/view/journals/024/1963/001/article-A004-en.xml#A04fn1
Fukao M (2003) Capital account liberalisation: the Japanese experience and implications for China. BIS Papers chapters. In: Bank for International Settlements (ed) China's capital account liberalisation: international perspective, vol 15. Bank for International Settlements, Basel, pp 35–57
Fukuyama F (2012) China and East Asian democracy: the patterns of history. J Democr 23(1):14–26
Fulcher J (1988) The bureaucratization of the state and the rise of Japan. Br J Sociol 39(2):228–254
Fung K (1991) Characteristics of Japanese industrial groups and their potential impact on US-Japanese trade In: Baldwin R (ed) Empirical studies in commercial policy. University of Chicago Press, Chicago
Gender Equality Bureau Cabinet Office (2020) 女性役員情報サイト[Women executive officer information side]. http://www.gender.go.jp/policy/mieruka/company/yakuin.html
Gerschenkron A (1962) Economic backwardness in historical perspective, a book of essays. Belknap Press of Harvard University Press, Cambridge, MA
Glawe L, Wagner H (2016) The middle-income trap—definitions, theories and countries concerned: a literature survey. Comp Econ Stud 58(4):507–538
Görger K (2001) Japan's financial reform. In: Holzhausen A (ed) Can Japan globalize? Studies and Japan's changing political economy and the process of globalization in honour of Sung-Jo Park. Springer, Berlin
Goto A (1982) Business groups in a market economy. Eur Econ Rev 19:53–70
Grabowiecki J (2019) Abenomics: from the "great stagnation" to the "three-arrows strategy." Int J Manag Econ 55(3):201–2011
Grad AJ (1948) Land reform in Japan. Pac Aff 21(2):115–135
Greenspan A (2002) Opening remarks. In: Rethinking stabilization policy, Federal Reserve Bank of Kansas City Jackson Hole Symposium, pp 1–10
Grimes WM (2018) In making the Japanese miracle: macroeconomic politics, 1985–2000. Cornell University Press, Ithaca, London
Hadley EM (1988) Remaking Japan: the American occupation as new deal by Theodore Cohen and Herbert Passin. J Jpn Stud 14(2):480–485
Hamada K (1985) Lessons from the macroeconomic performance of the Japanese economy. In: Argy VE, Nevile JW (eds) Inflation and unemployment: theory, experience and policy-making. George Allen & Unwin, London, pp 181–199
Hamada K, Hayashi F (1985) Monetary policy in postwar Japan. In: Ando A, Eguchi H, Farmer R, Suzuki Y (eds) Monetary policy in our times. MIT Press, Cambridge, MA, London, pp 83–121
Hamada K, Kasuya M (1992) The reconstruction and stabilization of the postwar Japanese economy: possible lessons for Eastern Europe? Center Discussion Paper, No 672. Yale University, Economic Growth Center, Hew Haven, CT

Hamada K (1996) Japan 1968: A reflection point during the era of the economic miracle. Center Discussion Paper No 764, Economic Growth Center, Yale University

Hamada K Kashyap A, Weinstein D (2011) Introduction. In: Hamada K, Kashyap A, Weinstein D (Eds) Japan's bubble, deflation, and long-term stagnation. The MIT Press, Cambridge

Hanley SB, Yamamura K (1977) Economic and demographic change in preindustrial Japan, 1600–1868. Princeton University Press, Princeton

Hausman JK, Wieland JF (2014) Abenomics: preliminary analysis and outlook. Brook Papers Econ Activity 1:1–63

Hayami Y, Ogasawara J (1999) Changes in the sources of modern economic growth: Japan compared with the United States. J Jpn Int Econ 13:1–21

Himino R (2021) The Japanese banking crisis. Palgrave Macmillan, Singapore

Horioka CY (1994) Japan's consumption and saving international perspective. Economic Development and Cultural Change 42(2):293–316

Horiuchi K, Otaki M (2017) Dr. Osamu Shimomura's legacy and the postwar Japanese economy. Springer, Singapore

Hoshi T, Kashyap A (2000a) The Japanese banking crisis: where did it come from and how will it end? In: Bernanke B, Rotemberg J (eds) NBER macroeconomics annual 1999

Hoshi T, Kashyap A (2000b) The Japanese banking crisis: where did it come from and how will it end? NBER Working Paper 7250, National Bureau of Economic Research, Cambridge MA

Hoshi T, Kashyap A (2010) Will the U.S. bank recapitalization succeed? Eight lessons from Japan. J Financ Econ 97:398–417

Hoshi T, Patrick HT (2000) Crisis and change in the Japanese Financial System. Springer, New York

Hoshi T, Kashyap A, Scharfstein D (1990a) The role of banks in reducing the costs of financial distress in Japan. J Financ Econ 27:67–88

Hoshi T, Kashyap A, Scharfstein D (1990b) Bank monitoring and investment: evidence from the changing structure of Japanese corporate banking relationship. In: Hubbard R (ed) Asymmetric information, corporate finance and investment. University of Chicago Press, Chicago

Hosono K, Takizawa M, Tsuru K (2016) International transmission of the 2007–2009 financial crisis: evidence from Japan. Jpn Econ Rev 67(3):295–328

Huang Y, Armstrong S (2014) Asian financial integration—impacts of the global crisis and options for regional policies. Routledge, New York

IFO Institute for Economic Research, Sakura Institute of Research (1997) A comparative analysis of Japanese and German economic success. Springer Science and Business Media

International Monetary Fund (IMF) (1999) Japan: economic and policy developments. International Monetary Fund, Washington DC

International Monetary Fund (IMF) (2016) Japan: 2016 Article IV consultation–press release; and staff report. International Monetary Fund, Washington DC

International Monetary Fund (IMF) (2017) Negative interest rate policies—initial experiences and assessments. IMF Policy Paper, August 2017, International Monetary Fund, Washington DC

Ishi H (1991) Land tax reform in Japan. Hitotsubashi J Econ 32(1):1–20

Ito T (1998) Japanese economic development: idiosyncratic or universal? In: Lin J (ed) Contemporary economic issues, Volume 1: Regional experience in system reform. Palgrave MacMillan, London, pp 18–37

Ito T (2013) Great inflation and central bank independence in Japan. In: Bordo MD, Orphanides A (eds) The great inflation: the rebirth of modern central banking. NBER-University of Chicago Press

Ito T, Hoshi T (2020) The Japanese economy. MIT Press, Cambridge MA, London

Iwaisako T (2010) Japanese macroeconomic policy management after the global financial crisis. Public Policy Rev 6(5):795–806

Iyoda M (2010) Postwar Japanese economy: lessons of economic growth in the bubble economy. Springer, New York

Kaizuka K (1967) Keizai Antei to Kinyu Seisaku (Economic Stabilization and Monetary Policy). In: Kinoshita K (Ed) Keizai Antei to Zaisei Kinyu Seisaku (Economic Stabilization and Fiscal-Monetary Policy), Nihon Keizai

Kan K, Kishaba Y, Tsuruga T (2016) Policy effects since the introduction of quantitative and qualitative monetary easing (QQE)—assessment based on the BoJ's large-scale macroeconomic model (Q-JEM). Bank of Japan Working Paper No. 16-E-15

Katz R (2003) Japanese Phoenix: the long road to economic revival. Routledge, London

Kawagoe T (1999) Agricultural land reform in postwar Japan: experiences and issues. Policy Research Working Paper 2111, The World Bank, Washington DC

Kawai M, Takagi S (2009) Why was Japan hit so hard by the global financial crisis? ADBI Working Paper No. 153. Asian Development Bank Institute, Tokyo

Kazui T, Videen SD (1982) Foreign relations during the Edo period: Sakoku reexamined. J Jpn Stud 8(2):283–306

Kennon J (2012) Democracy in Japan: from Meiji to MacArthur. Lehigh Rev 20:17–25

Kenourgios D, Ntaikou D (2021) ECB's unconventional monetary policy and bank lending supply and performance in the euro area. J Econ Finance 45:211–224

Kimura T, Small D (2006) Quantitative monetary easing and risk and financial asset markets. B E J Macroecon 6(1):1–54

Kiyota K, Okazaki T (2013) Effects of industrial policy on productivity: The case of import quota removal during postwar Japan. Discussion Paper No. 13-E-093, Research Instittue of Economy, Trade and Industry RIETI, Tokyo

Kiyota K, Okazaki T (2016) Assessing the effects of Japanese industrial policy change during the 1960s. Journal of the Japanese and International Economies 40(C):31–42

Kogiku KC (1977) Japan's "doubling national income plan" 1961–1970 and the 1976 plan. Weltwirtschaftliches Archiv 113(3):533–551

Komiya R, Okuno M, Suzumura K, Senta TKK (1988) Industrial Policy of Japan. Academic Press, San Diego

Kosai Y (1986) The era of high-speed growth: notes on the postwar Japanese economy. University of Tokyo Press, Tokyo

Kosai Y (1988) The postwar Japanese economy, 1945–1973. In: Duus P (ed) The Cambridge history of Japan, Volume 6: The 20th century. Cambridge University Press, Cambridge, pp 494–540

Kosai Y (1998) The postwar Japanese economic growth: 1945–1973. In: Smitka M (ed) Japanese economic history 1600–1960. Garland Publishing, New York, London

Kuttner K (2014) Monetary policy during Japan's great recession: from self-induced paralysis to Rooseveltian resolve. PIIE Briefing 14-04, Peterson Institute for International Economics, Washington DC

Lam WR (2011) Bank of Japan's monetary easing measures: are they powerful and comprehensive? IMF Working Paper 11/264. International Monetary Fund, Washington DC

Laver M (2011) The sakoku edicts and the politics of tokugawa hegemony, Cambria Press, New York

Lawrence R (1991) Efficient or exclusionist? The import behavior of Japanese corporate groups. Brook Papers Econ Activity 1:311–338

Lewis WA (1954) Economic development with unlimited supplies of labor. Manch School Econ Soc Stud 22:139–191

Lipscy PY, Takinami H (2013) The politics of financial crisis response in Japan and the United States. Jpn J Polit Sci 14(3):321–353. https://doi.org/10.1017/S1468109913000133

Maddison A (1998) Chinese economic performance in the long run. Second edition, revised and updated 960-2030 AD. OECD Development Centre, Paris

McBride J, Xu B (2018) Abenomics and the Japanese economy. The Council on foreign relations (23 March 2018). https://www.cfr.org/backgrounder/abenomics-and-japanese-economy

McCurry (2020) Japan is a democracy without women says ruling party MP, The Guarding. https://www.theguardian.com/world/2020/sep/23/japan-is-a-democracy-without-women-says-ruling-party-mp

Michaelis H, Watzka S (2017) Are there differences in the effectiveness of quantitative easing at the zero lower-bound in Japan over time? J Int Money Finance 70:204–233

Minami R (1994) The economic development of Japan: a quantitative study. St. Martin's Press, New York

Ministry of Health, Labour and Welfare (2019) 「平成30年度雇用均等基本調査」の結果概要 [The summary of FY2018 equal employment opportunity survey]. https://www.mhlw.go.jp/toukei/list/71-30r.html

Miyamoto M, Sakudo Y, Yasuba Y (1965) Economic development in preindustrial Japan, 1859–1894. J Econ Hist 25(4):541–564

Montgomery H, Volz U (2021) The effectiveness of unconventional monetary policy on Japanese bank lending. In: Stenfors A, Toporowski J (eds) Unconventional monetary policy and financial stability. Routledge, New York

Morck R, Nakamura M (2007) Business groups and the big push: Meiji Japan's mass privatization and subsequent growth. NBER Working Paper 13171, National Bureau of Economic Research, Cambridge MA. https://doi.org/10.3386/w13171

Morck R, Yeung B (2017) East Asian financial and economic development. NBER Working Paper 23845, National Bureau of Economic Research, Cambridge, MA

Nakamura T (1981) The postwar Japanese economy: its development and structure. University of Tokyo Press, Tokyo

Nakamura T, Odaka K (2003) Economic history of Japan 1914–1955: the deal structure. Oxford University Press, Oxford

Nakamura YT, Horimoto M (2021) Status of women leaders in Japan: challenges and opportunities. In: Nakamura YZ, Horimoto M, McLean GN (eds) Japanese women in leadership. Palgrave Macmillan

Nakano M (2016) Financial crisis and bank management in Japan 1997 to 2016. Palgrave Macmillan, London

Nakaso H (2001) The financial crisis in Japan during the 1990s: how the Bank of Japan responded and the lessons learnt. BIS Papers No 6, Bank for International Settlements, Basel

Nakatani L (1984) The world of financial corporate grouping. In: Aoki M (ed) Economic analysis of the Japanese firm. North Holland, New York

National Institute of Population and Social Security Research (IPSS) (2017) Population projections for Japan (2017): 2016 to 2065. Online available at: http://www.ipss.go.jp/pp-zenkoku/e/zenkoku_e2017/pp_zenkoku2017e.asp (Table 1-1)

Nishimizu M, Hulten CR (1978) The sources of Japanese economic growth: 1955–71. Rev Econ Stat 60(3):351–361

Noguchi Y (1998) The 1940 system: Japan under the wartime economy. Am Econ Rev 108 (2):404–407

OCED (2018) Balancing paid work, unpaid work and leisure. OECD. https://www.oecd.org/gender/balancing-paid-work-unpaid-work-and-leisure.htm; related database available online at: https://stats.oecd.org/Index.aspx?datasetcode=TIME_USE.

Oda N, Ueda K (2005) The effects of the Bank of Japan's zero interest rate commitment and quantitative monetary easing on the yield curve: a micro-finance approach. Bank of Japan working paper 05-T-6, Bank of Japan, Tokyo

OECD (2010) "Main Economic Indicators—complete database", Main Economic Indicators (database), http://dx.doi.org/10.1787/data-00052-en

Ohkawa K, Rosovsky H (1973) Japanese economic growth: trend acceleration in the twentieth century. Stanford University Press, Stanford

Ohno K (2017) The history of Japanese economic development: origins of private dynamism and policy competence. Routledge, London

Okada H (2014) Creating "a society in which women shine." APEC Women and the Economy Forum. Presentation by Hiroshi Okada, Senior Vice Minister of Cabinet Office Prepared for the High Level Policy Dialogue on Women and Economy, May 21-23, 2014, Beijing China. https://www.gender.go.jp/english_contents/international/apec/apec2014.html

Okazaki T (2019) Development state evolving: Japan's graduation from a middle income country. In: Takagi Y, Kanchoochat V, Sonobe T (eds) Developmental state building. Springer, pp 19–49

Okazaki T, Korenaga T (1999) The foreign exchange allocation policy in postwar Japan: its institutional framework and function. In: Ito T, Krueger A (eds) Changes in exchange rates in rapidly developing countries: theory, practice, and policy issues. University of Chicago Press, Chicago

Okina K, Shirakawa M, Shiratsuka S (2001) The asset price bubble and monetary policy: Japan's experience in the late 1980s and the lessons. Monet Econ Stud 19(S1):395–450

Okina K, Shiratsuka S (2004) Policy commitment and expectation formation: Japan's experience under zero interest rates. The North American Journal of Economics and Finance 15(1):75–100

Okita S (1951) Japan's economy and the Korean War. Far Eastern Survey 20(14):141–144

Okubo Y (2003) Of the financial sector reform in Japan: progress and challenges. In: Demaestri E, Masci P (eds) Financial crisis in Japan and Latin America. Inter-American Development Bank, Washington DC

Okuba T, Tomiura E (2012) Industrial relocation policy, productivity and heterogeneous plans: evidence from Japan. Reg Sci Urban Econ 42(1–2):230–239

Ouchi T (1966) The Japanese land reform: its efficacy and limitations. Dev Econ 4(2):129–150. https://doi.org/10.1111/j.1746-1049.1966.tb00776.x

Perkins DH (2013) East Asian development: foundations and strategies. Harvard University Press, Cambridge, MA

Prestowitz C (1988) Trading places: how we allowed Japan to take the lead. Basic Books, New York

Rosenstein-Rodan P (1943) Problems of industrialization of Eastern and South-Eastern Europe. Economic Journal 53(210/211):202–211

Ryota M (2014) The rise and fall of Taisho democracy: party politics in early-twentieth-century Japan. https://www.nippon.com/en/in-depth/a03302/

Shirai S (2013) Monetary policy and forward guidance and Japan. Speeches at the international monetary fund (September 19) and the board of governance is of the Federal Reserve system (September 20), Washington, DC. Bank of Japan. https://www.boj.or.jp/en/announcements/press/koen_2013/data/ko130921a1.pdf

Song J (2015) Economic empowerment of women as the third arrow of Abenomics. J Int Area Stud 22(1):113–128

Spiegel MM (2006) Did quantitative easing by the Bank of Japan "Work"? FRBSF Economic Letter 2006–28

Statistics Bureau of Japan (2021) Statistics Bureau, Ministry of Internal Affairs and Communications Website, https://www.stat.go.jp/english/

Stockwin A (2018) Explaining one-party dominance in Japanese politics. East Asia Forum (19 Jan 2018). https://www.eastasiaforum.org/2018/01/19/explaining-one-party-dominance-in-japanese-politics/

Suzuki T (2000) Japan's budget politics: balancing domestic and international interest. Lynne Rienner Publisher, Boulder, Colorado

Takagi S (1997) Japan's restrictive system of trade and payments: operation, effectiveness, and liberalization, 1950–1964. International Monetary Fund, Washington DC. https://www.elibrary.imf.org/view/journals/001/1997/111/article-A001-en.xml

Takayoshi M (1956) The development of democracy in Japan-Taisho democracy: its flowering and breakdown. Dev Econ 4(4):612–632

Takigawa T (1972) Historical background of agricultural land reform in Japan. Dev Econ 10 (3):290–310. https://doi.org/10.1111/j.1746-1049.1972.tb00283.x

Teranishi J (1994) Emergence and establishment of the financial system in postwar Japan: government intervention, indirect financing and the corporate monitoring system. EDI Working Papers 94-53, economic development Institute of the World Bank, Washington DC

Tipton FB (2008) Asian firms: history, institutions and management. Edward Elgar Publishing, Cheltenham

Tsuzuki C (2000) The pursuit of power in modern Japan 1825–1995. Oxford University Press, Oxford

Ueda K (2012) The effectiveness of non-traditional monetary policy measures: the case of the Bank of Japan. Japanese Economic Review 63(1):1–22

Ugai H (2007) Effects of the quantitative easing policy: a survey of empirical analyses. Monet Econ Stud 25(1):1–48

Vollmer U, Bebenroth R (2012) The financial crisis in Japan: causes and policy reactions by the Bank of Japan. Eur J Comp Econ 9(1):51–77

Wagner H (1989) Alternatives of disinflation and stability policy—costs, efficiency and implementation: a comparison between Japan and West Germany. BOJ Monet Econ Stud 7 (1):41–97

Wagner H (2010) The causes of the recent financial crisis and the role of central banks in avoiding the next one. Int Econ Econ Policy 7(1):63–82

Watanabe W (2007) Prudential regulation and the "credit crunch": evidence from Japan. J Money Credit Bank 39(2/3):639–665

Weinstein DE, Yafeh Y (1995) Japan's corporate groups: collusive or competitive? An empirical investigation of Keiretsu Behavior. J Ind Econ 43(4):359–376

Whalley J, Zhou W (2011) Technology upgrading in China's growth strategy to 2020. In: Whalley G (ed) China's integration into the world economy. World Scientific, Singapore

World Bank (2021) World Development Indicators. World Bank, Washington DC

Woronoff J (1992) Japanese targeting: successes, failures, lessons. Palgrave Macmillan, New York

Xu B (2014) Abenomics and the Japanese economy. The Council on foreign relations (29 April 2014). http://www.cfr.org/japan/abenomics-japanese-economy/p30383

Yamamura K (1967) Economic policy in postwar Japan: growth with this economic democracy. University of California Press, Berkeley, Los Angeles

Yokoi-Arai M (2002) Financial stability issues—the case of East Asia. Kluwer Law International, London

Yoshino N, Taghizadeh-Hesary F (2014) Three arrows of "Abenomics" and the structural reform of Japan: inflation targeting policy of the central bank, fiscal consolidation, and growth strategy. ADBI Working Paper No. 492. Asian Development Bank Institute, Tokyo

Yoshino N, Taghizadeh-Hesary F (2015) Japan's lost decade: lessons for other economies. ADBI Working Paper No 521, Asian Development Bank Institute, Tokyo

South Korea's Catching-Up Process

3

Abbreviations

ADB	Asian Development Bank
AFC	Asian Financial Crisis
ASEAN	Association of South East Asian Nations
BIS	Bank of International Settlements
CD	Certificate of Deposit
CDMA	Code Division Multiple Access
CDO	Collateralized Debt Obligation
CESP	Comprehensive Economic Stabilization Program
CMO	Collateralized Mortgage Obligation
CPI	Consumer Price Index
ED Plan	Economic Development Plan
EPB	Economic Planning Board
EXR	Exchange Rate
FDI	Foreign Direct Investment
FI	Financial Institution
FR	Foreign Reserves
FSC	Financial Supervisory Commission
FSS	Financial Supervisory Service
GDP	Gross Domestic Product
GFC	Global Financial Crisis
GNI	Gross National Income
GNP	Gross National Product
HAN	Highly Advanced National R&D

L. Glawe and H. Wagner, *The Economic Rise of East Asia*,
Contributions to Economics, https://doi.org/10.1007/978-3-030-87128-4_3

HCI	Heavy and Chemical Industry
HDTV	High Definition Television
IBTDP	Industrial Base Technology Development Project
ICT	Information and Communication Technology
IFS	International Financial Statistics
ILO	International Labor Organization
IMF	International Monetary Fund
ISI	Import Substitution Industrialization
KAIST	Korea Advanced Institute for Science and Technology
KAMCO	Korea Asset Management Corporation
KDI	Korean Development Institute
KDIC	Korea Deposit Insurance Corporation
KIST	Korea Institute of Science and Technology
LTD	Loan-to-Deposit Ratio
M&A	Merger and Acquisition
M2	Money Supply 2
M3	Money Supply 3
MBS	Mortgage Backed Securities
MIC	Ministry of Information and Communication
MOFE	Ministry of Finance and Economy
MOU	Memorandum of Understanding
NBFI	Non-Bank Financial Institution
NIF	National Investment Fund
NPL	Non-Performing Loan
NRP	National R&D Project
OECD	Organisation for Economic Co-operation and Development
OPEC	Organization of the Petroleum Exporting Countries
POSCO	Pohang Iron and Steel Company
R&D	Research and Development
SME	Small and Medium-Sized Enterprise
SOE	State-Owned Enterprise
SSA	Sub-Saharan Africa
TFP	Total Factor Productivity

USA	United States of America
WDI	World Development Indicators
ZBB	Zero-Based Budgeting

3.1 Introduction

About two decades after Japan's economic take-off, also South Korea underwent a period of extended economic growth and managed to rise to the ranks of high-income countries in the 1990s (according to the World Bank classification).[1] In 1996, South Korea became the 29th member of the OECD, the second Asian country after Japan. In the 1950s, however, there was still no sign of this exceptional economic performance: After the end of Japanese rule in 1945, Korea's per capita GDP was similar to that of poorer countries in Africa, and as a consequence of the Korean War, the country faced an even worse economic situation. In 1960, South Korea's per capita GDP (932 in constant 2010 US dollar) was only 83% of that of the group of sub-Saharan African countries and 8% of that of the group of OECD countries. As illustrated by Fig. 3.1, this picture changed dramatically over the next decades. South Korea reported an annual average per capita GDP growth rate of 7.3% over the period 1961–1997 (7.5% when excluding the oil crisis year 1980). In 1990, South Korea's GDP per capita was already 6.5 times as large as that of sub-Saharan African countries. Even though the South Korean growth rate dropped to 3.8% between 1999 and 2019, South Korea was still able to continue to gradually reduce the gap to the OECD average, and in 2019, it recorded a per capita income that was 70% of the average OECD income.

Different Stages of Development

The Korean economic development process can be subdivided into various phases, the historical roots—in particular, the Goryeo dynasty (918–1392) and the Joseon dynasty (1392–1897), the period under Japanese colonial rule (1919–1945), the period of liberation and state building (1948–1960), the period of economic take-off (1961–1979) with a focus on export promotion in the 1960s and on the heavy and chemical industries (HCIs) in the 1970s, the period of stabilization and liberalization (1980–1997) with the focus on the rationalization of the industrial structure in the 1980s and on liberalization in the 1990s, and finally the phase of economic crisis, new challenges, and maturation (1997/98–present) (cf. Kim 2016; Sakong and Koh 2010). The two periods "economic take-off" and "stabilization and liberalization" were both guided by government-led development plans. However,

[1] South Korea first became a high-income country in 1993, then briefly lost its position after the 1997 financial crisis, and in 1999, it regained high-income status.

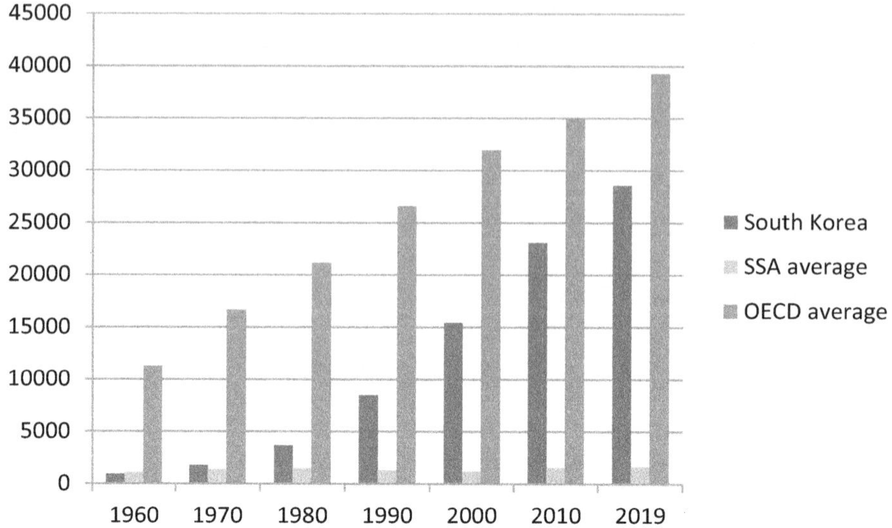

Fig. 3.1 South Korea's per capita income in comparison, 1960–2019. *Source* World Bank (2021). *Notes* GDP per capita in constant US$2010

while during the 1960s and 1970s, the government rather pursued a "growth first policy", the policy focus shifted to a more sustainable development strategy in the 1980s and 1990s. Among others, the government was more aware of the necessity of a balance between the government and private sectors. The final phase eventually presents the full-scale transformation into a market-driven, fully liberalized economy after the IMF bailout (cf. Yeon et al. 2016; Suh 2007).

Overview on the economic reforms

After Korea's independence from the Japanese colonial rule, the country was impoverished and faced very unfavorable economic conditions which were even further exacerbated by the Korean War between 1950 and 1953. Also in the years after the war, the South Korean economy saw only a slow recovery and reported very limited achievements with respect to infrastructure development because of resource scarcity and a rather small government budget. During the **1950s**, South Korea was heavily dependent on foreign assistance; however, foreign aid was misallocated (among others due to the problem of crony capitalism). The country was suffering from stagnation, inflation, and political volatility. Under Rhee Syngman (1948–1960),[2] South Korea pursued an **import substitution industrialization** policy, including overvalued foreign exchange rates, which had an adverse effect on South Korea's exports. However, two reforms that were installed over this period laid the foundation for the later industrialization process that triggered South

[2] For an overview of South Korea's presidents between 1948 and 2020, see Table 3.2.

Korea's economic take-off. The educational reform enabled the building up of a pool of relatively well-educated workers, and the land reform increased social equity and stability.

At the beginning of the **1960s**, South Korea was still a predominantly agricultural economy, which faced a similar income level than prior to its independence. When Park Chun-hee came to power in 1961, he implemented a "growth first strategy" with the aim of becoming independent from foreign assistance of the USA and also to compete against North Korea which was overtaking South Korea with respect to economic development and progress in industrialization. It was during the 1960s that the "Miracle of the Han River" started. The Park administration took control over banks and restructured the financial system in order to gain control over credit allocation. In addition, the government established 5-year economic development plans, which aimed at ending the vicious cycle of low savings, low investments, and low growth.

Under the direction of the newly created Economic Planning Board, the economy was redirected to an **export-led industrialization strategy** with a focus on light manufacturing in which South Korea had a comparative advantage due to its abundant cheap and relatively well-educated labor force. This strategy worked and between 1961 and 1970, the average annual GDP per capita growth rate was around 6.5% (see Fig. 3.2), the average annual savings rate increased from 11.1% over the period 1953–1960 to 15.5% between 1961 and 1970 and the investment ratio from 11.5 to 18.8% (see Table 3.1).

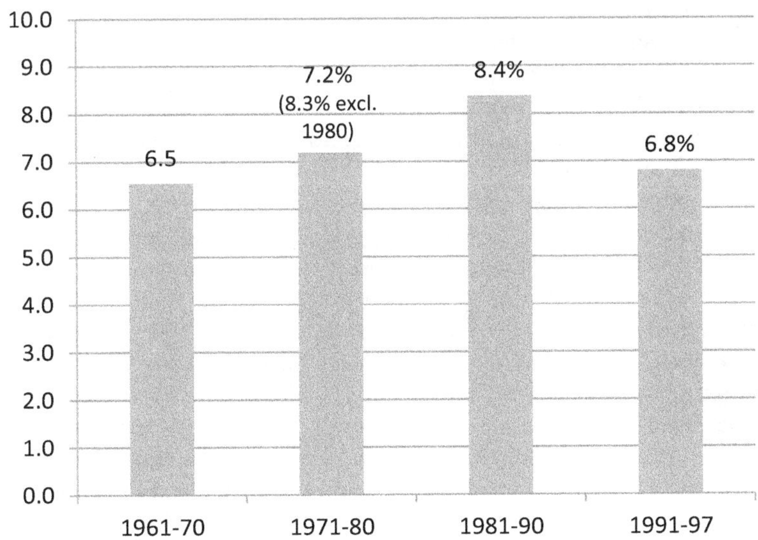

Fig. 3.2 Average growth rate, 1961–1997. *Source* World Bank (2021), own calculations

Table 3.1 Investment and savings rates, 1953–1997

	1953–60	1961–70	1971–80	1981–90	1991–97
Gross savings rate	11.1	15.5	23.8	34.0	37.6
Gross investment rate	11.5	18.8	29.6	33.9	38.9

Source Sakong and Koh (2010) for the periods 1953–60 and 1961–70; Bank of Korea, Economic Statistic System, for the remaining periods, own calculations

In the **1970s**, the South Korean government shifted its focus away from the promotion of labor-intensive export industries and started its **HCI drive** in the course of which six key industries (steel, machinery, chemicals, metals, shipbuilding, and electronics) were particularly favored. Industrial policy became more selective and targeted not only specific sectors but even specific companies. The Park regime turned more authoritarian, which further facilitated the realization of industrial policy. It was during the 1970s that the big conglomerates became more powerful. Large chaebols were heavily supported by the government (e.g. via preferential loans and other incentives) in order to minimize the time necessary for the development of a competitive heavy industry and also in order to exploit scale advantages inherent in HCI. The South Korean government also invested in upgrading the technology and technical workforce in order to meet the rising demand of skilled personnel required in HCI sectors. Overall, the reforms were successful in deepening the industrial structure and generated ongoing economic growth: GDP per capita growth was on average 7.2% over the 1971–1980 period. The average annual savings rate increased to 23.8%, and the average investment rate to almost 30%.

The unprecedented government support for the big conglomerates during the HCI drive and huge investments beyond the actual capacity of the South Korean economy also had various negative side effects, including and increasing concentration of power in the hands of few very large conglomerates, an increasing number of non-performing loans (NPLs), resource misallocation, a delay in the financial sector development, excess capacity, soaring inflation, and high foreign debt. These macroeconomic imbalances were further aggravated by an unfavorable external environment, including rising energy prices, high foreign interest rates, and a high dollar (the "three highs"). The growth model of the last two decades was not sustainable anymore, and in 1980, GDP growth turned negative for the first time in about 30 years. Consequently, the focus during the **1980s** was on **macroeconomic stabilization** and the "growth first" strategy was replaced by a stability-oriented development strategy. Stabilization measures included a tight monetary and fiscal policy, the restructuring of the HCI sector and industrial rationalization, a reduction of government intervention, the elimination of preferential lending rates along with the increasing (but still incomplete) liberalization of the financial market and accelerated import liberalization in order to increase international competitiveness. It was also during the 1980s that South Korea underwent the process of democratization. As a consequence, the labor–management relations changed significantly: workers' rights were strengthened and the number of labor unions increased drastically. Stabilization policies as well as progress in deregulation and liberalization turned out to be rather successful and South Korea was able to get back on its high-growth path: the average GDP per capita growth rate over the period 1989–1990 accounted to 8.4%.

In the **1990s**, South Korea pursued an intensified strategy of **globalization** under which the financial **liberalization** and the opening up of South Korea's capital markets were accelerated. The government announced the Four-Stage Interest Rate Liberalization Plan. However, contrary to the plan's initial intention, short-term interest rates and not long-term interest rates were liberalized first, significantly changing the structure of corporate sector financing. The stock market was opened to foreigners in 1992 and the number of South Korean financial institutions (FIs) that were allowed to engage in overseas activities increased significantly in the middle of the 1990s. Many chaebols took advantage of the increasing liberalization of the financial markets and gained control of still rather inexperienced non-bank financial institutions (NBFIs) to gain access to foreign capital without adequate state supervision. This generated an investment boom in the early years of the 1990s with an average investment ratio of almost 40% between 1991 and 1997. Chaebols took higher risks since they expected being bailed out by the government in the case of bankruptcy since they were "too big to fail". As a consequence, the debt to equity ratios of many chaebols became extremely high. In addition, the large majority of all foreign investment was on a short-term basis, while the chaebol-owned merchant banks lent on a long-term basis to the affiliates, resulting in a maturity structure mismatch, which made the financial sector extremely vulnerable to external shocks.

Overall, even though South Korea still achieved a relatively high average annual per capita income growth rate of 6.8% between 1991 and 1997 and also managed to become internationally competitive in the personal computer and semiconductor industries (as a result of the promotion of technological innovation), the country's corporate and financial sectors faced severe problems. These weaknesses eventually came to light when the external environment became extremely unfavorable in the mid-1990s. Among others, the oil price increased, the Japanese yen was depreciated, and the price of semiconductors declined. In addition, the **Asian Financial Crisis** started to spread over Southeast Asia and this increased the anxiety of foreign investors toward Asian markets, including South Korea. Creditors denied debt renewals and demanded fast loan repayments, causing a wave of chaebol bankruptcies in 1997. The South Korean government was forced to use its foreign exchange reserves to pay back loans; however, by November 1998, the country's reserves were almost depleted and South Korea had to apply for an **IMF bailout**. The IMF rescue package comprised $55 billion; however, it was tied to the implementation of various macroeconomic measures (particularly the tightening of monetary and fiscal policy) as well as a comprehensive structural reform program targeted at the financial sector, the corporate sector, the labor market, and the public sector. As a result of the monetary and fiscal retrenchment measures, the exchange rate was stabilized and the current account turned into a surplus in 1998. However, at the same time, the tightening of monetary and fiscal policies also deepened the

Table 3.2 Presidents in South Korea, 1948–2020

Year	President
1948–1960	**Rhee Syngman**
1960–1962	Yun Posun
1963–1979	**Park Chung-hee**
1979–1980	Choi Kyu-hah
1980–1988	**Chun Doo-hwan**
1988–1993	Roh Taw-woo
1993–1998	Kim Young-sam
1998–2003	Kim Dae-jung
2003–2008	Roh Moo-hyun
2008–2013	Lee Myung-bak
2013–2017	Park Geun-hye
2017–present	Moon Jae-in

recession. As a consequence of the structural reforms in the financial sector, the number of NPLs decreased and the BIS ratio of capital to risk-related assets improved significantly. Also the structural problems of chaebols could largely be solved. In 1999, South Korea again reported double-digit growth, and in 2001, the country was able to repay its IMF loan. Still, the average GDP per capita growth rate between 2001 and 2010 was "only" 4% per annum, raising questions of whether South Korea has adjusted to a new, lower steady-state growth path. However, declining average growth could also mean that South Korea is approaching the technological frontier and decreasing growth rates are only natural in the course of the convergence process postulated by neoclassical growth theory.

When South Korea was hit by the Global Financial Crisis in 2007/8, it was again its heavy reliance on a short-term foreign debt that made the country vulnerable to the global credit crunch. Also exports dropped considerably in 2009. Thanks to expansionary macroeconomic policy measures and the bank recapitalization strategy, South Korea managed to recover relatively fast from the crisis (also when compared with other OECD countries).

3.2 Historical Roots and Development Prior to 1945

While Korea engaged in international trade with Arabs, Japanese, Chinese, and Manchurians throughout the **Goryeo dynasty** (918–1392), this foreign policy changed dramatically in the **Joseon dynasty** (1392–1897) during which the Korean rulers tried to prevent foreign trade by closing the borders and only retained bilateral foreign relations with China, becoming a tributary state (so-called **foreign policy of sadae**, serve the great) (see Morck and Yeung 2017). South Korea became a Japanese protectorate around 1905 and eventually a Japanese colony in 1910. It stayed under **Japanese colonial rule** until 1945. During this time, the country underwent some industrialization; however, the respective economic policies were rather designed to benefit Japan (Kim and Kim 1997). For instance, the Japanese strategy favored the heavy and chemical industry, which reported a rising share from 32 to 51% over the period from 1931 to 1940, and not the traditional Korean, rather light manufacturing sectors which shrank by almost 20 percentage points over the same period (Kim and Roemer 1979). In addition, this development strategy was heavily dependent on Japanese capital, technology, and management and did not help Korea to achieve self-sustaining economic development (Kim and Kim 1997). After Japan's defeat in the World War II, also the colonial rule ended and the Peninsula was divided into North (controlled by the Soviet Union) and the South (controlled by the USA). In 1948, the Republic of Korea (South Korea) and the Democratic Party People's Republic of Korea (North Korea) were created.

3.3 The 1950s: Post-war Reconstruction

The period between 1945 until 1960 was characterized by economic stagnation. Figure 3.3, using Maddison data, displays the development of GDP over the period 1940–1960. There is a clear slump in GDP in the middle of the 1940s, that is, when Korea gained independence. There was a slight recovery until 1950; however, with the outbreak of the Korean War, GDP increased again significantly and it was not until 1955/56 that South Korea was able to recover and achieve a level of output similar to that prior to its independence. Regarding GDP per capita, the recovery

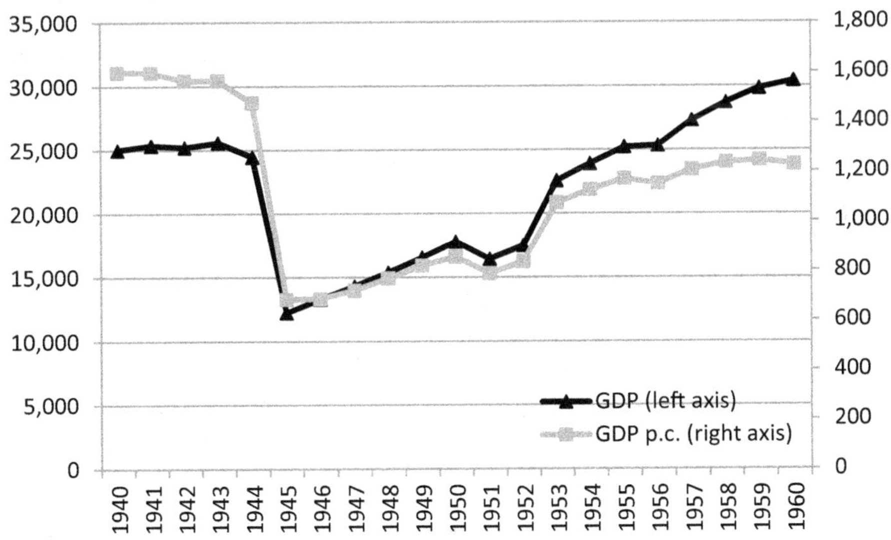

Fig. 3.3 GDP and GDP per capita, 1940–1960. *Source* Maddison Database

took even longer. The disastrous economic performance can to a large extent be attributed to very unfavorable initial conditions. First, when the Japanese occupation ended, also the Japanese labor force returned to Japan. However, the Korean factories now lacked engineers in order to run the machines since during the occupation, they had been heavily dependent on the Japanese technical manpower. In addition, Korea also lost Japan as the main trading partner, which had negative effects on Korean exports. The third point that probably distinguishes Korea from other previously colonized states such as India and Singapore is the division of the Korean Peninsula. Southern and Northern Korea had established a complementary industrial structure. While the northern part of the peninsula focused on heavy industries and produced more than 90% of electricity, the southern part was a predominantly agricultural economy that had a rather small industrial sector (with a focus on light manufacturing) that was not self-sustainable (Nam and Kim 1997). In 1940, the per capita net commodity product of North Korea was more than 60% bigger than that of South Korea. Also after the post-war recovery, North Korea's development initially appeared much more promising than that of South Korea (Krause 1997; Hwang 1993).

In addition to the rather disappointing growth performance, South Korea also did not undergo major structural transformation between 1953 and 1961 (which would have been usually expected during a post-war recovery period). For instance, in 1961, the value added of the agricultural sector—amounting to around 46%—was still the same as that of 1953. The light industry increased from about 9 to 16% and heavy industry from 2 to 4% while the share of services in GDP declined from 42% to around 31% (cf. Krause 1997).[3] That is, at the beginning of the 1960s, South Korea was still a rather agrarian economy.

The period between 1953 and 1961 was characterized by stagnation, inflation, government corruption (crony capitalism), heavy reliance on foreign assistance, and misallocation of aid funds (cf. Seth 2017). Moreover, the government pursued an import substitution policy. The most important policies and characteristics of this period will be briefly outlined in the next paragraphs.

3.3.1 Import Substitution Policy

In the post-war period, South Korea followed an import substitution industrialization (ISI) policy (Graham 2003a). In the 1950s and 1960s, import substitution-led industrialization was the standard policy recommended by economists that was followed by many developing countries (among others, in Latin America) (see Krueger 1997; ADB 2020). By replacing imports with domestically produced goods, the South Korean government aimed at reducing the foreign dependence and also to control the post-war hyperinflation (Ahn and Kim 1997). ISI policies included (a) currency overvaluation that enabled the cheap import of capital goods, (b) subsidies, particularly preferential bank lending for companies

[3] The output share of mining increased from 1.08 to 2.25%.

operating in targeted industries, as well as (c) protective barriers such as tariffs on imports that could be competing with domestically produced goods and an automatic approval rate (that is, the percentage items that can be imported without prior government approval) below 10% (Yoo 2017). Import substitution policies first focused on the so-called "three whites" (namely, sugar, wheat flour, and cotton, cf. Haggard et al. 1991), representing essential consumer goods, which were relatively easy to produce. At the end of the 1950s, South Korea was able to produce these goods self-sufficiently and turned to industrial products such as cement, radios, and electric fans. The ISI policy was successful in enabling South Korea to produce non-durable consumer goods on its own, and it paved the way for the subsequent export expansion in the 1960s by creating possibilities of improved capital utilization. However, it was not able to remove the country's reliance on foreign imports since those were still necessary for the raw materials and machines. In addition, the policies did not succeed in making the manufacturing sector the dominant one, and the overvalued currency resulted in an uncompetitive export industry and thus a widening trade deficit (cf. Yoo 2017; Ahn and Kim 1997; Kim and Roemer 1979; Kim 1991).

3.3.2 Foreign Aid Dependence

In the 1950s, South Korea was heavily reliant on foreign aid, primarily from the USA and to a lesser extent also from the United Nations. The foreign funds were used to finance the trade deficit, which was to a large extent the result of the ISI strategy: in the latter half of the 1950s, the average annual exports amounted to only $20 million while the average imports amounted to $370 million of which 80% were financed by foreign assistance (Yoo 2017). Foreign aid was also an important source of government revenues to which it contributed also approximately 80%. Foreign aid peaked in 1957, almost reaching US$400 billion and contributing more than 20% to GDP (Krueger 1982).

3.3.3 Corruption

One important reason for the facts that (1) (despite receiving huge amounts of foreign aid) South Korea remained poor with very low, rather stagnating per capita income levels and that (2) the ISI policies did not succeed in establishing a light industrial base, was **government corruption** (Graham 2003a). Singman Rhee channeled foreign aid flows into businesses of his cronies that were subsidized by ISI policies (Haggard et al. 1991; Seth 2017). This is the reason why South Korea's crony capitalism also created a new class of rich Koreans—of which some would later found chaebols that were decisive for South Korea's economic take-off in the next decades (cf. Graham 2003a; Jones and Sakong 1980).

Although the period between 1945 and 1960 was marked by economic stagnation, two major reforms took place under the Rheeman administration that contributed significantly to the country's economic take-off in the 1970s, namely, the land reform and the educational reform.

3.3.4 Land Reform

In 1945, over 70% of all farmers were tenant farmers who had to provide around 60% of their crop to the landlords (Pak 1956). The land tenure system had suppressed incentives for tenant farmers to increase investments in labor and input supply since production increases almost exclusively benefited the landlords (Shin 1976).

The land reform was carried out in two waves, the first in 1947 and the second around 1949/50 (Adelman 1997). In the course of the first reform, the US military government redistributed land that had been previously owned by Japanese (Ahn and Kim 1997; Kim 2016; Mitchell 1949). The second land reform was carried out by the Korean government. Land owned by large Korean landlords was redistributed to former tenant farmers, thus virtually abolishing tenancy (Adelman 1997; Gon and Gyun 2013).

In particular, the government purchased the land of large landlords (owning more than ca. 3 ha) in return for government bonds and then resold the land to small farmers at a favorable rate (Adelman 1997), usually 30% of the average annual output for 5 years (cf. Pak 1956). However, some argue that this price was still too heavy a burden for the farmers (Shin 1976). The landowners invested in business or established schools. The transformation of landlords into industrialists was, however, only partially successful since this process was interrupted by the outbreak of the Korean War (Seth 2017; Lie 1998). The proportion of farmland under tenancy decreased from 63.4% prior to the reform in April 1952 to only 8% after the reform in December 1950 (Moon and Sul 1997).[4]

The land reform had three major economic and social consequences: first, the land reform abolished the feudalistic landlords tenant system in favor of the private ownership of agricultural land by independent farmers and thus provided incentives for peasants to increase agricultural productivity and output (Jeon and Kim 2000). However, it is sometimes argued that the agricultural productivity only started increasing in 1958, that is, with a time lag (Shin 1976). Second, the land reform established social equality (Shin 1976; Adelman 1997). Finally, the land reform also provided a favorable setting for the advancement of democracy in South Korea (Shin 1976).

[4] According to Jeon and Kim (2000), the tenancy rate declined from 52.4% in 1944 to 5.2% in 1955.

3.3.5 Educational Reform

After the end of the Japanese colonial rule in 1945, the educational situation was rather worrisome with over 50% of the population aged 13 years and above being illiterate (cf. Lee et al. 2012). Enhancing the access to education was one of the main aims of the Basic Education Law that was passed in 1949 and that, among others, made 6 years of free compulsory elementary school education mandatory (Sorensen 1994; Lee et al. 2012). In 1964, elementary enrolment ratios had already passed 90%. At the same time, adult literacy programs and Citizens' Schools (kongmin hakkyo) were installed. These measures can also be considered as rather successful and illiteracy was largely eliminated in the 1960s (Sorensen 1994; Seth 2017). South Korea's educational achievements were especially remarkable given the country's still relatively low level of economic development. According to the findings of Harbison and Myers (1964), South Korea's educational performance at a per capita income level of $90 was almost that of a country with a per capita GNP of more than thrice this size. When South Korea's per capita income just passed the threshold of $100, its educational achievement was comparable with economies almost having a GNP per capita four times as big. Improvements in education outpaced economic growth. Even though the labor supply exceeded the labor demand at this stage of economic development, the labor surplus created under the Rhee administration would become decisive for the imitation drive in the 1960s and 1970s (Kim and Seong 1997).[5] According to Kim and Seong (1997), one unique feature of the South Korean economy is that it managed to expand education rather well-balanced at all levels early enough in order to support economic progress.[6]

Box 3.1 Summary: The South Korean Economy in the 1950s

Key features of the South Korean economy

- economic **stagnation**, **inflation**
- **import substitution policy** including currency overvaluation, subsidies, protective barriers such as tariffs and an automatic approval rate below 10%
- South Korea was still dependent on imports (→ widening trade deficit)
- dependence on **foreign aid**, especially from the USA
- problem of **corruption (crony capitalism)**

[5] However, such a rapid expansion of the educational system was also associated with problems such as overcrowded classrooms and double or even triple shifts in 40% of all classrooms (Lee 2008; Sorensen 1994). Therefore, some researchers argue that the rapid expansion came at the expense of quality (Lee 2012).

[6] See Park (2019) on synergy effects between land and educational reforms.

Land reforms (1947 and 1949/50) initiated by the US military government and subsequently enacted by the Korean government; abolishment of the feudalistic landlord-tenant system; increased agricultural productivity due to an improved incentive structure, established social equality, and building the foundations for democratic reforms.

Educational Reform (Basic Education Law 1949) increased the access to education; rapid expansion of primary schooling enrolment between 1945 and 1960; adult literacy program which eradicated illiteracy in the 1960s; one of the best educational achievements worldwide considering the income level; formation of labor surplus, which became decisive for South Korea's economic take-off.

3.4 The Second Republic (1960–1961)

The crony capitalism of the 1950s and the related economic stagnation led to a rising discontent among the population. Accusations of vote-rigging in 1960 were the final straw and on 26 April, the Rhee administration was overthrown in a student-led revolution (Kim 1983; Han 1974). In August 1960, Chang Myon was elected Prime Minister, forming a liberal democracy. However, the Second Republic was not able to solve the political and economic problems and led to further instability which Seth (2017) describes as a "rather chaotic experiment in parliamentary democracy" (for an overview on the evolution of democracy in South Korea, see also Box 3.2). Still, it was under Chang that the first economic development plan was designed, which was later (at least partly) used by the Park administration. The Second Republic only lasted a couple of months and was overthrown in the May 16 coup led by Park Chung-hee (Kim and Lee 1997). See Table 3.2 for an overview of South Korea's Presidents between 1948 and 2020.

Box 3.2 Evolution of Democracy in South Korea

South Korea's first democratic experiments started under the Rhee Syngman administration. However, the government turned more and more dictatorial and after accusations of vote-rigging 1960, the Rhee administration was overthrown in a student led revolution. However, also the second rather chaotic democratic experiment under Chang Myon did not succeed but induced more instability. After just 9 months, the Chang administration was overthrown by Park Chung-hee, and the new government became increasingly authoritarian. In 1972, the 1963 Constitution was suspended and the new Yushin Constitution was proclaimed, granting President Park de facto dictatorial powers. The South Korean economy experienced extraordinarily high growth rates during these years, and thus the South Korean middle class tolerated the rather authoritarian turn. After the assassination of President Park, Chun took over and filled the power vacuum. In contrast to Park, he did not even want to get popular support through elections. After the shooting of the Yonsei University student Lee Han Jol in 1987, a nationwide so-called "June democracy movement" started and eventually forced the government to amend the Constitution, leading to the establishment of the 6th Republic. That is, South Korea has seen a **bottom-up democratization process** driven by the civil society, that is, from within. Moreover, due to the authoritarian governments, the society was rather critical toward political institutions and had more trust in civil society organizations (Fukuyama 2012). However, more recently, there is evidence that generalized social trust in South Korea is positively associated with political trust (Lee and Yi 2018).

3.5 Foundation Building and Export Promotion of the 1960s Under the Park Administration

The primary goal of the Park administration was rapid economic progress (Krause 1997; Seth 2017; Park 2018). For this purpose, the government created the **Economic Planning Board** (EPB), which formulated 5-year economic development plans that laid out the main development strategy. The EPB overtook tasks previously conducted by the Ministry of Reconstruction, the Ministry of Finance, and the Ministry of Home Affairs and was under the leadership of the Deputy Prime Minister (Krause 1997).

Park's determination to initiate a South Korean economic take-off had two main motifs. First, South Korea wanted (and had) to get independent of the financial support by the USA (Seth 2017). In the late 1950s/beginning 1960s, the USA changed their foreign aid policies, reducing the amount of foreign assistance and providing it rather in the form of loans (Park 2018). At the same time, even though South Korea had successfully completed the import substitution of non-durable consumer goods, it was still heavily reliant on imports of raw materials and machinery, which had to be financed. Second, the Park administration was also competing with North Korea, which was challenging (and for short time even overtaking) South Korea economically (Seth 2017).

The **first 5-year economic development plan** (1962–1966) built upon the previous 3-year plan (Comprehensive Economic Reconstruction Plan) and was published rather hastily in 1961 to show the government's commitment to reform. Moreover, it provided the basis for the following economic plans (cf. Kim 1991).

For an overview of economic plans between 1962 and 2007, see Table 3.10 in the Appendix of this chapter.

The first version of the 5-year development plan underlined the importance of improving the general living standards, upgrading the industrial structure and building key industries, as well as improving the balance of payments by raising exports (Park 2018; Lee 1999a). Even though the plan mentioned export expansion as a desirable goal, the main focus was still on import substitution.[7] The plan was **revised in 1964**, eventually shifting the policy priority to **export-oriented industrialization** (Yoo 2017).[8]

In comparison to the development plan of the previous regime, the first 5-year plan under the Park administration assigned a much stronger role to the government (this is sometimes also referred to as "**guided capitalism**", cf. Park 2018). This was in sharp contrast to the recommendations of the USA, which favored the establishment of a market-based economy. Even after the transition to democracy in 1964, the power was rather centralized in the executive. The **centralization** was also reflected in the economic planning and decision-making process, which was the task of the newly formed EPB "super ministry" (Haggard et al. 1991).

As we will see later, centralization increased the range of policy instruments that the government could use in order to achieve the goals of the economic development plans (Haggard et al. 1991). Among others, the government intervened heavily in the financial system to foster industrialization (Cho 1989). For instance, the government **nationalized all commercial banks** in order to get control over credit and to enable targeted investment in specific sectors. Other related reforms include the **currency reform**, the **interest rate reform**, and the **exchange rate reform**. In addition, the **business–state relationships were restructured.** All the reforms mentioned above will be discussed in the following Sects. 3.5.1–3.5.6. Overall, this strategy was a top-down approach.

3.5.1 Export Expansion

One of the key success factors of South Korea's high growth in the 1960s can be attributed to the **rapid export expansion in manufacturing**. Whereas in the 1950s, the government had still pursued a rather inward looking import substitution strategy, the new slogan of the subsequent two decades was "nation-building through exports" (Krause 1997). This strategy change also appears reasonable against the background that South Korea was lacking natural resources and also only had a limited domestic market. Moreover, South Korea possessed a relatively well-educated labor force, and it seemed sensible to maximize the country's

[7] Cf. Economic Planning Board (1961).

[8] As we will see, also throughout the subsequent 5-year plans, the policy course changed according to the varying economic conditions as well as changing views on the role of the government and markets (Park 2018).

comparative advantage in labor-intensive manufacturing goods for export (Ahn 1990; Nam and Kim 1997).

Policy measures to promote export expansion included an **export import linkage system** in the course of which import licenses were distributed based on the export performance, **direct subsidies** for exports, **preferential export credits**, the **drawback system** (tariff exemptions on imports of raw material and intermediate inputs needed for export production), **indirect domestic tax exemptions** on **intermediate inputs** used for the production of exports, **direct tax reduction** on income earned from exports (until 1973), and the **exchange-rate reform** (cf. Nam and Kim 1997: 143; Frank et al. 1975: 40–51).

This change from import substitution driven to export-driven growth is also confirmed in the data: Between 1956 and 1960, import substitution contributed around 34% to economic growth, whereas the expansion of exports only made up 18%. Over the period from 1963 to 1973, the contribution of import substitution to growth was reduced to only 10% whereas the contribution of export expansion was more than three times as large (cf. Frank et al. 1975).[9]

According to Krueger (1977),[10] the main reason for why South Korea made a rather smooth transition from an import substitution to a rather export-oriented strategy was that "import substitution had not yet progressed to the development of high-cost intermediate and capital goods industries". Otherwise, pressure from domestic industries could have prevented duty-free imports of low-cost intermediate and capital goods for export production.

Especially in the beginning, the export expansion heavily focused on light industry, particularly the textile industry (clothing, footwear, etc.). This tendency was not really anticipated by the first economic development plan, which put emphasis on food and raw materials exports (in its initial 1961 version). While the share of products by materials in total exports was never intended to surpass 10% between 1962 and 1966, it in fact increased sharply, contributing more than 30%. In contrast, the contribution of food and raw materials which was suspected to lie above 70% for the entire period in fact decreased from 76% in 1962 to only 35% in 1966 (Kang et al. 2008, the data used to calculate the shares are presented in Table 3.3). President Park himself favored more prestigious products such as ships and heavy machinery. However, the EPB members succeeded to convince Park that South Korea (at this point) should use its comparative advantage of abundant cheap labor that it had in light manufacturing (Graham 2003a).

[9] Regarding the main driver of the rapid export expansion in the 1960s, there are partly **opposing views**. Early studies in the 1970s argue that the development strategies switch from import substitution to export promotion in the middle of the 1960s and the less interventional trade policy as well as increased liberalization were the main reasons for increasing exports (Cole and Lyman 1971; Frank et al. 1975; Hong and Krueger 1975; Krueger 1979). In the late 1980s, economists began to increasingly underline the importance of industrial policy, including subsidies, tax incentives, and administrative support (cf. Rodrik 1995). More recently, the foreign exchange system reform of 1961 came more in the focus of research (see Yoo 2017).

[10] Cited in Lal (1986).

Table 3.3 Export plan and actual realization (in million $)

	1962		1963		1964		1965		1966	
	Plan	Result	Plan	Result	Plan	Result	Plan	Result	Plan	Result
Food	20.1	21.9	23.2	18.1	27.6	26.3	31.6	28.2	35.8	35.1
Inedible raw materials	25.8	19.8	29.4	26.2	32.2	31.4	46.9	37.0	50.9	40.5
Products by materials	5.8	6.2	6.4	28.1	8.3	42.3	9.2	66.4	10	73.6
Machinery	–	1.4	–	4.1	–	2.2	–	5.5	–	8.4
Miscellaneous	4.6	2	7.3	6.4	9.1	13.2	9.9	34.5	12	52.2

Source Kang et al. (2008)

Box 3.3 Import Substitution and Export Promotion—East Asia Versus Latin America

Latin America and various East Asia countries, among others South Korea, Taiwan, Hong Kong, and Singapore, followed a very different strategy regarding the switch from import substitution to export promotion. Even though both country groups started with import substitution policies in lighter industries such as non-durable consumer goods in the 1950s, South Korea (and other East Asian economies) subsequently switched to an export promotion strategy in the 1960s. Moreover, during the initial import substitution phase, the level of protection of industries was lower compared with that in Latin American countries. Contrasting to the East Asian strategy, Latin America continued to rely on import substitution, extending the policies to capital and consumer durable goods. In South Korea, the focus switched again more to import substitution in the 1970s in the course of the HCI plan (cf. Sect. 3.6); however it was anticipated that the HCI industries would finally engage in exporting activities. The Latin American strategy of extended import substitution turned out to be problematic, resulting in lower growth and rising inequality, and it prevented industries from gaining efficiency. In the 1990s, Latin American economies eventual turned to an export promotion strategy. For more detailed information, see Baer (1984), and Ahn (1990).

3.5.2 Foreign Exchange Rate Reforms (1961–1965)

In the course of the foreign exchange rate reform in February 1961, the system of multiple exchange rates was abolished in favor of a unitary fixed rate (Yoo 2017). Even though multiple rates were again put in place in 1963, 2 years later, a fluctuating unified rate was introduced (Graham 2003a; Kim and Kim 1997). The

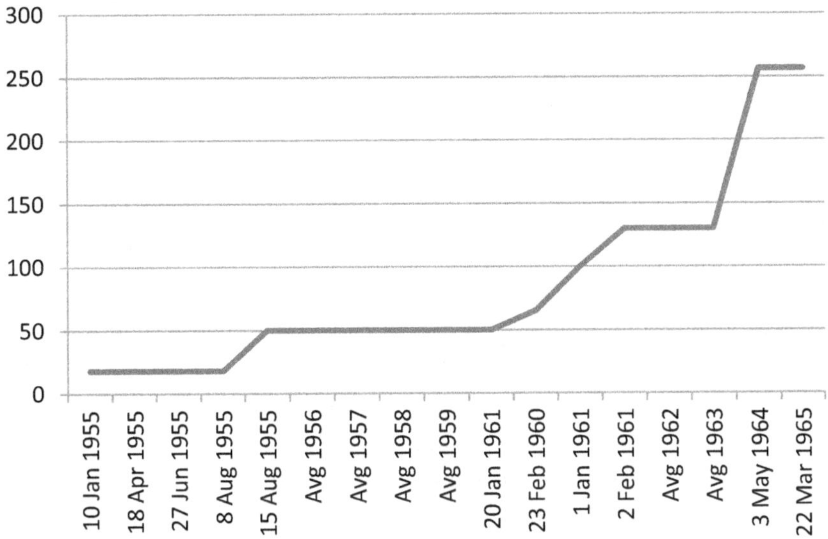

Fig. 3.4 Nominal exchange rate of the won to the US dollar. *Source* Frank et al. (1975), Yoo (2017)

exchange rate was also depreciated, which nearly eliminated the overvaluation of the won. In fact, there were three consecutive depreciations within 1 year (February 1960–February 1961); the first devaluation was rather initiated by the US government, whereas the other two were initiated by the South Korean government. The exchange rate was devalued by approximately 100% between 1960 and 1961 and again between 1963 and 1964 (see also Fig. 3.4).

3.5.3 Reducing the Savings–Investment Gap to Increase Exports

South Korea was able to even overfill the 5-year plans' GNP growth target, reaching an average growth rate of 7.8% between 1960 and 1966 (instead of the targeted 7.1%) and even 9.7% over the period from 1967 to 1971 (the target was 7%). However, as Table 3.4 shows, there was a mismatch between the investment rate and the savings rate, the latter being only half as large as the former. In order to realize the ambitious investment plans, the South Korean government undertook various measures to increase savings and mobilize capital. The government **nationalized all commercial banks**, and by **restructuring the banking system,** the Park administration gained increasing control over loan allocation (Seth 2017; Graham 2003a). Initially, credits were granted to every company that succeeded in exports, whereas later, the economic planning board started "picking winners". That is, it channeled low interest loans to firms operating in industries, which were

Table 3.4 First and second 5-year development plan—target and actual outcomes

	First 5-year development plan (1962–1966)		Second 5-year development plan (1967–1971)	
	Targets	Actual outcome	Target	Actual outcome
GNP growth	7.1	7.8	7.0	9.7
Investment rate	22.7	21.6	19.9	25.2
Savings rate	13.0	11.8	14.4	14.5
Export growth	28.0	38.6	17.1	33.8
Import growth	8.7	18.7	6.5	25.8
Unemployment	14.8	7.1	5.0	4.5
Inflation (CPI)		16.2		7.8

Source Kang (2000)

believed to become internationally competitive (Graham 2003a). In addition, the **currency reform** as well as an **interest rate reform** were installed in 1962 in 1965, respectively (see Sects. 3.5.4 and 3.5.5).

3.5.4 Currency Reform of 1962

In the course of the currency reform, the denomination was changed from hwan to won, having a face value 10 times higher than that of the hwan-dominated currency. Transactions in hwan-denominated currency were proscribed (Kim 1997: 199; Bank of Korea n.d.). The main objective of the reform was to reduce the informal sectors of the economy by channeling cash circulating in the underground into the market, particularly into industrial development. Prior to receiving new banknotes, it was mandatory to deposit the old currency at the banks within 7 days. An upper ceiling of 500 won per person was imposed on the immediate conversion, resulting in the freezing of bank deposits, which were intended to be used for funding economic development (Kim 1997). However, the amount of frozen funds turned out to be surprisingly small, and this, in combination with rising panic among the population, led to a lifting of the restrictions soon after. Overall, the reform turned out to be a failure, which worsened the inflationary pressure (Park 2018; Kim 1997).

3.5.5 Interest Rate Reform of 1965

In 1965, the government installed an interest rate reform in the course of which the maximum deposit interest rate was increased from 15 to 30% with the aim of encouraging savings and reducing inflation (Park 2018; Lee et al. 1984; McKinnon 1973). The reform was also encouraged by the USA (cf. Cole and Park 1983).[11]

[11] Moreover, Taiwan had succeeded to mobilize savings and stabilize inflation after increasing the interest rates (Cho 1989).

Prior to the reform, the South Korean government had pursued a low interest rate policy in order to reduce the financial costs for corporations. However, the low interest rates discouraged savings and the FIs had problems to mobilize funds (Park 2018; Kim 1997). Contrary to the currency reform, the interest rate reform was more positively evaluated, having been able to successfully increase the domestic savings rate (McKinnon 1973; Shaw 1973; both in Cho 1989). The financial sector experienced rapid growth with the M2/GNP ratio increasing from about 12% in 1965 to 35% in 1970. The significant increase was the result of funds flowing from the informal loan market to banks (cf. Cho 1989).

The mobilization of financial savings via the interest rate reform further increased the amount of resources that the Park administration could command since the banking system was under control of the government after it had been nationalized. Thus, the government could channel credits to private companies and thus expand its influence on them (Harris 1987; Cho 1989). Overall, the reforms provided the Park administration a "**discipline tool**" for the private sector since they could reward productive investment and punish poor performance of companies (Haggard et al. 1991; Amsden 1989 therein).

Starting in 1972, the government returned to a low interest rate policy since the high bank interest rate, in combination with the domestic recession had caused many loan-financed business firms being close to bankruptcy. The cut was also necessary due to the change in the industrial development strategy, increasingly favoring the HCI in the 1970s (Kim and Kim 1997; Lee 1991, see also Sect. 3.6). The successful establishment of the HCI required massive amounts of investment in **capital and technology,** which was only possible by granting low interest credit (Cho 1989; Cole and Park 1983). The general bank loan interest rate decreased from 23% in 1971 to 17.5% in 1972 and then stayed at 15.5% between 1973 and 1975 (Cho 1989) (Fig. 3.5).

3.5.6 External Capital Sources

The mixed (and partly disappointing) results of the currency and interest rate reform revealed that money mobilization inside Korea was limited, pointing to the necessity to mobilize external sources.

South Korea received $800 million from Japan as a **compensation** for the colonial era (between 1910 and 1945). This massive foreign capital inflow was largely used to support the economic development of the country. Among others, it was invested in infrastructure projects (such as Gyeongbu Expressway and the Soyang Dam) and used to support strategic industries. Another important factor of the external financing sources was **remittances money**. In the 1960s and 1970s, South Korea sent migrant laborers—nurses and miners—to **Germany** (Garz 2015). In addition, South Korea was actively engaged in the **Vietnam War**. Soldiers, civilian laborers, and technicians were sent to Vietnam, and construction companies were moved there (Baldwin 1975; Kim 1970). The workers and/or soldiers in Germany and Vietnam saved a large part of their earnings and sent it back to South

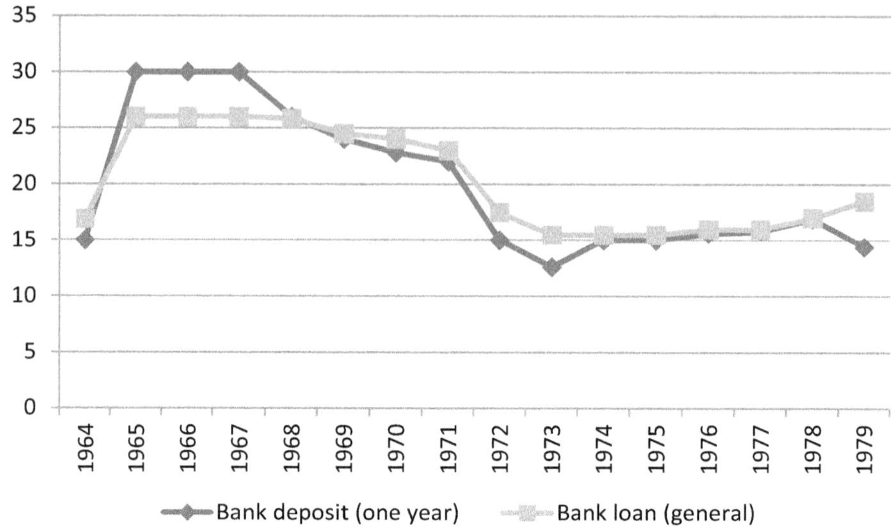

Fig. 3.5 Interest rates, 1964–1979. *Source* Cho (1989)

Korea. By the end of 1968, the earnings of the South Korean military amounted to $180 million, representing 16% of the overall receipt of foreign funds and almost 3% of South Korea's GNP (Kim 1970).

3.6 Heavy and Chemical Industrialization (HCI) Drive in the 1970s

In the 1970s, the focus of South Korea's development strategy shifted from the light to the heavy and chemical industry (HCI) (cf. Kim and Kim 1997; Lee 1991). Even though already the second 5-year economic development plan had focused on the promotion of the HCI, the policy announcement of 1973 by Park Chung-hee marked the actual starting point of the HCI drive. This policy change had several reasons: First, South Korea aimed at building up a military industry in order to become more self-defensive and independent of the USA. This was motivated primarily by the fact that the USA turned out to be a less reliable military partner (Seth 2017; Yoo 1990; Stern et al. 1995). The Nixon doctrine, underlining that the Asian ally nations were primarily responsible for their own security, raised fears that the USA would withdraw American forces out of South Korea.[12] This was

[12] The third point of the Nixon doctrine states: "Third, in cases involving other types of aggression, we shall furnish military and economic assistance when requested in accordance with our treaty commitments. But we shall look to the nation directly threatened to assume the primary responsibility of providing the manpower for its defense".

especially problematic because South Korea was still militarily inferior to North Korea and its northern neighbor had attacked South Korea multiple times in 1968. Moreover, the USA started to establish relations with China. Besides these *security problems*, there were also multiple *economic reasons* for which South Korea started intensively promoting the HCI policy in the 1970s (cf. Yoo 1990; Nam and Kim 1997). Since export promotion in the light industry had almost been completed, South Korea had to find new sources to stimulate growth. Due to rising wages, South Korea's price competitiveness in labor-intensive light industries was vanishing. The loss of the abundant low-cost labor comparative advantage is also one of the key mechanisms that can trigger a middle-income trap, a phenomenon which currently many (East) Asian emerging market economies are facing (cf. Glawe and Wagner 2016). At the same time, advanced countries undertook protective measures such as trade barriers for labor-intensive exports, which further weakened South Korea's export position. In addition, the light industries were more dependent on imports (for instance, on foreign raw materials and intermediate inputs). Thus, favoring HCI could improve South Korea's balance of payments and also increase the country's economic self-reliance (Kim and Kim 1997). Last but not least, HCI industries can have forward and backward linkage effects (Hirschman 1958).[13]

South Korea's strategy change was at least to some extent inspired by the Japanese experience. Japan had successfully promoted HCI in the 1960s (and before in the late 1940s), resulting in fast growth (cf. Sect. 2.5 and Park 2018). In addition, many advanced countries underwent a structural transformation process during which the share of HCI in manufacturing declined, particularly in the rather labor- and pollution-intensive steel and supporting industries. This opened up new opportunities for developing countries, which could fill this gap.

Box 3.4 Political and Institutional Background

Over the 1960s, the Park administration became increasingly **authoritarian**, culminating in the suspension of the 1963 Constitution in 1972 and the subsequent proclamation of the new Yushin constitution in October of the same year, which granted President Park de facto **dictatorial powers**. Park used this power to implement his plans for restructuring the economy, particularly the building up of the heavy industry. While the authoritarian turn might have facilitated the implementing of the industrial policy, it also built up imbalances between large companies and smaller firms and eventually led to political instability in the late 1970s. Many South Koreans became increasingly unhappy with autocratic direction of the regime, culminating in protests and the assassination of President Park on 26 October 1979.

[13] However, Lane (2019) finds that while South Korea's HCI policy positively impacted forward-linked industries it negatively impacted backward-linked industries.

3.6.1 HCI Plan

The HCI plan of 1973 targeted **six strategic industries**, namely, steel, metal, shipbuilding, machinery, chemical, and electronics. In contrast to the export promotion strategy of the 1960s, the HCI drive followed a more sector- and even firm-specific approach and each of the targeted industries had its own detailed plan and goals (Kim 1990). The building up of HCI requires enormous capital investments and the HCI plan of 1973 estimated a capital requirement of $9.6 billion over the period 1973–1981 (Stern et al. 1995; Horikane 2005). Key policy measures to promote HCI development included **financial support** of the government in order to allow for the necessary capital mobilization, **tax incentives**, a **foreign exchange rate reform**, **tariff protection**, the **provision of industrial parks** as well as various measures in order to **improve technical skills and the establishment of skilled technicians and engineers** required in HCI (Kim 1990; Kim and Kim 1997). The most important measures are briefly summarized in the following.

3.6.1.1 Financial Support

Even though South Korea still had to rely on foreign capital and technology, the increasing mobilization of domestic capital was emphasized (Horikane 2005). Among others, the government introduced new financial institutions to secure the necessary investment and loan funds to promote the HCI. Most importantly, the national investment fund (NIF) was established in 1974, and about two-thirds of its portfolio were directed to HCI projects (Kim 1990; Mah 2007). Other newly founded financing institutions include the **Export Import Bank** established in 1976, which provided the deferred payment loans to foreign buyers as well as **several special-purpose funds** such as the Machinery Utilization Fund, the Used Machinery Replacement Fund, and the Plant Localization Fund (Kim 1990; Galbraith and Kim 1998).[14] Since the NIF actually only made up a small proportion of total domestic credit, commercial banks played an important supporting financing role. About one-third of bank lending went into policy loans (Kim 1990; Galbraith and Kim 1998).

3.6.1.2 Protective Measures

The government undertook various other reforms in order to promote HCI development. For instance, the **Special Tax Reduction and Exemption Law** of 1974/5 supported the heavy industries by offering lower tax rates compared with the light industries (Kim and Kim 1997). Prior to 1973, the effective marginal tax rates of corporations of the light and heavy industries were roughly equal (fluctuating between 30 and 40%). However, after the enactment of the new tax law, the tax rate gap between both industries widened dramatically (cf. Fig. 3.6).

[14] The interest rates of the NIF and some of the special funds (Machinery Industry Promotion Fund) were 3–5% lower than the interest rates of general bank loans (cf. Cho and Kim 1997; Kim 1990).

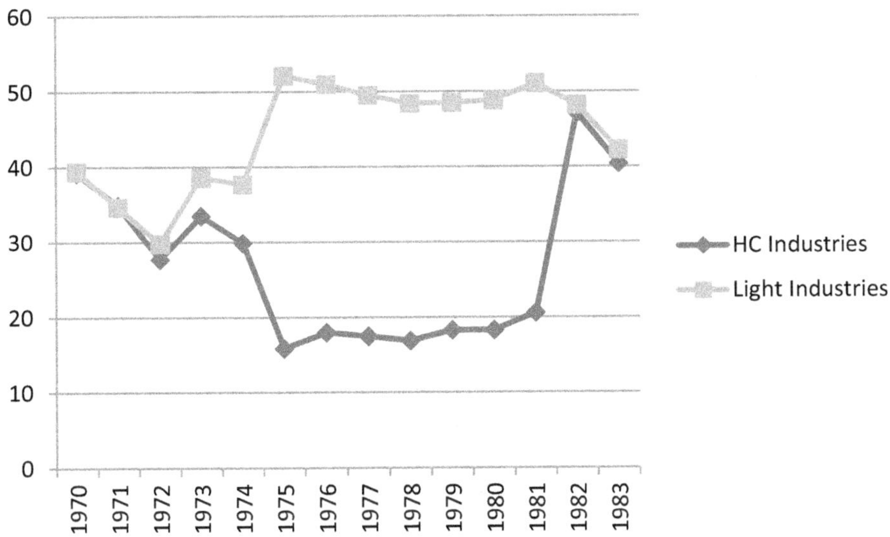

Fig. 3.6 Effective marginal tax rate of corporations. *Source* Kwack (1985), Yoo (1991)

While the effective tax rate of HCIs was reduced to below 20%, the respective rates for the light industries leveled off at around 50% during the second half of the 1970s. It was not before 1982 that the gap diminished rather abruptly. In addition, important raw materials and intermediate products used in HCI were exempted from custom duties under the **Revised Custom Law** (Park 2013, 2018).

The government also **fixed the exchange rate** to 484 won/$ over the period 1974–1979 in order to minimize the pressure on prices and to alleviate the burden of principal repayment on foreign loans (Park 2018; Kim 1990; see also Fig. 3.7).

In order to protect the HCIs, the government also used tariff barriers (Ahn and Kim 1997). In 1975, the **"Limited Tariff Drawback" system** was installed, which significantly reduced or even eliminated the tariff concessions for specific products. According to Kim (1990), the effective protection rate for HCI sectors was 71.2% in 1978 whereas that of light manufacturing sectors was −2.3%.

In 1978, the government **implemented import liberalization policies** with the intention of making domestic producers more efficient by increasing the competition with international companies. Correspondingly, the import liberalization ratio increased from 49.6% to 84.8% over the period from 1976 to 1984 (Kim 1990).[15]

3.6.1.3 Improving Technological Skills

HCI sectors usually require skilled engineers and technicians. To meet the rising demand for skilled personnel, the South Korean government undertook various

[15] The import liberalization ratio is defined as the automatic approval items divided by the total number of commodity class.

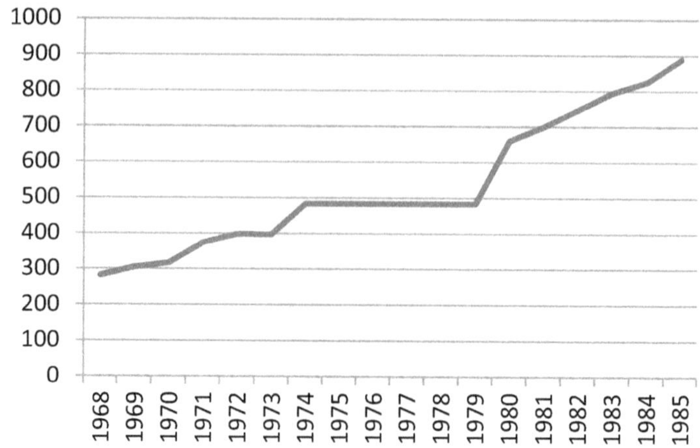

Fig. 3.7 Exchange Rate (won to US dollar), 1968–1985. *Source* Kim (1990)

measures. The focus was on expanding technical and vocational training as well as improving science and engineering education (Lim 2012). The **High School Equalization Policy** in the course of which entrance exams were replaced with standardized government examinations in each region was introduced in 1974 in Seoul and Busan and then gradually expanded to various other major cities. The main objectives of this policy measures were to normalize middle school curricula, promote vocational training, reduce quality differences among high schools, ensure a balanced educational development across regions, and reduce tutoring costs (cf. Kim and Lee 2002). The government also **raised the student admission quota** in the middle of the 1970s, thus increasing the number of students in higher education institutions (especially in those focusing on engineering and technical subjects). The measures significantly increased enrolment ratios of engineering and technical schools at various levels (Kim and Kim 1997: 22). The average years of schooling increased from around 6.4 in the 1970s to 6.9 in 1975 and further to 8 by 1980 (cf. Kim and Park 1985: 18). Moreover, the share of population with middle school education increased from 9.9% in 1962 to almost 24% in 1980, the share with high school education increased from 7.42% to almost 27% and the share with university degree from 1.3% to 7.4% over the same period (cf. Kim and Park 1985: 17). In addition, the government promoted the construction of research institutes to encourage HCI-related research and development (R&D) and established think tanks (Kim and Kim 1997: 22). In 1971, the government created the Korea Advanced Institute for Science and Technology (KAIST). The main research areas of the KAIST included energy, health, knowledge-based technology, and security whereas the 1966 founded Korea Institute of Science and Technology (KIST) focused on brain science, biomedical research, multidisciplinary convergence of materials, green city technology, future convergence research, and national agenda research (Jung and Mah 2013). According to the **Technology Development**

Promotion Law of 1972, tax incentives were given to the private sector in order to encourage R&D efforts (Lim 2012). One year later, the government passed the **Specialized Research Institute Promotion Law,** which promoted the establishment of industry-specific government research institutes (Jung and Mah 2013).

Policies concerning FDI, which is an important channel for technological transfer and spillovers from developed countries, were rather restrictive since the government doubted the positive impact of FDI and additionally feared that the country's political autonomy would be undermined (Seth 2017; Jung and Mah 2013). Instead, the government favored the direct import of technology (Kim 1992, 2020; Yoon 2006; see also Sect. 5.3.5).

Even though the HCI drive led to severe macroeconomic imbalances (see also the following paragraphs), it is hard to deny that it still played a significant role in building the foundation of various leading industries and paved the way for the transition from an imitation-driven to an innovation-driven development strategy.

Box 3.5 Summary: HCI Drive

The government shifted its focus to the heavy industry in the 1970s in order to become a self-reliant economy. The "HCI drive" was formally introduced in 1973. The six target industries selected for major financial support were steel, metal, shipbuilding, machinery, chemical, and electronics (Lee 1991). Since these sectors were highly capital-intensive, the government established various FIs for HCI-specific investment such as the national investment fund (NIF) in 1974 as well as various specially designed funds. Favorable policy-oriented loans of government-controlled banks played an important supporting role in the HCI financing. Other HCI promotion policies included tariff protection, tax incentives, the construction of industrial parks, exchange rate policy measures, the establishment of new research institutes as well as the expansion of technical and vocational training, and various measures aimed at providing students and workers the necessary technical skills.

3.6.2 Impact of the Reforms

As a result of the policy measures described above, the investment shares directed to heavy industries increased from 56.5% during the period 1971–74 to 82.5% in 1978. In addition, the growth rate of total investment rose steadily, starting at around 8.3% in 1974–75 to 26.6% in 1977 and eventually to 40.5% in 1978 (Kim 1990, see also Table 3.5). Between 1972 and 1977, the chemical industries' net capital stock quadrupled and the non-electric and electric machinery industries each increased more than fivefold (Krueger 1997).

Table 3.5 Investment growth, 1970–1978

	1970–71	1972–73	1974–75	1976	1977	1978
Investment growth	3.6	12.9	8.3	14.7	26.6	40.5
HCI share (in total investment)	56.5[a]			74.2	75.4	82.5
Light industries' share (in total investment)	43.5[a]			25.8	24.6	17.5

Source EPB (1981) and the Bank of Korea, National Account (1982), cited in Kim (1990)
Notes [a] During the period 1971–1974

The government's enormous investment support for sectors of the heavy industry led to rapid expansion of the HCI output and exports: The share of HCI in manufacturing value added and exports increased steadily in this period. The share of HCI industries in manufacturing value added increased from 36% and 1970 to almost 54% in 1983; the export share increased from 18% to almost 57% over the same period (see Figs. 3.8 and 3.9).

One of the major criticisms of the HCI policy is **the misallocation of capital** (via subsidized credits) toward few large companies operating in HCI (see e.g. Kwack 1984; Rhee 1987), resulting in inefficient resource allocation and capacity underutilization in the late 1970s (especially in the heavy machinery sector). The government-induced preferential treatment of HCIs consequently reduced the available resources—capital and skilled labor—in the remaining non-favored sectors such as light manufacturing (Rhee 1987). These industries suffered from decreasing capital–labor ratios and had to rely on more traditional technologies, which led to low productivity and low wages, and thus, to economic inefficiencies and also to a deterioration of the overall income distribution (Kwack 1984).

In addition, the HCI policies had a negative effect on **various macroeconomic indicators** (especially on inflation, the trade deficit, and the accumulation of foreign debt). Many of these adverse impacts were magnified by major domestic and worldwide **shocks** such as the assassination of President Park (in 1979) as well as the worldwide oil crises (Kwack 1984). The two oil price shocks had a particularly negative effect on the economy since South Korea did not have any substantial alternative energy sources and had to accept the high oil price. The main negative macroeconomic effects are briefly described in the following.

First, the expansionary macroeconomic policy led to **rising inflation rates** just at the moment when the two oil price shocks as well as the construction boom in the Middle East additionally built up inflationary pressures (Galbraith and Kim 1998). It has to be noted, however, that the construction boom in the Middle East also significantly helped the South Korean economy to rebound from the oil price shock since it provided a great opportunity for South Korean construction companies, which won contracts for infrastructure projects (Shim 2015; Collins and Park 1989).[16] As noted by Kwack (1984), consumer goods producers did not benefit

[16] According to Collins and Park (1989), this opportunity was "good fortune".

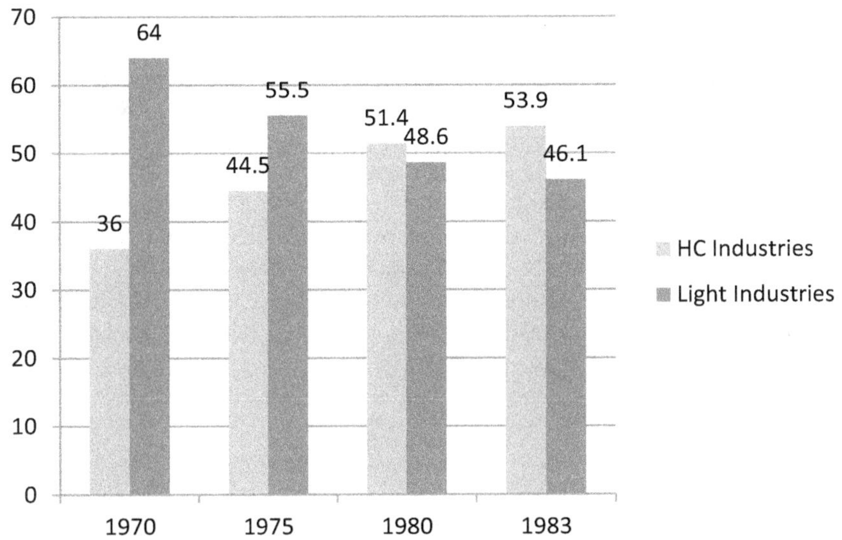

Fig. 3.8 Percentage of HCI in manufacturing value added. *Source* Lee (1991: 452)

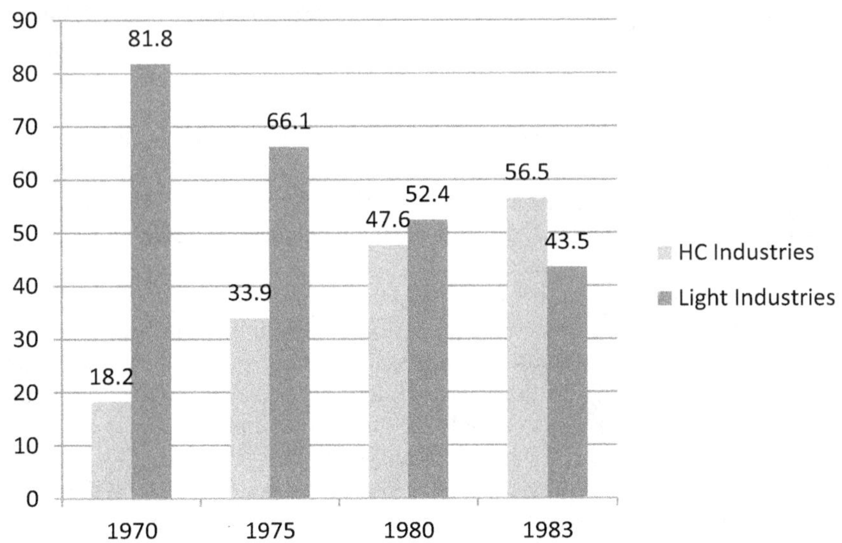

Fig. 3.9 Percentage of HCI in manufacturing exports. *Source* Lee (1991: 452)

from the preferential interest rates, leading to higher prices of these goods. Moreover, since HCIs were highly capital-intensive (cf. Lim 2012) and South Korea lacked the necessary raw materials and capital equipment, the imports of capital goods increased quickly, enlarging the **trade deficit**. This problem was magnified by the oil-shock-related recession on exports and by rising international inflation (Kim 1990). During the 1970s, the won (even though it was devalued by the government) was on average still overvalued by around 16% (cf. Park 1986); thus, South Korea's exchange rate was not internationally competitive. Finally, even though the savings rate of the South Korean economy was rising steadily, it could not keep pace with the soaring investment ratios. This gap had to be financed using current balance deficits. As a result, the ratio of **foreign debt** to GDP increased to 32.6% in 1973 and even surpassed 40% in 1975 (Corbo and Nam 1988). Between 1973 and 1978, the total amount of foreign debt increased by ca. 350% to almost $15 billion.

3.6.3 HCI and the Rise of the Chaebol

The HCI drive is also to a large extent responsible for the emergence of the **Korean conglomerates called chaebols** (lit. wealth clan) since the government concentrated its incentives on few very large companies in order to secure scale economies inherent in HCI. Chaebols are family-owned businesses that consist of a pyramid of subsidiary firms controlled by the main family (Lim 2001; Morck and Yeung 2017, see also Box 3.7 for a comparison between chaebol, keiretsu, and zaibatsu conglomerates). They are characterized by a high degree of diversification (Kim and Lee 1997). Most chaebols emerged after 1945 and only seven of the 22 largest business groups in 2000 have origins in the colonial era (including Hyundai, Samsung, and LG, cf. Lim 2012). However, these chaebols were still rather small in the beginning and engaged rather in the light industries (e.g. textiles). It was not until the Park administration that the chaebols switched their focus to the heavy industries and developed into the conglomerates of today (Park 2018). Not all the early conglomerates were able to survive; for instance, the chaebols Gaepoong, Samho, and Hwashin could not keep pace with their competitors, including newly founded conglomerates. Thus, there was a rather high fluctuation of the dominant chaebols (Seth 2017). For instance, only 22 of the top hundred firms in 1965 were able to sustain their position for the next ten years (Lew 2013).

As already mentioned in previous paragraphs, in the course of the HCI drive, the government particularly favored large companies, which were granted preferential loans and many other incentives to secure that the chaebols had sufficient access to the necessary capital and **technology**. In 1970, almost 90% of all manufacturing investment was directed to large companies (Lim 2012). As a consequence, the number of chaebols increased dramatically during the 1970s. Between 1971 and 1979, the 30 biggest chaebol companies established around 200 new firms and took over 135 existing companies (Park 2018). The number of affiliated companies in the heavy industry for Samsung increased from 9 in 1974 to 31 in 1978; most of the chaebols recorded similar increases. The 10 largest conglomerates accounted for 14% of GDP in 1973 and this number even further increased to 23.4% by 1978. The top 46 conglomerates even accounted for 43% of GDP (Kim 1991).

The alliance of large enterprises and the government were subject to the **performance principle**, meaning that chaebols received preferential loans and a favorable treatment regarding import duties on capital goods etc. as long as they used the state support efficiently which was ensured by constant monitoring of these companies (Seth 2017; Krueger and Yoo 2002). Moreover, the government encouraged competition among several chaebols in each industry to avoid inefficiencies. The relationship between the state and the chaebols changed over time: While in the 1960s, the government was still able to direct the conglomerates, their positions were reversed by the late 1970s (Luedde-Neurath 1986; Chibbers 1999). The economic power has increasingly been concentrated in the largest conglomerates.

Some chaebols tried to redirect HCI subsidies into other sectors (for instance, consumer electronics and automobiles) (Hundt 2008). This supported the simultaneous building up and extension of various complementary industries in the spirit of Rosenstein Rodan's (1943) complex network of interdependent firms considered crucial for rapid economic growth. Similar to the Japanese case, not the state but rather the private sector played a critical role in bringing forward this big push (even though it was supported by the state by preferential financing etc.). As argued by Park (2005), the government led the drive whereas the actual implementation was carried out by the private sector. The South Korean and also the Japanese experience thus differ from that of other developing countries. For instance, also Taiwan promoted the heavy industry since the beginning of the 1970s; however, the HCI development was mainly put forward by state-owned enterprises (Sakong and Koh 2010: 24). Overall, it indeed seems as if the successful Japanese zaibatsu-driven big push around the turn of the twentieth century served as a role model or at least inspiration for South Korea's chaebols (cf. Morck and Nakamura 2007; Morck and Yeung 2017).

The extreme favoring of the chaebols also resulted in **rising inequality** since the government neglected to stimulate the development in small and medium firms (Roemer 1994). Accordingly, the growth of large firms outpaced that of rather small ones. For instance, between 1967 in 1979, firms with five to nine employees recorded a manufacturing output growth rate of 11.1% and even a decline in manufacturing employment by 1.5%, whereas firms with more than 500 persons employed reported a growth rate of the manufacturing value added of 27.6% and an increase in employment by 15% over the same period (cf. Kim 1991). Overall, the enormous growth of the chaebols came at the expense of the small companies, particularly in the light industry. However, in the early 1980s, the government started to undertake countermeasures against the growing concentration of the economy and increased its support for small- and medium-size enterprises (Kim 1991).

Overall, even though the HCI drive enabled a continuation of high growth over the 1970s, the unprecedented government support for the chaebols had various negative side effects. As already mentioned above, there was a **concentration of**

economic power in the hands of **few very large companies** leading to a distorted competition and business environment as well as to rising inequality (see also the previous paragraph). Moreover, since the government directed the majority of resources into the heavy industry, the **development of a competitive financial sector literally came to a stop** and inefficiencies in financial intermediation increased (Graham 2003a: 29; Sakong and Koh 2010: 24).

Box 3.6 Chaebols

Chaebols are family-owned businesses characterized by a high degree of diversification. They consist of a pyramid of subsidiary firms controlled by the main family. The chaebols were supported enormously by the government (e.g. via preferential loans and other incentives) in the 1970s in order to minimize the time necessary for the development of a competitive heavy industry and also in order to exploit scale advantages inherent in HCI. The overall impact of the chaebols has led to debates among economists. While some argued that it was only thanks to the large conglomerates that South Korean companies successfully entered new industries within a short amount of time, others underlined that the disproportional favoring of chaebols also resulted in rising inequality, concentration of economic power in the hands of a few large conglomerates, a decelerated development of the financial sector, and (discussed more controversially) low TFP growth.

3.6.4 Evaluation of the HCI Drive

Economists that evaluate the overall success of the HCI drive in terms of productivity come to different conclusions. While some regard this policy rather as a failure (Yoo 1989; Noland 2004; Clifford 1994; Noland and Pack 2003), there are also various economists that come to a more positive judgment (including Amsden 1989; Zeile 1991; Sakong 1993; Cho 1994). An extensive discussion is provided in Graham (2003a, b) and Kwack (2000). One point of disagreement concerns the TFP in HCI sectors compared with non-favored sectors. Lee (1996) finds that heavily supported sectors had slower TFP increases than other manufacturing sectors. In contrast, Zeile (1991) shows that between 1972 and 1985, HCI sectors reported equally rapid or even faster increases in TFP than non-favored (manufacturing) sectors. However, in a subsequent paper of 1993, the author unveils that TFP increases in chaebol-dominated sectors were below average once controlling for economies of scale and R&D expenditures. One problem regarding the evaluation of the TFP growth in favored and non-favored sectors is that the measurement of TFP is highly sensitive to the methodology used and this is most likely responsible for the varying results.

Even though there are varying views on the effectiveness of the HCI drive, it cannot be denied that the HCI program facilitated the rapid expansion into new industries and thus upgraded the industrial structure and laid the foundations for many key industries (Sakong and Koh 2010). Moreover, some researchers argue that the building up of the industrial base during the 1970s enabled South Korea to make full use of the "three lows" of the next decade (low value of the won against the yen, low oil price, and low interest rates), including the deepening of the industrial structure and the improving export sophistication (Sakong and Koh 2010: 25).

Box 3.7 Differences and Similarities Between Chaebols, Zaibatsus, and Keiretsus

South Korean chaebols are often compared with the Japanese keiretsus (the successor of the zaibatsus); both constitute big business groups that consist of a collection of legally independent firms under common ownership. However, there exist various important differences between these two types of conglomerates, which are briefly discussed in the following:

Ownership: Chaebols are family-run businesses whereas the keiretsus are characterized by cross-shareholding relationships between member firms centered around a dominant bank and they are rather under control of a professional corporate management.

Relationship with an exclusive bank: At the center of (horizontal) keiretsus is the main bank that provides financial services across member firms and that also manages the relationships between them, while in chaebols, this task is performed by the dominant family. In fact, chaebols were prohibited from owning a bank.

Subsidiaries versus outside contractors: Keiretsus mostly relied on outside contractors for the production of components for export, whereas chaebols directed this task to subsidiaries.

In fact, the chaebols share more characteristics with the predecessor of the keiretsus, the zaibatsus, and are thus sometimes also referred to as **zaibatsu-style conglomerates**. For instance, zaibatsus and chaebols obtained a full-set diversification. Moreover, both, zaibatsus and chaebol firms preferred engaging in businesses with members within their respective conglomerate instead of concluding transactions with firms of other zaibatsus or chaebols, respectively.

Box 3.8 Success factor HCI in East Asia?

The effectiveness of industrial policy is heavily debated within the development and growth literature. The promotion of the heavy industry (including directed credits and import protection) was an important part of the development strategy in Northeast Asia, particularly in Japan, South Korea, and

Taiwan. In contrast, for most of the remaining countries in (South) East Asia including Hong Kong, Singapore, Thailand, Malaysia, China, and Indonesia, HCI policies were not the key success factors for fast economic growth:

"it [the promotion of HCI] surely was not the common denominator that accounts for the rapid growth across East and Southeast Asia. Instead, the common denominator was manufactured exports, supported by a regime best characterized as free trade for exporters. The varied experiences of the countries of East and Southeast Asia indicate that both an open market and a more interventionist approach that offsets other distortions can be made to work, as long as manufacturers face the acid test of operating on world markets, both for imported inputs and exports. East Asia's successful industrial policy strategy was to support labor-intensive manufactured exports, not capital intensive heavy industries."—Radelet et al. (1997)

Further Reading: Radelet et al. (1997), Roemer (1994), Hill (1996) (on Indonesia).

3.6.5 The Role of Japan

The transformation of South Korea's economy benefited significantly from investments and technology transfers from Japan (Seth 2017; Castley 2006; Kim 1998b). One prominent example is the success of Pohang Iron and Steel Company (POSCO), which enjoyed the supply of plants and equipment from Japanese steel firms (Kim 1998b). Between 1962 and 1979, 60% of foreign technology was provided by Japan (Lone and McCormack 1994). The collaboration of South Korea and Japan appeared reasonable since the former could provide cheap labor whereas the latter supplied essential capital and technology; accordingly, the trade between the two countries expanded rapidly after the normalization of relations in the corresponding treaty in 1965 (Seth 2017). Japan provided the development role model for successful modernization and industrialization as an alternative to the development strategies postulated by Western countries, and South Korea dropped the US model already in the 1960s (Pecotich and Shultz 2006). The South Korean motto was "Do what the Japanese have done, but do it cheaper and faster." (Kang 1989: 23). Nonetheless, the USA presented an attractive market for South Korean exports (Seth 2017).

3.7 Macroeconomic Imbalances at the Turn of the 1980s and Stabilization Measures

South Korea found itself in a rather difficult position at the turn of the 1980s, facing severe macroeconomic imbalances. While some of the reasons for the economy's problematic situation originated from inside the South Korean economy, their negative effects were intensified by non-favorable external conditions. As a result, in 1980, GDP growth turned negative for the first time in about 30 years.

3.7.1 Main Factors of the Slowdown

With respect to the main causes of the growth slowdown, it can be distinguished between internal and external factors, which will be outlined in the following.

Internal factors. First, the economy was confronted with political instability after the assassination of President Park in October 1979. Second, due to the unusually cold weather, the South Korean economy faced an extremely bad rice harvest in 1980 and the government had to import over 3 million tons of rice grains (Choi et al. 2016). However, most importantly, the country still had to cope with the negative side effects of the HCI drive of the previous decade, including soaring inflation, excess capacity, an increasing number of non-performing loans, diminishing competitiveness in the international markets, resource misallocation, a delay in the financial sector development, and high foreign debt (Morck and Yeung 2017; Cho 1989). That is, South Korea's growth in the 1970s had come at the cost of serious macroeconomic imbalances, which were further worsened by certain developments in the external environment described in the next paragraph.

External factors. First, energy prices were rising after the second oil crisis. Second, many developed countries kept interest rates high in order to fight inflation which had negative side effects for South Korea because of the country's large stock of foreign debt, particularly in dollars. Third, the dollar remained high, which further aggravated the situation with respect to South Korea's foreign debt.

3.7.2 Stabilization Measures

The necessity of macroeconomic stabilization was already recognized during the Park administration and particularly put forward by younger generations of government officials of the EPB in cooperation with KDI economists, resulting in the announcement of the Comprehensive Economic Stabilization Program (CESP) in April 1979. The proponents of this program were convinced that the high reliance on the market economy and the adoption of a comprehensive stabilization program were crucial (Sakong and Koh 2010; Cho and Kang 2013). However, it was not until President Chun came in charge in 1980 that the CESP was seriously implemented (an extensive overview on the stabilization policies under President Park and his passive implementation see Cho and Kang 2013). The "growth first" strategy was eventually replaced by a "stability oriented" development strategy that also relied (or at least aimed at relying) more on private sector-led than government-led growth. Policy measures included a restrictive monetary and fiscal policy, industrial rationalization, as well as financial and trade liberalization. The most important measures are summarized in the following.

3.7.2.1 Restrictive Monetary and Fiscal Policy

With respect to **tight monetary policy,** the government managed to bring the **M2 growth down** significantly: while the M2 still grew at an average annual rate of 36% between 1976 and 1978, the M2 growth slowed down to an average of 25% over the period 1979–1989 and even reached an average growth rate of 14% between 1983 and 1985 (Kim 1997: 216). With respect to **tight fiscal policy,** South Korea adopted a **zero-based budgeting** (ZBB) approach in 1982/3 in order to optimize government expenditures by evaluating the justification of every spending thoroughly on an annual basis (always starting again from zero) (Cho and Kang 2013; Park 2018; Kim 1997).[17] In 1984, the budget for government expenditures was even frozen at the level of the fiscal year 1983 (Cho and Kang 2013). As a consequence, the fiscal balance eventually recorded a surplus in 1987 (Sakong and Koh 2010). The financial retrenchment measures proved rather effective, and in combination with decreasing oil prices around 1981, inflation was brought under control, decreasing from almost 29% in 1980 to only 3.4% in 1983, and also economic growth soon regained momentum (World Bank 2021).

3.7.2.2 Industrial Restructuring and Rationalization

The restrictive monetary and fiscal policy were accompanied by the **restructuring of the HCI sector** to address the serious negative side effects of the HCI drive, including misallocation of capital, excess capacities, as well as the deteriorating profitability and decreasing international competitiveness of HCI companies (particularly in the car and electricity generation equipment industries). The **industrial rationalization policy** included various anti-competitive measures such as **the restriction or prohibition of new market entries** and the **encouragement of company mergers** (leading to a further concentration of power). The government also provided assistance in the form of tax support and by granting relief loans. In addition, capacity expansion schedules were postponed or withheld (for instance, in the machinery and shipbuilding industries) (cf. Mah 2007). Industrial targeting that previously had guaranteed an almost unlimited protection was limited to industries in need for 3 years (Hamilton and Kim 1993).

3.7.2.3 Trade and Financial Liberalization

Since the middle of the 1980s, the government increasingly **promoted import liberalization**. The main motivation for this reform was to **increase the international competitiveness** of domestic industries **by improving productivity** (Ahn

[17] According to Sakong and Koh (2010), the ZBB most likely also had an announcement effect.

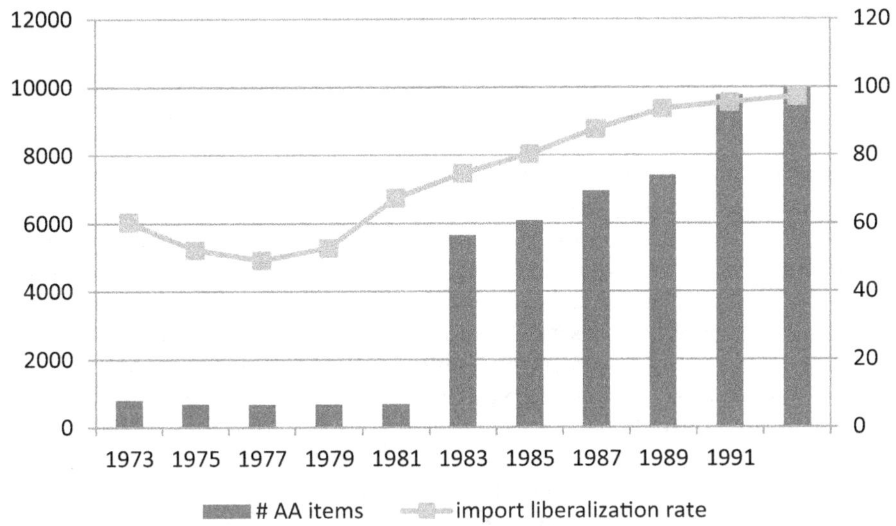

Fig. 3.10 Import liberalization rate, 1973–1991. *Source* Nam (1993: 156, Table 6.1). *Note* "AA" stands for automatic approval

and Kim 1997; Lee 1991). In particular, the government forced South Korean companies to compete against multinational firms in the export market and additionally in the domestic market by raising the import liberalization ratio and by cutting the average tariff rate (Kim and Seong 1997): The import liberalization ratio (in the sense of an automatic approval list) increased from 52.1% in 1973 to 87.7% in 1985 and even surpassed 95% in 1989 (Nam 1993, see also Fig. 3.10). In 1994, it was very close to 100%.[18] In addition, the government reduced the average tariff rate by 4.3 percentage points to 22.4% between 1984 and 1988 and by another 14.5 percentage points until 1994 (Kim and Seong 1997).[19]

These measures were accompanied by the relaxing of non-tariff trade barriers such as regulations on product quality by special laws and the abolishment of various administrative requirements (Kim and Kim 1997). However, in order to protect the South Korean economy against the possibility of a boundless flood of imports and thus an exaggerated bilateral trade imbalance, the government also put into place an import monitoring program as well as an import-source diversification program (Kim and Kim 1997). Trade liberalization was expedited by the favorable international economic conditions referred to as the "three lows", which will be described in Sect. 3.7.3. Moreover, the USA put pressure on the South Korean economy to open up its markets for foreign investors and goods due to the growing trade deficit between the two countries (particularly between 1984 and 1988). Even

[18] Namely 98.6%, cf. Kim and Seong (1997).

[19] Nam (1993) reports even lower levels for the 1980s (23.7% for 1983 and 19.3% for 1987).

though import liberalization progressed steadily over the 1980s, this development accelerated since 1989 (see also Sect. 3.8.1).

As already mentioned above, the **financial sector development** was retarded due to the policy measures undertaken in the course of the HCI drive (in combination with adverse external events such as the oil price shocks). The South Korean government undertook various reform measures in order to reduce its interventions; however, it also faced some critical constraints that prevented an immediate full and comprehensive liberalization of the financial sector (see also the next paragraph). Important policy measures to enhance financial liberalization included the **privatization of commercial banks** between 1981 and 1983 as well as the **elimination of preferential lending rates** until 1982 (Kim and Kim 1997). In addition, the government **lowered the entry barriers into the financial industry** and **allowed a broader spectrum of financial services** (Cho 1989). Also the **scope of national investment fund (NIF) loans was reduced** considerably from around 25% in 1979 to 5% in 1991 (Cho and Kim 1997).

As indicated above, a full-fledged financial liberalization could not be accomplished in the 1980s due to various constraints (Dalla and Khatkhate 1995). First, the restructuring and rationalization measures as well as the large number of NPLs made government intervention in the credit markets necessary in order to maintain stability (Cho 1989). Second, the government increasingly supported small- and medium-sized enterprises, which had been heavily disadvantaged during the HCI drive in the 1980s. As a consequence, the share of SME loans and total loans increased from 33% in 1983 to almost 60% in 1994 while the share of loans going to large conglomerates decreased. This change in the structure of loan recipients was motivated by the democratization movement, which called for greater social equity (Kim and Kim 1997; Lee 2005: 295). Therefore, the government first focused predominantly on the deregulation of non-bank financial institutions (NBFIs) and the securities market instead of further liberalizing banks (Cho 1989). This is also depicted in the share of NBFI loans relative to bank loans: while in 1976, NBFI loans only accounted for slightly above 25% of all loans, at the end of the 1980s, NBFI loans and bank loans both had almost equal shares (cf. Park 2018).

External pressure regarding the opening up of the South Korean capital market intensified in the 1980s. In 1981, the South Korean government announced a policy to gradually open its capital market (Hamilton and Kim 1993). However, until the beginning of the 1990s, the capital market still stayed largely closed to foreigners, and only the Three Stage Finance Liberalization Market Opening Plan promulgated in June 1993 marked the start of more genuine capital market liberalization (see also Sect. 3.8.1).

In the beginning, the government restricted capital account liberalization measures to the capital inflows. The main motivation behind this was the financing of the current account deficit. It was not until the second half of the 1980s that also the capital account outflows were freed, primarily in order to reduce the pressures for won appreciation caused by a current account surplus and difficulties in monetary management (Leiteritz 2014; Kim and Kim 1997). At the same time, the government put in place restrictions regarding capital inflows until 1989, when the current account balance again showed a deficit.

Important measures included the establishment of the Korea Fund in 1984 that enabled foreigners to indirectly invest in South Korean companies (until the early 1990s, direct investment was prohibited and loans had to be intermediated by SOEs, cf. Leiteritz 2014; Park 2018). In 1985, South Korean companies were allowed to issue overseas convertible bonds (Kim and Kim 1997). In 1988, the Ministry of Finance eventually set up a timetable for the gradual opening up of the capital market (Kim 1997: 222).

Box 3.9 South Korea's Foreign Exchange Controls

One of the reasons why South Korea had strict foreign exchange controls for a relatively long time was because the South Korean economy faced a chronic current account deficit until the mid-1980s. This control was ensured via the South Korean Foreign-Exchange Concentration System and the Foreign Exchange Management Act. The former secured that all foreign exchange had to be consigned to the central bank, whereas the latter put strict limitations on the use of foreign exchange such as limits on overseas remittance funds, overseas real-estate acquisitions, and even on foreign tourism expenditures. Large trade surpluses in the second half of the 1980s created excess liquidity and pushed the government to undertake measures by scaling this excess liquidity down. Even though the trade surpluses disappeared, increasing capital inflows in the 1990s provided justification for the continued raising of the ceiling and foreign exchange holdings.

With respect to foreign direct investment, the severe restrictions were lifted in the 1980s in order to encourage competition and in order to acquire advanced foreign technologies. In 1983, the government revised the Foreign Capital Inducement Law. One major change was the switch from a positive to a negative list system and the almost complete opening up of the manufacturing sector to FDI (Nicolas et al. 2013). In addition, the government pushed forward the simplification of administrative procedures (Kim and Wang 1996). The average amount of FDI increased from an average of $130 million between 1980 and 1983 to $920 million at the end of the 1980s (Kim and Kim 1997).

Box 3.10 Summary: Liberalization Measures in the 1980s

Import Liberalization

Measures: rise in import liberalization ratio, reduction of the average tariff rate, loosening of non-tariff trade barriers (regulations on product quality, administrative requirements).

Security measures: import monitoring program, import-source diversification program.

Reasoning: increasing international competitiveness by improving productivity, US pressure.

Financial Liberalization

Measures: privatization of commercial banks (1981–1983), elimination of preferential lending rates (until 1982), lowering of the entry by years into the financial industry, permission of a broader spectrum of financial services, reduction of the scope of NIF loans, deregulation of NBFIs and securities market.

Restrictions: restructuring measures and large number of NPLs made government intervention in credit markets necessary, support of SMEs, domestic opposition.

Capital Account Liberalization

Measures: Korea Fund (1984), permission to issue overseas convertible bonds (1980), presentation of a timetable for the gradual opening up by the Ministry of Finance (1988); liberalization measures were first restricted to capital inflows in order to finance current account deficits, liberalization of outflows only started in the latter half of the 1980s.

Scope: the domestic capital market was still largely closed for foreigners.

FDI measures: revision of the Foreign Capital Inducement Law (1983), switch to a negative list system, almost complete opening up of the manufacturing sector to FDI, simplification of administrative procedures.

3.7.3 The "Three Lows"

In the mid-1980s, the external economic conditions became extremely favorable for the South Korean economy. The so-called **"three lows"** refer to the low value of the won against the yen, low oil price, and low interest rates (see also Table 3.6). This—in combination with the successful economic stabilization measures of the early 1980s—enabled South Korea to achieve again strong, double-digit economic growth in the second half of the decade.

The appreciation of the yen after the Plaza Accord significantly increased the price competitiveness of South Korean exports since the value of the won quickly fell against the yen. As a consequence, South Korean exports increased on average 20% per year between 1986 and 1988 (Park 2018); and between 1986 and 1989, the country eventually achieved current account surpluses ($4.7 billion in 1986 and

Table 3.6 External macroeconomic environment and development of the S. Korean economy

	1981	1983	1985	1986	1987	1988	1989	1990	1991	1992	1993	1994
	Panel A: External macroeconomic environment											
EXR ₩/$[b]	681	776	870	882	823	732	672	708	733	788	808	789
EXR ₩/100 ¥[b]	308	326	364	522	568	534	487	488	543	633	722	774
EXR ¥/$[b]	221	238	239	169	145	128	138	145	135	124	112	102
Oil price[c]	34.1	28.8	26.7	14.2	16.9	13.9	15.8	20	18.6	17.8	15.8	14.8
Foreign interest rate	16.5	9.6	8.3	6.8	7.1	9.4	8.4	7.7	4.3	3.4	3.4	6.1
	Panel B: Development of the South Korean economy											
GNP growth	5.9	12.6	7	11.9	12.3	12	6.9	9.6	9.1	5	5.6	8.2
Investment ratio[a]	29.9	29.2	30.3	29.2	30	31.1	33.8	37.1	39.1	36.8	34.4	32
Current account	-4.6	-1.6	-0.9	4.6	9.9	14.2	5.1	-2.2	-8.7	-4.5	0.5	-4.7
Net foreign debt	24.5	30.9	35.5	32.5	22.4	7.3	3	6.4	11.9	11.1	7.9	10.5

Source Cho (1995)
Notes [a] Gross Domestic Investment Rate, [b] period average, [c] crude import unit price: $/barrel (Unit: interest rate of Euro dollar: 90-day and US $ billions in current prices). For earlier data on various indicators, see also Collins and Park (1989)

almost $35 billion in the last 3 years).[20] This allowed South Korea not only to foster economic growth but also to repay its foreign debt, and the amount of foreign loans as a percentage of GDP started to decrease in 1986 and had been reduced to 18.1% by 1990.

3.7.4 Transition to Democracy

In June 1987, a nationwide democracy movement started after the shooting of the Yonsei University students Lee Han Jol by the riot police. The protests (referred to as the "June democracy movement") eventually forced the government to amend the Constitution, leading to the establishment of the Sixth Republic in 1988 (Krause 1997).[21] South Korea's political democratization also had various economic

[20] However, the strong yen also led to an increase in the prices of capital imports from Japan for South Korean companies, which, in general, had a negative effect on the current account balance. As shown in the data, the positive effect of the yen appreciation outweighed the adverse impacts (Cho 1995).

[21] Perkins (1997) distinguishes between four phases of economic policy experience. While the first two phases are marked by President Park, the third phase with the election of President Roh in 1987 and President Kim in 1993 are the cornerstones for the fourth phase of increasing democracy. However, as Perkins (1997) notes, the increasing democratic influence was based on reform ideas that were already developed in the previous phase.

consequences, including the rise of labor unions, which demanded higher wages (Kim and Kim 1997). The number of unions as well as the labor union participation rate increased significantly, so did the number of labor disputes. Prior to 1987, the number of disputes was far below thousand per year; however, in 1987, this number shot up to almost 4000 (Park 2018). In 1988, the government enacted the Minimum Wage Law and also introduced the national pension system. One year later, the nationwide medical insurance system was installed (Suh 2007).

South Korea increasingly lost its low labor cost advantage with wages increasing at double-digit rates, surpassing 25% in 1989 (Park 2018). These increases were not only limited to the time immediately after the transition to democracy but also continued in the 1990s. As a consequence, labor productivity was declining and companies started losing their competitiveness. Moreover, inflation was rising again. In addition, the democratic reforms resulted in a higher demand for welfare services and social equity. This led to rising government expenditures on welfare, which rose at an average annual rate of 30% between 1987 and 1991 (Kim and Kim 1997).

3.8 Kim Administration: Globalization, Liberalization, and Promotion of High-Technology Innovation

The Kim administration (1993–1998) followed a strategy of globalization (segye-wha) under which the financial liberalization and the opening up of South Korea's capital markets were intensified. Moreover, the government strived to accomplish more successfully the transition to a private sector-led economy and promoted high-technology innovation.

In 1993, the authorities announced the **5-year financial liberalization plan** that focused, among others, on interest rate deregulation, the reduction of entry barriers to financial activities, the phasing out of policy loans, and on enhancing the managerial autonomy of banks (Chang et al. 1998). The most important aspect of the plan was, however, **the capital account liberalization**, which was a necessary condition in order to realize the intended OECD accession in 1996 and which had been neglected in previous liberalization plans in order to avoid a destabilization of the South Korean macroeconomic environment (Lee et al. 2000).[22]

3.8.1 Financial Liberalization

In 1991, the government announced the **Four-Stage Interest Rate Liberalization Plan**, which aimed at accelerating financial liberalization by freeing interest rates. According to Cho and McCauley (2003), the plan followed the principles of a

[22] An excellent overview of the most important financial liberalization measures during the 1990s is provided by Chang et al. (1998: 737, Table 1).

gradual move from (a) long-term to short-term interest rates, (b) securities markets to bank interest rates, and (c) large-denomination to small-denomination instruments. However, the actual implementation of this plan deviated significantly from these principles, and while many interest rates (including bank interest rates) were not liberalized until 1996/97, interest rates on commercial papers, that is, rather short-term market instruments, were liberalized relatively fast (Cho 2002a). This development induced the shift of funds toward the short-term market, and commercial papers became increasingly important in the financing of the corporate sector with their share in total corporate financing rising from 2.5% in the early 1990s to 17.5% in 1996 (Cho 2002a). This development weakened the financial soundness of companies and banks (Park 2018, see also Sect. 3.8.2).

3.8.2 Capital Account Liberalization

The **stock market was opened to foreigners in 1992**, however, still with restrictions on equity purchases, which were only gradually relaxed (Suh 2007). Moreover, non-residents were only allowed to invest in very few types of fixed income securities under strict purchase limits (Leiteritz 2014). The number of South Korean FIs that was allowed to engage in overseas activities increased significantly in the mid-1990s. For instance, between 1994 and 1996, the number of merchant banks increased from 6 to 30 (Kihwan 2006) and domestic banks opened 28 foreign branches (Sakong and Koh 2010). The capital account liberalization measures helped the private sector, particularly the large conglomerates, to finance their international expansion by granting them access to the international capital markets (Leiteritz 2014). However, this strategy also held many potential problems, which eventually led to a growing instability of the financial system, which will be described in Sect. 3.8.3.

3.8.3 Liberalization and Chaebols—A Capital Structure and Maturity Structure Mismatch

Many chaebols gained control of NBFIs (especially merchant banks) that were still rather inexperienced. In combination with the government-induced deregulation of these institutions, this gave the conglomerates the opportunity to make use of foreign capital without adequate state supervision, resulting in an investment boom in the early 1990s. Due to the gradual elimination of state loans and a diminishing active industrial policy, the chaebols could make investment decisions more independently from the government and the domestic banks. At the same time, the conglomerates took higher risks because they still expected that the state would bail them out in case of a bankruptcy since they were "too big to fail" (Kwon 1998). This moral hazard problem had dramatic consequences when the Asian Financial Crisis hit the country. The chaebols financed their investments primarily with debt instead of raising equity, which was reflected in an extremely high debt-to-equity ratio of over 500% for the largest 30 chaebols at the end of 1997 (Kim 1998a). Between 1995 and 1997, the chaebols Halla, Jinro, Hanwha, and New Core reported debt to equity ratios between 1000 and more than 3000%. Among the top three chaebols (of 1995), Hyundai's debt-to-equity ratio increased from 376% in 1995 to 579% in 1997, Samsung reported an increase from 206 to 371% and LG from 313 to 506% (Kim 1998a). Moreover, the chaebols invested rather in new industries than in product improvement or innovation. However, due to the increasing general sophistication level of the industry, entering new industries required comprehensive and costly investments in advanced human resources and technical know-how, while at the same time, wages and land prices were increasing (Park 2018). This led to a declining profitability of most chaebols. For instance, the profitability of the 6th to 10th largest chaebols was only around 1% between 1993 and 1995 and even dug into negative area between 1996 and 1997. The 11th to 30th largest chaebols also recorded on profitability around or below zero over the entire 1993–1997 period. Only the top five chaebols managed to achieve on average higher profitability ratios (around 2.4% between 1993 and 1997, cf. Park 2018). Overall, there existed a **severe capital structure mismatch** (Kihwan 2006).

In addition, about 90% of all foreign investment was on a short-term basis, while the chaebol-owned merchant banks lent on a long-term basis to their affiliates, resulting in a severe discrepancy in the maturity structure between the borrowings and lendings (Leiteritz 2014; Chang 1998; Chang et al. 1998). On the part of foreign investors, short-term investment was considered as being safer, and on the part of South Korean companies and FIs, short-term debt was preferred due to the relatively low interest rates (Park 2018). In addition, long-term borrowing faced stricter regulations (Cho 2002b; Kim and Shin 2003; Sakong and Koh 2010; Cho and McCauley 2003). The share of short-term foreign loans in total foreign loans already stood at 43.7% in 1993 and eventually surpassed 58% at the end of 1996 (Chang et al. 1998; Cho 2002a; Park 2018; see also Figs. 3.11 and 3.12). In contrast, the share of short-term foreign debt was only around 20% for the non-OPEC developing countries prior to the 1980s debt crisis (Koener et al. 1986). That is, South Korea's main problem was the **maturity structure of its foreign debt** rather than its total amount: even though foreign debt increased quickly, South Korea's debt to GNP ratio was still relatively modest in international comparison (it remained less than 30%; the critical threshold of the World Bank separating a less indebted from a moderately indebted country lied at 48%) and also its debt service ratio did not surpass 6% and, thus, was below the World Bank's critical threshold of 18% (Chang et al. 1998; Kihwan 2006).

Despite the fast expansion of short-term financing and a worsening maturity structure, the government did not enhance the supervision since it believed that macroeconomic stability could be ensured sufficiently via discretionary intervention through banks (Sakong and Koh 2010). In addition, the fragmentation of the supervisory authorities and their lacking coordination prevented a strengthening of the supervision (Cho 2002a). As a consequence, the accounting and disclosure standards of South Korean FIs were below international best practices. The lack of an adequate financial market infrastructure in combination with the high

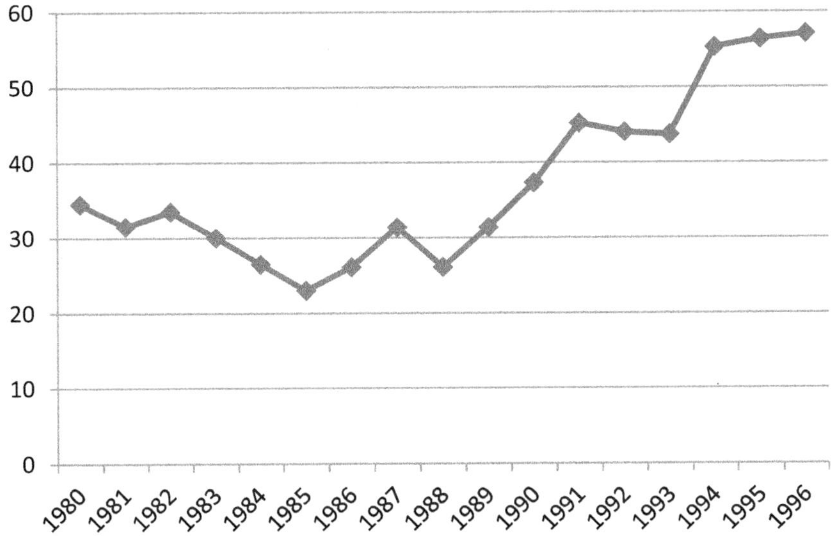

Fig. 3.11 Short-term debt (% of total debt), 1980–1996. *Source* Cho (2002a: 50)

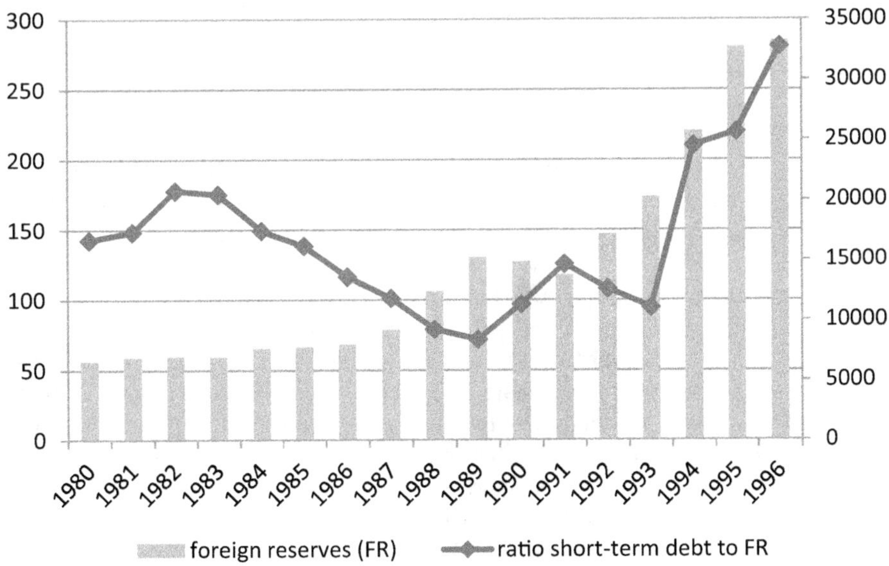

Fig. 3.12 Foreign debt structure, 1980–1996. *Source* Cho (2002a: 50)

dependence of chaebols on bank financing led to an increasing concentration of risks within banks (Kihwan 2006).

Some researchers argue that the inconsistent implementation of the liberalization policies was indeed due to the lacking understanding of the necessity of an adequate prudential regulation that should accompany deregulation. The "de-control without de-protection" (cf. Lim 2001: 15) increased the vulnerability of the financial sector during the Asian financial crisis (Lim 2001; Sakong and Koh 2010).

Box 3.11 Summary: Liberalization Prior to the Asian Financial Crisis

Financial liberalization

Interest rate deregulation in four stages (the liberalization of all lending and borrowing rates was mostly accomplished by 1997); actual implementation deviated considerably from the plan (short-term interest rates were liberalized first while the liberalization of bank interest rates was postponed → shift of corporate finance toward the short-term market, especially, commercial papers).

Foreign exchange liberalization

Foreign-Exchange Reform Plan 1994, significant relaxation of the Foreign-Exchange Concentration System in 1995.

Capital market liberalization

1992 opening of South Korean stock markets to foreign investors (with ownership ceilings, gradually relaxed until around 1996); mid-1990s: significant increase in the number of South Korean FIs that were allowed to engage in overseas activities.

Rising financial instability and the role of Chaebols

Many chaebols gained control of (rather inexperienced) NBFIs (especially merchant banks) to get access to foreign capital. In that context, the government did not anticipate the arising **moral hazard problem**: Since the deregulation of FIs was not accompanied by an adequate financial market infrastructure, particularly a sufficient prudential regulation, chaebols did not face state supervision regarding their financing activities. Since the chaebols thought they were (regarded as) "too big to fail", they engaged in riskier activities (in anticipation of a state bailout in the case of bankruptcy). This resulted in an extremely high debt to equity ratio of most chaebols and thus, a severe **capital structure mismatch**. In addition, the large majority of all foreign investment was on a short-term basis, while the chaebol-owned merchant banks lent on a long-term basis to their affiliates, resulting in a severe **maturity structure mismatch**. On top, the **profitability** of many chaebols **declined** since they expanded in new industries, which required large investments, while facing rising wages at the same time, resulting in a deteriorating cost structure.

3.8.4 Technology Development

The South Korean government shifted the focus of industrial policy away from sector-specific assistance to a rather function-oriented support for R&D (Mah 2007; Lee et al. 1989). The corresponding Industrial Development Law was approved at the end of 1985. In 1989, the South Korean government established the 5-year plan for development of cutting-edge industries and promised funding and support for related projects.

Since the middle of the 1990s, South Korea switched gradually from an imitation-based to a rather innovation-led growth strategy. The focus of technology development in the 1990s shifted to the ICT sector, which experienced a rapid expansion. South Korea managed to become internationally competitive in the personal computer industry as well as the semiconductor industry. The successful establishment of the ICT sector also provided a new development vision for the heavy industry (Sakong and Koh 2010).

The state-financed research institutes founded in the 1960s and 1970s played a key role in enabling South Korea to develop its own technologies (in collaboration with the large conglomerates). In this context, important projects were the Industrial Base Technology Development Project (IBTDP), the National R&D Project (NRP), and the Highly Advanced National R&D (HAN or G7) project R&D (see Box 3.12) (cf. Kim and Seong 1997). R&D activities of private enterprises started in the 1980s (still with government support), and since the 1990s private firms (particularly chaebols) began to create various private-sector research institutes and engaged more in R&D on their own. In addition, they opened branch offices in the USA and Japan to enable a "leapfrogging into state-of-the-art technologies" (Kim and Seong 1997; Kim 1993). Moreover, many conglomerates developed ties with multinationals via joint ventures and licensing agreements in high-technology industries (Kim and Seong 1997). The number of private research institutes sevenfold between 1990 and 2000 and many major companies formed strategic alliances with foreign companies to join international networks and gain access to frontier technology (examples include Hyundai's acquisition of A&T's GIS micro-electronics division and Samsung's acquisition of AST research) (Sakong and Koh 2010; Ahn and Kim 1997).

The active government promotion of the building up of ICT infrastructure was decisive for the South Korean success in the ICT sector since it fostered the widespread ICT usage. In 1994, the government founded the Ministry of Information and Communication (MIC) and its Information Promotion Fund with the aim of establishing high-speed broadband internet access. This facilitated, among others, the development of the TX telephone switching technology as well as that of the CDMA wireless system.

R&D investments increased from 1.7% of GDP in 1990 to 2.4% in 1997. In addition, the role of the South Korean government and the private sector in R&D efforts had reversed at the turn of the 1990s. While in 1980, the government still contributed almost 65% of total R&D investment, the private sector was responsible for 80% of total R&D in the 1990s (Ahn and Kim 1997; Mah 2007).

Box 3.12 R&D Projects in the 1990s

The following three projects were funded by the government and carried out by the government research institutes in collaboration with private companies.

Industrial Base Technology Development Project (IBTDP):

Focus on current problems in existing technology areas with high economic externalities (especially the import substitution of Japanese components in the electronics and machinery industries).

National R&D Project (NRP):

Focus on future problems in new technology areas with high risk of failure or with high economic externalities (e.g. new materials development, new chemical development, biotechnology development).

Highly Advanced National R&D (HAN or G7) Project:

Focus on lifting South Korea's technological capability to the level of G7 countries between 1997 and 2001.

part A: product technology development projects (new drugs and chemicals, broadband integrated services digital network, next-generation vehicle technology, HDTV).

part B: fundamental technology development projects (ultra-large-scale integrated circuits, advanced manufacturing systems, new materials for information, electronics, and energy industries, …).

Based on Kim and Seong (1997).

3.9 The 1997 Financial Crisis and Its Aftermath

The weaknesses in South Korea's corporate and financial sector, previously hidden behind the impressive growth performance (with a sevenfold income increase between 1965 and 1996), eventually came to light when the **external environment** changed in the mid-1990s (Radelet et al. 1998). These changes included **increasing oil prices**, the **depreciation of the Japanese yen** in the third quarter of 1995 as well as **declining prices for semiconductors** in 1996 (Chopra et al. 2001). As a consequence, South Korea's terms of trade weakened and the current account deficit worsened (Park 2018). The deficit had to be financed with foreign debt.

The **Asian Financial Crisis**, which started in Thailand and soon spread to Indonesia and Malaysia, increased the anxiety of foreign FIs toward Asian markets, and international credit rating agencies lowered South Korea's sovereign rating. As a consequence, creditors denied debt renewals and demanded loan repayments in a relatively short amount of time. The size of the net private capital outflows in the last quarter of 1997 amounted to around 6% of the country's GDP (Lee 2017a). The massive and rather unexpected withdrawal of funds led to a wave of bankruptcies starting with the Hanbo group in January 1997. In June 1997, six of the top 30 chaebols went bankrupt. In order to pay back loans, the South Korean government had to use its foreign exchange reserve, which was almost depleted by November 1997, falling to only $6 billion. Among the East (and South East) Asian countries, South Korea, together with Indonesia and Thailand, was most severely hit by the Asian Financial Crisis (Radelet et al. 1998).

The **internal factors** that accelerated the foreign currency crisis in Korea were partly discussed in Sect. 3.8.3. Due to the fact that financial deregulation was not accompanied by an adequate prudential regulation, in combination with the strong belief that the government would bail out big companies if needed, the chaebols invested recklessly by gaining control over NBFIs, particularly merchant banks that provided them with foreign capital. The composition of the private sector debt in the 1990s was very different from that in the early 1970s and 1980s. In particular, there was an extremely large share of short-term debts provided by foreign creditors (Lim and Hahm 2006). The cross-subsidization among affiliated chaebol firms was not sufficiently regulated and the accounting and auditing practices lacked credibility and transparency. This made risk assessments of individual companies difficult (Cho 2002a). The **high debt to GDP ratio in the corporate sector** as well as the **maturity mismatch** made the South Korean economy extremely vulnerable to external shocks.

Even though **the change in the structure of debt** was probably the main difference, there were also various other aspects that distinguished 1997 crisis from the two crises of the early 1970s and early 1980s. For instance, the development of the 1997 crisis was extremely sudden and much larger in its magnitude. Thus, the government was not able to adopt the previous strategy of directly reducing the debt service by reducing interest rates and rescheduling loans as well as by supporting commercial banks by preferential central bank loans (Cho 2002a).

3.9.1 IMF Bailout

Due to the depleted foreign exchange reserve, South Korea was forced to apply for a bailout from the IMF. The IMF rescue package comprised US$55 billion, of which US $21 billion was provided by the IMF, the World Bank contributed US$10 billion and the ADB US$4 billion; the USA, Japan, and some other countries[23] provided the remaining US$20 billion as a "second line of defense".[24] The rescue package was tied to the implementation of various **macroeconomic measures**, including an increase in the interest rates and in the exchange rates, as well as the implementation of other retrenchment measures, accompanied by a comprehensive long-term structural reform program focusing on (1) the financial sector, (2) the corporate governance, (3) the labor market, and (4) the public sector (Park 2018; Radelet et al. 1998).

[23] Among others, Australia, Britain, Canada, France, and Germany.

[24] Cf. New York Times (1997) 04.12.1997.

3.9.2 Tight Monetary and Fiscal Policies

In order to restore the confidence of investors and stabilize financial markets, the IMF program included various macroeconomic policies. The aim of the prescribed austerity course was to avoid a depreciation-inflation spiral and the stabilization of the won (Chopra et al. 2001; IMF 2000a). Concrete policy measures included an increase in the interest rates (the overnight call rate was immediately increased from 15 to 25% and subsequently to over 30%, cf. Chopra et al. 2001 and Bank of Korea 2002)[25] and the reduction of the M3 growth rate (from 16.3% at the end of November 1997 to 13.9% at the end of December 1997, Lee 1999b). The interest rate increase was supposed to reduce capital outflows and additionally attract foreign investment (Kim 2000). With respect to fiscal policy, the government was required to generate a small surplus in 1998.[26]

The monetary and fiscal retrenchment measures managed to stabilize the exchange rate in the Q2 of 1998, and the current account turned into a surplus (Sakong and Koh 2010). However, the tight monetary and fiscal policies also aggravated the recession. The initial tightening of monetary policy is considered as having been too harsh by some economists, particularly if a liquidity problem is regarded to have been the main cause of South Korea's financial crisis. In this context, a high interest rate policy can bring about huge social costs and makes it difficult for highly leveraged but viable firms to obtain credits, making bankruptcies of these firms more likely (the so-called "credit crunch" view) (Lee and Rhee 2007).

The South Korean government started relaxing the retrenchment policies in May 1998. Interest rates were gradually increased and the South Korean government also raised public spending (Lee and Rhee 2007).

Box 3.13 Summary Retrenchment Policies

Monetary policy: increasing call rates to over 30%, reducing M3 growth rate to 9% in Q1 of 1998, afterward allowing cautious reduction of call rates (4th MOU; agreed on 7 February 1998).

Budgetary policy: maintaining the small budget surplus (1st MOU), allowing budget deficits up to 0.8% of GDP (4th MOU).

*MOU = Memorandum of Understanding (between IMF and South Korea).

See also Shin and Chang (2003).

[25] Lee (1999b) reports that the call rate was first raised by 8.4 percentage points between the 1st and 3rd December 1997 (from 12.3 to 20.7%). On the 23rd of December, it then further increased to 30.1%.

[26] However, this policy was subsequently reversed and the South Korean government was allowed to maintain a budget deficit of up to 0.8% of GDP (Shin and Chang 2003).

3.9.3 Structural Reforms of Four Sectors

In the following, we will discuss the structural reform program with a focus on the financial and corporate sector reforms. Overall, the structural reforms aimed at laying the foundation for a sustained recovery and preventing future crises (Chopra et al. 2001).

3.9.3.1 Corporate Sector Reform

The reform of the corporate sector was guided by the **five principles of business structural adjustment**, which were agreed upon by President Kim Dae-jung and chaebol leaders during a meeting in January 1998. These five principles included (1) **improving the transparency of corporate management**, (2) **eliminating mutual debt guarantees** between subsidiaries,[27] (3) **improving the financial structure of corporations**, (4) **the focus of conglomerates on core business operations/activities**, (5) **increasing the accountability of controlling shareholders and the management**. A selection of concrete policy measures to achieve these objectives is presented in Table 3.7.

Principles (1) and (5) were preliminary designed to strengthen the market discipline and to cope with the problem of the "arbitrary imperial rule" by the chaebol bosses (Sakong and Koh 2010; Lim 2010). The remaining three principles seemed to focus on breaking up the "convoy-style management" of the chaebols and presented rather temporary measures as long as the market principle was not yet working properly (Sakong and Koh 2010; Lim 2010).

In August 1999, the government added **three supplementary principles** in order to prevent chaebols from exploiting NBFIs under their control to escape restructuring, namely (1) improving the governance structure of the NBFIs, (2) limiting circular equity investment by chaebol affiliates, and (3) prohibiting irregular inheritance and gift-giving (Heo and Woo 2006; Mo and Moon 2003; Sakong and Koh 2010). Concrete policy measures included limits on cross-equity holding at 7%, a cap on the total amount of equity investment of 25% of net assets, and the amendment of related laws.

The restructuring measures were **differentiated by tiers**; in particular, it was distinguished between the top five chaebols (Hyundai, Daewoo, Samsung, SK, and LG), heavily indebted medium-sized chaebols, and the financially extremely weak SMEs (Kwon 2016). Even though companies of all three tiers were confronted with relatively similar problems, they varied significantly regarding their degree of indebtedness and access to capital (Chopra et al. 2001).

First-tier chaebols: Since the five largest chaebols were regarded to have sufficient financial and managerial resources for restructuring themselves, the government enforced the so-called "**big deals**", that is, business swaps and mergers

[27] These guarantees are also referred to as cross-debt guarantees. One affiliate guarantees to pay back the debt of another affiliate in case that this affiliate is not able to repay the debt on its own (Graham 2003a).

Table 3.7 Overview of policy measures (five principles of business structural adjustment)

Objective	Policy measures
Enhancing of transparency	• Mandatory consolidated financial statements (reviewing the financial situation of all affiliates) • Adoption of international accounting principles • Protection of minority shareholders • Compulsory appointment of outside directors (50%)
Eliminating of cross-debt guarantees	• Resolution of existing cross-debt guarantees • No new cross-debt guarantees between subsidiaries
Improving of financial structure	• Reduction of Debt Equity Ratio to 200% • Agreement with banks to improve the capital structure • Removing restrictions on capital infusion • Excluding income tax deductions on interest payments on excessive borrowings • Introducing asset-backed securities
Focusing on core business activities	• Adoption of corporate-split system • Liberalization of foreign ownership of real estate • Full liberalization of M&As • Streamlining of bankruptcy procedures
Strengthening accountability	• Introduction of a cumulative voting system • Strengthening the legal liability of controlling owners • Allowing voting rights of institutional investors

Source Haggard et al. (1999)

among chaebols operating in overlapping industries in order to reduce overcapacities and over-leveraging (Lee 1999b; Haggard et al. 1999).[28]

Second-tier chaebols: The highly leveraged second-tier chaebols (the 6th to 64th largest ones) that lacked access to bank credit and the capital markets were regarded as too weak to restructure themselves. Therefore, the government established the so-called **out-of-court workout programs**. These bank-sponsored rehabilitation programs are, in general, more flexible regarding rescheduling negotiations between a firm and its creditors and enable the company to continue operating (Sakong and Koh 2010; Baudino and Yun 2017; Lee 1999b). The South Korean out-of-court workout program was inspired by the "London approach" of the Bank of England (for an extensive comparison of the South Korean workout program with that of other countries see Kwon 2016).

Third-tier small companies: SMEs were most severely hit by the crisis. The government initiated various measures, including an expansion of the capacity of credit guarantee funds and the establishment of various short-term lending facilities (Chopra et al. 2001).

[28] Six swaps of businesses among the chaebols that were actually implemented included (1) the annexation of Kia motors by Hyundai motors, (2) the takeover of Samsung motors by Renault, (3) the merging of Aerospace portions of Hyundai, Samsung and Daewoo into the Korea Aerospace Industries, (4) Semiconductor portion of LG went to Hyundai, (4) the takeover of power components of Samsung Heavy Industries and Hyundai industries by Korea Heavy Industries and Construction (Hanjung) (cf. Heo and Woo 2006).

3.9.3.2 Financial Sector Reform

To **improve financial regulation**, particularly to monitor the banking, securities, and insurance industries, the Financial Supervisory Commission (FSC) was established in April 1998. In addition, the Financial Supervisory Service (FSS) was created in January 1999 to act as an executive arm of the FSC. Even though being formally separate, the FSC and the FSS were supposed to operate as a single supervisory authority and were the sole supervisory agency for banks and non-banks (Kim and Lee 2006). The Bank of Korea gained substantial independence from the government and was assigned the primary goal of controlling price stability (Kwon 1998).

The FSC, together with the MOFE, established the principles to distinguish non-viable FIs from viable ones, defined clear exit strategies for the former, and developed **restructuring** plans for those judged to be salvageable (Lee 2017b). Exit strategies included the transfer of business units of non-viable FIs, purchase and assumptions, mergers between non-viable banks, and mergers between sound and non-viable banks (Lee and Rhee 2007; Graham 2003b). A key indicator to evaluate the soundness of the banking sector was the BIS capital adequacy ratio (a ratio of capital to risk-related assets), which should have been above 8% according to the IMF guidelines (Heo and Woo 2006; Chopra et al. 2001). Between 1998 and 2004, five weak banks had closed through purchase and assumption, and nine banks had been merged with others (Lee 2017a). In the course of the restructuring process, the government injected huge amounts of public funds into the financial sector, especially in the banking sector, in order to reduce the number of NPLs and to enhance the recapitalization of banks (cf. Kim et al. 2006). The total amount of public funds used for financial restructuring amounted to 160.5 trillion won, of which around half were injected into troubled FIs through the Korea Deposit Insurance Corporation (KDIC) for recapitalization, and around one-fourth was used to purchase NPLs through the Korea Asset Management Corporation (KAMCO), which had been reorganized and expanded in August 1997 (Lee and Rhee 2007).

The government also **accelerated the liberalization of capital markets and foreign direct investment** by (a) eliminating ceilings on foreign investment in equity, bond, and money markets, (b) lifting restrictions on corporate borrowing abroad, (c) fully liberalizing foreign ownership in most industries including financial services, (d) establishing a "one-stop service" to simplify the approval process for foreign investment, (e) removing hostile takeover rules and other anti-takeover devices to protect existing management, and (f) eliminating restrictions on foreign investors to purchase land for investment projects (Chopra et al. 2001; IMF 2000b). The main objectives of these reforms were (1) to attract foreign capital and reduce the excessive amount of short-term debt—particularly through the implementation of the reform steps (a) and (b)—and (2) to impose greater market discipline on corporations—through reform steps (c)–(f). As a consequence of the reforms described above, portfolio investment and FDI in South Korea picked up sharply in 1998; the latter increased from $2.8 billion in the previous year to $5.1 billion (IMF 2000b). Moreover, the lifting of restrictions on overseas borrowing led to a reduction of short-term borrowings of domestic FIs (from US$63 billion to US$31 billion between the end of 1997 and the end of 1999). By contrast, the long-term external liabilities of domestic corporations grew from US$25 billion to US $30 billion over the same period (Chopra et al. 2001). An extensive overview of the financial sector reform can be found in the IMF (2000b). As argued by Shin and Chang (2003), many financial reform measures were designed in close coordination with the corporate reform program, because the NPL problem was closely related to the performance of the corporate sector.

3.9.3.3 Labor Sector Reform

The financial and the corporate sector reforms required greater labor market flexibility (Chopra et al. 2001). However, the necessary reforms faced strong resistance from labor unions. To achieve consensus, the South Korean government formed the Tripartite Commission in January 1998 to promote cooperation among the government, labor unions, and employers. In February, the Tripartite Commission reached an agreement on a restructuring program (Coe and Kim 2002). In order to increase the flexibility of the labor market, the South Korean government legalized layoffs of workers for "urgent managerial need" (including mergers and acquisitions) and reduced restrictions on the use of temporary dispatched labor. In exchange, labor rights were enhanced, including the guarantee of the right of public servants and teachers to unite (the former in workplace associations and the latter in unions), as well as the permission of political participation of labor unions (Sakong and Koh 2010; ILO 2012). It has to be noted that, even though the layoffs for managerial reasons were legalized, companies that intended to dismiss employees were required to follow strict guidelines aimed at minimizing actual layoffs (IMF 2000b). The Ministry of Labor had to be informed about layoff plans, and companies were obliged to provide severance payments (IMF 2000b). In addition, the social safety net was strengthened (Chopra et al. 2001).

As a consequence of the labor market reform and the IMF prescribed austerity course, the unemployment rate increased sharply (from around 2–3% prior to the crisis to about 7% in 1998 and 6.3% in 1999) and the number of unemployed people shot up (from 568,000 in 1997 to 1,490,000 in 1998 and 1,374,000 in 1999) (Kim 2010). Especially the youth unemployment rate skyrocketed (Lee et al. 2005). Also the share of irregular (part-time or temporary) workers increased steadily from 45.7% in 1997 to 56.6% in 2002 (Heo and Woo 2006; Lee et al. 2005; Yang 2006). According to Kim (2002), this increase rather reflected the companies' temporary attempts to cut labor costs and not their efforts to achieve long-term efficiency gains. Income inequality increased, reflected by a rising Gini coefficient (from 0.268 in 1997 to 0.303 in 1998). Also the poverty rate rose from 9.3% in 1997 to 13.1% in 1999. Prior to the crisis, both measures had been relatively stable (Kim 2010).

As a consequence of the expansion of the social safety net, the coverage of the unemployment insurance system was expanded significantly, in July 1999 even to temporary and part-time workers; however, due to the lack of collective bargaining power, only 26% of irregular workers were effectively covered by the employment insurance scheme in 2003 (Yang 2006).

3.9.3.4 Public Sector Reform

The South Korean government undertook various reforms to increase the efficiency of the public sector. These measures included a reorganization of the central government ministries, the privatization of public enterprises, and a reduction of the employment in central and local governments. In addition, government regulations were reduced significantly (Sakong and Koh 2010; Shin and Chang 2003).

3.9.4 Back to Normal?

The various reforms and macroeconomic adjustment policies as well as their impacts and evaluation have been already discussed in the previous sections. In the following paragraphs, we will briefly summarize the recovery process of the South Korean economy (after 1998).

The South Korean government started relaxing the retrenchment policies in May 1998, and the high interest rates were gradually reduced. In addition, public spending was increased. As a consequence, GDP growth reached again double-digit area in 1999 (10.7%), and in August 2001, South Korea managed to repay its IMF loan completely. However, even though GDP growth recovered relatively fast after the crisis, the average growth rate for the post-crisis period was significantly lower than that experienced in the decades prior to the crisis ("only" around 4.5% between 2001 and 2005). According to Lee and Rhee (2007), one main reason was the slower investment growth, which, in turn, resulted from the increased risk aversion of corporations as a side effect of the corporate and financial sector reform. However, these developments could also mean that South Korea had adjusted to a new, lower steady-state growth path (Lee and Rhee 2007; Lee 2005; Suh 2007). However, it cannot be neglected that the immediate macroeconomic adjustment policies and also the comprehensive structural reforms facilitated the recovery process. As a consequence of the structural reforms in the financial sector, the NPL ratio of commercial banks declined from the peak value of 13.6% at the end of 1999 to only 2% by the end of 2004. The BIS ratio (ratio of capital to risk-related assets) increased from 7.0% in 1997 to 11.3% in 2004 (Kim et al. 2006, see also Table 3.8). As a consequence of the accelerated liberalization, the South Korean economy reported a rise in FDI.

Firms' debt-to-equity ratios also improved significantly and chaebols focused on becoming more profitable and started making investment decisions in a more prudent and transparent way (Sakong and Koh 2010). The punishment of the

Table 3.8 NPL and BIS ratio

	1997	1998	1999	2000	2001	2002	2003	2004
NPL ratio	6.1	7.4	13.6	8.8	3.3	2.4	2.7	2.0
BIS ratio	7.0	8.2	10.8	10.5	10.8	10.5	10.4	11.3

Source Kim et al. (2006)
Notes "NPL" stands for non-performing loans

management of the Daewoo chaebol in 1999 as well as the demise of other conglomerates signaled that the government would not continue to tolerate questionable/dubious business practices of chaebols.

3.10 The Global Financial Crisis

Around 10 years after the Asian Financial Crisis, the South Korean economy was exposed to another severe crisis. The 2008 **Global Financial Crisis (GFC)** was partly caused by the **subprime mortgage crisis,** which started in 2007: The US' lax banking sector regulation and supervision as well as the low interest rate policy had resulted in a **housing price bubble**. At the same time, the credit risks of US banks were increasingly transferred to third parties via **financial derivatives** such as mortgage backed securities (MBS), collateralized debt obligations (CDOs), and collateralized mortgage obligations (CMOs). These complex financial products were all interrelated so that the default of one product could cause a chain reaction. The situation was further aggravated by the **pursuit of short-term profits** by actors of the financial sector (Wagner 2010). The Global Financial Crisis hit the South Korean economy in two phases (cf. Lee and Rhee 2012; Yoon 2011). Each phase will be briefly outlined in the following.

3.10.1 The First Phase of the 2008 Crisis

The first phase of the crisis was characterized by **large capital outflows** due to the **confidence loss of foreign investors**. Initially, the South Korean government did not expect that the South Korean economy would be hit severely by the crisis. After considerable restructuring efforts after the Asian Financial Crisis (cf. Sect. 3.9.3), the situation of South Korea's financial and corporate sector had improved significantly, and abundant foreign exchange reserves had been accumulated. However, after the collapse of Lehman Brothers in September 2008, the situation in South Korea deteriorated much worse than anticipated. As a consequence of the credit crunch in the global market, banks in advanced economies started to withdraw funds from Asian banks, which caused a liquidity problem in the foreign exchange market. South Korea was especially hard hit. In the fourth quarter of 2008, South Korea's capital account recorded a deficit of US$42.6 billion, which corresponds to 20% of GDP (Lee and Rhee 2012; Lee 2017a). The won depreciated sharply against the US dollar with the won/dollar exchange rate increasing from 944.69 in January 2008 to 1390.09 in November 2008, which corresponds to a 47% increase (IMF IFS 2021, see also Fig. 3.13).

The liquidity strain in the foreign exchange markets also caused a deterioration of the domestic financial markets. Financial institutions stopped lending to each other, which led to a credit crunch in the money market. The credit default swap premium increased by 559 basis points, from 116 at the end of August 2008 to 675

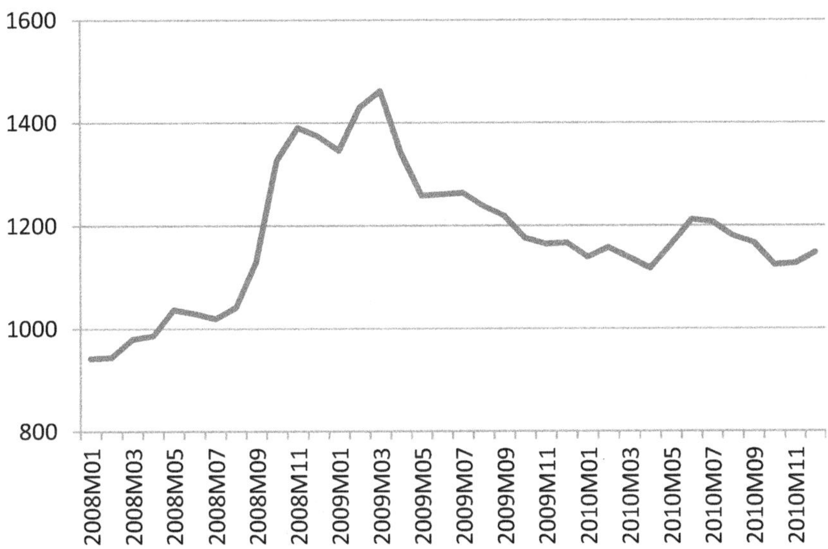

Fig. 3.13 Won/dollar exchange rate (monthly). *Source* IMF, International Financial Statistics (IFS) (2021). *Note* Won per U.S. dollar, period average

at the end of October 2008. Stock prices plummeted by almost 30% between the beginning of 2008 and the end of October 2008 (Chung 2009).

The particularly severe situation in South Korea (compared with other Asian economies) can be explained by global investors' sudden loss of confidence in the South Korean economy. Besides the **stigma from the 1997 crisis,** South Korea's **heavy reliance on short-term external debt** was a driving force for this development since it increased the country's vulnerability to the global credit crunch. The short-term external debt increased from US$65.9 billion in 2005 to almost US $190 billion in the third quarter of 2008, thus accounting for around 45% of the total external debt, which was very close to the share reported in 1997, namely, 48% (Lee and Rhee 2012). Accordingly, the short-term external solvency worsened significantly with the ratio of foreign exchange reserves to the sum of the short-term external debt and the 3-month import amount declining from around 170% in September 2004 to only around 80% in September 2008 (Lee 2017a). In addition, the **loan-to-deposit ratio (LTD ratio)** that relates the total loans granted by banks to their total deposits for the same period had increased to almost 120% by the end of 2008, thus being significantly higher than the LTD ratios in other Asian countries, which were usually less than 100%.

However, a closer look into the country-specific characteristics of these indicators reveals that the situation was far less severe than suggested by the actual numbers; however, this was not taken into account by global investors once the crisis had started. For instance, a non-negligible part of South Korea's external debt was in fact risk-free because it was either **non-obligatory**[29] or **owed to branches of foreign banks**. In 2008, activities of foreign bank branches accounted for about 40% of the banking sector's foreign debt.[30] Of this debt, only a rather small amount was balanced by foreign assets (Tsutsumi et al. 2010). Moreover, the share of short-term foreign borrowing of foreign bank branches was considerably higher than that in domestic banks. The South Korean regulators did not expect that the monitoring of the short-term liquidity of foreign bank branches was actually necessary since they believed that these branches could easily access liquidity from the headquarters—especially since the global banks usually had a much higher credit rating (Lee and Rhee 2012). In addition, the LTD ratio would have been lower if the deposits of South Korean banks would have also included certificates of deposits (CDs), which has been common practice in other countries including the USA.

The South Korean government initiated various policy measures to counteract the above-described liquidity problems, to stabilize the foreign exchange market, and to restore global investors' confidence. Among others, it **provided payment guarantees for foreign currency borrowing of South Korean domestic banks** and **supplied liquidity to domestic financial markets** to mitigate the credit crunch. In addition, the Bank of Korea utilized around US$60 billion of the foreign exchange reserves to ensure financial institutions' foreign exchange liquidity (cf. also Fig. 3.15). However, the foreign exchange reserves were not fully exploited in order to be able to better react to shortages of trade finance at a later time. In addition to these measures, the South Korean government also tried to explain the structural difference between the 1997 crisis and the 2007/08 crisis (Lee and Rhee 2012).

However, all these measures turned out to be rather ineffective and it was not until the Bank of Korea entered into a **US$30 billion currency swap arrangement with the US Federal Reserve** in October 2008 that financial markets stabilized (as at least temporarily). This was rather ironic, since the crisis had originated in the USA (Lee and Rhee 2012). Swap lines are transactions in the course of which a supplying central bank (here the Federal Reserve) offers a credit line to a foreign central bank (here the Bank of Korea) for a pre-set time and interest rate (Aizenman et al. 2011). Thanks to the swap arrangement with the US Fed, the Bank of Korea's international reserve position was augmented; it now had the option to borrow US $30 billion. This also alleviated the necessity to set aside more reserves to replace the US$60 billion chunk that South Korea had utilized during the first phase of the crisis (Aizenman et al. 2011). In December 2008, the Bank of Korea also engaged in currency swap arrangements with the People's Bank of China (amounting to ¥118 billion) and the Bank of Japan (amounting to US$20 billion) (cf. Chung 2009).

---

[29] That is, this debt was not subject to any repayment burden.

[30] The increasing presence of foreign bank branches was the consequence of the liberalization measures installed after the Asian Financial Crisis (see also Sect. 3.9.3.2).

3.10.2 The Second Phase of the Crisis

Even though the swap lines temporarily succeeded in stabilizing financial markets, this effect, unfortunately, did not last long, and already starting from the middle of November 2008, credit crunch problems again became more severe.

While the problems of the first phase had been rather short-term and primarily caused by the—partly unjustified—lack of trust of global investors, the problems of the second phase were rather long-term and structural (Lee and Rhee 2012). The main concern was Asia's heavy reliance on exports to advanced Western countries, which made most Asian economies particularly vulnerable to a contraction of global demand. Indeed, the global recession led to a collapse of exports, and thus, the Global Financial Crisis also soon spilled over to the real sectors of Asian countries: The declining exports were responsible for the cooling down of economic activity in Asian economies. This, in turn, potentially deteriorated the balance sheet of Asian banks and thus increased the danger of a banking crisis (Lee and Rhee 2012). Also China (at least initially) suffered from a decrease in exports and consequently faced a collapse of growth (Cho 2009). In the fourth quarter of 2008, Chinese exports contracted by 13.3% and imports even by 26% (q-o-q growth rate, IMF IFS 2021); Chinese GDP growth declined to only 6.3%. Since China was also South Korea's largest trading partner (South Korea's exports to China accounted to around 22% of its total exports prior to the crisis, cf. Cho 2012), South Korean exports suffered not only from the shrinking demand of Western countries but also from that of its Asian trading partners, which also had to cope with declining growth rates due to the export collapse. As we will see later, it was, however, also thank to China's quick economic recovery that the South Korean economy was able to relatively fast regain momentum. However, initially, the South Korean exports collapsed in the fourth quarter of 2008. While in September, year-over-year export growth was still 27.6%, in November, this number declined to 7.8%, and eventually plummeted to −19.5% in November 2008 (Cho 2009). In the first quarter of 2009, the year-over-year export growth then almost fell to −25% (Lee and Rhee 2012). Between 2008 and 2009, South Korea's exports to China decreased by 5% (from US$91.4 billion to US$86.7 billion) and that to the ASEAN region by 20% (from US$49.3 billion to US$41.0 billion) (cf. Cho 2012; see also Fig. 3.14).

As a consequence of the steep decline in exports and considerable contraction of domestic demand, GDP growth decreased by more than 5% in the fourth quarter of 2008, which was the second-worst performance since 1970 and around two-thirds of the worst record, namely, −7.8% in the first quarter of 1998 (Cho 2009; Chung 2009).

In order to revive the real economy and stabilize the vulnerable financial sector, the South Korean government adopted a proactive monetary and fiscal policy. In addition, it initiated the restructuring of the corporate sector, also with the aim of preventing a contagion of the banking sector. Banks' recapitalization measures were primarily installed to prevent bank panics and not because of an inadequate capitalization. In the following, the main policy measures will be briefly discussed.

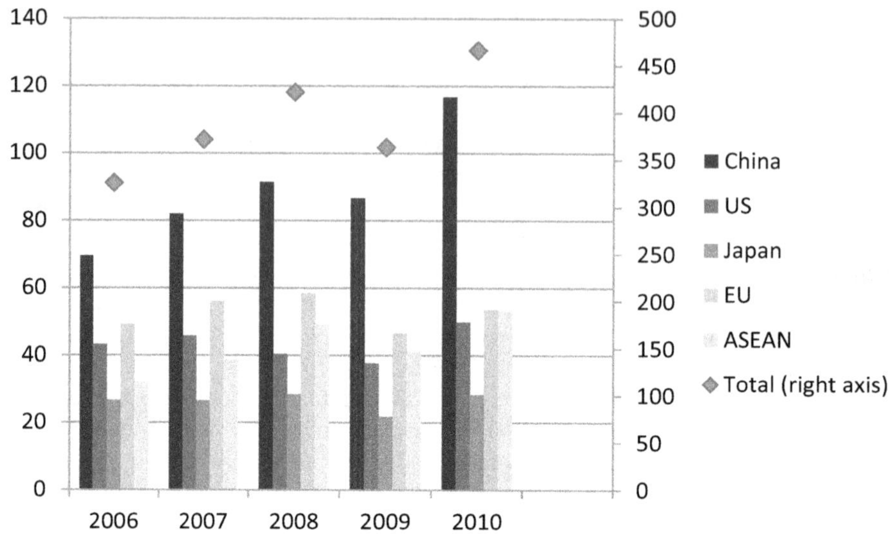

Fig. 3.14 South Korean exports to selected countries and regions, 2006–2010, in US$ billion. *Source* Ministry of Foreign Affairs and Trade (MOFAT) data, Cho (2012: 11, Table 3). *Notes* ASEAN = Association of Southeast Asian nations; EU = European Union

The government launched a **large fiscal stimulus package** to curb the adverse effects of the crisis and to stimulate domestic demand. The total package for the years 2008 and 2009 amounted to 49.6 trillion won; key elements of South Korea's fiscal policy were **tax reductions** (16.4 trillion won) and increased **government spending** (33.2 trillion won) (cf. Yoon 2011). Even though the fiscal stimulus package adopted in the course of the 1997 crisis also had been considerably large in its magnitude, it had only been gradually introduced, whereas the new fiscal expansion was immediately announced. Thus, the South Korean government managed to have a comparatively short implementation time lag and was able to maximize the positive effects of its fiscal policy measures (Cho 2009). Around 60% of the stimulus package was executed by the first half of 2009 (Lee and Rhee 2012). Already in November 2008, the government announced a supplementary budget amounting to 11.2 trillion won (corresponding to slightly more than 1% of GDP) (Cho 2009). South Korea's fast policy reaction was only possible thanks to the country's relatively solid fiscal balance: central government debt was around 30% in 2006, which was significantly below the average public debt level of the OECD (Lee and Rhee 2012; Yoon 2011).

South Korea also adopted an **expansionary monetary policy**. Between October 2008 and February 2009, the Bank of Korea **lowered its base rates** successively in six steps **from 5.25% to only 2.00%** (Chung 2009). This considerable interest rate cut should support economic and financial market stabilization. This monetary policy reaction was very different from that of the 1997 crisis when monetary policy

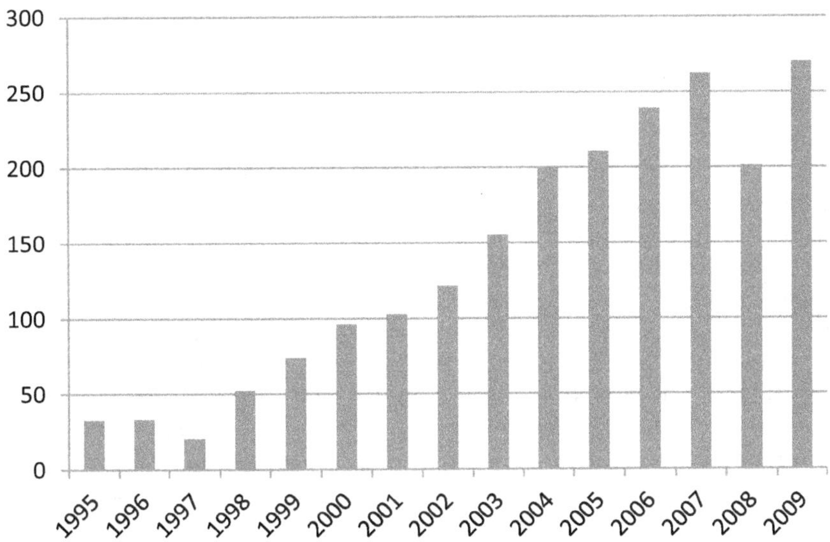

Fig. 3.15 South Korea's foreign exchange reserves (in US$ billions). *Source* Yoon (2011)

was initially tightened as part of the IMF program (see also Sect. 3.9.3). In particular, the base interest rate was then raised to almost 30%. The tremendously contrasting policy reactions can be partly explained by the fact that the foreign exchange liquidity situation was fundamentally different. While at the onset of the Global Financial Crisis, South Korea had accumulated considerable foreign exchange reserves, it had almost depleted its foreign reserve in 1997 and thus, the main policy goal at that time had been to prevent the worst-case scenario, namely, a sovereign default (Cho 2009; Lee and Rhee 2012; Kihwan 2006, see also Fig. 3.15).

The South Korean government also **expanded the liquidity supply**. Through **open market operations**, the Bank of Korea provided liquidity amounting to **18.5 trillion won** (Chung 2009). Moreover, the government established the **10 trillion won Bond Market Stabilization Fund** to support SMEs and construction companies suffering from liquidity shortages (Yoon 2011; Lee 2017a). Also the **eligible securities and counterparties for open market operations were broadened**. The eligible securities were expanded to include not only treasury bonds but also bank debentures and some government agency bonds. The eligible counterparties were expanded by 12 additional securities companies (Chung 2009; Lee and Rhee 2012).

The credit supply capacity of banks was supported by a more than **50% rise in the aggregate credit ceiling** between November 2008 and March 2009, and a **one-off interest payment** on banks' required reserved deposits by the Bank of Korea totaling 500.2 billion won. Interestingly, South Korean banks were actually adequately capitalized—at the end of 2008, the BIS capital ratio stood at 12.8—however, the media and the markets put the South Korean government under pressure to further enhance the capital basis of banks (Lee and Rhee 2012). The South Korean government created the **Bank Recapitalization Fund** in December 2009, which was endowed with **20 trillion won** (Yoon 2011). Its main cause was to provide a safety net in order to forestall bank panics and to ensure that banks would continue to provide credits to SMEs (Lee and Rhee 2012; Yoon 2011). Even though the Bank Recapitalization Fund provided an effective safety net, it did not cause any financial burden since it was not used. However, this was rather negatively perceived by the media which in early 2010 assessed the fund as a failure due to its disuse. Therefore, the government was to some extent "forced" to enjoin the banks to actually utilize the fund (Lee and Rhee 2012).

The above-described reforms to combat the Global Financial Crisis were accompanied by a corporation restructuring program. Creditor financial institutions evaluated the credit risks of corporations in struggled industries such as construction and shipbuilding. These industries were particularly severely affected by the Global Financial Crisis since they were rather sensitive to the general economic conditions. In general, **creditor financial institutions graded companies** according to their future liabilities **from A to D**. Companies belonging to group A ("normal") and B ("temporary liquidity shortage") received continued liquidity support, whereas companies that fell under the category C ("signs of insolvency but viable") and D ("nonviable") were subject to either creditor institution-led workout programs or liquidation/bankruptcy procedures, respectively (Lee and Rhee 2012; Koo 2011). The first round of credit assessments for the construction and shipbuilding industries was conducted in January 2009, followed by the second round in March. With respect to the construction industry, 24 companies received a grade C rating and 5 a grade D rating; regarding the shipbuilding industry, 5 companies were assigned to category C and 2 to category D. In 2010, another 16 companies were targeted for restructuring in the construction sector. In contrast, the shipbuilding industry had undertaken heavy restructuring and only 3 companies were targeted for restructuring in 2010. The number of companies with a total credit exposure over 50 billion won which did not belong to the construction, shipbuilding and shipping industry, and that were assigned to the categories C or D, increased significantly in 2009 and 2010 (to 33 and 45, respectively, see also Fig. 3.16). In the course of the first round of credit ratings for SMEs in July 2009 (for SMEs with a credit exposure from 5 to 50 billion won), 113 firms were classified as grade C (68%) or D (32%).[31] The government also enacted the **Fast Track program** in October 2008. It accelerated the classification process and provided 18 trillion won to SMEs by the middle of 2009. Liquidity was provided among others, through the extension of new bank loans, swapping debt for equity, and rolling over existing loans at lower interest rates (Tsutsumi et al. 2010).

[31] Please note that all information on the number of firms assigned to each grade is obtained from Koo (2011).

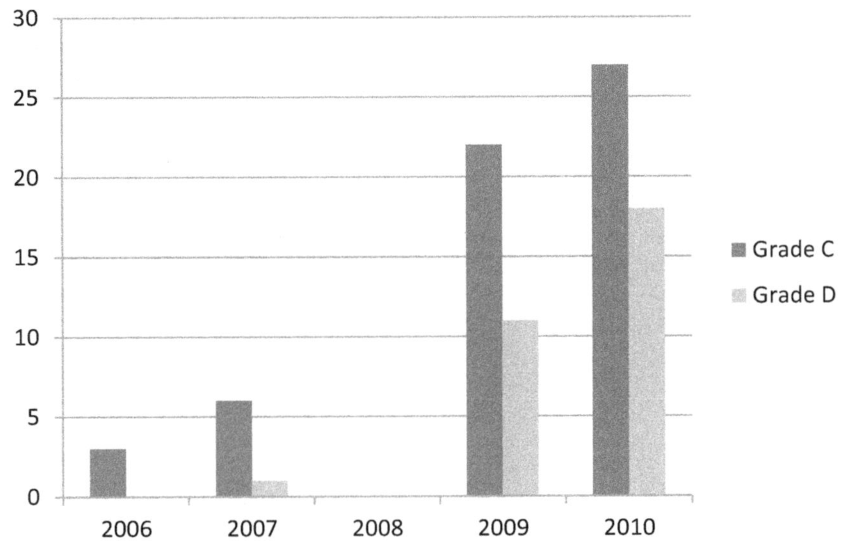

Fig. 3.16 Firms targeted at restructuring 2006–2010 (credit exposure > 50 billion won, excluding construction, shipping, and shipbuilding industry). *Source* Koo (2011). *Notes* Grade C: "signs of insolvency but viable"; Grade D: "nonviable"

3.10.3 What Helped in the GFC: Lessons Learnt from the AFC and Crisis Recovery

During and after the Asian Financial Crisis, South Korea underwent a painful restructuring process. The adopted measures aimed at making the South Korean economy more resistant to future crises. Among others, financial markets were liberalized and the regulation and supervision of financial institutions were enhanced. Overall, the financial sector became much sounder and also more profitable. As already discussed in Sect. 3.9.4, the BIS capital ratio had improved significantly since the early 2000s and also the return on equity ratio of the banking sector which had plummeted to around −50% during the Asian Financial Crisis was fluctuating between 0 and 20% during the 2001–2008 period (Cho 2009). There was also considerable improvement regarding the financial position and profitability of the corporate sector. In the course of the restructuring progress, transparency and accountability were enhanced, financial structures improved, cross-debt guarantees eliminated, and the focus on core business activities strengthened (see also Sect. 3.9.3). Between 1997 and 2008, the average debt to equity ratio in the manufacturing sector fell from more than 400% to only slightly above 100% (Cho 2009). The return on equity in the early 2000s was above 10%, whereas in 1998, it was only about −15%. Overall, the soundness of the financial and corporate sector had been enhanced significantly. In addition, South Korea's foreign reserve position had considerably improved and at the onset of the crisis, reserves amounted to around US$260 billion (in 1997, it had stood at only US$20 billion). Table 3.9 summarizes the key similarities and differences between the Asian Financial Crisis (AFC) of 1997 and the onset of the Global Financial Crisis (GFC) of 2008.

Table 3.9 Overview AFC and GFC

	Asian Financial Crisis 1997/98	Global Financial Crisis 2007/08
Cause	External crisis but primarily domestic problems	External crisis
Overall economic situation		
Corporate and financial sector	Severe problems	Rather sound (considerable improvement due to restructuring after the AFC)
BIS-ratio	7.0 (1997)	12.8 (end 2008)
External debt	High level of short-term external debt in 1997: US$174 billion total external debt; 33.7% of GDP; 57.6% short-term debt	High level short-term external debt in 2007: US$382 billion total external debt; 39.4% of GDP; 41.8% short-term debt
Foreign exchange reserves	Almost depleted (1997): US$20,405 million	Abundant reserves (2007): US$262,224 million
Economic impact		
Growth rate (q-o-q)	−7.8% (1Q1998)	−5.6% (4Q2008)
Capital withdrawal	December 1997: US$6.4 billion	October 2008: US$25.5 billion
Policy reaction		
Monetary policy	Initial tightening, base interest rate initially raised to 30%, since mid-1998 gradually declining interest rates	Fast successive lowering of the base interest rate to only 2%
Fiscal policy	Large but delayed fiscal stimulus program (initial IMF requirement: balanced budget)	Large and fast fiscal stimulus program
Recovery	V-shape recovery, driven by exports and government spending	V-shape recovery, driven by exports (also to emerging market economies) and government spending

Sources Own representation based on data of: Jeon (2012) (external debt); Cho (2009) (capital withdrawal, growth rate (q-o-q)); Yoon (2011) (foreign exchange reserves); Lee and Rhee (2012) and Kim et al. (2006) (BIS ratio). For the remaining information, see the sources cited in the main text. *Notes* The BIS capital adequacy ratio is a ratio of capital to risk-related assets. See also Sect. 3.9

Thanks to the fast implementation of monetary and fiscal policy measures, the carefully designed bank recapitalization strategy (which was possible because of the newly built-up legal and financial infrastructure), as well as the accumulated experience with corporate restructuring processes during the Asian Financial Crisis, South Korea recovered relatively fast from the 2008 financial crisis. Exports presented another important factor that facilitated the recovery of the South Korean economy. They had already played a significant role in the 1997 crisis recovery; however, this time, South Korea also exported increasingly to emerging market economies. Especially, China's fast economic recovery propelled South Korean exports to China which even exceeded the pre-crisis level (recall Fig. 3.14 in Sect. 3.10.3).

Figure 3.17 depicts South Korea's GDP growth rates in comparison to selected OECD countries. It becomes apparent that, similar to the 1997 crisis, there was a kind of V-shape recovery process (cf. also Yoon 2011). Also a closer look into South Korea's quarterly real GNI growth rates (at constant 2015 prices) in Fig. 3.18 illustrates closely resembling V-shape patterns for both crises periods (with the main exception that the drop in GNI growth was more pronounced during the Asian Financial Crisis).

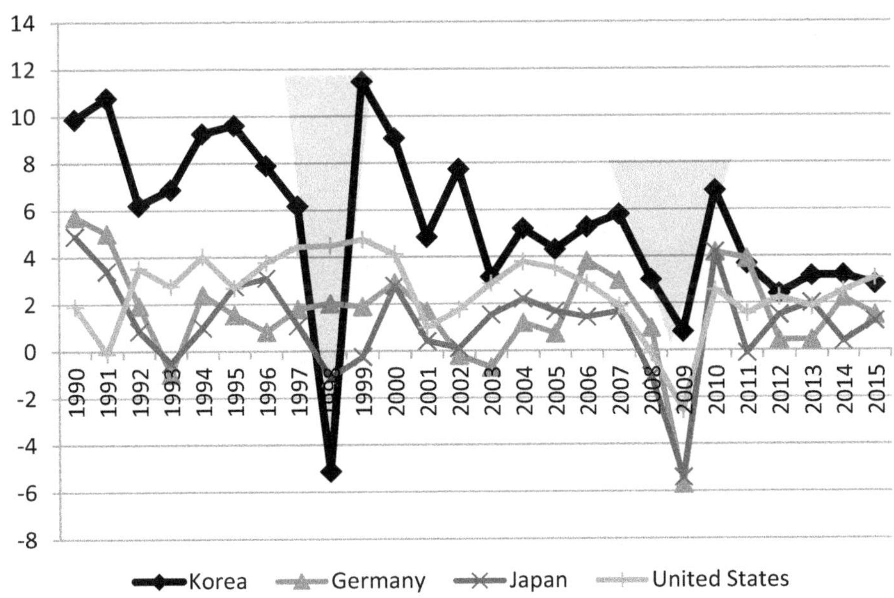

Fig. 3.17 GDP growth in comparison. *Source* IMF, Global Economic Outlook

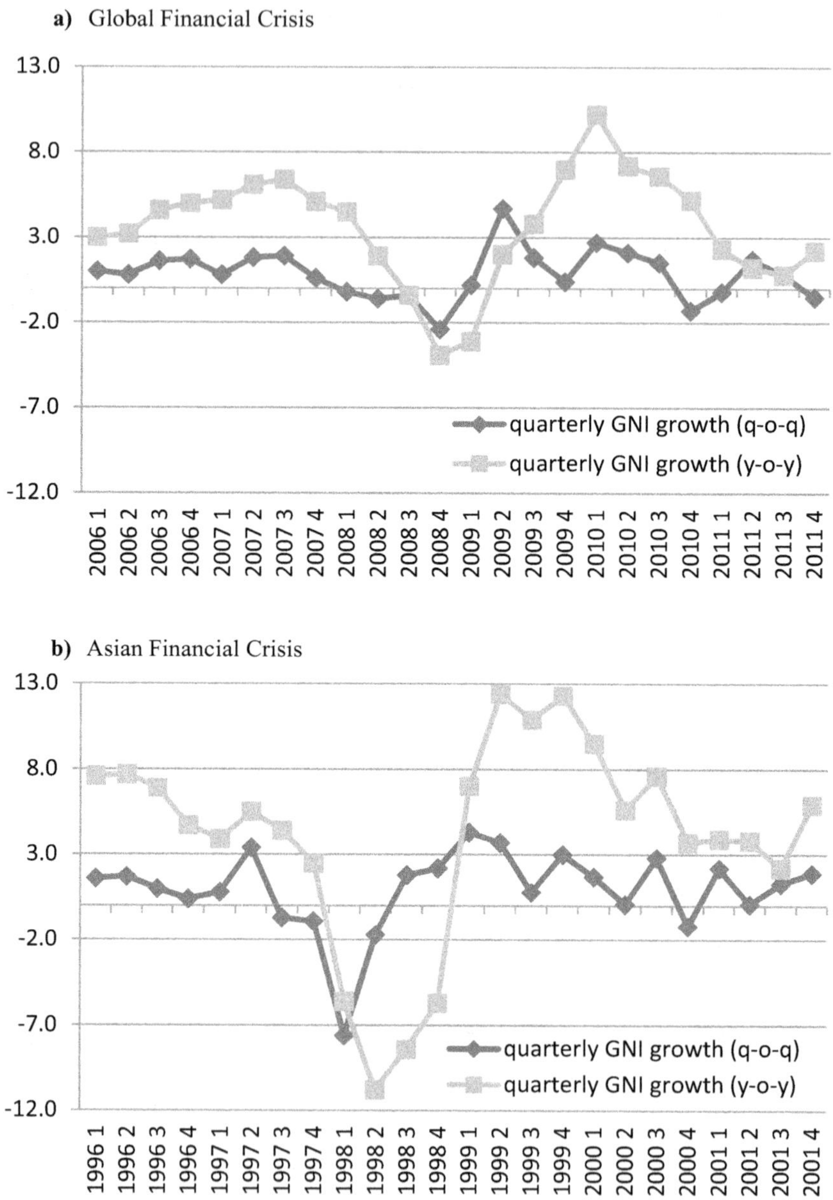

Fig. 3.18 Quarterly GNI growth rate (constant 2015 prices). **a** Global Financial Crisis, **b** Asian Financial Crisis. *Source* Bank of Korea

Overall, South Korea managed to significantly improve the resilience of its financial system. The various reforms installed to cope with the adverse impacts of the Asian Financial Crisis and the Global Financial Crisis will most likely reduce the negative effects of future global crises on the South Korean economy. However, this does not imply that South Korea can rest on its laurels; in fact, the country's financial market development still lags greatly behind that of other advanced economies. Even in 2015, it ranked only 80th in this category according to the Global Competitiveness Index of the World Economic Forum, lower than Liberia (ranked 74th) and only slightly better than Senegal (ranked 88th) and Zambia (ranked 84th). That means there is still a lot of room for improvement here. In order to become even better, it is above all relevant to further improve so-called "regulatory governance" (on the role of regulatory governance for financial stability, see Mohr and Wagner 2012, 2013).

Appendix

See Table 3.10.

Table 3.10 Economic Development (ED) Plans, 1962–2007, overview

Development regimes	Government-led industrialization	Government-led industrialization	Transforming to market-led growth	Transforming to market-led growth	Balanced growth
Period	1962–1981	1982–1992	1993–1996	1997–2002	2003–2007
Major plans	1st to 4th 5-year ED plans	5th and 6th 5-year ED plans	7th New economy ED plan	Knowledge-based economy development plan	National fiscal management plan
Key features of plans	Mobilization and allocation of national resources	Rationalization and restructuring	Private sector's participation in government planning	Crisis management and institutional reform	Long-term fiscal planning
Focuses of government policies	Export promotion, subsequently HCI drive (particularly in the 3rd 5-year ED plan)	Strengthening industrial competitiveness	Internationalization and economic liberalization	Four-sector reform and moving toward the knowledge-based economy	Maintaining social equity and sectoral/regional balances
Key targets of fiscal policies	Supporting industrialization, strengthening defense capabilities	Restoring fiscal prudence, priorities on education and social welfare	Strengthening industrial competitiveness, priorities on economic sectors	Assisting reforms, expanding welfare spending	Harmonizing growth and welfare

Source Suh (2007)

References

Adelman I (1997) Social development in Korea, 1953–1993. In: Cha DS, Kim KS, Perkins DH (eds) The Korean economy 1945–1995: performance and vision for the 21st century. Korea Development Institute, Seoul, pp 509–540

Ahmad J (1978) Import substitution—a survey of policy issues. Dev Econ 16(4):355–372. https://doi.org/10.1111/j.1746-1049.1978.tb01070.x

Ahn CY (1990) Recent economic transition of South Korea: comparative perspectives with Latin America. J Econ Dev 15:27–46

Ahn CY, Kim J-H (1997) The output-looking trade policy and the industrial development of South Korea. In: Cha D-S, Kim KS, Perkins DH (eds) The Korean economy 1945–1995: performance and vision for the 21st century. Korea Development Institute, Seoul, pp 339–382

Aizenman J, Jinjarak Y, Park D (2011) Evaluating Asian swap arrangement. ADBI Working Paper 297, Asian Development Bank Institute, Tokyo

Amsden A (1989) Asia's next giant: South Korea and late industrialization. Oxford University Press, New York

Asian Development Bank (2020) Asia's journey to prosperity: policy, market, and technology over 50 years. Asian Development Bank, Manila

Baer W (1984) Industrialization in Latin America: successes and failures. J Econ Educ 15(2):124–135

Baldwin F (1975) America's rented troops: South Koreans in Vietnam. Bull Concern Asian Sch 7 (4):33–40. https://doi.org/10.1080/14672715.1975.10406389

Bank of Korea (2002) Monetary policy in Korea. Bank of Korea, Seoul

Bank of Korea (n.d.) From the Second Currency Reform in 1953 to Third Currency Reform in 1962. Bank of Korea, Seoul. https://www.bok.or.kr/eng/main/contents.do?menuNo=400117

Baudino P, Yun H (2017) Resolution of non-performing loans-policy options. FSI Insights on Policy Implementation No 3, Bank for International Settlements, Basel

Castley RJQ (2006) The role of Japan in Korea's acquisition of technology. Asia Pac Bus Rev 3 (1):29–53

Chang H-J (1998) Korea: the misunderstood crisis. World Development 26(8):1555–1561

Chang H, Park H, Yoo CG (1998) Interpreting the Korean crisis: financial liberalization, industrial policy and corporate governance. Camb J Econ 22(6):735–746

Chibber V (1999) Building a developmental state: the Korean case reconsidered. Polit Soc 27 (3):309–346

Cho D (2009) The Republic of Korea's economy in the swirl of global crisis. ADBI Working Paper 147, Asian Development Bank Institute, Tokyo

Cho D, Kang Y (2013) 2012 modularization of Korea's development experience: Korea stabilization policies in the 1980s. Ministry of Strategy and Finance, Sejong, KDI School of Public Policy and Management, Sejong

Cho H (2012) Korea's experience with global financial crisis. The North-South Institute, Ottawa

Cho JH (1995) External debt and policy controversy in Korea. South Econ J 62(2):467–480

Cho S (1994) The dynamics of Korean economic development. Institute for International Economics, Washington

Cho YJ (1989) Finance and development: the Korean approach. Oxford Rev Econ Policy 5(4):88–102

Cho YJ (2002a) Financial repression, liberalization, crisis and restructuring: lessons of Korea's financial sector policies. ADB Institute Research Paper 47, Asian Development Bank Institute, Tokyo

Cho YJ (2002b) The political economy of financial liberalization in South Korea. In: Lee CH (ed) Financial liberalization and the economic crisis in Asia. Routledge, London, pp 82–103

Cho YJ, Kim JK (1997) Credit policies and the industrialization of Korea. Korea Development Institute (KDI), Seoul

Cho YJ, McCauley RN (2003) Liberalising the capital account without losing balance: lessons from Korea. In: China's capital account liberalisation: international perspectives. BIS Working Paper 15, Bank for International Settlements, Basel, pp 75–92

Choi S, Dyck J, Childs N (2016) The rice market in South Korea. USDA Rice Outlook RCS-16I-01, United States Department of Agriculture, Economic Research Service, Washington DC

Chopra A, Lang K, Karasulu M et al (2001) From crisis to recovery in Korea: strategy, achievements, and lessons. IMF Working Paper No 01/154, International Monetary Fund, Washington DC

Chung HC (2009) The Bank of Korea's policy response to the global financial crisis. BIS Papers 54, Bank of International settlement, Basel

Clifford ML (1994) Troubled tiger: business, bureaucrats & generals in South Korea. M.E. Sharpe, Armonc NY

Coe DT, Kim S (eds) (2002) Korean crisis and recovery. International Monetary Fund, Korea Institute for International Economic Policy, Washington DC

Cole D, Park YC (1983) Financial development in Korea, 1945–1978. Harvard University Press, Cambridge

Cole DC, Lyman PN (1971) Korean development: the interplay of politics and economics. Harvard University Press, Cambridge

Collins SM, Park W (1989) External debt and macroeconomic performance in South Korea. In: Sachs JD (ed) Developing country debt and the World economy. University of Chicago Press, Chicago IL

Corbo V, Nam SW (1988) Korea's macroeconomic prospects and policy issues for the next decade. World Dev 16:35–45

Dalla I, Khatkhate D (1995) Regulated deregulation of the financial system in Korea, World Bank Discussion Paper 292. World Bank, Washington DC

Economic Planning Board (1961) The first 5-year economic development plan 1962–1966 (in Korean). Economic Planning Board, Seoul

Frank, CR, Kim KS, Westphal LE (1975) Foreign trade regimes and economic development. NBER, South Korea, New York

Fukuyama, F (2012) China and East Asian democracy the patents of history. Journal of Democracy 23(1):14–26

Galbraith JK, Kim J (1998) The legacy of the HCI: an empirical analysis of Korean industrial policy. J Econ Dev 23:1–20

Garz D (2015) Going away. Going home! Coming home? The migration of Korean nurses and miners to Germany and their return in retirement to Korea's German village—together with their German husbands. OMNES: J Multicult Soc 6(1):161–183. https://doi.org/10.15685/omnes.2015.07.6.1.161

Glawe L,Wagner H (2016) The middle-income trap - definitions, theories and countries concerned: a literature survey. Comp Econ Stud 58(4):507–538

Gon CS, Gyun PT (2013) Suggestions for new perspectives on the land reform in South Korea. Seoul J Korean Stud 26(1):1–21

Graham EM (2003a) The miracle with a dark side: Korean economic development under Park Chung–hee. In: Reforming Korea's industrial conglomerate. Peterson Institute for International Economics, Washington DC

Graham EM (2003b) The 1997–98 crisis and its aftermath. In: Reforming Korea's industrial conglomerate. Peterson Institute for International Economics, Washington DC

Haggard S, Kim B-K, Moon C-I (1991) The transition to export-led growth in South Korea: 1954–1966. J Asian Stud 50(4):850–873. https://doi.org/10.2307/2058544

Haggard S, Pinkston D, Seo J (1999) Reforming Korea Inc.: the politics of structural adjustments under Kim Dae Jung. Asian Perspect 23(3):201–235

Hamilton N, Kim EM (1993) Economic and political liberalisation in South Korea and Mexico. Third World Q 14:109–136

Han S-J (1974) The failure of democracy in South Korea. University of California Press, Berkeley

Harbison FH, Myers CS (1964) Education, manpower, and economic growth. McGraw-Hill, New York

Harris L (1987) Financial reform and economic growth: a new interpretation of South Korea's experience. In: Harris L et al (eds) New perspectives on the financial system. Croom Helm, London

Heo U, Woo J-Y (2006) South Korea's experience with structural reform: lessons for other countries. Korean Soc Sci J 33:1–24

Hill H (1996) Indonesia's industrial policy and performance: "orthodoxy" vindicated. Econ Dev Cult Change 45(1):147–174

Hirschman AO (1958) The strategy of economic development. Yale University Press, New Haven

Hong W, Krueger AO (eds) (1975) Trade and development in Korea. Korea Development Institute, Seoul

Horikane Y (2005) The political economy of heavy industrialisation: the heavy and chemical industry (HCI) push in South Korea in the 1970s. Mod Asian Stud 39(2):369–397

Hundt D (2008) Korea's developmental alliance: state, capital and the politics of rapid development. Routledge

Hwang E-G (1993) The Korean economies; a comparison of north and south. Clarendon Press, Oxford

ILO (2012) Republic of Korea—development of national employment policies through two economic crises: lessons from its experiences. International Labour Office, Geneva

IMF (2000a) Recovery from the Asian crisis and the role of the IMF. International Monetary Fund, Washington DC. https://www.imf.org/external/np/exr/ib/2000/062300.htm#box2

IMF (2000b) Republic of Korea: economic and policy developments. IMF Staff Country Report No 00/11, International Monetary Fund, Washington DC

IMF (2021) International financial statistics. https://data.imf.org/?sk=4c514d48-b6ba-49ed-8ab9-52b0c1a0179b

Jeon BN (2012) from the 1997–98 Asian financial crisis to the 2008–09 global economic crisis: lessons from Korea's experience. MPRA Working Paper 36469

Jeon Y-D, Kim Y-Y (2000) Land reform, income redistribution, and agricultural production in Korea. Econ Dev Cult Change 48(2):253–268

Jones LP, Sakong I (1980) Government, business, and entrepreneurship in economic development: the Korean case. Harvard University Press, Cambridge, MA

Jung J, Mah JS (2013) R&D policies of Korea and their implications for developing countries. Sci Technol Soc 18(2):165–188. https://doi.org/10.1177/0971721813489435

Kang K, Lee Y, Choi S (2008) Korean policymaking systems during the rapid development period: Economic Planning Board and policy implementation. Korean Development Institute, Seoul

Kang TW (1989) Is Korea the next Japan?: understanding the structure, strategy, and tactics of America's next competitor. The Free Press, New York

Kang G-H (2000) Five year economic development plan (in Korean). Seoul University Press, Seoul

Kihwan K (2006) The 1997–98 Korean financial crisis: causes, policy response, and lessons. Paper presented at the high level seminar on crisis prevention in emerging markets, International Monetary Fund and The Government of Singapore, Singapore, 10–11 June 2006

Kim C, Shin I (2003) Economic liberalization of Korea for an advanced market economy. Working Paper 2003-03, Korea Development Institute, Seoul

Kim D (2002) The Korean labor market: the crisis and after. In: Coe DT, Kim S-J (eds) Korean crisis and recovery. International Monetary Fund, Washington DC, Korea Institute for International Economic Policy, Seoul, pp. 261–292

Kim DK, Seong HW (1997) Science and technology: public policy and private strategy. In: Cha D-S, Kim KS, Perkins DH (eds) The Korean economy 1945–1995: performance and vision for the 21st century. Korea Development Institute, Seoul, pp 383–425

Kim H-B, Lee CH (2006) Financial reform, institutional interdependency, and supervisory failure in postcrisis Korea. J East Asian Stud 6(3):409–431

Kim I (2016) Land reform in South Korea under the U.S. military occupation, 1945–1948. J Cold War Stud 18(2):97–129. https://doi.org/10.1162/JCWS_a_00639

Kim JD, Wang Y (1996) Toward liberalisation of international direct investment in Korea: retrospects and prospects. KIEP Working Paper, No 96-02, Korea Institute for International Economic Policy, Seoul

Kim JH (1990) Korean industrial policy in the 1970's: the heavy and chemical industry drive. Korea Development Institute, Seoul

Kim J-K (1998a) Debt and financial instability in Korea. ERI Working Paper No 69, Economic and Social Research Institute, Tokyo

Kim K (1998b) Technology transfer: the case of the Korean electronics industry. Paper presented at the thirty-first Hawaii international conference on system sciences, Kohala Coast, HI, 9 January 1998. https://doi.org/10.1109/HICSS.1998.654779

Kim KM (2020) The Korean development state. Palgrave Macmillan, Singapore

Kim KS (1991) The Korean miracle (1962–1980) revisited: myths and realities in strategy and development. Kellogg Institute Working Paper 166, University of Notre Dame, Helen Kellogg Institute for International Studies, Notre Dame IN

Kim KS (2000) The 1997 financial crisis and governance: the case of South Korea. Kellogg Institute Working Paper 272, University of Notre Dame, Helen Kellogg Institute for International Studies, Notre Dame IN

Kim K-S, Park J-K (1985) Sources of economic growth in Korea: 1963–1982. Korea Development Institute, Sejong City

Kim KS, Roemer M (1979) Growth and structural transformation. Harvard University Council on East Asian Studies, Cambridge, MA

Kim L (1993) National system of industrial innovation: dynamics of capability building in Korea. In: Nelson J (ed) National innovation and technology learning

Kim P-J (1997) Financial policies and evolution. In: Cha D-S, Kim KS, Perkins DH (eds) The Korean economy 1945–1995: performance and vision for the 21st century. Korea Development Institute, Seoul, pp 186–237

Kim Q-Y (1983) The fall of Syngman Rhee. Institute of East Asian Studies, Korea Research Monograph #7, University of California, Berkeley

Kim S, Lee J-H (1997) Industrial relations and human resource development. In: Cha D-S, Kim KS, Perkins DH (eds) The Korean economy 1945–1995: performance and vision for the 21st century. Korea Development Institute, Seoul, pp 586–622

Kim S, Lee J-H (2002) The secondary school equalization policy in South Korea. Unpublished Working Paper, University of Wisconsin-Milwaukee, W and KDI School of Public Policy and Management, Seoul

Kim SJ (1970) South Korea's involvement in Vietnam and its economic and political impact. Asian Surv 10(6):519–532. https://doi.org/10.2307/2642884. https://www.jstor.org/stable/2642884

Kim SK, Kim J-K (1997) Korean economic development: an overview. In: Cha D-S, Kim KS, Perkins DH (eds) The Korean economy 1945–1995: performance and vision for the 21st century. Korea Development Institute, Seoul, pp 3–56

Kim S-M, Kim J-Y, Ryoo H-T (2006) Restructuring and reforms in the Korean banking industry. In: BIS (ed) The banking system in emerging economies: how much progress has been made? Bank for International Settlements, Basel, BIS Papers No 28, pp 259–68

Kim ST (2010) Korea's unemployment insurance in the 1998 Asian financial crisis and adjustments in the 2008 global financial crisis. ABDI Working Paper No 214, Asian Development Bank Institute, Tokyo

Kim Y-S (1992) Korea's technology policy for industrialization: imported technology for economic development. Korea J Popul Dev 21:85–98

Koener P, Maass G, Siebold T, Tetzlaff R (1986) The IMF and the debt crisis: a guide to the Third World's dilemma. Zed Books, London

Koo J-H (2011) corporate restructuring in Korea following the global financial crisis. Wkly Financ Rev 20(10):1–10

Krause LB (1997) The political economy of South Korea: 50 years of macroeconomic management, 1945–1995. In: Cha D-S, Kim KS, Perkins DH (eds) The Korean economy 1945–1995: performance and vision for the 21st century. Korea Development Institute, Seoul, pp 101–142

Krueger AO (1979) The developmental role of the foreign sector and aid. Council on East Asian studies. Harvard University, Cambridge, MA

Krueger AO (1977) Growth, distortions and patterns of trade among many countries. Princeton Studies in International Finance, no. 40. International Finance Section, Dept. of Economics, Princeton University, Princeton

Krueger AO (1982) Comparative advantage and development policy 20 years later. IUI Working Paper No 65, The Research Institute of Industrial Economics (IUI), Stockholm

Krueger AO (1997) Trade policy and economic development: how we learn. Am Econ Rev 87 (1):1–22

Krueger AO, Yoo J (2002) Chaebol capitalism and the currency-financial crisis in Korea. In: Edwards S, Frankel JA (eds) Preventing currency crises in emerging markets. University of Chicago Press, Chicago

Kwack S (2000) Total factor productivity growth and the source of growth in Korean manufacturing industries, 1971–1993. J Korean Econ 1(2):229–265

Kwack T (1984) Industrial restructuring experience and policies in Korea in the 1970s. KDI Working Paper 84-08, Korea Development Institute, Sejong-City

Kwack T-W (1985) Depreciation allowance and capital income taxation (in Korean). Korea Development Institute, Seoul

Kwon O-K (2016) Corporate restructuring in Korea. Korea Development Institute, Sejong City

Kwon OY (1998) The Korean financial crisis: diagnosis, remedies and prospects. J Asia Pac Econ 3(3):331–357. https://doi.org/10.1080/13547869808724656

Lal D (1986) Ideology and Industrialization in India and East Asia. Development Research Department Report 218, World Bank, Washington DC. https://documents1.worldbank.org/curated/en/593101468266445242/text/DRD21800Box37700India0and0East0Asia.txt

Lane N (2019) Manufacturing revolutions—industrial policy and industrialization in South Korea. Working Paper. https://nathanlane.github.io/assets/papers/ManufacturingRevolutions_Lane_Live.pdf (author's homepage). A summary is available at VoxDev. https://voxdev.org/topic/firms-trade/manufacturing-revolutions-role-industrial-policy-south-korea-s-industrialisation

Lee B-C (1999a) Park Chung-hee administration and a developing country model formation (in Korean). J Korean Econ Dev 5(2):141–187

Lee CH, Lee K, Lee K (2000) Chaebol, financial liberalization, and economic crisis: transformation of quasi-internal organization in Korea. Working Papers 200004, University of Hawaii at Manoa, Department of Economics, Honolulu HI

Lee CJ (2008) Education in the Republic of Korea: approaches, achievements, and current challenges. In: Fredricksen B, Tan JP (eds) An African exploration of the East Asian education experiences. World Bank, Washington DC, pp 157–217

Lee CJ, Kim Y, Byun S-Y (2012a) The rise of Korean education from the ashes of the Korean War. Prospects 42:303–318. https://doi.org/10.1007/s11125-012-9239-5

Lee D, Sohn C-K, Kim Y-Q (1984) Recent developments of financial system in Korea. Economic Research Institute Discussion Paper 30, Economic Planning Agency, Tokyo

Lee J (1996) Government interventions and productivity growth. Journal of Economic Growth 1 (3):391–414

Lee H, Rhee C (2012) Lessons from the 1997 and the 2008 crisis in the Republic of Korea. ADB Working Paper 298, Asian Development Bank, Manila

Lee H-H (1999b) Korea's 1997 financial crisis: causes, consequences, and prospects. Agenda: J Policy Anal Reform 6(4):351–363

Lee J-W (2017a) Twenty years after the financial crisis in the Republic of Korea. ADBI Working Paper 790, Asian Development Bank Institute, Tokyo

Lee J, Yi D (2018) Still a new democracy? Individual-level effects of social trust on political trust in South Korea. Asian Journal of Political Science 26(2):201–220

Lee J-W, Rhee C (2007) Crisis and recovery: what we have learned from the South Korean experience? Asian Econ Policy Rev 2:146–164. https://doi.org/10.1111/j.1748-3131.2007.00061.x

Lee K, Kim B-K, Lee CH et al (2005) Visible success and invisible failure in post-crisis reform in the Republic of Korea: interplay of global standards, agents, and local specificity. World Bank Policy Research Paper 3651, World Bank, Washington DC

Lee K-S (2017b) The Korean financial crisis of 1997: onset, turnaround, and thereafter. World Bank, Korea Development Institute, Washington DC, Seoul

Lee S, Kim S, Han S-H (1989) Industrial policy of Korea (in Korean). Korea Institute for Industrial Economics and Trade, Seoul

Lee S-C (1991) The heavy and chemical industries promotion plan (1973–1979). In: Cho L-J, Kim YH (eds) Economic development in the Republic of Korea: a policy perspective, chapter 17. East-West Center, University of Hawaii Press, Honolulu, Hawaii, pp 431–471

Lee Y (2005) Participatory democracy and Chaebol regulation in Korea: state-market relations under the MDP governments, 1997–2003. Asian Surv 45(2):279–301

Leiteritz RJ (2014) Capital account policy in South Korea: the informal residues of the development state. Colomb Int 83:235–265. https://doi.org/10.7440/colombiaint83.2015.09

Lew, SC (2013) Confucian Capitalism of Park Chung Hee: possibilities and limits. In: Lew SC (ed) The Korean economic developmental path. Palgrave Macmillan, New York. https://doi.org/10.1057/9781137347299_5

Lie J (1998) Han unbound: the political economy of South Korea. Stanford University Press, Stanford CA

Lim U (2001) Ownership structure and family control in Korean conglomerates. In: Choi JJ (ed) Asian financial crisis financial, structural and international dimensions (International Finance Review, Vol. 1). Emerald Group Publishing Limited, Bingley, pp 379–410. https://doi.org/10.1016/S1569-3767(00)01016-5

Lim W (2010) Corporate restructuring in post-crisis Korea. Ministry of Strategy and Finance, Republic of Korea and Korea Development Institute, Seoul

Lim W (2012) Chaebol and industrial policy in Korea. Asian Econ Policy Rev 7:69–86. https://doi.org/10.1111/j.1748-3131.2012.01218.x

Lim W, Hahm J-H (2006) Turning a crisis into an opportunity: the political economy of Korea's financial sector reform. In: Mo J, Okimoto DI (eds) From crisis to opportunity: financial globalization and East Asian capitalism. Walter H. Shorenstein Asia Pacific Research Center, Stanford CA, pp 83–120

Lone SP, McCormack G (1994) Korea since 1850. Longman, Melbourne, Australia

Luedde-Neurath R (1986) State intervention and export-oriented development: a reassessment of the South Korean case. Westview Press, Boulder CO

Mah JS (2007) Industrial policy and economic development: Korea's experience. J Econ Iss 41:77–92

McKinnon R (1973) Money and capital in economic development. The Brookings Institute, Washington

Mitchell CC (1949) Land reforms in South Korea. Pac Aff 22(2):144–154

Mo J, Moon C-I (2003) Business-government relations under Kim Dae-jung. In: Haggard S, Wonhyuk Lim W, Kim E (eds) Economic crisis and corporate restructuring in Korea. Cambridge University Press, New York, pp 127–149

Mohr B, Wagner H (2012) Regulatory governance and the framework for safeguarding financial stability. In: Tavidze A (ed) Progress in economics research, vol 23. Nova Science Publishers, New York, pp 1–32

Mohr B, Wagner H (2013) A structural approach to financial stability: on the benefical role of regulatory governance. J Gov Regul 2(1):7–26

Moon PY, Sul KE (1997) Agricultural policies and development. In: Cha D-S, Kim KS, Perkins DH (eds) The Korean economy 1945–1995: performance and vision for the 21st century. Korea Development Institute, Seoul, pp 468–508

Morck R, Nakamura M (2007) Business groups and the big push: Meiji Japan's mass privatization and subsequent growth. Enterp Soc 8(3):543–601

Morck R, Yeung B (2017) East Asian Financial and Economic Development. NBER Working Paper 23845, National Bureau of Economic Research, Cambridge, MA

Nam C-H (1993) The role of trade and exchange rate policy in Korea's growth. In: Ito T, Krueger AO (eds) Growth theories in light of the East Asian experience. University of Chicago Press, pp 153–179

Nam S, Kim J-I (1997) Macroeconomic policies and evolution. In: Cha D-S, Kim KS, Perkins DH (eds) The Korean economy 1945–1995: performance and vision for the 21st century. Korea Development Institute, Seoul, pp 143–185.

New York Times (1997) Crisis in South Korea: The Bailout; Package of Loans Worth $55 billion is set for Korea (04.12.1997)

Nicolas F, Thomsen S, Bang M-H (2013) Lessons from Investment Policy Reform in Korea. OECD Working Papers on International Investment 2013/02, OECD Publishing, Paris. https://doi.org/10.1787/5k4376zqcpf1-en

Noland M (2004). Selective intervention and growth: the case of Korea. Working Paper Series WP04-3, Peterson Institute for International Economics

Noland M, Pack H (2003) Industrial policy in an era of globalization: lessons from Asia. Peterson Institute for International Economics, Washington DC

Pak KH (1956) Outcome of land reform in the Republic of Korea. J Farm Econ 38(4):1015–1023

Park J-D (2019b) The essence of the Korean model of development. In: Park J-D (ed) Re-inventing Africa's development. Palgrave Macmillan, Cham. https://doi.org/10.1007/978-3-030-03946-2

Park S-J (2013) Development state in Korea (60–70ties) revisited: institution-building for the making of 'coordinated market'. Ordnungspolitische Diskurse 2013-2, Ordnungspolitisches Portal (OPO)

Park Y (2018) Modern Korean economy 1948–2008. The Academy of Korean Studies, Seongnam

Park YC (1984) Korea's experience with industrial adjustment in the 1970's: promotion of heavy and chemical industries. Paper presented at the International Forum on Industrialization and Urban-Rural Linkages, Seoul, 16–25 October 1984

Park YC (1986) Foreign debt, balance of payments, and growth prospects: the case of the Republic of Korea, 1965–88. World Dev 14(8):1019–1058

Park Y-K (2005) Structural changes and the drive to heavy and chemical industry. In: Lee D (ed) New Korean economic history: from the late Joseon period to the high growth period of the 20th century (in Korean), Seoul, pp 403–428

Pecotich A, Shultz CJ (2006) Handbook of markets and economies: East Asia, Southeast Asia, Australia, New Zealand. Routledge, London

Perkins DH (1997) Structural transformation and the role of the state: Korea, 1945–1995. In: Cha DS, Kim KS, Perkins DH (eds) The Korean economy 1945–1995: performance and vision for the 21st century, Chapter 12. Korea Development Institute, Seoul, pp 57–98

Radelet S, Sachs J, Cooper RN et al (1998) The East Asian financial crisis: diagnosis, remedies, prospects. Brook Papers Econ Activity 1:1–90

Radelet S, Sachs J, Lee J-W (1997) Economic growth in Asia. Harvard Institute for International Development, Cambridge, MA

Rhee S (1987) Policy reforms of the eighties and industrial adjustments in Korean economy. KDI Working Paper 8708, Korea Development Institute, Seoul

Rodrik D (1995) Getting interventions right: how South Korea and Taiwan grew rich. Econ Policy 10(20):55–107

Roemer, M (1994) Industrial strategies: outward bound. In: Lindauer DL, Roemer M (eds) Asia and Africa: legacies and opportunities in development. Institute for Contemporary Studies Press, San Francisco

Rosenstein-Rodan PN (1943) Problems of industrialisation of Eastern and South-Eastern Europe. Econ J 53(210/211):202–211

SaKong I (1993) Korea in the world economy. Institute for International Economics, Washington DC

Sakong I, Koh Y (eds) (2010) The Korean economy: six decades of growth and development. Korea Development Institute, Seoul

Seth MJ (2017) South Korea's economic development, 1948–1996. Oxford research encyclopedias. Asian Hist. https://doi.org/10.1093/acrefore/9780190277727.013.271

Shaw E (1973) Financial deepening in economic development. Oxford University, New York

Shim U-S (2015) South Korean workers and the Middle East construction boom in the 1970s. J Contemp Korean Stud 2(1):37–56

Shin J-S, Chang H-J (2003) Restructuring Korea Inc. Routledge Curzon, London

Shin Y-H (1976) Land reform in Korea, 1950. Bull Popul Dev Stud Center 5:14–31

Sorensen CW (1994) Success and education in South Korea. Comp Educ Preview 38:10–35

Sta. Romana LL (2014) Some lessons from Korea's industrialization strategy and experience. MPRA Paper No 58250, Munich Personal RePEc Archive, Munich

Stern J, Kim JH, Perkins DH (1995) Industrialization and the state: the Korean heavy and chemical industry drive. Harvard University Press

Suh S (2007) The influence of foreigners' stock investment on Korean stock prices and its implications. Bank Korea Econ Papers 9(2):123–161. Bank of Korea, Seoul

Tsutsumi M, Jones RS, Cargill TF (2010) The Korean financial system: overcoming the global financial crisis and addressing remaining problems. OECD Economics Department Working Papers 796, OECD, Paris

Wagner H (2010) The causes of the recent financial crisis and the role of central banks in avoiding the next one. Int Econ Econ Policy 7(1):63–82

World Bank (2021) World development indicators. The World Bank, Washington, DC.https://data.worldbank.org/products/wdi

Yang J-J (2006) Corporate unionism and labor market flexibility in South Korea. J East Asian Stud 6(2):205–231

Yeon J-I, Pyka A, Kim T-Y (2016) Structural shift and increasing variety in Korea, 1960–2010: empirical evidence of the economic development model by the creation of new sectors. Hohenheim Discussion Papers in Business, Economics and Social Sciences, No 12-2016, Universität Hohenheim, Stuttgart

Yoo J (1989) The Korean experience with industrial targeting policy. Korea Institute for International Economic Policy, Seoul

Yoo J (2017) Korea's rapid export expansion in the 1960s: how it began. KDI. J Econ Policy 39 (2):1–23. https://doi.org/10.23895/kdijep.2017.39.2.1

Yoo, J (1990) The industrial policy of the 1970s and the evolution of the manufacturing sector in Korea. KDI Working Paper No. 9017, Korean Development Institute, Seoul

Yoo J (1991) The effect of heavy and chemical industry policy of the 1970s on the capital efficiency and export competitiveness of Korean manufacturing Industries (in Korean). Korea Dev Rev 13(1):65–113

Yoon DR (2011) The Korean economic adjustment to the worst financial crisis. Asian Econ Papers 10(1):106–127

Yoon J-H (2006) Korean technology policy (in Korean). KyungMun Publishing, Seoul

Zeile W (1991) Industrial targeting through government rationing: the Korean experience in the 1970s. Program in East Asian Culture and Development Research Working Paper Series, No. 41. Institute of Government Affairs, University of California, Davis CA

4 The Rise of China

List of Abbreviations

ABC	Agricultural Bank of China
ADBC	Agricultural Development Bank of China
AMC	Asset-Management Company
AML	Anti-Monopoly Law
BIC	Beneficial International Cycle
BMI	Basic Medical Insurance
BOC	Bank of China
BOCOM	Bank of Communications
CBRC	China Banking Regulatory Commission
CCB	China Construction Bank
CDBC	China Development Bank Corporation
CDS	Coastal Development Strategy
CEIB	China Export–Import Bank
CFETS	China Foreign Exchange Trading System
CHN	Chinese
CIS	Commonwealth of Independent States
CJV	Contractual Joint Venture
CPC	Communist Party of China
CPI	Consumer Price Index
EEBP	Enterprise Employee Basic Pension
EJV	Equity Joint Venture
EPZ	Export Processing Zone
ETDZ	Economic and Technological Development Zone
FDI	Foreign Direct Investment

L. Glawe and H. Wagner, *The Economic Rise of East Asia*,
Contributions to Economics, https://doi.org/10.1007/978-3-030-87128-4_4

FEAC	Foreign Exchange Adjustment Center
FIE	Foreign Invested Enterprise
FTC	Foreign Trade Corporation
GATT	General Agreement on Tariffs and Trade
GDP	Gross Domestic Product
GIP	Government Institution Pension
HRS	Household Responsibility System
Hukou	Household Registration System
ICBC	Industrial and Commercial Bank of China
IMF	International Monetary Fund
IPO	Initial Public Offering
IT	Information Technology
ITA	Information Technology Agreement
JSCB	Joint-Stock Commercial Bank
JV	Joint Venture
KMT	Kuomintang
M&E	Machinery and Electronic Equipment
MLP	Medium- and Long-Term Program of Science and Technology
MLSP	Minimum Living Standard Program
MOF	Ministry of Finance
NBFI	Non-Bank Financial Institution
NCMS	Rural Cooperative Medical Schemes
NDRC	National Development and Reform Commission
NEV	New-energy Vehicle
New M&A Regulations	Regulations Concerning the Merger and Acquisition of Domestic Enterprises by Foreign Investors
NPL	Nonperforming Loan
NUP	New-type Urbanization Plan
PBC	People's Bank of China
PC	Personal Computer
PPP	Purchasing Power Parity
PRC	People's Republic of China
R&D	Research and Development
RDA	Regionally decentralized authoritarian
RMB	Renminbi
RRC	Rural Credit Cooperative
SASAC	State-Owned Assets Supervision and Administration Commission
SAT	State Administration of Taxation
SCM	Subsidies and Countervailing Measures
SEI	Strategic Emerging Industry
SEZ	Special Economic Zone

SOE	State-Owned Enterprise
SRC	System Reform Commission
TFP	Total Factor Productivity
TSS	Tax Sharing System
TVE	Township and Village Enterprise
UCC	Urban Credit Cooperative
URBMI	Urban Residents Basic Medical Insurance
URRSP	Urban–Rural Resident Basic Social Pension Scheme
US	United States of America
VAT	Value-Added Tax
WFOE	Wholly Foreign Owned Enterprise
WTO	World Trade Organization

4.1 Introduction

China presents probably the most astonishing growth miracle in modern world history. In 1978, China was still one of the poorest countries in the world with a per capita income even lower than that of many poor African countries (for instance, it was only 60% of that of Niger according to World Bank data, constant US$2010, see also Fig. 4.1). The population living in absolute poverty was as high as 97.5% (UNDP 2019).[1] However, since the beginning of reforms under Deng Xiaoping in 1978, more than 850 million people have been lifted out of poverty, and in 2016, the share of the Chinese population living at less than $1.90 a day accounted to only 0.5% (World Bank 2020).[2]

During the reform process, the Chinese economy has seen phenomenal growth with an average growth rate of almost 9% between 1978 and 2010, leading to an almost 15-fold increase in per capita income (see also Fig. 4.2). Today, China accounts for the largest share in global GDP (18.56% vs. 15.98% of the USA, based on PPP, IMF WEO 2020).

Interestingly, China was once already one of the world's leading economic and technological nations, namely, prior to the Industrial Revolution. Around 1000, that is, during the Song dynasty, China's GDP per capita was even above that of Western Europe according to estimates of Angus Maddison. However, by 1820, China had a GDP per capita of only 50%[3] of that of Western Europe, and by 1973, this number has further decreased to 7.3% (see Brandt et al. 2014).

[1] UNDP https://www.cn.undp.org/content/china/en/home/ourperspective/ourperspectivearticles/2019/what-changes-after-china-defeats-poverty-.html.

[2] See also https://www.worldbank.org/en/country/china/overview#1.

[3] This view is challenged by Pomeranz (2000) who argues that per capita income in Western Europe and China has been roughly equal until 1800. See also Sect. 4.2.

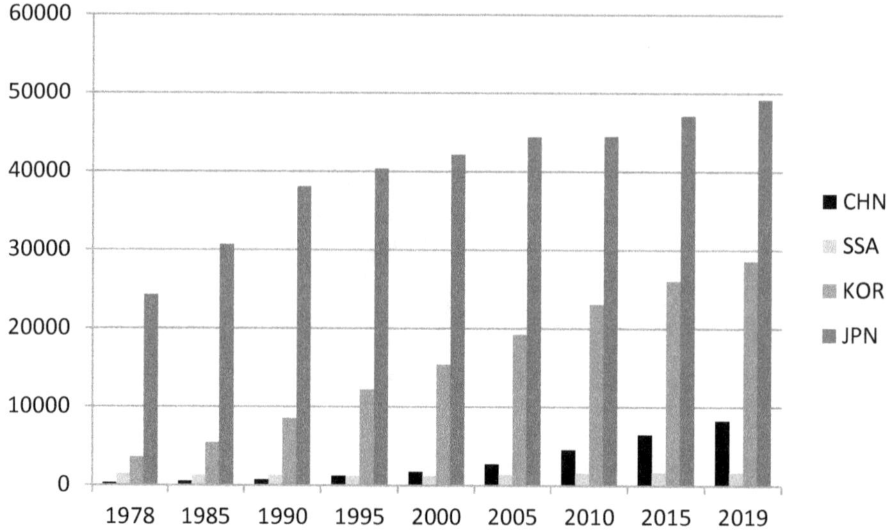

Fig. 4.1 China's per capita income in comparison, 1978–2019. *Source* World Bank (2021). *Notes* GDP per capita in constant US$2010. "SSA" stands for Sub-Saharan Africa

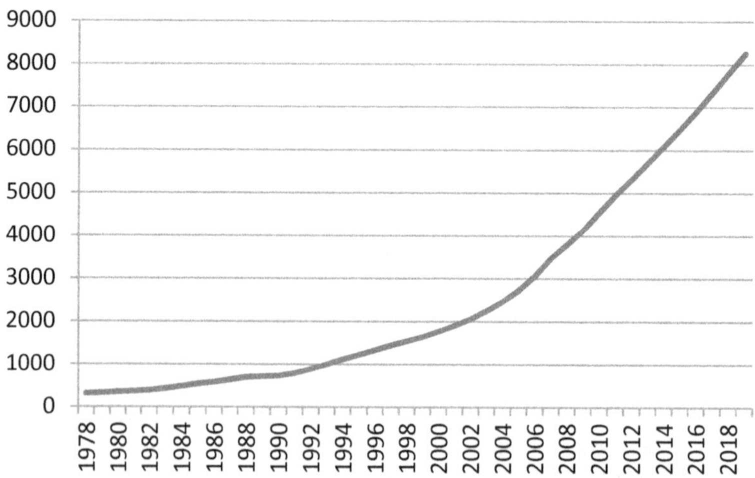

Fig. 4.2 China's per capita income, 1978–2019. *Source* World Bank (2021). *Notes* GDP per capita in constant US$2010

Phases of economic development

China's economic development process can be subdivided into various phases, very broadly speaking into the **historical roots** (here we cover the Song dynasty (960–1279) as well as the Ming (1368–1644) and Qing (1636–1911) dynasties), the **pre-1978-reform era** (in particular the phase of the Republic of China (1912–1949) and the phase of the centrally planned economy under Mao Zedong (1949–1977)), and the **post-1978 reform era** on which we focus primarily in this Chapter.

The **post-1978 reform era** can itself be subdivided into various sub-phases, the initial phase with a focus on agricultural reforms (1978–1984), the industrial reform with a special focus on Township and Village Enterprises and the dual-track strategy (1985–1992), the phase of extensive liberalization and institutional restructuring (including the reform of the fiscal and tax system, the banking and financial system, and the SOEs reform) (1992/3–2003), the phase of reform slowdown and return of industrial policy (starting from 2003). Sometimes, researchers also insert a reform phase starting from 2001 onwards (the year when China joined the WTO). More recently, researchers also identify a phase of "re-balancing" that started around 2011/2012 when Xi Jinping came to power (cf. Wagner 2019).

Hofman (2019) distinguishes between only three broader reform phases, namely, the phase of market-seeking reforms (1978–1993), the phase of market-building reforms (1993–2003), and the phase of market-enhancing reforms (since 2003). This broader classification does however not contradict the one presented above, it just summarizes some of the smaller sub-phases.

Characteristics of the Chinese reform approach since 1978

Under Deng Xiaoping, China followed a **gradualist, evolutionary, and experimental reform strategy** (Prasad and Rajan 2006: 331; Rawski 1994: 272). Deng aptly described the economic reform process by the metaphor "crossing the river by feeling the stones", reflecting that there was **no blueprint** when the reforms started in 1978, but the reform strategy rather resembled "a process of trial and error". The main goal was known ("crossing the river", that is, reforming the country toward a market economy), but not the steps necessary in order to achieve it. Reformers focused on making the first step ("stone") and once this was successfully accomplished, the situation was re-evaluated and the next reform step was adapted to the changed environment. As put by Naughton (2018: 156), "the genius of China's transition process was not that it was gradual—after all, walking slowly is not better than walking faster if you know where you are going—but rather the specific policy packages are well suited to the specific requirements of rapidly changing institutions". Deng Xiaoping had also a rather **pragmatic approach** to reform, captured by the famous quote: "It doesn't matter whether a cat is black or white, as long as it catches mice". Economic development was regarded as essential for the survival of the regime and thus became top priority (Xu 2011).

China's economic reforms followed a "**stop–go cycle**" (Zhang and Yi 1997; Wang 1993). According to Naughton (2018), the first reform phase (1978–1984) can be interpreted as an initial (rural) breakthrough, which was followed by two phases of accelerated market reforms (from 1984 to 1989 and from 1993 to 1999). Reforms were more cautious after the Tiananmen Square political crisis in 1989 as well as the rising inflation at around the same time. Between 1989 and 1992, conservatives tried to even reverse reform measures. However, the earlier initiated reforms unfolded an unexpected positive economic dynamism that even surprised the reform critics. In addition, no major social group had incurred economic losses during this period. It was for these reasons that the reform soon gained momentum at the beginning of the 1990s. Over all, the reform pullbacks were less than the forward measures, and over time the gradual reforms accumulated into a radical change (Zhang and Yi 1997).

Another key feature of China's reform approach was the **regionally decentralized authoritarian (RDA) regime**, a term coined by Xu (2011). The RDA regime presented a "combination of political centralization and economic regional decentralization". While political power was delegated to subnational governments which were responsible for executing economic reforms, the career paths of regional officials were controlled by the central government, presenting a powerful incentive mechanism (Xu 2011). In particular, the central government appointed and promoted provincial leaders, which in turn controlled municipal leaders. It was through this "nested network" that the central government's personnel control was extended to officials at all levels (Burns 1994). Each subnational government level had to fulfil performance criteria which were usually broader for higher level officials and more precisely defined for officials in lower level governments. Rotation and cross-region transfer were employed to ensure the diffusion of successful regional experimentation (and probably also to prevent local officials from becoming too popular in a specific region). See also Xu (2011) for an excellent discussion of these aspects.

The centrally controlled regional decentralization had various benefits. Among others, it allowed **experimenting** with new reforms at the regional level. Since these experiments often involved high political risks, restricting them to certain areas ensured that in case of a failure, the stability of the overall economy would not be seriously affected. Instead, the negative effects would be restricted to the region in which the experiment was conducted. Moreover, since the central leaders usually implicitly tolerated these reforms instead of clearly committing to them, they would not be seriously responsible for any adverse effects and thus their legitimacy would not be threatened. In addition, Chinese leaders were not really experienced in conducting market-oriented reforms. Therefore, a geographically restricted implementation (for instance, in the so-called special economic zones which served as a kind of reform "laboratories", see also Sect. 4.4.6) allowed to test the effectiveness of the reforms before applying them nationwide. Finally, after the initial reforms proved successful, the opposition to reform was significantly reduced. This strategy of regional experimentation also led to another characteristic of the China's reform process, namely, that there has been great regional variation with respect to the reform progress (Zhang and Yi 1997). In particular, the reforms started in the coastal regions and then spread to the interior. This is also reflected in the starkly varying level of economic development across Chinese provinces.

Box 4.1 Characteristics of the Chinese Reform Strategy Since 1978

(1) **gradualist**, **evolutionary**, and **experimental** reform strategy

- "a process of trial and error" meaning that there was no blueprint
- "crossing the river by feeling the stones".

(2) **pragmatic approach** to reform

- "It doesn't matter whether a cat is black or white, as long as it catches mice".

(3) **stop–go cycle**

- initial (rural) breakthrough (1978–1984)
- accelerated market reforms (1984–1989)
- more careful reforms, rising conservatism (1989–1992)
- accelerated market reforms (1993–1999)
- especially since 2003 reform slowdown.

(4) **regionally decentralized authoritarian (RDA) regime**

- combination of political centralization and economic regional decentralization
- diffusion of successful regional experimentation through cross-region transfer of officials
- allowance of experimenting (geographically restricted implementation is less risky).

China's gradual economic reform stands in sharp contrast to the "big bang" approach adopted by the Eastern European countries and the former Soviet Union after 1991 (McMillan and Naughton 1992; Jefferson and Rawski 1994; Hofman 2019). According to Wang (1993), a big bang strategy can be understood as a comprehensive reform program implemented with one stroke. The standard reform package of the Washington Consensus postulated by international organizations such as the World Bank and the IMF included privatization, liberalization, and macroeconomic stabilization. In contrast, a gradualist reform strategy implies that the reform program is implemented in a sequential and evolutionary fashion. In China, privatization and reforms of the state sector were only introduced in later reform stages. Also, price liberalization occurred rather gradually under the dual-track system. Institutions were adapted if necessary and kept otherwise.

Box 4.2 Big Bang Versus Gradualism

Wei (1997) surveys the main arguments in favor of the big bang and gradualist reform approach, respectively:

Arguments in favor of a big bang approach

- critical mass of privatization can be achieved (increases efficiency of private firms) (Roland and Verdier 1994).
- increased reform credibility (Lipton and Sachs 1990a, b).
- reform opponents have no time to organize themselves (Krueger 1993).
- not afflicted by time inconsistency problems (in case that the program needs consensus approval) (Martinelli and Tommasi 1995).
- benefits unfold faster (World Bank 1991).

Arguments in favor of a gradual approach

- avoids excessive costs (for the government budget) (Dewatripont and Roland 1992; Nielsen 1993).
- avoids an excessive reduction in living standards at an early reform stage (Wang 1992).
- enables room for experimentation (trial and error processes) and adjustment of policies (World Bank 1991).
- government can gain incremental credibility (Fang 1992).

Figure 4.3 compares the growth rate of China which followed a gradual approach with that of Russia and Commonwealth of Independent States (CIS) countries after the beginning of reforms (1978 for China and 1991 for Russia and the CIS countries). Strikingly, China's transition was relatively smooth whereas the growth rate of Russia and the CIS countries plummeted during the first years.

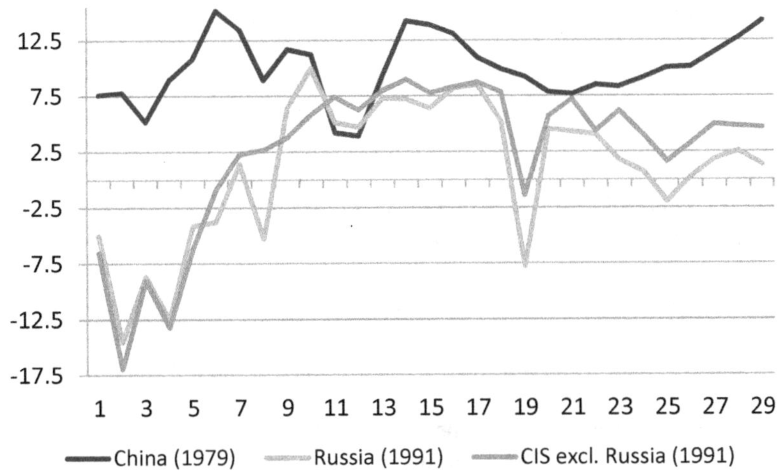

Fig. 4.3 Growth rates since the start of reforms—gradualism versus big bang. *Source* World Bank (2021). *Notes* Growth rate of GDP in constant US$2010. "1" denotes the initial year of economic reforms. "CIS" stands for "Commonwealth of Independent States"

According to Hofman (2019), China benefited greatly from the fact that the state and the ruling party remained intact which allowed the country to focus primarily on the economic reforms whereas many former Soviet Union and Eastern European countries had to cope additionally with the collapse of the political system.

4.2 Historical Roots

> China has long been one of the richest, that is, one of the most vital, best cultivated, most industrious, and most populous countries in the world. It seems, however, to have been long stationary (Smith 1776).

In this section, we will briefly summarize China's economic history between 960 and 1927. An excellent overview of China's historical roots is provided by Brandt et al. (2014).

During the Song (960–1279) dynasty and the preceding Tang (618–907) dynasty, China underwent not only a significant institutional change but also experienced major technological progress. Important innovations include gunpowder, woodblock printing, magnetic compass, and shipbuilding (Brandt et al. 2014). The latter two technological advances also enabled an extensive overseas trade. Central institutional reforms included the strengthening of emperor's political control, the introduction of a tax system based on registration and privately held land assessment, a merit-based civil service staffed by commoners, the selection of officials according to written examinations, and the large-scale development of private commerce (cf. Brandt et al. 2014). Various economists argue that the Song period was characterized by significant increases in per capita income and urbanization (cf. also Jones 1988; Maddison 2001; Brandt et al. 2014; however this "Song peak" hypothesis is disputed among researchers).

Agriculture was extremely productive thanks to the "traditional triad" of foreign technology which was developed in a trial and error process and that consisted of selected seed varieties, organic fertilizer, and sophisticated irrigation systems (Naughton 2018). These technological breakthroughs were largely responsible for the economic and cultural development in Southern Song. However, this agricultural system was highly labor-intensive and the labor productivity was relatively low.

However, between 1500 and 1800, China's per capita income stagnated, whereas Western Europe experienced continued growth. One main reason is that innovation and commercial activities in China were hampered because of the more centralized and inward looking political system that developed during the Ming and Qing dynasties (the former lasting between 1368 and 1644 and the latter between 1644 and 1911) (cf. Zhu 2012). It has to be noted that some economists and historians argue that it was not until the Industrial Revolution that China started to fall behind Western Europe (cf. Pomeranz 2000; Brandt et al. 2014; see also Box 4.3). Moreover, Pomeranz (2000) emphasizes that comparing specific Chinese and European *regions* with each other (rather than focusing on entire countries) could provide more informative insights with respect to the living standards at that time. More recent studies followed this approach, including Allen et al. (2011) and Li and Van Zanden (2012). Overall, the results of these studies indicate that China's relatively well-developed regions (including the Yangtze River Delta) could compete globally but were still outpaced by the most advanced countries such as Great Britain and the Netherlands (Naughton 2018).

Box 4.3 Why Did the Industrial Revolution Not Originate in China?

The fact that the Industrial Revolution did not originate in China despite the various technological innovation is often referred to as the "Needham puzzle" (Lin 1995).[4] Overall, during various phases of China's history, the country was technologically innovative and the agricultural productivity in fertile areas such as the Yangtze Delta was sufficiently high to support a dense population (Acemoglu 2009: 867). However, China's imperial system of governance and the hierarchically organized society structure prevented the entry of new entrepreneurs into business and thus a potential important source for initiating a process of creative destruction; economic activity (including internal and external trade) was strictly regulated (Knight and Ding 2012). In order to maintain political and social stability, China's elite even accepted a worsening economic performance. For instance, property rights and contracting institutions as well as a strong autonomous middle class which

[4] Also referred to as "The Needham Question" (after Joseph Needham who conducted research on the history of science and technology in China, particularly regarding the question of why China had been overtaken by the West, cf. Needham 1969).

usually can promote economic growth were not developed (Acemoglu 2009; Elvin 1973; Mokyr 1990; Wong 1997). Brandt et al. (2014) list five key aspects for why China's imperial systems prevented China to undergo an Industrial Revolution, namely (1–3), the lack of vision, fiscal capacity, and growth-enhancing administrative structures (state capacity), (4) patronage structures which enhanced corruption and impeded innovative activities, and (5) the interlocking of elite interests (imperial households, members of bureaucracy, the intellectual/commercial/landed elites) which made the imperial system resistant to change that could have threatened the position of the elites. According to Pomeranz (2000), Western Europe (particularly Great Britain) also had various region-specific advantages compared to China, including the access to coal and colonies (and thus, to land-intensive products) (Brandt et al. 2014).

Various wars since the middle of the nineteenth century eventually led to the collapse of the Qing dynasty (Zhu 2012). Foreign powers increasingly gained more impact on China's policy and economy. The most important developments will be briefly described in the following.

The **two opium wars** (the first from 1839 to 1845 between Qing and Great Britain and the second from 1856 to 1860 between Qing and Britain and France) weakened the Qing dynasty considerably. British merchants illegally sold Indian opium to China, particularly since 1820. The widespread opium addiction among the Chinese population led to increasing economic and social problems and the Chinese government thus forbade the opium trade. Consequently, the British government sent gunboats to China and quickly defeated the Chinese military forces that had technologically inferior weapons. China's first unequal treaty of 1842 (the Treaty of Nanking) forced the country to open up five ports, to concede British merchants extraterritorial legal rights, and to cede Hong Kong to Britain (Naughton 2018; Morck and Yeung 2017).

The following **Taiping Civil War** between 1850 and 1864 was initiated by Hong Xiuquan who considered himself as "Jesus' little brother". The underlying causes of the civil war were the dissatisfaction with the economic problems, China's defeat in the first opium war as well as ethnic conflicts. The civil war resulted in the loss of at least 20 million human lives and was one of the most devastating civil wars in human history (Naughton 2018). Regional leaders were able to suppress the rebellion eventually, however the civil war had further worsened China's overall situation (Morck and Yeung 2017).

After China had again been defeated in the second opium war, the country was forced to open more ports to foreign trade, to legalize Christianity, and to allow the import of opium. Various military conflicts followed. China was once more defeated in the **first Sino-Japanese War (1894–1895)** and Taiwan became a Japanese colony. Korea, which had been a tributary state of China, was declared as independent. Because of the various military defeats and humiliations by foreign nations, an **anti-foreign sentiment** manifested in China (Morck and Yeung 2017). However, there was also a growing awareness that China had to modernize in order to change its deteriorating position. This "self-strengthening movement" strongly depended on the adoption of foreign ideas. China's situation at that time is comparable to that of Japan in the mid-nineteenth century. However, in China, the debate between the pro-reformers and the traditionalists that were resistant to reform and rejected the embracement of foreign ideas continued for a much longer time (Morck and Yeung 2017). For instance, the Emperor Guangxu (1871–1908) (strongly influenced by his advisor Kang Youwei) initiated a comprehensive economic, political, educational, and military reform (inspired by the Japanese reforms during the Meiji era), the so-called **Hundred Days Reform** (or Wuxu Reform, wuxu bianfa) that lasted from the 11 June to the 22 September 1898. The reforms were rather radical and implied an unprecedented overhaul of the existing social and institutional structures, including a modernization of the educational system with a stronger focus on science-related topics and a government reform in order to make the tax collecting system more efficient and to better fight against corruption (Eckel 1948). However, the conservatives, led by the Dowager Empress Cixi, strongly opposed these reform measures since they weakened the position of the entrenched elites which greatly profited from the "old system". On 22 September 1898, Guanxu was eventually overthrown in a **coup d'état** and subsequently imprisoned until his death. Dowager Empress Cixi became the central figure in the anti-Western, anti-Christian **Boxer Rebellion** originating in Shandong in 1899. She used the "Boxers" to fight against the influence of Europeans in China and issued various decrees that supported them. Many foreigners and Chinese Christians were killed during the rebellion, and the Boxers eventually reached the capital Beijing. In 1901, Western and Japanese troops came to Beijing in order to put down the rebellion and rescue foreigners. On 7 September 1901, the signing of the Boxer Protocol ended the rebellion. After this military defeat, Dowager Empress Cixi eventually embraced **modernizing reforms**, including a constitutional monarchy with national and subnational parliaments, military modernization, and the abolishment of the Confucian civil service examination. These reforms shared many similarities with the Guangxu reforms and resembled the Japanese Meiji reforms (Brandt et al. 2014; Jin and Liu 2011). Guangxu died in 1908, followed one day later by Dowager Empress Cixi. As a consequence of the transfer of political and fiscal power to the provincial level in the course of the late modernizing reforms, the Qing dynasty eventually collapsed in 1911, followed by a "**Warlord era**" which was characterized by fragmentation, political instability, and a weak center (Brandt et al. 2014). However, this also provided an opportunity for new ideas and institutions that according to Brandt et al. (2014) were decisive for China's long-term development. During this era, democracy, science, etc. gained increasing prominence and the first Shanghai industrial tycoons emerged. However, the state was too weak to provide a stable, reliable environment and thus Chinese entrepreneurs relied on informal institutions, including private contracting and social networking.

Box 4.4 Overview on the Dynasties (since Tang) and Key Events of the Qing Dynasty

Tang dynasty (618–907)–**Song dynasty** (960–1279)–**Yuan dynasty** (1272–1368)–**Ming dynasty** (1368–1644)–**Qing dynasty** (1644–1911)–**Warlord era**.

(Selected) key events of the Qing dynasty

- First Opium War (1839–1845)
- Second Opium War (1856–1860)
- First Unequal Treaty (Treaty of Nanking) (1842)
- Taiping Civil War (1850–1864)
- First Sino-Japanese War (1894–1895)
- Hundred Days Reform under Emperor Guanxu (1898)
- Emperor Guanxu (1871–1908) is overthrown in a coup d'état (1898)
- Boxer Rebellion (central figure: Dowager Empress Cixi) (1899–1901)
- Modernization reforms under Cixi (since 1901)
- Death of Guangxu and Cixi (1908)
- Collapse of the Qing dynasty (1911).

4.3 The Republic of China (1927–1949) and the Centrally Planned Economy Under Mao Zedong (1949–1978)

In 1927, the Nanjing government (led by Kuomintang, KMT)[5] was created, eventually re-unifying China (Naughton 2018). After the defeat in the First Sino-Japanese War (in 1895), there had been a rising inflow of foreign investment into China, paving the way for an initial industrialization which was led by foreigners in the beginning. However, industrialization was first restricted to enclaves in the Treaty Ports with a focus on light consumer goods, especially textiles. In the 1930s, China was then not dependent on textile imports anymore. At that point, Chinese firms (especially those that had relationships with foreign businesses) had also grown in importance and accounted for the lion share of the factory output value (Naughton 2018). The industrialization pattern in the Northeast of China (Manchuria) differed significantly from this enclave industrialization (see Naughton 2018 for a detailed overview). Foreign investment came mainly from Japan, the Japanese industry was the biggest outlet market (unlike the Chinese domestic market in the enclaves), and the focus was on the heavy industry. Moreover, there

[5] Since 1925, it was led by Chiang Kai-shek. Together with the Chinese Communist Party, it presents one of the two historical parties in China.

were fewer backward linkages and only a very limited skill transfer. Literacy rates improved steadily and Chinese students went abroad, primarily to Japan but also to the USA and Europe. The foreign influence enabled advancements in technology.

Starting from 1931, Japan began taking control of the Manchurian provinces. After the Marco Polo Bridge incident in 1937, the Japanese invasion expanded and the Japanese captured Beijing, Shanghai, and Nanjing in the same year.[6] Between 1927 and 1937, there was also a civil war between nationalists and communists, in particular between the KMT-led government of the Republic of China and the Communist Party of China (CPC). The inner Chinese conflicts facilitated the Japanese invasion. Starting from 1937, the KMT and the CPC combined their forces in order to fight Japan. China also received military support from the Soviet Union and the USA. However, after Japan surrendered in 1945, the Civil War soon continued.

In **1949**, Chiang Chang had to withdraw to Taiwan after losing the Civil War against the CPC. In the same year, the **People's Republic of China was established**. In the course of the first 3 years, the class of landlord tenancy system was abolished. Except for that, the transition was relatively peaceful and people's freedom was not significantly reduced. This changed in 1952. The CPC implemented a socialist planning system inspired by the Soviet Union model.[7] However, China's planning system was less extensive and more decentralized compared to that of the Soviet Union (Brandt et al. 2014; Wong 1985; Xu 2011). Reforms included the reorganization of the educational system, the nationalization of all businesses and the related abolishment of private markets, and restricted cross-border trade (Chow 2007; Naughton 2018; Brandt et al. 2014).

In 1958, the **Great Leap Forward** was launched under Mao Zedong. Under this campaign, China should be rapidly transformed from an agrarian economy to a modern industrialized society that was able to compete with Western powers. China's agricultural and industrial sectors should be developed at the same time; increasing grain and steel output were the top priorities. One key reform was the collectivization of agriculture in the course of which farmers were organized into collective units (renmin gongshe). With the restructuring in communes, the Chinese government believed that the food problem was permanently solved and thus transferred many rural laborers from the agricultural to the industrial sector. However, it in fact decreased the incentives of farmers to work efficiently (see also Sect. 4.4.1 for an extensive discussion). More than 16 million peasants were relocated into cities to support the industrialization in 1958, and 100 million farmers were assigned to the construction of "backyard iron furnaces" (in order to bring industrialization to the countryside) as well as to irrigation and land reclamation

[6] This so-called "Second Sino-Japanese War" lasted from 1937 until 1945.

[7] Various factors supported the rise of the socialism in the late 1940s (cf. Naughton 2018): As a consequence of the Civil War, China's economic infrastructure and industrial capital were seriously damaged and the economy was plagued by hyperinflation. Due to various wars in the past, including the opium wars and the Sino-Japanese war, China regarded Western institutions and ideas critically. The Chinese population had suffered substantially under the Civil War and was more likely to accept strong government in order to restore stability.

projects (Li and Yang 2005). Between 1957 and 1958, the agricultural labor force declined from 193 to 155 million (Li and Yang 2005). Due to unreasonable output targets, local officials often falsified harvest statistics. Massive grain procurement led to a significant decrease in the per capita grain retained in rural areas (between 1957 and 1959, it shrank by 80 kg to only 193). Between 1957 and 1960, the estimated calorie intake was reduced from 2100 to only 1500 kcal which had a negative effect on labor productivity (Ashton et al. 1984; Strauss 1986). The situation was worsened by bad weather, wasteful food consumptions in the communes mass dining halls, and also inappropriate policies (including growing grain in unsuitable areas and the killing of birds, cf. Chow 2007; Chang and Wen 1998). Overall, the Great Leap Forward was a massive failure and finally was stopped in 1961; Mao consequently lost political power. In 1963, Premier Zhou Enlai announced the **Four Modernizations**, namely, agriculture, industry, defense, and science and technology; however, they were not carried out immediately because of the start of the **Cultural Revolution** launched by Mao in **1966** in order to restore his power (Chow 2007).[8] The main goal of the Cultural Revolution was to remove capitalist, bourgeois, and traditionalists' influences in the society that were regarded as hindering the social revolution. Moreover, Mao used this movement in order to restore his power that had suffered because of the adverse effects of the Great Leap Forward (Morck and Yeung 2017). Students organized into groups called the "Red Guards" attacked intellectuals as well as people considered belonging to the elite. They also destroyed historical sites and artifacts in order to eliminate the "Four Olds" (that is, old ideas, old customs, old culture, and old habits). The Cultural Revolution lasted for a decade and further aggravated the economic situation in China. Estimations show that the output and consumption per worker in 1992 would have been twice as large as the actual values if the Great Leap would not have taken place; without the Cultural Revolution, output and consumption would have been 1.2 times as large (Chow 2007; see also Kwan and Chow 1997).[9]

Mao died in 1976. His successor Hua Guofeng ended the Cultural Revolution and arrested the Gang of Four (including Mao's wife Jiang Qing, Zhang Chunqiao, Yao Wenyuan, and Wang Hongwen) that had played an important role in carrying out the Cultural Revolution. Hua Guofeng's policy orientation was still heavily based on Maoism and is often described as the two whatevers ("Whatever Mao said, whatever Mao did") (cf. Hofman 2019). Deng Xiaoping regained increasing political influence after Mao's death and eventually took over the power from Hua Guofeng, becoming the (de facto) leader of the People's Republic of China in 1978 (Chow 2007).[10] This year marks an important turning point regarding China's reform orientation and its economic development, as we will see in the following sections.

---

[8] However, they later played a key role under the reforms initiated by Deng Xiaoping in the late 1970s.

[9] In the absence of both events, output and consumption would have been 2.7 times as large.

[10] Deng Xiaoping never served as Chairman or General Secretary of the CPC (see also Shambaugh 1993).

Box 4.5 Selected Key Events of the Mao Zedong Era (1949–1978)

Great Leap Forward (1958–1961) campaign launched by Mao Zedong to collectivize agriculture and accelerate the industrialization (among others through the development of small backyard steel furnaces). In combination with adverse weather condition, it was one of the main causes of the **Great Famine (1959–1961)** during which tens of millions of people died of starvation.

The **Four Modernizations** (namely, agriculture, industry, defense, and science and technology) were introduced in **1963** by Zhou Enlai but only adopted after Mao's deaths.

Cultural Revolution (1966–1976) was a campaign launched by Mao that aimed at removing capitalist, bourgeois, and traditionalists' influences in the society to preserve Chinese communism (and at restoring his power).

4.4 Phase of Market-Seeking Reforms (1978–1992/3)

The Third Plenary Session of the 11th National Congress of the CPC in December 1978 marks the beginning of reforms under Deng Xiaoping. Deng put economic pragmatism before political ideology and his approach to reform turned out to be an unprecedented success (Morck and Yeung 2017). He promoted Zhao Ziyang to Premier who became responsible for the implementation of economic policy (Naughton 1993).

The reforms started at the countryside and their enormous success paved the way for more comprehensive reform policies in other sectors. Market institutions were stepwise introduced; during this process, China was able to gradually build up reform experience (Hofman 2019). Very often, unconventional "second-best" institutions were adopted (at least according to a Western understanding at that time). The usually postulated first-best solutions were unlikely to be successful in a heavily distorted environment as in China (see also Rodrik 2008). Deng's experimental approach to reform allowed identifying institutional arrangements that could work in such a setting. Critical reforms that would very likely have faced more opposition and that could potentially have threatened social stability (such as the reform of state-owned enterprises and privatization as well as comprehensive financial reforms) were postponed to later reform stages.[11] The success of the reforms during this phase significantly reduced skepticism and reinforced the credibility in the reforms.

[11] This was also partly due to the conservative politicians, including important figures such as Chen Yun (who opposed the SEZs reform) and Li Xiannian (see Chow 2007 for a more detailed discussion).

Box 4.6 Macroeconomic and Reform-Policy Cycles in the 1980s

During the 1980s, phases of accelerated reform were accompanied by inflation and increased imbalances. As depicted in the Figure below, there have been three inflation spikes, namely, in 1980, 1985, and 1988. Usually, these unfavorable macroeconomic outcomes were followed by an episode of increased skepticism regarding the reform efficacy by conservatives, and reform efforts were suspended. That is, macroeconomic cycles and reform-policy cycles were closely interrelated (Naughton 2018). However, at least in the beginning of the reforms, these episodes with high inflation were relatively fast brought under control by the government.

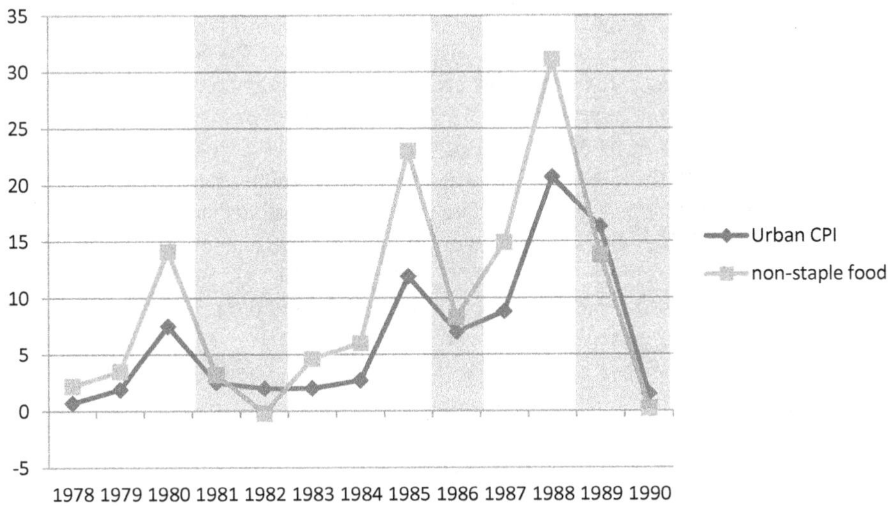

Urban CPI (percentage increase), 1978–1990. *Source* Naughton (1991). *Notes* The grey shaded areas mark periods of more cautious and even suspended reform efforts

4.4.1 Agricultural Reforms

The reforms started in the agricultural sector and encompassed the following key reforms: (1) a rise in state procurement prices in 1979, (2) the decollectivization of Chinese agriculture via the household responsibility system (HRS) reform, (3) the expansion of free markets for agricultural commodities (intensified in the mid-1980s).

There are various reasons for why the Chinese government decided to first reform the agricultural sector (cf. Glawe and Wagner 2017). First, the majority of the population lived in rural areas (Yao 1999)—around 82% in 1978 (NBS, own calculations). Second, China intended to ensure food security, in particular after the food crisis of the Great Leap Forward (Zhu 2012; Brandt et al. 2014). Third, among all three sectors, the agricultural sector was the least centralized and thus, reforms in this sector would not have been regarded as affecting the Chinese socialist orientation (as long as they did not involve changes in the state sector, see Guo 2013 and Yao 1999).

Price reform

Shortly before the reforms started, the Chinese government set procurement prices for 113 agricultural commodities and controlled sales and prices for 158 commodities at the retail level (Yang and Li 2008; CRDR 1994). There existed two distinct prices in the state commercial system: *quota procurement prices* and *above-quota procurement prices*. The former applied to crops sold in fulfilment of procurement obligations, whereas the latter applied to crops sold in excess of the quota (Lin 1992). Above-quota prices were higher than quota prices in order to provide extra production incentives to the farmers (beyond the fulfilment of the quota); however, both prices were much lower than potential market prices (Yang and Li 2008).

In 1979, quota prices for grain, oil crops, cotton, sugar crops, and pork were increased by 17.1% on average (Lin 1992); the price-premium for above-quota sales was even raised from 30 to 50% of the quota prices (McMillan et al. 1989; Kueh 1984). Overall, the weighted average increase in procurement prices for major crops amounted to 22.1% (Lin 1992). The price rise stimulated food production by enhancing the incentives of farmers to work more efficiently, and also increased the income of rural households (Zhu 2012; Yang and Li 2008). In addition, the availability of purchased inputs increased considerably and the prices of agricultural machinery, fertilizers, and pesticides were reduced by 10–15% (Lin 1992; Yang and Li 2008).

Market and planning reform

During the Mao era and particularly during the Cultural Revolution, the government emphasized **regional grain self-sufficiency** (Naughton 2018) which required an extensive planning of agricultural production (including the acreage for each crop, the amount of inputs that should be used, etc., cf. Lin 1992). China followed a strict **"grain first" policy** under which agricultural collectives were under constant pressure to produce basic crops (rice, wheat, corn) independent of soil suitability, etc.[12] This led to dramatic losses in allocation efficiency since the planners neglected considerations with respect to the profitability and a region's comparative advantage (Lin 1992).[13] The mandatory grain procurement at a low price can be

[12] A famous slogan of the Cultural Revolution was "take grain as a key link" (yiliang weigang) (cf. Naughton 2018).

[13] The grain first policy sometimes resulted in what Naughton (2018) refers to as a "perverse 'reverse specialization'", meaning that areas were growing more of the crops from which they had the *least* comparative advantage. To meet the quota, regions that were in fact ineligible for grain production had to devote all their land to the production of grain in order to compensate for the missing comparative advantage, whereas regions that were particularly suitable for grain production fulfilled the quotas easily and used some of the remaining land to grow cash crops instead.

regarded as an implicit tax that financed the building up of China's heavy industry (Naughton 2018).

The regional grain self-sufficiency policy during the Mao era had resulted in severe allocation efficiency losses (cf. Sect. 4.3) that the authorities could no longer neglect. The government reduced grain procurement quotas and the number of planned product categories while increasing grain imports in order to give a greater role to markets (McMillan et al. 1989).[14] In combination with the rise in agricultural prices and the loosening of restrictions on interregional trade and agriculture products, this allowed new patterns of specialization to emerge (Lin 1992). Between 1978 and 1984, the area devoted to cash crops[15] increased from 9.6 to 13.4% of total sown area while the area devoted to grain crops decreased from 80.4 to 78.3% (Lin 1992, Table 3).

The announcement of the elimination of agricultural procurement quotas and the introduction of the dual-track system in 1985 marks an important point in the process of agricultural market reforms. The enormous success of the agricultural price and market reforms during the first phase had convinced Chinese reformers that market forces were crucial for raising agricultural production and thus ensuring food security. The expansion of free markets in agriculture was, however, also fostered by the rising financial burden of the government. Since procurement prices were raised but retail prices in grain remained unchanged, the government provided in fact a price subsidy to urban residents. Until 1984, the price subsidies had increased from 8.4 to 24.6% of the state budget (Lin 1992). By giving up control, the government could reduce the financial burden arising from the state-financed price subsidy (Yang and Li 2008). In the course of the 1985 reform, the mandatory quotas were replaced by procurement contracts that were negotiated between the government and farmers. Under this new "dual-track pricing" system, the farmers delivered the contracted outputs at the contract price which was the weighted average of the basic quota price and the above-quota price (Lin 1992). The remaining output could be sold in the free market (Yang and Li 2008).

Decollectivization of agriculture: the household responsibility system (HRS) reform

Prior to 1978, all land was collectively owned by production teams, comprising 20–30 households, which were the basic accounting and production organizing unit (Johnson 1982). The production teams were supposed to be self-sufficient and had to fulfil production targets set by upper government levels. The income of a production team was distributed among its members according to a work point system which should reflect the quality and quantity of work of each team member (McMillan et al. 1989, see also Box 4.7). However, due to the nature of agricultural

[14] As argued by Naughton (2018), the rural reforms entailed the costly trade-off, especially since China faced a shortage of foreign exchange. Because of the rise in grain imports, the government had to defer the technology import program of the "leap outward".

[15] In his study, Lin (1992: 48) counts 12 cash crops (namely, cotton, peanuts, rapeseed, sesame, jute, ramie, sugar cane, sugar beets, tobacco, tussah silk cocoons, mulberry silk cocoons, and tea) as well as seven grain crops (namely, rice, wheat, corn, potatoes, sorghum, millet, and soybeans).

production, it is extremely difficult to monitor the individual efforts in a team. Therefore, in reality, the workers received a rather fixed amount of work points independent of their individual efforts. As a consequence, the incentives to work and to increase agricultural productivity and output were relatively low (Lin 1988).

Box 4.7 Work Point System

The production team distributed income among its members on the basis of contribution estimates via a **work point system**. In particular, the quantity of work was measured in terms of labor days and the work quality was captured by work points received per labor day. Dependent on their skill level and work capacity, the team members were assigned to different grades and each grade had a different amount of work points attached to it. The individual income was calculated as follows: the production teams' total income at the end of the agricultural year was divided by the sum of work points of all members of the team. Thus, it was possible to determine the value of one work point, which was then multiplied by the number of working points of each farmer (see McMillan et al. 1989 for more details).

Under the new HRS, collectively owned land was assigned to the individual households with contracts up to 15 years (Lin 1992: 37). After selling a fixed quota of grains to the government at official prices, it was left up to the household to sell any extra grain at market prices or to keep it for its own consumption (Cau and Birchenall 2013: 167; Zhu 2012: 112–3; Chow 2007).

It is important to note that in order to increase agricultural output, the government initially only planned to modify the management methods within the collective; the subdivision of collectively owned land was never intended and even prohibited since it was considered to be opposed to socialist principles (Lin 1992).

The HRS can be traced back to some areas in Anhui province, which were frequently plagued by floods and droughts and that had suffered greatly during the Great Leap Forward (Lin 1988). In December 1978, a small number of production teams made a secret, illegal agreement to dissolve their collective and divide up the farmland into individual family plots (Kroeber 2016: 28). The results were spectacular and nearby production teams also adopted the household responsibility system, soon outperforming the teams that still worked under the system of collective farming (Chen 1981; Lin 1988, see also Fig. 4.4). Due to the enormous success, the central government conceded the HRS but restricted it to poor and geographically disadvantaged areas (in Anhui and Sichuan). However, this restriction was not effective and also relatively rich provinces soon adopted the HRS. In late 1981, it eventually received universal recognition.

It is important to note that the property rights in rural China were still incomplete. Even though property rights were *exclusive* and *enforceable* (only one

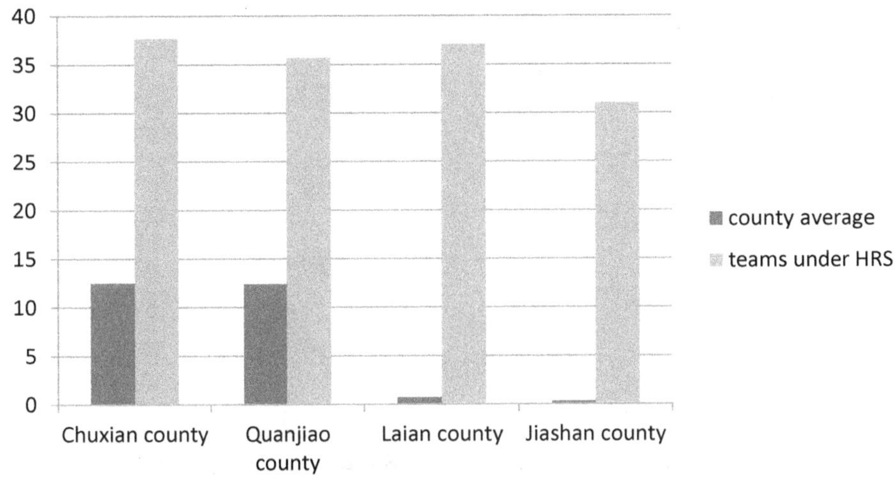

Fig. 4.4 Grain output increase, selected counties. *Source* Chen (1981)

household had the right to use a particular land area; violations of this allotment would be disciplined by the government), they were not fully *secure* and also not *transferable* (cf. Perkins 1994 for an in-depth discussion). The contracts were made on a 15-year basis with a (rather vague) promise of extension afterwards. However, due to the political instability prior to the beginning of reforms, there was a credibility problem and farmers therefore did not want to invest in major capital improvements. It was also very difficult to sell land which prevented many farmers to migrate to urban areas since they had to take care of the acreages.

The reforms in the agricultural sector had a strong effect on farmers' incentives to exert effort and thus, increase productivity and agricultural output growth. Lin (1992) argues that the productivity improvements between 1978 and 1984 can be mainly attributed to the shift to the HRS which, according to the author's estimations, alone produced almost half of the output growth (namely, 48.69%, which is as much as the combined effects of input increases, cf. Lin 1992). In the same vein, McMillan et al. (1989) find that the productivity gain in the agricultural sector can be attributed to 78% to the HRS reform, in particular through the resultant incentive effects, and to 22% to the price reform. According to Huang et al. (1998), the implementation of the HRS augmented rice yields by 35.6% over the period 1978–1984.[16] At the lower end of the spectrum, Fan (1990) finds that 26.6% of production growth can be attributed to the institutional change over the period

[16] They report a 0.4% increase for the period 1985–1990 and a 22.3% increase for the period from 1975 to 1990.

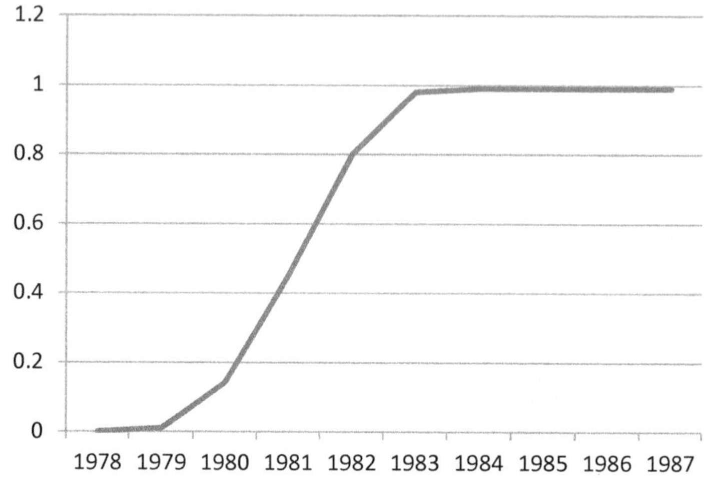

Fig. 4.5 HRS adoption rate in China, 1978–1987. *Source* Lin (1992)

1965–1985 (via TFP improvements); however, input growth accounted for around 57.7% of total production growth. At the regional level, the institutional change was most pronounced in Northern and Southern China while it was the lowest in Northeastern China.[17]

There was a trend reversal around 1985, when the agricultural output growth and TFP growth declined substantially (Zheng et al. 2009, see Wen 1993 for an overview of different studies). Whereas the agricultural growth rate was around 7.3% between 1978 and 1984, it accounted for only 3.1% between 1984 and 1988 (cf. Perkins 1994). This development can be mainly attributed to the fact that the HRS reform was completed in 1984 when 99% of the former production teams had adopted the HRS (Lin 1992; Zhu 2012, see also Fig. 4.5).

According to Zhu (2012), the efficiency gains induced by the institutional reform were rather *static* and there was no significant change in the production technologies used in agriculture during the first reform phase (see also Glawe and Wagner 2017). Therefore, the HRS only enabled a temporary surge in agricultural productivity (Perkins 1994: 27, refers to this as a "one-shot affair") after which crop production reverted to its long-term growth rate. According to Huang (1993), this development can also partly be explained by the fact that farmers decided to increasingly invest their resources in the rural industry.

[17] Northeast China: Heilongjiang, Liaoning, and Jilin provinces; Northern China: Municipalities of Beijing and Tianjin as well as the Hebei, Henan, Shandong, Shanxi, Shaanxi, and Gansu provinces; Southern China: Guangxi autonomous region plus the Fujian and Guangdong provinces.

Box 4.8 Summary: Agricultural Reforms (1979–1984)

Reasons for why the reforms started in the agricultural sector: most people lived in rural areas; ensuring food security; agricultural sector was least centralized.

Key reforms

- **rise in state procurement prices** in 1979 (around 22.1% on average)
- decollectivization of Chinese agriculture via the **household responsibility system (HRS) reform:** collectively owned land was assigned to the individual households with contracts up to 15 years; any extra grain beyond a fixed quota could be sold at market prices
- **expansion of free markets** for agricultural commodities (intensified in the mid-1980s).

4.4.2 The Reform of the Township and Village Enterprises (TVEs)

Chinese Township and Village Enterprises (TVEs; xiangzhen qi ye) were not only a major growth engine of the 1980s/90s but also significantly pushed forward the transformation from a command to a market economy, provided room for institutional experimentation, and were the driving force for making China the world's factory (Xu 2011). A typical TVE is an enterprise that is collectively owned by all residents of the village or township in which it is located. However, the communal collective owners were usually represented by the local township and village government which controlled and managed the TVE and which was thus the de facto executive owner (Byrd and Lin 1990).[18] Thus, TVEs were neither public enterprises nor state firms (Jin and Qian 1998). The collective character made them ideologically much safer than private firms (Naughton 2018). Since the property rights of TVEs are only vaguely defined, it would be usually expected that they are rather unproductive according to traditional wisdom. Therefore, their enormous success presents a paradox to the traditional property rights theory (Weitzman and Xu 1994).

It is noteworthy that, somehow similar to the HRS reform, the success of the TVEs in China was neither planned nor anticipated by the Chinese government. Deng Xiaoping noted in 1987 that "all sorts of small enterprises boomed in the countryside, as if a strong army appeared suddenly from nowhere". Their rapid emergence "was not something I had thought about. Nor had the other comrades.

[18] That is, TVEs presented local community public firms which were owned and controlled by the township or village government (Chang and Wang 1994; Che and Qian 1998; Jin and Qian 1998).

This surprised us" (Zhou 1996). Even though the development of TVEs was tolerated during the initial reform phase, it was only actively encouraged when the Chinese government realized that they effectively absorbed the majority of the rural labor surplus and helped to increase rural incomes in the 1980s (Jin and Qian 1998; Perotti et al. 1998).

Box 4.9 Property Rights in TVEs

Weitzman and Xu (1994) refer to TVEs as "*vaguely defined cooperatives*" because of their special semi-public ownership structure with only poorly developed property rights. In particular, neither residence nor executive owners

(1) have exclusive ownership rights and there are legal restrictions that prevent the transformation of TVEs into private companies,
(2) have the full right to consume or dispose of the after-tax income,
(3) can sell, transfer, or inherit TVE assets.

The collective character of TVEs made them ideologically safe (Naughton 2018).

There are various **factors** that contributed to the success of the TVEs. The most important ones will be briefly summarized in the following.

First, the Chinese government created a favorable environment for the TVEs. Among others, a number of **preferential policies** were installed which, inter alia, allowed TVEs to **enter previously protected industries**. Due to the increased market liberalization, TVEs were able to participate in the monopoly rents of SOEs in some activities and especially early entrants benefited greatly from windfall profits. However, as more and more TVEs emerged, monopoly profits vanished gradually (see also the paragraph on the impact of TVEs on SOEs below).

Second, TVEs faced a **harder budget constraint** compared to SOEs. They were less subsidized and thus faced factor prices that mirrored much better China's true factor endowment (namely, abundant labor and scarce capital). Moreover, capital could only be borrowed at market interest rates or via internally generated funds at high opportunity costs (Knight and Ding 2012: 33). Consequently, TVEs had more pressure to be efficient than state firms. This tendency was reinforced by the enormous regional competition.[19] Moreover, the much lower wages (compared to SOEs) and the more flexible employment policies enabled TVEs to successfully generate a comparative advantage in labor-intensive industries.

Third, the imperfect markets and particularly the absence of sufficient property right protection gave an important **function** to **community governments** which

[19] The local government could not install trade barriers to prevent competition with other townships since the local market was usually too small *to offer all necessary goods* (Perotti et al. 1998).

could provide TVEs with access to capital (via bank loans) since they acted as debt guarantors. The local government had an incentive to develop productive TVEs since the "money stayed local": due to preferential tax treatment, the majority of profits could go into an extra-budgetary fund which had not to be shared with the upper-level governments and which was primarily used for reinvestments or the provision of public goods and services (Naughton 2018). The **decentralization** of economic decision-making that enabled these incentives of local government was crucial for rural industrialization. Even though the government supported TVEs, there was still a responsibility for bad investment decisions; however, this risk was spread over the entire local community. Even though the budget constraint was much harder compared to that of SOEs (see point 1), it was still not *completely* hard since the local government provided a certain sense of security to the community and to some extent a kind of insurance to new firms which could therefore enter with a larger size and thus benefit more from some form of scale economies (Naughton 2018). Since the community government organized and executed the collective financing and debt repayment system, it could borrow the funds required for a TVE start-up from already existing TVEs and also organize internal reorganizations, etc. (Sun 1997; Perotti et al. 1998).

Fourth, TVEs could **fill empty market niches** with respect to various light consumer goods (e.g. food, clothing, etc.) since the production of many SOEs focused on rather capital-intensive products and thus did not meet the demand of local residents. This effect was further enhanced by the rising rural incomes and also by the self-contained character of China's regional economies which also ensured a sufficient input supply (Xu 2011).

Fifth, there were **close links between TVEs and urban SOEs** and many rural industries concentrated in coastal areas (Naughton 2018). The connections with the urban economy, often in the form of long-term subcontracting relationships (Jin and Qian 1998; Otsuka and Banerjee 1998), enabled important technology and knowledge spillover effects (Xu and Zhuang 1998). This was further facilitated by family relationships, underlining the important role of informal institutions (such as relational contracting) for the development of TVEs (Xu 2011; McMillan and Woodruff 2002). Also, SOEs could benefit from this corporation. Since they were forced to also reduce their costs due to the increasing competition, they appreciated the cheap labor and land use. Moreover, subcontracting enabled them to escape to some extent the tight control of the state sector (see also the last point). In addition, TVEs in coastal regions, especially those located in Guangdong, Fujian, Zhejiang, and Jiangsu, were well connected to Hong Kong, Taiwan, and South East Asia and could profit from the benefits of foreign investments including the transfer of advanced technology (Perotti et al. 1998).

Finally, also the **organizational diversity** contributed to the success of TVEs since they could relatively easily adapt to the local conditions (Naughton 2018). In addition, most TVEs were relatively **small in size** (on average 73 employees per township and 26 employees per village firm) which further contributed to this versatility (Perotti et al. 1998). Moreover, compared to state firms, TVEs had relatively flexible financial and bookkeeping systems.

The essence of these points is that the political and institutional environment provided TVEs with both, incentives and discipline, in the form of a relatively hard budget constraint (Perotti et al. 1998). Moreover, the special semi-public structure made TVEs so successful since it allowed combining "entrepreneurial energy with political patronage" (Kroeber 2016).

As already mentioned above, the TVEs were one of the main drivers of economic growth in the second reform phase. Especially from 1983/1984 onwards, when the official policy became more tolerant toward TVEs, their growth was explosive (Kroeber 2016; Zhu and Elbern 2002). The number of TVEs increased from 1.5 million in 1978 to 23 million in 1996. Over the same period, TVE employment increased from 28 million to over 130 million (Zhu and Elbern 2002; Wang 1999). TVEs' value-added share in GDP, accounting to below 6% in 1978, increased to 26% in 1996 (Naughton 2018). This is especially remarkable since also GDP growth was extremely fast over this period. TVEs played an especially important role in the industry sector: Between 1978 and 1991, the state sector's share in industrial output decreased from 78 to 53%, whereas the non-state sector's contribution increased from 22 to 47% of which around 4/5 was produced by TVEs (cf. Weitzman and Xu 1994). The average annual growth rate of TVEs was around 25.3%, more than 16% points above that of state firms. Also, TFP growth was three times as fast compared to that of SOEs (12% vs. 4%) (Weitzman and Xu 1994). The TVEs helped to absorb the labor force that was set free because of the HRS reforms and increased rural income.

When private property rights improved around the middle of the 1990s, the advantages of TVEs diminished and they were increasingly privatized (Kung and Lin 2007). In particular, the supportive role of community governments lost the importance due to the development of functioning markets. Moreover, TVEs faced increasing competition from reformed SOEs and also from the newly established private sector in urban areas (Knight and Ding 2012). According to Jefferson and Singh (1999), the private sector had overtaken both the TVEs and SOEs with respect to their share in gross industrial output in 1996 (see also Fig. 4.6).

TVEs did not only enable rapid economic growth but also played an important role for pushing forward the **marketization process** in the entire Chinese economy. They brought prices in alignment with costs, and the entry of TVEs into formally protected markets significantly increased the competition for SOEs which were gradually outcompeted and outgrown (Weitzman and Xu 1994; Knight and Ding 2012).

In addition, TVEs provided room for **institutional experimentation** (Naughton 2018). Moreover, the institutional structures had a lasting impression on China's corporate governance (Xu 2011): Some key features of TVEs such as informal institutional arrangements and the involvement of the local government in business are still relevant and have shaped entrepreneurship in China. For instance, these structures enabled the formation of **clusters** consisting of many small specialized (private) firms in various (coastal) townships. These enterprises received regulatory support of the local government which strategically managed the respective cluster, and they were closely coordinated by networks of informal arrangements (see Xu

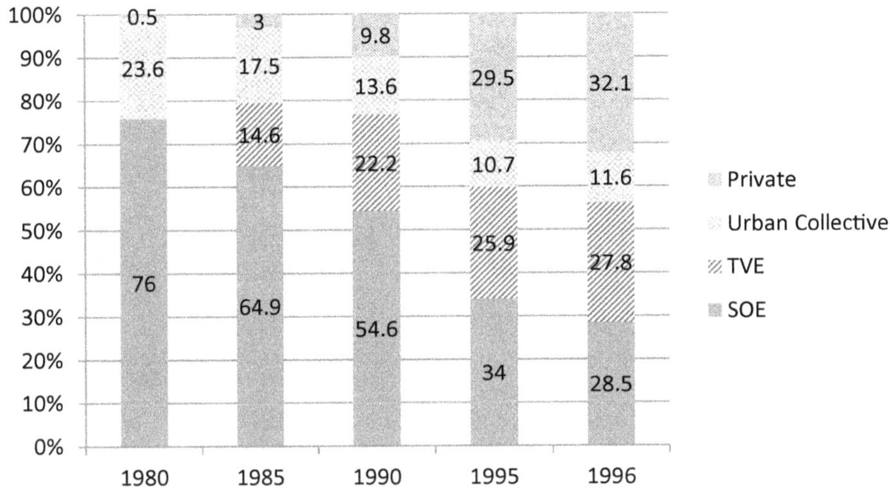

Fig. 4.6 Gross industrial output, 1980–1996. *Source* Jefferson and Singh (1999), Table 1.3

2011 for a more extensive discussion). These townships ultimately made China the **world's workbench** (Xu 2011; Xu and Zhang 2009).

Box 4.10 Summary: Township and Village Enterprises

Definition and characteristics: enterprise that is **collectively owned** by all residents of the village or township in which it is located; de facto executive owner is however the local township and village government; neither a public enterprise nor a state firm; vaguely defined property rights.

Factors that made TVEs successful

- **preferential policies** (e.g. entering previously protected industries)
- **harder budget constraints** (compared to SOEs), but not completely hard
- important **function of community government** (provided TVEs with access to capital by acting as debt guarantor)
- local governments had **incentives** to develop productive TVEs ("money stayed local")
- TVEs **filled empty market niches** (light consumer goods)
- close **link** between **TVEs** and **urban SOEs** (long-term subcontracting relationships enabled **technology spillovers**)
- organizational diversity and rather small size allowed **easy adaptation to local conditions**.

→ **Incentives paired with discipline**

Role of TVEs

- absorbed rural labor surplus
- main drivers of growth (on average more productive than state firms)
- pushed forward the marketization process (e.g. increased competition for SOEs)
- provided room for institutional experimentation
- institutional features enabled formation of clusters in coastal townships.

4.4.3 Reform of State-Owned Enterprises (SOEs)

State-owned enterprises (SOEs) are enterprises that are officially "owned by all citizens of China"; however, the actual control resides in government. Very often, the goals of SOE managers are closely aligned with that of the government since former government officials are often recruited as managers and vice versa (Wang 2012).

Some advantages of SOEs are that they can to some extent maintain social stability and also allow the government to maintain control over key elements of the Chinese society. In addition, government interventions can be necessary to create capital-intensive industries at an early development stage (Lin et al. 1998; Lin and Tang 1999). SOEs had a relatively easy access to key materials and credit (however, these benefits diminished gradually over time). Probably most importantly, SOEs assume many functions that go beyond pure profits seeking, including the political support of the government and also the provision of social services (such as education, housing, health insurance, and pension provision, cf. Chow 2007).

SOEs also have various shortcomings which are partly closely related to the advantages described above. First, the fact that SOEs are no pure economic actor can significantly reduce their profitability, e.g. because of the hiring of redundant workers (which in fact accounted for around 20% of the total workforce, Bell et al. 1993). According to Xiao (1991), 40% of the profitability differences between SOEs and TVEs can in fact be attributed to social welfare provisions (such as the provision of public goods) (cf. Perotti et al. 1998). Moreover, lacking profitability can easily be attributed to the imposed policy burdens since it is very difficult to judge whether weak firm performance is due to the fulfilment of social goals or rather due to a lack of effort and/or talent of SOE managers (Lin et al. 2020). Efficiency is also hampered as a consequence of the soft budget constraint, a term coined by Kornai (1986). The soft budget constraint occurs when there is a relaxation of the strict relationship between expenditure and earnings. In particular, a financially insolvent firm expects to be bailed out by the state via fiscal subsidies, etc. The incentives of SOE managers are thus separated from firm performance and the firms are in general less responsive to price signals and market rules (Lin et al. 2020; Song 2019).

First cautious reforms between 1978 and 1984

During the initial reform phase between 1978 and 1984, first tentative reform steps were undertaken in order to expand the autonomy of SOEs and to thus improve their efficiency. The decision responsibility was increasingly shifted to the SOE managers while the firms were still owned by the state (Groves et al. 1994). These rather cautious measures were assessed critically from Western economists; one main argument was that the reforms were incomplete since they were lacking a comprehensive reform of the price system and thus were prone to be ineffective (Johnson 1988). In October 1978, first experiments were conducted in six SOEs in Sichuan province (Zhang 2019b; Song 2019): the local government slightly increased the decision-making rights of these SOEs by granting them control over marketing decisions and technical innovation (Lin et al. 2020). Moreover, SOEs were now allowed to retain part of their profits and to deposit them into three different funds, namely, welfare, bonus payments, and investment funds (prior to the reforms, all profits had to be remitted to the state) (Naughton 1995). Money out of the funds was among others used for paying bonuses to workers in order to boost their incentives to work more efficiently (Zhang 2006; Naughton 1995). SOEs were also allowed to engage in production beyond mandatory plan targets, and decentralized, semi-market transactions were encouraged (Jefferson and Rawski 1994). In addition to these measures which focused on the domestic market, the new open-door policy additionally reduced barriers to international trade and investment. Especially state firms located in Southern provinces were granted incentives to expand foreign economic contracts, and exporting SOEs could retain some of the foreign exchanges (Jefferson and Rawski 1994; Lin et al. 2020). The program was quickly expanded to include more state firms, and by 1980 about 6,600 SOEs participated. This number increased to 42,000 in 1981, and by 1983 almost all industrial state enterprises had adopted the program (Huang 1999).

Reforms since mid-1980s

The second reform round of SOEs encompassed two main measures, the dual pricing system and the enterprise contract responsibility system.

The **dual-track system** was characterized by the coexistence of two coordination mechanisms, namely, a traditional plan and a market channel for the allocation of a given good (Jefferson and Rawski 1994; Naughton 2018). After having fulfilled the output obligations under the compulsory plan, most SOEs were allowed to sell above-quota output and buy out-of-plan inputs at market prices which increasingly responded to the forces of demand and supply (Li and Putterman 2008). As a consequence, SOEs had to adapt more and more to the market and became more efficient. Moreover, state firms gained the permission to engage in business relations with non-state firms. Through subcontracting with TVEs, they were able to reduce their production costs with respect to labor and land (Naughton 2018). Since the government also committed to freeze the plan track (in absolute terms) which consequently became proportionately less and less important, the economy was able to "grow out of the plan" (Naughton 1995, 2018). This also had an important effect on SOEs' incentives since, even if many transactions were initially with other state units, SOEs faced "market prices on the margin" (Byrd 1991). Still, the state could to a certain extent continue to stabilize state firms through the planned component and thus ensure that SOEs were able to meet their obligations to workers. The market liberalization via the dual-track approach thus also helped to reduce opposition to reform.

With respect to enterprise financing, budgetary appropriations were gradually replaced by bank loans repayable with interest which became the main investment finance in the 1980s (cf. Jefferson and Rawski 1994; Fan and Woo 1993). In addition, a set of industrial and commercial taxes (tax-for-profit reform; li gai shui) that has already been introduced in 1983 was extended in 1984, replacing all profit remittances of SOEs (Prime 1991; Hofman 2019).

During the 1980s, the share of output as well as inputs traded through the market increased significantly, ranging between 27 and 54% points for the latter and between 11 and 53% points for the former (Jefferson and Rawski 1994).

The second key reform was the **enterprise contract responsibility system** which was introduced in the mid-1980s and expanded nationwide until 1988 when 93% of state firms had adopted the system (Lin et al. 2020; Zhang 2019b). Employment contracts specified a set of obligations that the enterprise manager(s) had to fulfil (involving targets for total profits, productivity increases, etc.) in order to receive an extensive operational control over the enterprise, including production planning, worker payment and recruitment, and often complete retention of excess profits (Song 2019; Jefferson and Rawski 1994). The reform aimed at incentivizing the managers to increase production while at the same time assuring that the government obtained enough revenue (Zhang 2019b). Overall, the contract responsibility system presented an alternative to privatization that was less radical and thus ideologically more acceptable.

The reforms further increased the autonomy of SOEs (even though with certain limitations),[20] created a more competitive market environment, and increased the incentive of SOE managers and workers. The urban SOE reform thus showed parallels with the rural reform, particularly the HRS. However, while empirical studies state a positive effect of the increased market competition on SOE productivity (cf. Jefferson and Rawski 1994; Huang 1999), the financial performance deteriorated continuously with profit rates decreasing by 12% points to only 6% in the early 1990s (Song 2015). In this context, the soft budget constraint became increasingly problematic and the subsidies grew from below 2% of GNP in 1980 to 10% in 1992 (Huang 1999). According to Naughton (1992), this declining profitability can be among others attributed to the increased market entry of non-state

[20] For instance, government officials sometimes tried to prevent SOE managers from exerting their newly acquired decision-making authority; but also state firm managers tried in some instances to retain the SOEs' profits but expected the state to take care of financial losses (Jefferson and Rawski 1994).

firms. Moreover, the separation of ownership and control in the course of the contract responsibility system reform gave rise to the problem of insider control and made the monitoring of SOE managers rather difficult. This principal-agent problem encouraged managers to maximize their own benefits at the expense of the benefits of the government, for example, by extracting resources from SOEs (Zhang 2019b). Continued intervention of government officials in SOE businesses as well as the SOEs' social welfare responsibilities for state firm employees (due to the absence of a social safety net) further impeded the monitoring process (Perotti et al. 1998). These problems exacerbated in the next reform stages (Song 2019).

Box 4.11 Summary: State-Owned Enterprises (First Reform Phase)

Definition: enterprises that are officially "owned by all citizens of China"; however, the actual control resides in government.

- multiple functions/goals that go beyond pure profit seeking (e.g. political support for the government, provision of social services)
- potential efficiency losses due to the soft budget constraint.

Reforms

1978–1984: first cautious reforms

Decision responsibilities were increasingly shifted to SOE managers; part of the profits could be retained and deposited into different funds, semi-market transactions were encouraged; incentives to expand foreign contracts; exporting SOEs could retain some of the foreign exchanges.

Since mid-1980s: two key reforms

(1) **dual-track system**: coexistence of two coordination mechanisms, namely, a traditional plan and a market channel; above-quota output could be sold at market prices.
(2) **enterprise contract responsibility system**: introduced in the mid-1980s and expanded nationwide until 1988; employment contracts specified a set of obligations that the enterprise manager(s) had to fulfil in order to receive an extensive operational control over the enterprise.

→ **SOE reforms showed parallels with the agricultural reforms.**

4.4.4 Fiscal Reform

China has a multilevel administration hierarchy with the **central government** at the top and **four subnational levels of government** ("local governments"), namely (i) the **provincial level** (consisting of 22 provinces (excluding Taiwan), four municipalities, five autonomous regions, and two special administrative regions (namely, Hong Kong and Macao)), (ii) the **prefectural level** (over 300 divisions), (iii) the **county level** (over 2,800 divisions), and (iv) the **township level** (several tens of thousands of divisions) (see also Chan 1994; Shen et al. 2012).

Prior to 1978, financial relations between the central and local governments were organized under the "**unified revenue collection and unified spending**" (tongshou tongzhi) system which is also known as "*eating from one big pot*" (chi daguofan). It presents a centralized system in which the central government collects all revenues and then reallocates them down to each level of government. The local governments did not have a separate budget and lacked discretionary power (Lin and Liu 2000). Profit remittances of state enterprises were the main source of government revenues (around 50%). The tax system was rather simple. While this set up was suitable for a centralized economy, it was incompatible with market-oriented reforms: First, SOEs faced a growing competition from the rising non-state sector (e.g. TVEs) which could now enter formerly protected industries. An increasing number of SOEs recorded losses and thus, the main revenue source was eroded, posing a huge burden for the fiscal system. Second, local governments had no incentives to promote economic growth and improve tax collection under the unified system since they were not allowed to keep any of their local revenues. Third, the tax administration had difficulties dealing with the newly arising mixed ownership forms of enterprises (cf. Lin and Liu 2000; Shen et al. 2012).

As a consequence, the share of fiscal revenue in GDP declined significantly, so did the share of central government revenue of total revenues. Sufficient provision of public goods by the local governments could no longer be ensured. A restructuring of the fiscal system appeared indispensable. During the 1980s, Chinese policymakers hence installed various reform measures in order to decentralize the fiscal system. In particular, the old unified system was replaced by a **fiscal revenue-sharing system** under which, as implied by the name, revenues were shared by the central and provincial governments. The reform is therefore often described as "*eating from separate kitchens*" (fenzao chifan). The main goal of the **fiscal decentralization** was to promote local economic development (by increasing the responsibilities and autonomy of local governments) while at the same time guaranteeing an adequate revenue flow from subnational governments to the central government. There were three different waves of reforms between 1980 and 1993.[21]

First reform wave (1980–1985). The central government and the local governments adopted the first revenue-sharing system in 1980. The revenues were classified into three different categories, namely, **central fixed revenues**, **local**

[21] To be precise, first experiments were already conducted in 1977 in Jiangsu province, cf. Lin and Liu (2000).

fixed revenues, and **shared revenues**. The shared revenues were divided between central and local governments according to pre-determined sharing schemes. Between 1980 and 1984, the central government received 80% of these shared revenues while the rest stayed with the local governments. By being able to retain part of the revenue, local governments had an incentive to ameliorate their tax collection efforts. In addition, they supported local economic development and acted as "helping hands" for enterprises (instead of "grabbing hands"). This incentive was further reinforced by the design of the promotion system which was based on local growth achievements. While the reform was able to raise revenue collection, it worsened the inequality between rich and poor provinces.

Second reform wave (1985–1988). In 1985, the revenue-sharing arrangement was modified to include varying schedules based on localities' budget balances of the previous year. However, since richer provinces had to contribute more revenues, this reduced their incentives for broadening the tax base (Shen et al. 2012). The modifications also made sure that the two fixed revenues only constituted a rather small part of the total budget, whereas shared revenues accounted for the main part (Lin and Liu 2000). There was also a reform of the tax system in the course of which SOEs' profit remittances were replaced by income taxes (cf. also Sect. 4.4.3).

Third reform wave (1988–1993). The fiscal contracting system was finally implemented between 1988 and 1993. Each government level contracted with its subordinate government levels' specific revenue and expenditure targets. In the course of this reform step, six types of central-provincial revenue-sharing methods were established, namely, (i) contracted sharing rate with a fixed yearly growth rate of revenue, (ii) fixed local shared rate in total revenue, (iii) fixed local shared rate in total revenue plus incremental fixed shared rate, (iv) contracted remittance with fixed annual growth rate, (v) fixed contracted remittance, and (vi) fixed contracted grants (for a detailed overview will see Shen et al. 2012, Table 2).

During the 1980s, provincial marginal revenue retention rates increased remarkably and by 1989, around 70% of all provinces had a rate amounting to 100%. Jin et al. (2005) find a positive correlation between marginal revenue retention rates and development of non-state enterprises as well as reform efforts in SOEs. Ma (2000) and Lin and Liu (2000) also show that fiscal decentralization had been conducive to economic growth, whereas Zhang and Zou (1998) report a negative effect of fiscal decentralization on economic growth.

Fiscal decentralization had various advantages. For instance, if adequately designed, it could increase local incentives to raise revenues. In addition, subnational politicians could make better use of local information. It also enabled experimentation which had proved as extremely useful for the reform of the agricultural sector and of TVEs. However, even though the fiscal reforms during the 1980s put local governments on the self-financing basis for the first time, they were not able to solve the **financial problems** of the **central government**. The budgetary revenue share in GDP as well as the central to total budgetary revenue share declined steadily; the latter fell from 33 to 22% between 1988 and 1993 (Shen et al. 2012). This constrained the center's support for the provision of basic public services and also interfered with the central government's function to moderate regional fiscal disparities. The transfer of fiscal responsibilities **undermined the center's fiscal power**. The local tax collection was under de facto control of local government officials who often abused their newly obtained power. For instance, local governments frequently **granted tax reductions and exemptions** to locally owned SOEs. Moreover, subnational governments **reallocated budgetary funds into extra-budgetary funds** in order to further reduce the amount of revenues that they had to share with the center (Wang 1997; Martinez-Vazquez 2006). Lou (2008) aptly compared the fiscal strength of the center compared to that of local governments to the picture of a "weak trunk with strong branches". There was also a **growing climate of distrust** between central and subnational governments, and each side made the other responsible for behaving inappropriately. From the local government perspective, the frequent changes in the revenue sharing rules implied planning uncertainty and they aspired for a greater commitment of the central government to ensure solid local finances (Shen et al. 2012). On the other hand, the central government of course realized that the subnational governments were trying to circumvent remittances, eroding fiscal revenues at the national level. Macroeconomic control was hampered. The fact that state firms' revenues were assigned to either the central fixed revenue or the local fixed revenue based on SOE ownership aligned the fiscal interests of subnational governments with those of locally owned state firms, leading to **distorted competition** as well as **local protectionism** and increasing **interregional rivalry**. As already mentioned above, the fiscal decentralization also led to **increasing regional inequality,** and especially poor provinces suffered economically from the reforms of the fiscal system (Lou and Wang 2008). Finally, it complicated coordination of investment projects in which multiple provinces were involved.

Box 4.12 Summary: Fiscal Reforms

Prior to 1978: **unified revenue collection and unified spending system**

Central government collects all revenues and reallocates them down to each level of government; "*eating from one big pot*" (chi daguofan) → incompatible with market-oriented reforms; declining share of fiscal revenue in GDP.

After 1978: **fiscal revenue-sharing system**

Revenues were shared by the central and provincial governments; "*eating from separate kitchens*" (fenzao chifan); three waves of reforms: 1980–1985, 1985–1988, 1988–1993.

4.4.5 Foreign Trade Reform

The opening up of the Chinese economy to international trade and investment was a key element of the China's economic reform process and both went in fact hand in hand, as implied by the slogan "reform and opening up" (gaige kaifang). Within only 40 years, China managed to transform from an isolated economy into the world's leading exporter and trading nation.

Prior to economic reforms, China had a Soviet-style foreign trade regime which represented an extreme example of import substitution (Lardy 1992). The state heavily controlled all foreign trade activities and the state's corresponding foreign trade plan was implemented by foreign trade corporations (FTCs). The Soviet Union became China's biggest trading partner; however, China's main goal was to become eventually economically self-reliant. In 1955, the director of the Ministries Import Bureau stated that "*the purpose of importing more industrial equipment from the Soviet Union is to lay the foundation of China's industrial independence, so that in the future China can produce all of the producer goods it needs and will not have to rely on imports from the outside*" (Zhang Huadong in Mah 1968: 672–3). China imported grain as well as industrial materials and intermediate goods that could not be produced domestically but which were necessary for the heavy industry development strategy that China pursued during the 1950s. Exports were the "inevitable evil" to earn sufficient foreign exchange to pay for the imports (Naughton 2018). Thus, the main role of imports was to overcome domestic bottlenecks and contribute to China's socialist industrialization while exports mainly financed imports (Lardy 1992). That is, international trade was not regarded as a potential source that could drive economic growth and development by specializing in one's comparative advantage or by enhancing product quality because of the increased competition. There were "two airlocks" that ensured that the center was able to control the flows of goods and money, namely, (i) the centrally controlled foreign-trade monopoly and (ii) foreign-exchange system (Naughton 2018). With respect to (i), centrally controlled FTCs exercised monopolies over imports and exports. Regarding (ii), imports that went through FTCs were repriced in order to reflect Chinese domestic prices, and thus could not fulfil their allocative and incentive functions (Lardy 1992). In addition, the Chinese currency was not convertible and there was an extensive system of rigid exchange controls. Producers were not allowed to retain their foreign exchange income from the sales of goods abroad, there were strict controls on the outflow of foreign capital, and the individual's right to hold foreign currency was subject to tight limitations (Branstetter and Lardy 2014). In 1955, the official exchange rate amounted to ¥2.46/US dollar and it remained almost unchanged for two decades. In order to subsidize the import of capital goods, the exchange rate was highly overvalued which made it financially unattractive to engage in export activities. In 1955, the average cost of earning one US dollar in foreign exchange was ¥3.08 which was 36% above the official exchange rate; by the early 1960s, this premium has increased to 170% (with an average cost of ¥6.65 per US dollar, cf. Lardy 1992).

In the mid-1970s, the economic situation in China began to recover from the aftermath of the Cultural Revolution and China started to export light manufacturing consumer goods (primarily textiles) and oil. The foreign exchange earnings were used to buy technology from Japan and Western countries in the course of an ambitious technology-import program, especially during 1977/78. However, China soon ran out of foreign-exchange, particularly after domestic production grew much more slowly than expected (Naughton 2018; Lardy 2002). It became more and more obvious that China's traditional foreign trading system was inappropriate for the opening of China to the outside world and that a comprehensive reform of the system was inevitable. The course of the reforms, however, was very uneven and there were phases of only incremental reform measures in alternation with phases of accelerated reforms. Especially in the beginning, reforms were carefully executed.

The **open-door policy** was officially announced in December 1978 at the third plenary session of the 11th central committee of the CPC. As argued by Tzeng (1991), the logic of the open-door policy was not equivalent to the logic of trade liberalization. Whereas the latter aimed at eliminating tariff and non-tariff barriers for the promotion of international free trade, the former focused on the absorption of foreign technology and investment to enable the self-reliant national construction. In 1981, Deng Xiaoping stated that "the door is being opened because the Four Modernizations require it" (People's Daily, 4 December 1981, p. 124, cited in Tzeng 1991). Beside the increased technological exchange with other economies, the open-door policy should also enhance the entry of Chinese products into the world market.

The Coastal Development Strategy (CDS) was the "vehicle" to carry the open-door policy through China's coastal regions (Tzeng 1991). During the first 2 years of reform, the government allowed for the opening of new trade channels in Guangdong and Fujian. The reason for the choice of these two provinces was the proximity to Hong Kong. In 1980, four special economic zones (SEZs, jiangji tequ) were established in Guangdong and Fujian. These enclaves provided special tax provisions and other incentives in order to attract FDIs (see also Sect. 4.4.6). In 1984, 14 coastal cities were opened to foreign investment, soon followed by the creation of various economic zones (in Yangtze River Delta, Pearl River Delta, and the Min Nan region). The CDS was officially confirmed as a key element in economic policy in February 1988 at the fourth Meeting of the Political Bureau of the CPC. Its main goal was to allow China to expand its exports and compete in the global market.

Box 4.13 The Origin of the CDS

The original concept of the coastal development strategy was put forward by Wang Jian. In his beneficial international cycle (BIC) framework, he emphasized the necessity to link the traditional rural sector and the more developed urban sector through export-oriented and labor-intensive industrialization.

The four key ideas of the BIC concept were:

(1) focus on export-oriented and labor-intensive industrialization promotion in coastal areas
(2) active involvement of industries in global competition and the earning of foreign exchange
(3) use of these earnings to attract more foreign investment and technology for the promotion of the heavy industry
(4) once (3) is completed, funds should be used to facilitate agricultural development.

The BIC was intended to be implemented in three main stages, starting with the development of the export-oriented and labor-intensive industry in coastal areas in stage 1. During stage 2, also products manufactured by companies located in the inland provinces would be introduced into international markets. Foreign exchange earnings were intended to support the development of the basic industrial infrastructure. Over the third stage, the earnings would then be primarily employed to support the heavy processing industry.

For an extensive discussion see Tzeng (1991).

Since the mid-1980s, especially between 1984 and 1988, Chinese policymakers gradually liberalized the main national trading system (Naughton 2018; Bin 2015; Shujin et al. 1998). The key elements of this reform episode will be briefly described in the following.

Demonopolizing/Decentralization of the foreign trade authority

The central government **decentralized the authority to engage in foreign trade** by granting greater powers of export administration to provincial governments, national production ministries, and some large enterprises if they supplied more than $3 million annually in export products ($1 million for firms in Guangdong) (Lardy 1992). The **number of companies** that were allowed to engage in foreign trade transactions increased from 12 in 1979 to around 800 in 1985 and further to 5000 three years later (Branstetter and Lardy 2014; Wang 2008; see also Fig. 4.7). Even though this increase is remarkable, the monopoly position of the national trade corporations was reduced only slowly. The national corporations still controlled 91% of exports and 87% of imports in 1981. By 1984, the share still amounted to 79% and 65%, respectively (World Bank 1988). The decentralization was accompanied by a **phasing out of the national foreign trade plan**. Prior to the foreign trade reforms, the plan extensively specified quantities for export and import commodities. However, the scope was decreased stepwise, and by 1988 the planned share of exports had decreased to 45% and that of imports to 40% (Lardy 1992; Working Party 1988). In addition, the foreign trade plan was partitioned into

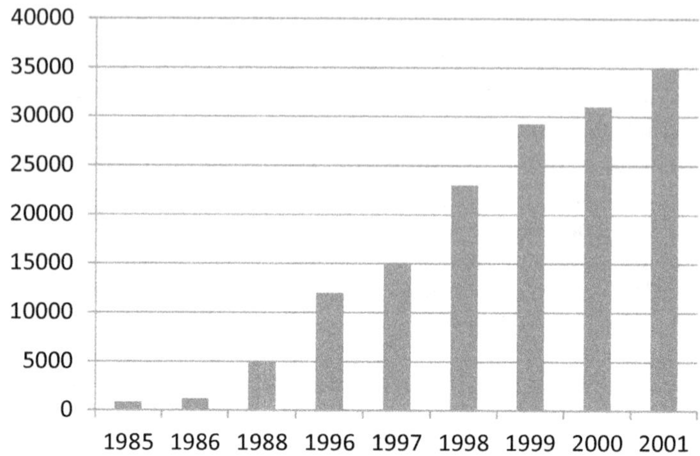

Fig. 4.7 Number of trading companies. *Source* Wang (2008), Branstetter and Lardy (2014), Lardy (2002)

a **mandatory plan component** (zhilingxing jihua) and a **guidance plan component** (zhidaoxing jihua). The targets of the latter plan increased local trading corporations' flexibility in composing the specific import/export product mix. Moreover, the **agency system** (daili zhi) was encouraged. Under this system, FTCs at the national and local level provided international trade services to firms engaged in the export and/or import of goods. However, unlike in previous arrangements, the domestic prices of traded commodities were linked to international prices (through the exchange rate) and the firms now were responsible for profits and losses of the transaction (Lardy 1992).

Tariffs and non-tariff barriers

While the central government decentralized foreign trade and reduced the scope of the state's foreign trade plan, it imposed high tariffs, complemented by significant non-tariff barriers. In 1982, the average statutory import tariff rate amounted to 56% and after a slight cut in 1985 (in the course of the new customer regulation that revised the tariff schedule), it fluctuated around 43% until 1992 (see also Fig. 4.8). In addition, according to the World Bank (1994), 51% of imports were subject to at least one of four overlapping non-tariff barriers. As depicted in Fig. 4.9, the number of imports subject to licensing increased from 21 in 1982 to 53 in 1989. The number of export goods subject to licensing grew even more rapidly from 24 in 1981 to 173 in 1989, peaking at 235 in the mid-1980s. Tariff revenues amounted to almost ¥50 billion between 1980 and 1985 which was more than twice the amount collected between 1953 and 1979 (Lardy 1992).

While the introduction of tariff and non-tariff barriers usually reflects foreign trade limitations, in the Chinese case, they can be rather interpreted as liberalization

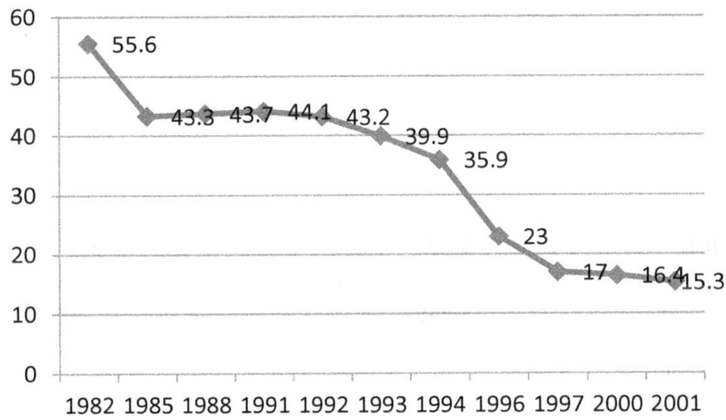

Fig. 4.8 Average statutory import tariff rate. *Source* Lardy (2002) and sources within

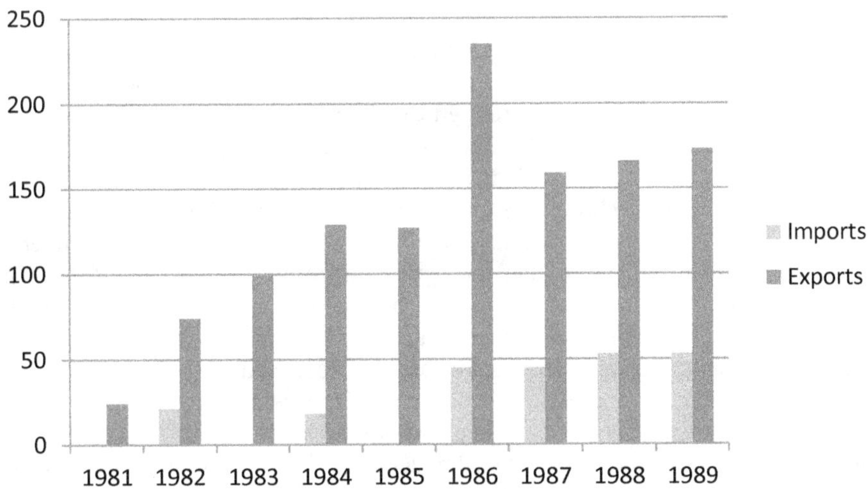

Fig. 4.9 Imports and exports subject to licensing. *Source* Lardy (1992) and sources cited within

measures since they replaced the direct planning system of the entire trade (Wang 2008; Lardy 1992, 2002). According to the 5-phase trade regime evolution classification of Krueger (1978) and Bhagwati (1978), during the first trade regime development stage, there is an across-the-board imposition of quantitative controls, whereas throughout the second phase the control system becomes increasingly complex (see also Edwards 1993 for an overview). China's increasing use of import and export licensing and other measures such as import duties, export subsidies, etc. thus fitted well into the transition from stage one to stage two according to Krueger (1978) and Bhagwati (1978). This strategy allowed Chinese policymakers to protect specific domestic industries and improve the imbalance between rising import demand and limited foreign exchange while phasing out the states' foreign trade plan.

Exchange rate reform

As outlined above, China had an overvalued currency prior to reforms. In 1981, the official exchange rate amounted to ¥1.5 per dollar. This enabled a relatively cheap import of important capital goods that could not be produced domestically. However, overvaluation also made export activities unprofitable and thus created an excess demand for foreign exchange. As a consequence, there were extensive exchange controls. With the beginning of reforms, the government started to relax these restrictions.

At the beginning of the 1980s, the central government issued interim regulations for exchange control. A key modification was that also banking institutions other than the Bank of China were allowed to handle foreign exchange transaction (before, the Bank of China had held a monopoly position). At the end of 1980, around 90 banks and financial institutions were authorized to engage in foreign exchange business (Lardy 1992; IMF 1989). Moreover, the tight restrictions of individuals' right to hold foreign currency (e.g. remittances from relatives abroad or saved foreign currency from study trips, etc.) were relaxed and around the mid-1980s, individuals were allowed to open foreign exchange accounts (Lardy 1992). Probably most importantly, the 100% foreign exchanges surrender requirements for exporting companies were relaxed (Branstetter and Lardy 2014). In 1979, the state introduced a **foreign exchange retention system (waihui liucheng zhidu)** that allowed export producing enterprises at the subordinate level of governmental administration to retain part of the foreign exchange earnings (Lardy 1992). The structure of the retention rates incentivized the exploitation of **new types** of trade. For instance, the retention rates for compensation trade and for the processing and assembly of foreign components accounted for 15% and 30% of all earnings, respectively, whereas for most export commodities it was only allowed to retain exchange rate earnings above the level of exports achieved in 1978. In addition, the retention rate for commodities produced under local management was twice as high as for that produced under ministerial management (40% vs. 20%), thus incentivizing the newly permitted provincial and local trade corporations and supporting the decentralization of foreign trade outlined above.

During the 1980s, the government established **dual exchange rate systems**. In 1981, the government introduced an internal settlement rate which amounted to ¥2.8 per dollar in order to provide greater incentives for exporters (Lardy 1992; Naughton 2018). This rate only applied to trade transactions whereas non-trade transactions including foreign remittances and tourism expenditures still were subject to the official rate. Also, the official exchange rate was devalued gradually and when it reached ¥2.8 in 1984, internal settlement rate was abrogated (Lardy 2002).

In 1986, the government introduced a formal secondary market for foreign exchange (often referred to as the "**swap market**") and the dual exchange rates began to re-emerge. Foreign-funded enterprises in SEZs and major coastal cities were permitted to trade foreign exchange among themselves in **foreign exchange adjustment centers** (FEACs, waihui tiaoji zhongxin) at rates agreed between buyers and sellers (Mehran et al. 1996). The first FEAC had been already opened in 1985 in Shenzhen as a kind of initial experiment. Around 1985/86, there was a growing trade deficit accompanied by the depletion of the foreign exchange reserves. Because of this foreign exchange crisis, the State Council announced additional controls on how retained foreign exchange could be used in order to dampen imports and promote exports. As a consequence, the swap market initially only increased slowly. In 1988, the controls on the swap market were abolished and it was opened to domestic firms (first in Shanghai on a trial basis in April and 5 months later officially, cf. Lardy 1992). After the lifting of the previous restrictions, the swap market became increasingly important. The number of FEACs increased steadily, reaching 39 in 1988 and around 80 in the following year. Also, the foreign exchange transaction volume expanded rapidly, reaching more than $6,000 billion in 1988 and increasing further to around $8,600 billion in 1989. At the end of 1989, the official exchange rate was devalued by 21.2%, followed by minor adjustments in the following years (Lardy 2002).

Overall, the dual exchange rate systems (the internal settlement rate and the swap market) presented another application of the dual-track reform strategy in the area of foreign trade (Naughton 2018).

Export processing trade and dualist trade regime

In 1979, the state introduced a legal framework for export processing activities (Branstetter and Lardy 2014). Export processing includes, among others, the processing of imported raw materials for export and the assembly of imported components to produce exportable final goods (Lardy 1992). Firms located in coastal provinces that engaged in these activities were granted special privileges. These incentives were expanded in 1987, including the duty-free import of all raw materials and components used for the production of export goods. In addition, wholly foreign-owned companies and joint ventures were also authorized to import capital goods duty-free (Branstetter and Lardy 2014). These privileges presented not only a considerable cost advantage but also allowed exporters to bypass the intricate ordinary trade regime (Naughton 2018). By the late 1980s, China had in fact two separate trading regimes, (i) the **export processing trade regime** which was restricted to foreign enterprises and domestic firms engaged in export processing that was very open and (ii) the **ordinary trade regime** that applied to all other enterprises and that was much more restrictive (Fig. 4.10). This "one country, two systems" regime also caused two potential problems. First, there could be a welfare reducing effect since domestic Chinese enterprises could be crowded out by foreign companies because of their special legislative privileges, even if the domestic firms had a comparative advantage in the production of certain export processed goods. Second, a large part of the Chinese economy was still protected from international competition. However, with respect to the second problem, it has to be noted that some goods containing duty-free imports were illegally channeled into the domestic Chinese market and US goods were smuggled. Striking examples

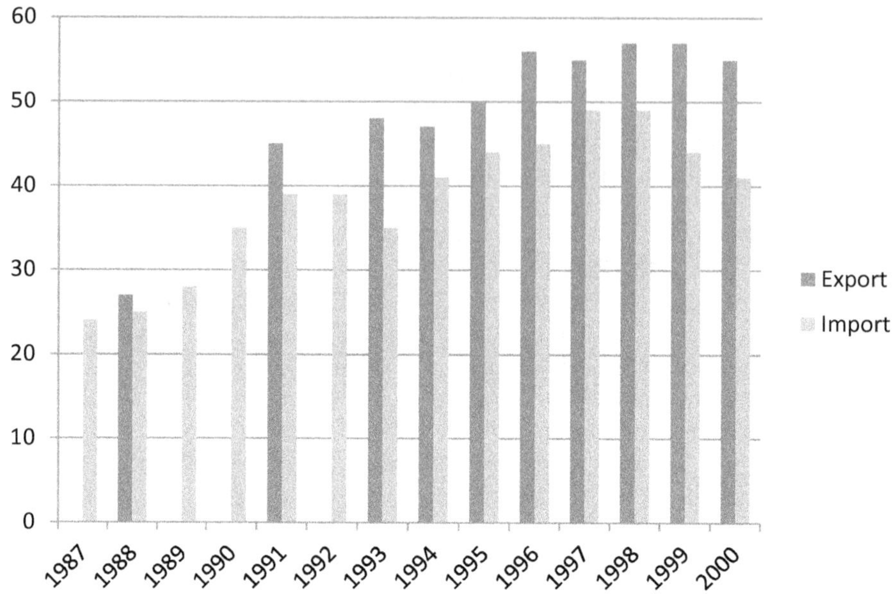

Fig. 4.10 Share of processing in total trade. *Sources* Lardy (2002)

include oranges and cigarettes (cf. Branstetter and Lardy 2014; Lardy 2002). Thus, the de facto degree of openness of the Chinese economy (including the interior) was much higher.

This dualist trade regime was established in the course of the Coastal Development Strategy, and the export processing trade zone encompassed the entire coastline (Tzeng 1991). Thus, even though the Chinese export processing shows certain similarities with the development strategies of Japan and South Korea, the sheer size of the Chinese export processing zone is rather unique (Naughton 2018).

Over the course of time, the role of the dualist trade regime had changed. Initially, Hong Kong businesses used the Chinese cheap labor in order to assembly export goods. However, when processing trade gained increasing importance in the production of electronics hardware, the trade regime became an important part of global high-technology production networks (Naughton 2018, see also Sect. 4.5.3.1).

Box 4.14 Summary: Open-Door Policy and Trade Reforms

Open-door policy (official announcement in December 1978).

Focus on the absorption of foreign technology and investment to enable the self-reliant national construction; **Coastal Development Strategy** (CDS) as a "vehicle" to carry the open-door policy through China's coastal regions.

Gradual liberalization of the national trading system (especially between 1984–1988)

Decentralization of the foreign trade authority

Phasing out of the national foreign trade plan; partitioning of the foreign trade plan into a mandatory plan component and a guidance plan component (the latter increased the flexibility of local trading firms), encouragement of the agency system.

Introduction of tariff and non-tariff barriers

Replaced the direct planning system of the entire trade.

Relaxation of foreign exchange restrictions

Foreign exchange retention system (1979), dual exchange-rate system (1980s), "swap markets" and foreign-exchange adjustment centers (mid-1980s).

Dual trade regimes

Export processing trade regime and ordinary trade regime.

4.4.6 Foreign Direct Investment (FDI)

1978, the year of the beginning of the reforms, marks an important milestone for the role of foreign investment in China. Even though FDI had played a significant role in China's early industrialization in the 1930s, it had been almost non-existent in China after 1949 (with the exception of few joint ventures with socialist countries; cf. Naughton 2018). Significantly departing from this self-reliance policy during the Mao period, in 1978, Deng Xiaoping underlined the importance of attracting foreign direct investment in order to acquire advanced technology (Chen 2019). Allowing foreign companies into the domestic market was the central point of China's "open door policy".

However, especially in the beginning, there was substantial political opposition to opening up the Chinese economy to foreign investment flows. Many politicians were afraid that FDI would come at the cost of giving up national sovereignty. Letting in foreign investors was regarded as "selling the nation" (Xu 2011). This was especially due to China's rather negative historical experiences (see also Sects. 4.2 and 4.3). At this point, allowing FDI would also have not been in line with the Chinese Constitution (Xu 2011). In addition, it was feared that opening the country to FDI would increase inequality (Zhao 2009). However, the Chinese economy still suffered heavily from the aftermath of the Cultural Revolution and FDI could help to speed up the economic development process.

In 1979, officials of Guangdong province proposed the idea of establishing special economic zones to attract FDI in an experimental manner in Shenzhen and Zhuhai (Cai et al. 2008; Xu 2011). In case that the experiments were successful, other cities could follow. Still, there was high degree of skepticism toward this approach among the top leadership. Eventually, small-scale experiments in four cities were approved in the same year. In 1980, **four special economic zones** (SEZs, jiangji tequ) were established, three in Guangdong (Shenzhen, Zhuhai, and Shantou) and one in Fujian (Xiamen). All cities were located far away from the political center in Beijing. Thus, it was ensured that (a) the political interference was rather small and (b) in case of a failure of the experiments, this would be less associated with the central government. In addition, all four cities were located in coastal areas and in close proximity to Hong Kong, Macao, and Taiwan. This enabled them a good access to ports, railways, etc. Shenzhen probably had the highest strategic location advantage since it is bordering Hong Kong which already had a well-functioning market economy and management expertise (Zheng 2010; Yeung et al. 2009). Hong Kong and Shenzhen (and later also other SEZs in the Pearl River Delta region) complemented each other perfectly: while Hong Kong provided access to world markets, advanced technology, capital, and management know-how, the Chinese special economic zones were endowed with land and abundant cheap labor (Yuan et al. 2010).

Foreign investment in SEZs was actively encouraged by favorable tax rates (including tax holidays for 3 years), inexpensive land, simplified administration procedures, and rapid customs clearance. Moreover, foreign enterprises could import raw materials and components used for the production of export goods duty-free (see also Sect. 4.4.5). They also had to pay a significantly lower statutory rate on profits (15% compared to 30% for domestic enterprises). In addition, the SEZs provided a good infrastructure and business services to foreign enterprises and thus attracted FDIs (cf. Naughton 2018; Enright et al. 2005).

One key advantage of the SEZs was that they could be easily monitored and presented less threat to the overall national economy (Naughton 2018). After the initial SEZs proved to be highly successful, growing at an annual rate ranging from 9% for Shantou to even 58% for Shenzhen, the opposition visibly diminished. In fact, the SEZs gradually increased the credibility of the reform process. In 1984, 14 coastal cities were opened to foreign investment (duiwai kaifeng chengshi),[22] and 1 year later, economic zones were created in Yangtze River Delta, Pearl River Delta, and Southern Fujian (in particular, in the Min Nan region).[23] In 1988, the

[22] Dalian, Qinhuangdao, Tianjin, Yantai, Qingdao, Lianyungang, Nantong, Shanghai, Ningbo, Wenzhou, Fuzhou, Guangzhou, Zhanjiang, and Beihai.

[23] To be precise, these cities were economic and technological development zones (ETDZs) which were smaller than SEZs (cf. Zheng 2010).

Shanghai Pudong New Development Zone was opened to FDI, followed by the entire coastal area.

In 1979, the **Foreign Equity Joint Venture Law** was promulgated and the Chinese government committed itself to install policies to attract FDIs. FDIs were granted legal status in China and ensured foreign investors' rights and benefits (Chen 2019; Dang 2008).

The **Law of Foreign Invested Enterprises** of 1986 and the **Law on Chinese Foreign Contractual Ventures** of 1988, together with the Foreign Equity Joint Venture Enterprise Law of 1979 provided the first basis for China's foreign investment regulatory regime (Li 2019).[24]

Box 4.15 Summary: FDI Reforms

Creation of economic zones

- 1980: creation of four special economic zones (SEZs) in Guangdong and Fujian
- 1984: opening up of 14 coastal cities to foreign investment
- 1985: creation of various economic zones (in Yangtze River Delta, Pearl River Delta, and the Min Nan region).

Measures to encourage foreign investment in SEZs: favorable tax rates, simplified administration procedures, duty-free imports of raw materials used for the production of export goods, lower statutory rates on profits, good infrastructure.

First legal basis for China's foreign investment regulatory regime

- 1979: Foreign Equity Joint Venture Law
- 1986: Law of Foreign Invested Enterprises
- 1988: Law on Chinese Foreign Contractual Ventures.

According to Naughton (2018), SEZs shared many similarities with the export processing zones (EPZs) that emerged in Asia in the 1970s (e.g. in South Korea and Taiwan, cf. Chen 1997). EPZs provided very similar advantages to foreign enterprises, including a favorable tax treatment, simplified administrative procedures, etc. Thus, they promoted exports while at the same time domestic companies were still protected. Through the EPZs, Asian countries could accumulate foreign exchange earnings and the zones also contributed to the creation of new jobs; however, at the cost of giving up potential tax revenues and linkages to the domestic economy.

[24] These three laws are also known as "sanzi qiye fa" (Li 2019).

While this is in general also true for the Chinese SEZs, they have been even more "special". In contrast to many Asian countries establishing EPZs, China was still a planned economy at the end of the 1970s. Thus, the difference between SEZs and the rest of the economy was even more pronounced than for the EPZs in the rest of Asia. Also, the functions went far beyond that of EPZs. The responsible local governments had an exceptionally high degree of autonomy and were allowed to retain most of the SEZs' earnings. Moreover, they were allowed to develop municipal laws and regulations along the basic lines of national regulations which provided them with more freedom to experiment with policy reform measures (Zheng 2010). Probably, the most prominent example in this respect is Shenzhen which pushed forward various institutional innovations, including a wage reform, a minimum wage, and a social insurance package.

Until a certain threshold (US$30 million prior to 2004), local governments could approve FDI projects without approval from the national level. However, this also led to the artificial subdivision of FDI projects into smaller segments that just met the threshold requirement (Lubman 2006). Regional competition also incentivized local government leaders to provide an environment favorable to foreign investment because it could use local output and employment and thus, also provide them with a better position in the national promotion procedure.

SEZs were also much bigger in size. While EPZs in Taiwan, Malaysia, Indonesia, and the Philippines usually ranged between 0.7 and 36.6 km^2, Zhuhai and Xiamen accounted for an area of more than 100 km^2, Shenzhen was even larger than 300 km^2 (all numbers are for 1990, cf. Naughton 2018). SEZs were some kind of experimental "laboratories" in which reforms could be first tested before they were implemented on a bigger scale once they proved successful (Xu 2011; Naughton 2018). Thus, they provided space, the "window to the world" but also a kind of buffer for the skeptics by keeping the effects within bounds (Dang 2008; Chen 1997).

Even though FDI increased steadily over the first and second reform phase—FDI inflows accounted on average US$1.8 billion per annum—its share in GDP was still below 1% (see Fig. 4.14 in Sect. 4.5.4.2). This can partly be attributed to the fact that the Chinese government only gradually opened the economy to FDIs but also because of the cautiousness of foreign investors. The number of SEZs increased to 77 in 1985 and further to almost 300 in 1990 (see also Fig. 4.11).

4.4.7 Financial Reform

Prior to the economic reforms in 1978, China had only one national bank, namely, the **People's Bank of China (PBC)** which served both, central and commercial banking functions (Huang and Wang 2019). It controlled more than 90% of the total financial assets and was responsible for almost all financial transactions (Allen et al. 2014). However, between 1979 and 1984, the government started to divest the PBC of all its commercial activities which were taken over by four state-owned specialized banks, namely, the Agricultural Bank of China (ABC), the China

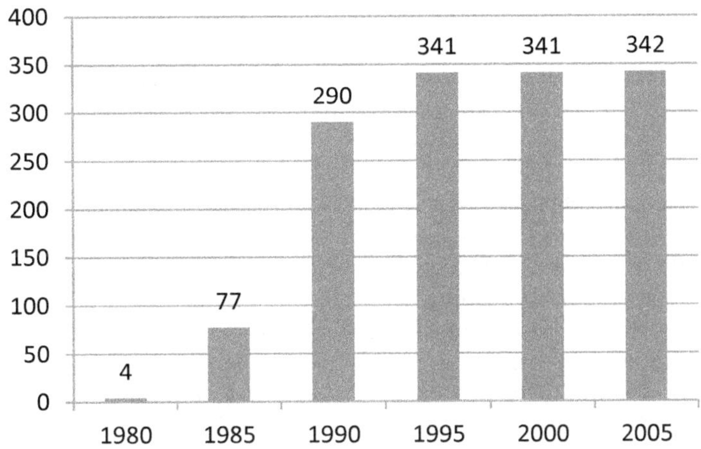

Fig. 4.11 Number of SEZs. *Source* Xu (2011)

Construction Bank (CCB), the Bank of China (BOC), and the Industrial and Commercial Bank of China (ICBC). These banks which obtained monopoly positions are often referred to as the "**Big Four**" (Naughton 2018; Zhang 2019a). The BOC handled transactions related to foreign trade and investment, the ABC was responsible for the banking business in rural areas, providing rural development loans and primarily financing agriculture, the CCB was specialized in transactions related to fixed investment (including infrastructure and manufacturing projects), and the ICBC was responsible for commercial transactions (Allen et al. 2014). Freed from its commercial activities, the PBC became China's **central bank** with the role of carrying out monetary policy and monitoring financial markets (Huang and Wang 2019). However, it is important to note that the PBC was part of the State Council and thus not independent from the government. According to the Provisional Regulation Relating to Bank Management of 1986, the PBC also had the responsibility to manage the state firms' demand for operating capital (Okazaki 2007).

Commercial banks were required to make deposits of legal reserves in the central bank which created the need for short-term borrowing and lending of funds (cf. Zhang 2019a). In 1984, specialized banks were allowed to lend and borrow money from each other and 2 years later, the PBC officially established rules for **interbank lending**.

In 1979, foreign banks were authorized to establish representative offices in China (Li et al. 2015). In 1981, the Chinese government authorized foreign banks to establish operating institutes in SEZs, and 1 year later the first operating institutes of the Nanyang commercial bank was set up in Shenzhen (Zhang 2019a). The 1980s also saw the rise of non-bank financial institutions such as trust companies, security companies, and insurance companies. This will be more extensively discussed in the section of financial reforms during the second reform phase.

Overall, the most striking financial reform during the first reform period was the abolishment of the "monobanking" system.

The main focus of financial reforms since 1984 was on the establishment of new banks and securities markets (Okazaki 2007).

During the mid-1980s, the central bank lifted restrictions on new entries in the banking sector (Rehman et al. 2016). Several **joint-stock commercial banks (JSCBs)** were set up in order to create competition in the banking sector. **JSCBs** are held by corporations (including non-state entities) and not directly by the state. Even though they are not completely privately owned, the Chinese government's stakes in them are considerably less compared to the big state-owned commercial banks (Amstad et al. 2020). In 1986, the **Bank of Communications (BOCOM)** was re-established and 1 year later, the China CITIC Bank and the China Merchants Bank were created (Zhang 2019a). Various local shareholding banks emerged after 1986 (for instance, the Shenzhen Development Bank). By 1992, around a dozen shareholding banks were created (Zhang 2019a).

Rural Credit Cooperatives (RRCs), defined as grass-root branches of the ABC, and their urban equivalent, the Urban Credit Cooperatives (UCCs) were set up during the 1980s (Allen et al. 2014; see also Nan et al. 2018, He and Ong 2014 on RCCs).

The 1980s also saw a rapid development of various **non-bank financial institutions**, including **trust and investment companies** as well as **securities companies**. Trust companies were an important source for local governments to finance local development. In addition, banks used trust companies to circumvent restrictions of the credit plan. Due to the increasing amount of credits and illegal fund operations, the central government conducted various rounds of clean-up over the 1980s (cf. Zhang 2019a). The first securities company was created in 1987 (the Shenzhen Securities Company).

Due to difficulties for private enterprises to obtain loans from the big state-owned commercial banks, an underground private financial system emerged and the first underground banks were established in Wenzhou (in the coastal province Zhejiang) (Zhang 2019a). They either engaged with illegal deposits and lending (collecting funds from relatives and friends) or with the illegal buying and selling of foreign-exchange. Besides that, there existed pawn shops and privately offered funds (Zhang 2019a).

Box 4.16 Summary: Financial Reform

Abolishment of the "monobanking" system (1979–1984)

Agricultural Bank of China (**ABC**), the China Construction Bank (**CCB**), the Bank of China (**BOC**), and the Industrial and Commercial Bank of China (**ICBC**), the so-called **"Big Four"**, take over the commercial activities of the People's Bank of China (**PBC**); PBC becomes China's **central bank**.

Establishment of new banks and securities markets (since 1984)

Lifting of restrictions on new entries in the banking sector by the central bank; establishment of joint-stock commercial banks (JSCBs), re-establishment of the Bank of Communications (BOCOM) (1986), establishment of Rural and Urban Credit Cooperatives; development of non-bank financial institutions (trust investment companies, securities companies).

4.5 Phase of Market-Building Reforms Starting from 1992/3

As already argued in Sect. 4.1, the Chinese reforms followed a stop-and-go pattern, and accelerated reform episodes (in 1979/80, 1984, and 1987/88) alternated with more cautious phases (in 1981/82, 1986, and 1989/90) during which conservative policymakers raised skepticism about the efficacy of reforms. The reform enthusiasm always cooled down after macroeconomic imbalances occurred as a consequence of the accelerated reform phases; however, at least after the first two slowdown episodes, reforms resumed relatively fast. The situation around 1989/90 turned out to be more severe. Inflation increased to 9% in 1987 and even 27% in the following year, the highest value since the beginning of reforms (Cheng 1991; see Box 4.6).[25] Consequently, conservatism ascended again and many questioned the reform and opening up policies (Naughton 2018).

Another, partly related development exacerbated the situation: At the end of 1986, student demonstrations had started, demanding further political and economic liberalization. The Chinese leadership was highly critical toward these protests. After the death of Hu Yaobang in 1989, a pro-reformer and former general secretary who had been forced to resign, the situation escalated and many students gathered at the Tiananmen Square in Beijing to mourn him. The demonstrations were suppressed with military force and subsequently, many pro-reform politicians were removed (including Zhao Ziyang and some of his advisers) (cf. Chow 2007).

Between 1989 and 1999, conservatives tried to reverse the reforms. The soaring inflation was seen as a sign that the economic reforms installed earlier were not successful. However, this was a severe misjudgment by the conservative hard-liners, and the whole attempt to rollback reforms turned out to be a failure. In fact, the market track even recovered much faster than the plan track, and the reforms of the 1980s aroused an enormous dynamic that surprised the conservatives

[25] The underlying reason for this inflation spike was the unrestrained enterprise spending on capital investment and wage increases which was financed by banks which unreservedly extended credits (Cheng 1991). According to Naughton (1991), these inflation spikes could therefore have been avoided if the restructuring of the fiscal system would have occurred earlier.

(Naughton 2018). In 1991, economic reforms again picked up speed and during Deng Xiaoping's Southern Tour from 18 January to 21 February 1992, he recommitted to the nationwide implementation of the "reform and opening up" policy. The subsequent reforms during the 1990s were more comprehensive compared to that of the previous decade (see also Box 4.17) and also advanced to critical areas such as finance and state enterprises.

Box 4.17 1980s Versus 1990s Reforms

The two periods of accelerated transition had very different characteristics. Zhao Ziyang, appointed by Deng Xiaoping, was responsible for the economic policymaking in the 1980s. Because of the political environment, his policymaking was rather cautious and consensual. By contrast, Zhu Rongji who was in charge of the reforms during the 1990s followed a much bolder and rapid reform approach. Also, the focus of the reforms during these two phases differed dramatically: In the course of the 1980s reform, markets were introduced (with a focus on agriculture and industry) with the help of the dual-track system. In contrast, the 1990s reform focused more on the strengthening of the market institutions (with a focus on finance and regulation) after the economy had grown out of the plan (meaning that the dual-track had served its time). It was not until the 1990s that privatization began and comprehensive SOEs reforms were installed. One decade earlier, competition was rather created by entry of new actors such as the TVEs and via the dual-track system. While political power had been decentralized during the 1980s, the 1990s saw a recentralization. Finally, the reforms of the 1980s did not impose losses on any major social group ("reform without losers", Lau et al. 2000), while the 1990s reforms created losers (for instance, SOE workers).

Source Naughton (2018), Table 5.1.

4.5.1 Enhanced Reform of State-Owned Enterprises (SOEs)

The contract responsibility system reform during the second half of the 1980s helped to improve the performance of SOEs for a while; however, it was not able to solve the principal-agent and soft budget constraint problems. Consequently, state firms recorded substantial losses. The deteriorating financial situation was the driving force for more comprehensive SOE reforms at the beginning of the 1990s (Garnaut et al. 2006). There was a rising awareness among policymakers that an adequate institutional framework had to be developed in order to solve the SOE problem. As specified in the 14th National Congress of the CPC, the core element for the establishment of a modern enterprise system for the socialist market economy was the **ownership transformation (gaizhi)**. As argued by Song (2019), gaizhi was in fact a euphemism for privatization. The **Company Law of 1994** was an important milestone for establishing a regulatory framework for "corporatizing" SOEs, a process during which traditional SOEs were one by one converted into the legal form of a corporation, either joint stock companies or, for smaller state firms, limited liability companies (Naughton 2018; Chavance 2017). The Company Law helped significantly to improve the corporate governance procedures of state firms. In the course of the reform, the shareholders' meeting, the board of directors, and the supervisory board became the three main bodies of Chinese companies with the board of directors being the supreme authority.

At the 15th National Congress in 1997, SOE reforms were further accelerated through the adoption of the **"grasping the large, letting go of the small"** (zhua da fang xiao) reform. Under this policy, small and medium-sized SOEs were restructured into private-sector firms (via employee shareholding, open sales, public offerings, leasing, mergers, joint ventures, or bankruptcies; cf. Garnaut et al. 2006), whereas large SOEs were retained by the state. The motivation for this reform was the following: by retaining control of large SOEs, the government was able to control strategic industries such as finance, infrastructure, energy, transportation, and the heavy industry. At the same time, it could divest small, inefficient SOEs (Morck and Yeung 2017).

The closing of small and medium-sized state firms was accompanied by mass layoffs (xiagang policy), and between 1998 and the middle of 2001, around 28 million workers lost their job, creating the first generation of reform losers (Zhang 2019a; Song 2019; Jefferson 2016). The private sector helped to absorb the laid-off workers.

Another important reform was the establishment of the **Shanghai and Shenzhen stock exchanges** in 1990 and 1991 that created the preconditions for the **Modern Enterprise System** since they enabled the listing and financing of SOEs in the capital market, that is, allowing corporatized SOEs to raise funds by issuing shares (Zhang 2019a; Allen et al. 2015). The implementation of the **Securities Law in 1999** formalized the legal status of China's capital markets for the first time and facilitated their development (Qi 2008). Another related reform was the establishment of a social security system in 1997 (Song 2019).

The reforms since 2003 focused on large and important SOEs. In 2003, the State-Owned Assets Supervision and Administration Commission (SASAC), which is directly under the State Council, was set up in order to better manage SOEs' assets and in order to improve governance (Lam and Schipke 2017). On behalf of the central government, it fulfilled the role of shareholder for large SOEs (Lin et al. 2020). Shortly afterwards, corresponding provincial SASACs were established, performing similar functions at lower government levels (Holz 2018; Perkins and Rawski 2014). In 2003, the SASAC initiated the board reform of central SOEs. It supervised the board of directors and raised the number of outside directors in order to strengthen the board's monitoring and advising role.

In the course of the third Plenum of the 18th National Congress in 2013, the directions for future SOEs' reforms were defined, including the promotion of mixed ownership, the shift from asset management to capital management, and the definition of SOEs' functions to determine levels of state ownership and control (Song

2019; Zhang 2019a). However, it was not until the publishing of the "Guiding Opinions and Deepening the Reform of State-Owned Enterprises" by the CPC Central Committee and the State Council in 2015 that the implementation of these reforms seriously started. The Guiding Opinions were accompanied by various supplementary files. This pattern is also referred to as "1+N" (Naughton 2017). With respect to the promotion of mixed ownership, the policies were sector specific: While for SOEs in competitive sectors, the mixed ownership was to be pushed forward steadily and state capital and non-state capital should both engage in the SOEs' operations, SOEs in strategic sectors "should remain state-controlled", however, "share-holdings of non-state parties" were encouraged (State Council 2015; Song 2019). According to Song (2019), the Chinese government has adopted a "picking the winner" approach regarding its mixed ownership reform. Successful large private companies were allowed to take a stake in large SOEs in sectors that had previously been restricted (such as Alibaba, Baidu, Tencent, and JD in China Unicom in 2017). Under the 2015 Guiding Opinions, SOEs were either classified as commercial or public service SOEs (Lin et al. 2020). Commercial SOEs were further subdivided into those in strategic sectors and those in competitive sectors. SOEs falling into the public category usually received more resources from the government than commercial SOEs; the latter were also allowed to compete with private enterprises (Lin et al. 2020). Finally, there was a reorganization of central SOEs, and between 2012 and 2018, there were a total of 20 mergers, and at the end of 2018, the number of SOEs had dropped to 96 (Lin et al. 2020).

Box 4.18 Summary: SOE Reforms (II)

Ownership transformation (gaizhi) (1992–2003)

- **"grasping the large, letting go of the small"**: small and medium-sized SOEs were restructured into private-sector firms; large SOEs were retained by the state (in order to retain control over strategic industries)
- Establishment of the **Shanghai and Shenzhen stock exchanges (1990, 1991)**: enabled the listing and financing of SOEs in the capital market
- **Company Law (1994)**: establishment of an institutional framework for the modern enterprise system and for "corporatizing" SOEs
- **Securities Law (1999)**: formalization of the legal status of China's capital markets; facilitation of capital market development

Restructuring large SOEs and organizational change (2003–2013)

- Creation of **State-Owned Assets Supervision and Administration Commission (SASAC) (2003)** (directly under the State Council) as the regulator and funder of SOEs
- Division of industries into three groups **(2006)** (key, pillar, and normal industries)

Renewed mixed-ownership reform (since 2013)

- **2013 announcement** of further reforms (to promote mixed ownership)
- **Issuance** of the "**Guiding Opinions** and Deepening the Reform of State-Owned Enterprises" (**2015**): 1+N policy system (one guiding core document supplemented by supporting policies); implementation of 2013 announcements; sector-specific: classification of SOEs as (a) commercial SOEs (divided into (i) strategic sectors or (ii) competitive sectors) or (b) public services SOEs.

4.5.2 Fiscal Reforms—Tax System Modernization

In order to deal with the problems introduced by the fiscal decentralization, particularly the centers' continuing declining revenues, the government adopted the **tax sharing reform in 1994** which fundamentally changed the Chinese tax system. The three main components of the fiscal reform were (a) tax modernization, (b) tax administration, and (c) tax sharing (see Wong and Bird 2014 for an excellent overview of the 1994 reform). Each component will be briefly described in the following.

Tax modernization: The tax structure was simplified considerably in order to increase transparency. The turnover-based product tax was replaced by the value-added tax (VAT) which amounted uniformly to 17%. Previously, turnover taxes had created severe distortions since the government expanded local enterprises which had an above average product tax rate such as in the liquor and tobacco sector even though the profit rates were low (cf. Zhou 2000; Wong and Bird 2014). In addition, an excise tax was introduced on 11 products, including cigarettes, alcohol, and several luxury consumer goods. Even though in the beginning a local business tax was still applied to services (at a rate of 5% turnover), it was gradually replaced by the VAT across all sectors.

Tax sharing system: The introduction of the **Tax Sharing System (TSS) (fenshuizhi)** was the core element of the tax reform. In particular, the previously negotiated system of general revenue-sharing was replaced by a mix of rule-based tax assignments and tax sharing. Even though taxes were still classified into three categories (centrally fixed, locally fixed, and shared taxes), these assignments were not subject to bargaining anymore (Arora and Norregaard 1997), reducing dramatically the discretionary powers of local governments. The revenues from the VAT were shared between the central government (75%) and local governments (25%) (cf. Wang 1997). The central government, in turn, ensured that local revenues would not fall short of a certain "basic amount".

Tax administration: The tax reform was complemented by the establishment of a national tax administration system. Previously, local tax offices were responsible for collecting all taxes. Under the new system, central and local tax administrations were separated. The newly created **State Administration of Taxation (SAT)** was responsible for collecting central and shared taxes (including the VAT and all taxes of centrally owned state enterprises), whereas the local governments were responsible for the collection of local taxes (Lou and Wang 2008; Wong and Bird 2014).

The central governments' revenue share in total revenues jumped up dramatically in 1994 (from 22 to 55.7%, see Fig. 4.12). According to Shen et al. (2012), this increase can be to a large extent attributed to the central collection of VAT which contributed to 42% of total government revenue in 1994. In addition, thanks to the creation of the SAT, local governments could not introduce tax reductions or exemptions without approval from the center. This eventually stopped the steady fall of the share of government revenues in GDP. The revenue-to-GDP ratio recovered steadily since 1996, increasing from 10.9 to 18.5% in 2003. This increase is particularly remarkable since GDP was also growing fast over this period. Between 1994 and 2005, the national fiscal revenue increased from ¥521.8 billion to ¥3161.8 billion which corresponds to an average annual growth rate of almost 18% (Shen et al. 2012).

The simplification of the tax system led to a more transparent tax assignment and at least to some extent corrected the incentives for local governments. Among others, excise taxes were assigned to the central government and business taxes to subnational governments, which reduced the incentives of local governments to

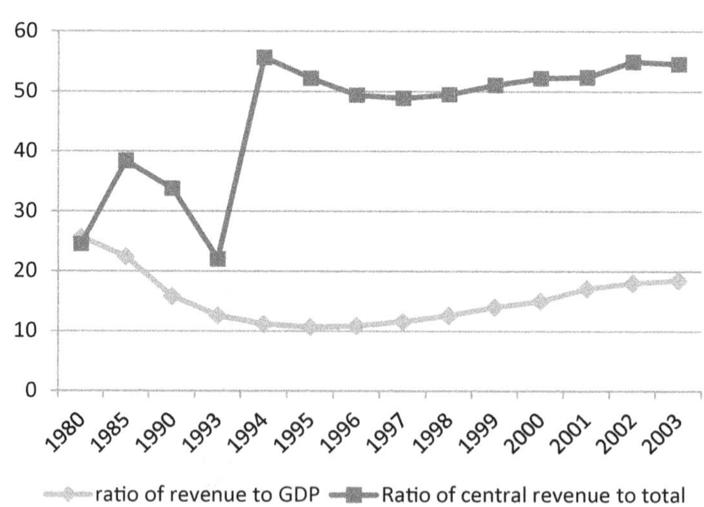

Fig. 4.12 The "two ratios" revenue. *Source* Martinez-Vazquez (2006)

favor disproportionally enterprises with higher tax returns, including the above-mentioned alcohol and tobacco industries (Shen et al. 2012; Zhang and Martinez-Vazquez 2003). Even though the incentive structure improved, there were still various unsolved problems. First, even though the central fiscal control increased considerably, there were persisting income disparities across provinces. Second, there was a lack of local government revenue sources and subnational governments tried to cope with this problem by increasing revenues in a variety of ways, some of them being de facto illegal (Chow 2007). Among others, the local governments raised revenues by leasing land-use rights to developers (Fan and Wan 2016). Third, China's VAT was of production-type and not of the consumption-type, implying that input VAT paid on purchase of fixed assets could not be used to offset the purchaser's output VAT. A production-type of tax can be detrimental to export competitiveness and it discourages new investments (Chow 2007). Especially in the course of the WTO accession, it appeared more and more urgent to align the Chinese VAT with international standards. However, the change to a consumption-type VAT came at a certain cost, because of the heavy reliance of China's growth on investment.

From 2004 onwards, first experiments were conducted in Northeastern China to transition to a consumption-based VAT that does not discourage investment (Cai and Harrison 2011). The reform was intended to evolve gradually, following the typical Chinese approach of a trial and error process; however, at the end of 2008 the government announced somewhat unexpectedly that the reform would be extended nationwide in the following year. When the "Revised VAT Regulations" became effective in January 2009, all enterprises could deduct the input VAT on equipment from the VAT on sales (Chen et al. 2019). This lowered the tax cost of investment, and according to Chen et al. (2019), the reform increased investment in domestic Chinese firms by 36% (relative to foreign firms).

Box 4.19 Summary: Tax Sharing Reform (1994)

(1) **Tax modernization** (simplification of the tax structure; replacement of return over-based product tax by value-added tax)
(2) **Tax sharing system** (mix of rule-based tax assignments and tax sharing; reduction of the discretionary powers of local governments)
(3) **Tax administration** (separation of central and local tax administrations; creation of the state administration of taxation).

4.5.3 Increased Liberalization—China Becomes a WTO Member

4.5.3.1 Trade Reforms in the 1990s

Trade reforms intensified in the 1990s. In 1994, China issued its first Foreign Trade Law which provided the legal foundation for modern Chinese trade policy (Bin 2015). Key aspects of the Trade Law included transparency and uniformity in order to meet the WTO requirements. The reforms undertaken during this reform stage (including a significant reduction of tariff and non-tariff barriers) indeed made the Chinese trade system increasingly consistent with the WTO guidelines (Song 2012). The most important reforms will be briefly described in the following.

Exchange rate

In 1994, the official **exchange rate** and the swap rate were **unified** and set to ¥8.7. The new unified rate was determined in China's newly established interbank foreign-exchange market, the **China Foreign Exchange Trading System (CFETS)** which became operational in Shanghai in April 1994. While initially only US Dollar and Hong Kong Dollar were traded at the CFETS, the Japanese Yen followed in the next year (Guijun and Schramm 2003; Song 2012). After a slight appreciation, the foreign exchange rate was fixed to ¥8.3 in 1995, and until 2005 the exchange rate fluctuated in a narrow range around this value. According to the IMF, the Chinese currency lost over 70% of its real value between 1980 and 1995. In 1996, China accepted the IMF's Article VIII obligations regarding current account convertibility (Lardy 2002; Guijun and Schramm 2003).

Tariff and non-tariff barriers

In the early 1990s, the average statutory import tariff rate was still relatively high, amounting to 43%. However, starting from 1992, it was decreased significantly, reaching 23% in 1996 and 15.3% in 2001. Also, import licensing was cut considerably during the 1990s. The share of imports regulated by licensing decreased to 18% in 1992 and then further to 8.45% in 2001 (Lardy 2002). China announced to abolish its import substitution list in 1992/93 (Li and Jiang 2018) and to instead rely on tariffs and exchange rates in order to adjust imports, consistent with the rules of the WTO (Song 2012). From 1997 onwards, various domestic institutions and firms could also enjoy duty-free imports on a wider range of imported goods. Examples include scientific research and teaching institutions and, starting in 2000, Chinese software companies.

After the number of commodities that were subject to export licensing had increased significantly during the 1980s, rising from 24 in 1981 to 235 in 1991 and thus principally covering around two-thirds of all exports, they declined steadily over the 1990s. The commodities covered by export licensing decreased by 30.5% to 114 commodities in 1993 and then further to 59 in 1999 before reaching 50 in 2000. This was possible thanks to the prize liberalization which eliminated the differences between domestic and international prices (Lardy 2002).

As a consequence of the growing share of duty-free imports (because of the expansion of FDI, the rising importance of export processing, and the extension of duty drawbacks on a broader product range) and fraud (e.g. the illegal resale of components imported duty-free), the tariff collection rate plummeted to around 3% in 1994. There it stayed for around 4 years until the Chinese customer service followed the firmer approach to smuggling, and the tariff collection rate increased to 24.2% (which was still relatively low compared to other developing countries) (Lardy 2002, 2000).

Still, there have been some measures to control imports, including the automatic registration for the import of special commodities (introduced in 1994 and applied throughout the 1990s), the use of tendering for specific products, as well as quality and safety standards (see Lardy 2002 for a detailed discussion).

Trading rights

The number of Chinese companies that were allowed to engage in foreign trade further increased to 15,000 in 1997 and surpassed 30,000 at the turn of the century (Wang 2008). The first Sino-foreign joint venture trading companies were authorized in 1997, and 1 year later, the first private trading companies were allowed to start business operations. Starting from 1999, scientific research institutes were permitted to engage in foreign trade, large industrial companies could apply for trading rights which were issued in a relatively short amount of time (within 15 days if the firm met the respective criteria), and private firms received assurance that they would face lower size requirements to qualify for trading rights registrations (see Lardy 2002). Even though the number of firms with trading rights was still very small, companies without these rights could assign specialized trading companies with the task to handle their trade transactions. According to Lardy (2002), the rising market offering international trading services was presumptively rather competitive with low transaction costs and could enhance efficiency. Lardy also argued that the share of import commodities that exhibited limited or monopolized trading rights was probably a more insightful measure of trade openness in this environment. While this ratio still accounted at around 40% in 1988, it fell by almost 30% points over the next decade.

A changing export processing regime

As already mentioned in Sect. 4.4.5, export processing trade enjoyed a special treatment already during the 1980s. Its importance increased further in the 1990s when more and more electronic goods were assembled in China, enabling the country's integration into the high-tech goods production network. Thanks to the duty drawback on inputs used in processing exports, China became the assembly site for many Taiwanese companies. One prominent example is the computer industry. In 1993, around one-third of all offshored Taiwanese computer hardware production took place in China. In the second half of the 1990s, also desktop PCs became more important, and by the end of the 1990s almost 30% of Taiwan's PCs were produced in China. Only 1 year later, this number had surpassed 40%. Also, an increasing number of Taiwanese firms relocated their production entirely to

China, and consequently, China's IT hardware production surged in the late 1990s. Soon, also semiconductor manufacturers and chip design and packaging companies chose China as production location. For an excellent description see Lardy (2002).

Institutional reforms

At the end of the 1990s, the Chinese government also introduced various **institutional reforms**. In 1997, China promulgated the Antidumping Regulations which were mostly consistent with the WTO principles. Moreover, in order to enhance efficiency in the expenditure of public funds, the State Council announced the Provisional Regulations on Government Procurement in 1999, and in the same year, the formal Competitive Bidding Law (focusing particularly on engineering projects) was adopted (Tang 2005). Also in this respect, the Chinese regulations and laws were in general in line with the WTO principles.

Box 4.20 Summary: Trade Reforms (Selection)

- **Foreign Trade Law** 1994 (legal foundation for modern Chinese trade policy)
- **Unification** of the **official exchange rate and the swap rate** (1994)
- Establishment of the **China Foreign Exchange Trading System** (CFETS) (Interbank foreign-exchange market)
- Accepting **IMF's Article VIII** obligations regarding current account convertibility (1996)
- **Reduction of tariff and non-tariff barriers** (e.g. decrease in the average statutory imports tariff rates, reduction of import licensing, reduction of commodities subject to export licensing)
- Increasing number of Chinese companies were allowed to engage in foreign trade
- **Institutional reforms**: promulgation of the Antidumping Regulations 1997, Provisional Regulations on Government Procurements 1999, Competitive Bidding Law 1999.

4.5.3.2 China's WTO Membership

In 1986, China applied to rejoin the WTO's precursor, the **GATT**. While initially this process did not appear to be a major obstacle, it in fact took China 15 years to eventually become a **WTO member** on **11 December 2001**. Various events led to this postponement, including the suppression of the Tiananmen Square protests in 1989, the unilateral publication of details of the Chinese concessions of the 1999 bilateral agreement without prior consultation with China, and the US bombing of the Chinese Embassy in Belgrade (Yee 2004; Lardy 2002). In addition, the breakup of the Soviet Union in 1991 which led to an increasing number of potential new

GATT members from Eastern Europe for which China's membership could be seen as a template, and China's exceptional export performance which was not in line with the typical developing countries' characteristics, were responsible that China had to face more extensive commitments. In the course of the **Uruguay Round,** there had been significant shifts in the scope of negotiations. There was the so-called "**grand bargain**" (cf. Ostry 2000) between developed countries and developing ones. While developing countries agreed to adopt domestic regulations in new areas including the trade of services and intellectual property which would engender increased purchases from developed countries, the developed countries would in turn open up in the areas of agriculture and textiles (Finger and Nogués 2001; Finger 2001; Cine 1995).

China had to make significantly stricter commitments in order to become a member of the WTO than other developing countries (and even than some of the advanced economies) (cf. Branstetter and Lardy 2014; Scott and Wilkinson 2013). According to the premier Zhu Rongji, China's WTO membership was a key element of the overall reform strategy since increased competition could put pressure on state firms and banks to embrace comprehensive structural reforms (Branstetter and Lardy 2014). Moreover, the WTO membership was expected to increase confidence of foreign investors that China was a stable, open economy. Thus, the WTO accession could provide "external pressure" to enforce marketization and reform (Breslin 2006). However, it has to be noted that not the entire leadership in China advocated a WTO membership; various politicians were afraid that further liberalization would provide outsiders more power on China's internal affairs (Scott and Wilkinson 2013). In addition, it was feared that Chinese industries were not able to compete with foreign firms (Naughton 2018).

The key points of the WTO accession agreement are summarized in Table 4.1.

4.5.3.3 Development of China's Foreign Trade

The above-described trade liberalization and foreign exchange rate system reform measures made import and export behavior more responsive to market prices (Lardy 2002). The reform measures incentivizing exports, including benefits enjoyed in the processing trade as well as exchange rate devaluation, engendered the significant expansion of exports which in turn provided the foreign-exchange necessary to finance imports. During the 1990s, China's share in world exports increased at an annual average rate of 10%; China's share in world trade increased from below 1% prior to reforms to almost 4% in 2000 (Lardy 2002). Since 1992, the trade share in GDP was always above 30% with a peak around 2006 (World Bank 2021; cf. Fig. 4.13).

As the Chinese economy became more open for foreign investment, and labor-intensive production moved from other Asian countries to China, the share of labor-intensive light manufacturing goods, especially textiles, clothing, footwear, and toys, increased rapidly. Between 1980 and 1998, the share of textile exports in worldwide exports almost doubled; that of clothing export almost quadrupled. Over the same period, the share of toy and footwear exports even eightfold and tenfold, respectively (see also Table 4.2).

Table 4.1 WTO accession agreement (selection)

Tariffs	• reduction of the average tariff rate for industrial products to 8.9% • reduction of the average tariff rate for agricultural products to 15% • elimination of all tariffs on Information Technology Agreement (ITA) covered products
Textiles	• Agreement on Textiles and Clothing • abolishment of WTO members' quotas on Chinese textile exports 2004 (but safeguard mechanism until end of 2008)
Agriculture	• limitation of subsidies for agriculture production to 8.5% of the value of farm output • reduction of duties on agricultural products from 22 to 17% (on US priority products from 31 to 14%)
Trading and distributional rights	• allowing domestic and foreign enterprises to trade all goods in China except for cereals, tobacco, and fuel products • lifting of joint venture restriction on large department stores and all chain stores
Import/export licensing and quota	• maintenance of a transparent, predictable, uniform, fair, and non-discriminatory system and fair procedure for trade licensing
Subsidies and countervailing practices	• Subsidies and Countervailing Measures (SCM) Agreement • elimination of export subsidies and import substitution subsidies
Antidumping and China's market economy status	• China will not be regarded as a market economy for 15 years with regard to antidumping cases • bringing antidumping rules into accordance with the WTO agreement • earlier initiating of sunset reviews (compared to standard WTO rules)

Source Wang (2008)

The growing importance of the manufacturing sector for China's growth in the second reform period is also supported by the changing export structure depicted in Table 4.3. In the first phase of reforms, primary and manufacturing exports had approximately equal shares (around 50% each).[26] Since the mid-1980s, the primary export share decreased steadily accounting to only 25.6% in 1990, whereas the manufacturing sector saw a constant rise (to almost 75% in 1990) (see NBS 1997, 2020).

In the mid-1990, there has been another major change in the export structure which in particular concerned the composition of the manufacturing exports. Machinery and electronic equipment (M&E) became the principal export category, replacing garments the relative importance of which began to decrease (see Chan et al. 1999: 14–16, 33 and also Table 4.4). Between 1990 and 1992, M&E exports more than tenfold and between 1992 and 1995, they grew at an average annual rate of around 40% (Chan et al. 1999: 16). Thus, China managed to move to higher-value-added activities during the second phase of reforms.

[26] However, this was still a quite high share for the manufacturing sector compared to other developing countries which focused primarily on agricultural exports.

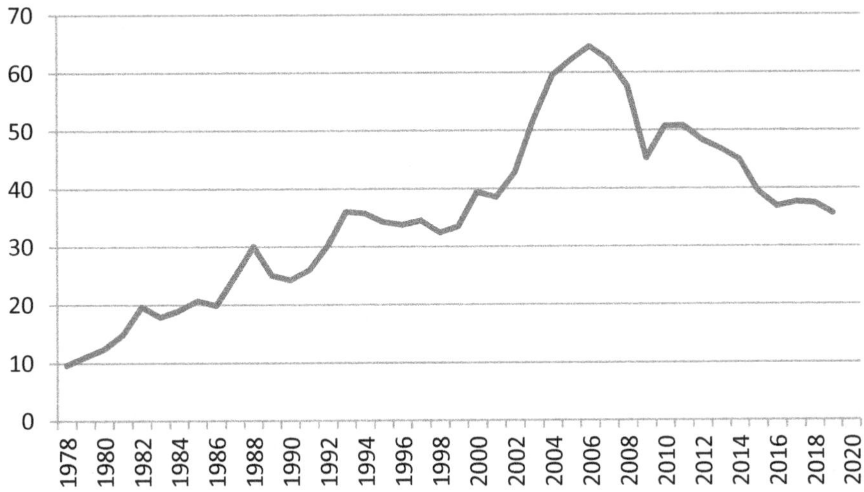

Fig. 4.13 Trade share in GDP. *Source* World Bank (2020)

Table 4.2 Share of Chinese exports in total world exports, labor-intensive manufactured goods (1980 vs. 1998)

	1980	1998
Textile exports	4.5	8.5
Apparel/Clothing	4.0	16.7
Toys	2.3	17.9
Footwear	1.9	20.7

Source Lardy (2002)

Table 4.3 Export structure in China (primary and manufacturing exports)

	Primary exports	Manufacturing exports
1980	50.30	49.70
1985	50.56	49.44
1990	25.59	74.41
1995	14.44	85.56
2000	10.22	89.78
2005	6.44	93.56
2010	5.18	94.82
2015	4.57	95.43

Source NBS (1997, 2020)

Notes Share of primary and manufacturing exports in total exports

Table 4.4 M&E exports of manufactured goods

	1980	1985	1988	1990	1992	1994	1995
M&E exports in billion US $ [% of total exports]	0.3 [1.7]	0.2 [0.7]	0.8 [1.7]	1.5 [2.4]	16.1 [19]	26.1 [21.6]	43.9 [29.5]

Source Chan et al. (1999: 15–16)
Notes "M&E" stands for machinery and electronic equipment

4.5.4 Accelerated FDI Reforms

4.5.4.1 The Nationwide Implementation of FDI-Enhancing Policies

Deng Xiaoping's southern tour and his reaffirmed commitment to the open-door policy bolstered confidence of foreign investors. In 1992, the term "socialist market economy" was officially adopted during the 14th National Congress of the CPC, solving the long debate on "market versus socialism". In 1993, the Chinese Constitution was accordingly amended and the term planned economy was replaced (Chen 2008). Article 15 now states that "The State practises socialist market economy". "The State strengthens economic legislation, improves macro-regulation and control, and prohibits in accordance with law any organization or individual from disturbing the socio-economic order".[27]

During the 1990s, there was a series of new reforms, laws, and regulations. Most importantly, there was now a **nationwide implementation** of FDI-enhancing policies by opening the inland region to FDI and by extending the preferential policies to inland cities. Moreover, the government aimed at a more consistent and systematic regulatory framework for foreign investment. Fifty-two cities, enjoying the same preferential policies as the 14 coastal cities, were opened to foreign investors, among them almost all inland provincial capitals and major cities were located near the Yangtze River (Chen 1997).[28] The establishment of duty-free zones was enhanced in the coastal areas. Moreover, a number of new sectors were opened to foreign investors, including some service industries, on an experimental basis (for instance, aviation, telecommunication, banking, retailing, etc.) (Chen 2019). Finally, certain foreign business people were allowed to buy land-use rights for building infrastructure facilities (Chen 2019).

In 1995, the first "Foreign Investment Industrial Guidance Catalogue" was issued. It classified foreign investment projects into four categories, namely (1) encouraged, (2) permitted, (3) restricted, and (4) discouraged/prohibited. The catalogue was revised in 2002 and from then on every 2–4 years. The revisions reflected China's economic and industrial development strategy which increasingly selectively encouraged certain industries (and also a gradual shift away from regional priority, cf. also Chen 1997). In the course of the 2002 revision, also many service sectors moved from the fourth to the third category.

[27] USC US-China Institute (1993).
[28] With the exception of Lhasa and Urumqi, cf. Chen (1997).

In the wake of China's WTO accession, there was a major revision of the three central laws. The Wholly Foreign Owned Enterprise Law and the Contractual Joint Venture Law were amended in 2000, followed by the Equity Joint Venture Law in 2001. Among others, restrictions on wholly foreign-owned enterprises were relaxed since they were not forced to adopt advanced technology or engaged primarily in exporting (Chen 2019). In 2004, the upper ceiling on investment projects that needed government approval increased to US$100 million for the categories (1) and (2) and to US$50 million for the category (3) projects (Lubman 2006).

During the 1990s and beginning 2000s, China established the foundation of the modernized commercial legal system by issuing various laws, including the Company Law, the Contract Law, and the Anti-Monopoly Law. The New Company Law, issued in 2005, provided the necessary basis for modernizing China's corporate governance. It simplified the requirements for the establishment of companies and expended shareholders' rights (Chen 2019). In 2006, new "Regulations Concerning the Merger and Acquisition of Domestic Enterprises by Foreign Investors" ("New M&A Regulations") were issued. They allowed foreign investors to acquire equity interests held by shareholders of a Chinese domestic company, and thus were more consistent with international practices (OECD 2006). After a 13 year-long drafting process, China eventually adopted the Anti-Monopoly Law (AML) in August 2007 (Wu 2008). It went into effect in the following year. Prior to the AML, China did not have any special laws dealing with anti-monopoly issues; however, there have been various rules with some anti-monopoly content (cf. Xian-Chu 2009).[29]

However, starting from the second half of the 2000s, there was a kind of normalization of special policies favoring SEZs. The preferential tax treatment of foreign capital was phased out starting in 2008 (under the new Enterprise Income Tax Law). The tax rates for foreign and domestic enterprises were unified at 25% and many tax incentives such as tax breaks for foreign investors were abolished (cf. Chen 2019). The normalization of the rules in SEZs was among others due to the fact that Chinese domestic enterprises gained strength (Naughton 2018).

Box 4.21 Summary: FDI Reforms (II)

- **Deng Xiaoping's southern tour** in 1992 (re-commitment to the open-door policy)
- **Nationwide implementation** of FDI-enhancing policies (opening up of the inland region to FDI, extending preferential policies to inland cities)

[29] For instance, the administrative regulations on price, the provisional rules on the development and protection of supportive socialist competition, the administrative regulations during the 1980s and the anti-unfair competition law, the consumer rights and interests protection law, the price law, the bidding law, the foreign trade law in market economies activities, etc. during the 1990s, cf. Xian-Chu (2009).

- First **Foreign Investment Industrial Guidance Catalogue** (1995; revision in 2002) (four categories: encouraged, permitted, restricted, and discouraged/prohibited foreign investment projects)
- **Major revisions** of the Wholly Foreign Owned Enterprise Law (2000), the Contractual Joint Venture Law (2000), and the Equity Joint Venture Law (2001)
- Foundation of the modernized commercial legal system (Company Law, Contract Law, Anti-monopoly Law)
- New M&A Regulations (2006)
- **Normalization** of special policies favoring SEZs in the second half of the 2000s.

4.5.4.2 FDI Development Since the 1990s

Magnitude/Extent of FDI

As shown in Fig. 4.14, there was an enormous increase in FDI in the early 1990s. Between 1991 and 1992, FDI inflows more than doubled, reaching US$11.2 billion (World Bank 2021; see also Fig. 4.14). In the same year, 48,858 FIEs were established and their realized amount was almost US$200 billion (Li 2019). Also in the next year, FDI inflows grew by 250%, and a record high of 83,595 newly

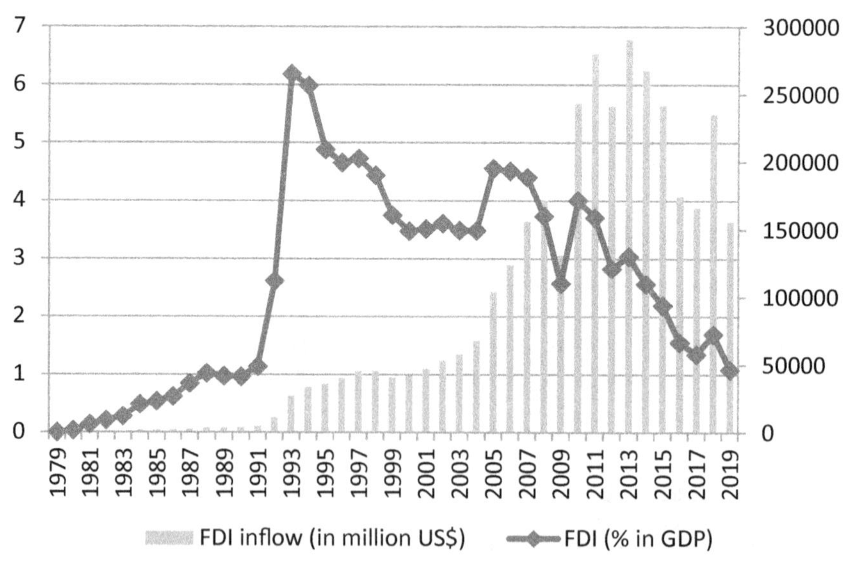

Fig. 4.14 FDI inflows in million US dollar and FDI share in GDP. *Source* World Bank (2020)

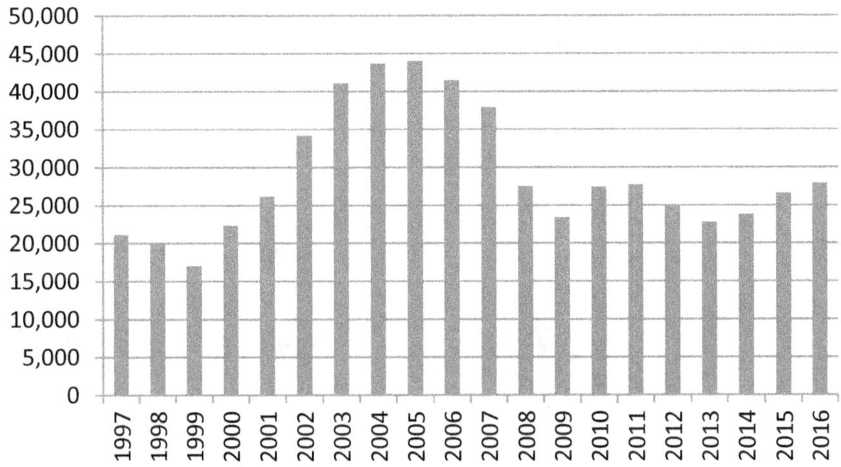

Fig. 4.15 Number of foreign invested enterprises (FIEs). *Source* Li (2019)

established FIEs was reached, their realized amount surpassing US$400 billion (see also Fig. 4.15). Also the FDI share in GDP shot up from 1.1% in 1991 to 2.6% in 1992 and subsequently to 6.2% in 1993. Over the next years, FDI continued to rise even though at a somehow lower speed. The FDI share in GDP fluctuated around 5%. At the end of the 1990s, the number of FIEs fell below 20,000 and also FDI inflows showed a declining tendency. This interruption can mainly be attributed to the negative consequences of the Asian Financial Crisis which negatively affected some of China's main foreign investment partners. However, the WTO accession gave new impetus and FDI increased again steeply until the Global Financial Crisis in 2009. While China managed to recover during the next 2 years since 2013, FDI inflows have exhibited a steady downward trend. For the sectoral composition of FDI, cf. Fig. 4.16.

Ownership structure

With respect to the ownership structure, there were three main different types of foreign invested enterprises, namely, equity joint ventures, cooperative joint ventures, and wholly foreign-owned enterprises. An equity joint venture (EJV) is established through a joint investment by foreign and local partners. EJVs require a minimum share of foreign ownership and are organized in the form of a separate limited liability company. Profits are shared according to each partner's capital contribution. In contrast, the contractual joint venture (CJV, also referred to as corporative joint venture) is not a separate legal entity. Profits are shared as specified in the contract agreement. The same applies to the degree of foreign control, the company's management mode, and responsibilities for risks and debts. In the case of wholly foreign-owned enterprises (WFOEs), the foreign firm has the sole ownership (100%) (see Yuan and Tsai 2000; Jiang et al. 2018).

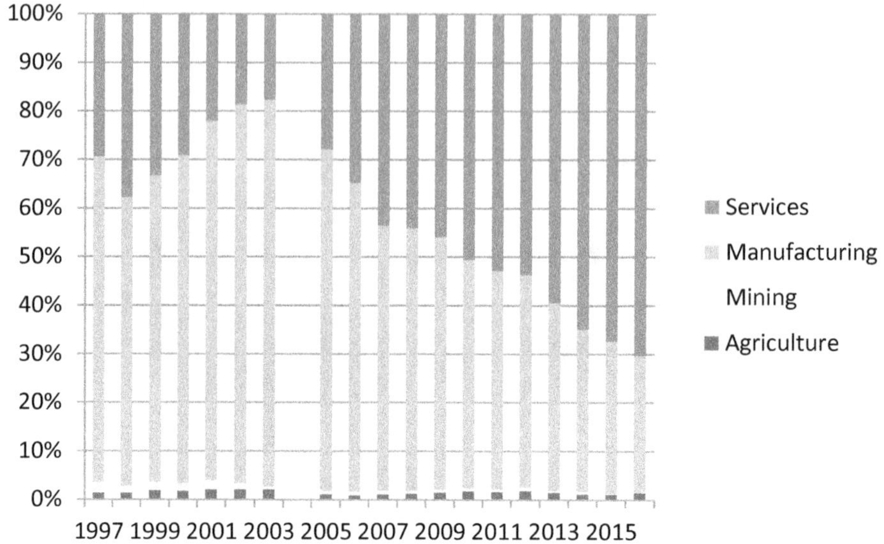

Fig. 4.16 Types of FDI, 1997–2016. *Source* Li (2019), Chap. 8. *Note* No data available for the year 2004

Over the course of the reforms, the composition of these three types has changed significantly. In the beginning, EJVs dominated FDI in China, accounting for 43% of total FDI inflows in 1997. Together, EJVs and CJVs even accounted for more than 60%. However, starting from 2000, the share of WFOEs expanded rapidly. Between 1997 and 2002, it increased from 36 to 60%, and by 2012, it had almost reached 80%. Only in recent years, the number of equity joint ventures is again increasing slightly.

Because of its enormous size, the Chinese market is very attractive to foreign investors. Therefore, China had the power to dictate the conditions for foreign investment. By establishing joint ventures, Chinese companies could better profit from foreign advanced technologies that the foreign partner was "forced" to transfer. In specific industry sectors, it was mandatory to form international joint ventures (prominent examples included the pharmaceutical and automobile industry). The increasing dominance of WFOEs since the turn of the century can be partly attributed to the regulatory liberalization, in particular the relaxed requirements that foreign investors have to form a joint venture with the domestic firm (in the course of China's WTO membership, see also Sect. 4.5.3), but also because of mistrust by foreign investors (Jiang et al. 2018). For the positive impact of FDI and economic development see also Sect. 4.5.4.3.

With respect to the regional distribution of FDI, there was a concentration of foreign investment in eastern provinces. Guangdong and Jiangsu province accounted each for almost 15% of total FDI between 1983 and 2014. Henan

Table 4.5 Share of provincial FDI in total national FDI for selected provinces (in percent)

Province	Share in national FDI
Guangdong	14.6
Jiangsu	14.5
Liaoning	8.7
Shanghai	7.1
Shandong	6.5
Fujian	5.9
Zhejiang	5.9
Tianjin	5.3
Beijing	3.7
Henan (central)	3.3
Sichuan (western)	2.7

Source Chen (2019)

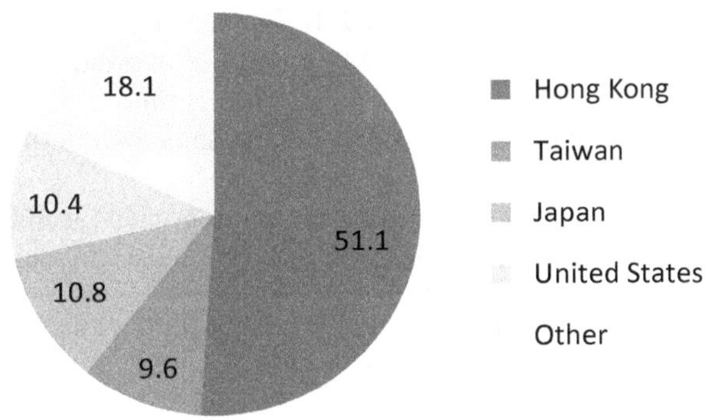

Fig. 4.17 China's main joint venture partners 1998–2007. *Source* Jiang et al. (2018)

attracted the largest amount of FDI inflows among the central provinces (3.3% of total FDI) and Sichuan was the top performer of the Western region (2.7% of total FDI) (cf. Chen 2019; see also Table 4.5).

China's main joint venture partner between 1998 and 2007 was Hong Kong (accounting for around half of all joint ventures). Taiwan, Japan, and the USA each accounted for around 10% (see also Fig. 4.17).

4.5.4.3 Beneficial Effects of FDI for Economic Development

FDI can be beneficial for both, the domestic and the foreign partner. The domestic partner can help the foreign partner to cope better with local regulatory, cultural, and administrative complexities. Moreover, in the Chinese case, joint ventures were the only opportunity to gain access to the Chinese domestic market (at least in the beginning). In addition, the foreign partner could benefit from lower production costs and the favorable economic conditions in SEZs such as preferential tax rates and a good infrastructure (see also Sect. 4.4.6). The host country can of course also benefit greatly from FDI. Especially in a capital scarce country such as China, FDI has been essential to increase fixed capital formation which promotes economic growth (empirical evidence is provided among others by Chen et al. 1995; Chen 2011). FDI has also provided new employment possibilities for Chinese workers (Chen 2019). Probably even more important, the Chinese domestic firm can profit greatly from the transfer of advanced technology and management methods via spillover effects (cf. also the general literature on technology spillover effects, e.g. Javorcik 2004; Keller 2010; Keller and Yeaple 2013). Dees (1998), Chen (2011, 2017), Xu and Sheng (2012), and Jiang et al. (2018) find that FDI has increased China's economic growth through knowledge/technology spillover effects. Moreover, FIEs can generate export spillovers to domestic firms by reducing the export costs and by increasing productivity (both thanks to knowledge and technology spillovers) and by integrating them into international product specialization (by strengthening domestic industry linkages) (see Chen 2019 for a more detailed discussion). This positive effect is well documented for China (e.g. in the empirical studies of Sun 2011; Zheng et al. 2004; Buck et al. 2007). As argued by various studies, the positive effects of FDI have usually been greater in eastern/coastal regions (cf. Yao and Wei 2007; Sun 2009).

In the following, we will describe in more detail how spillover effects can take place and to which extent technological transfers occurred in the Chinese economy. We refer particularly to the study of Jiang et al. (2018) that so far provides the most up-to-date analysis.

There are multiple channels through which technology transfers can occur (see Fig. 4.18). The first and probably the most obvious possibility is that the foreign partner firm passes its knowledge to the newly formed joint venture. Jiang et al. (2018) label this the ***internal*** technology transfer. This transfer is (at least to some extent) also in the interest of the foreign firm setting up the joint venture because the foreign partner of course wants the joint venture to be successful. The second channel refers to the transmission of technology from the joint venture to the Chinese domestic partner firm. This effect is called the ***intergenerational*** technology transfer. Third, also ***external*** Chinese domestic firms operating in the same industry can benefit from technology spillovers, either from the newly founded joint venture but also from the Chinese partner firm that set up this joint venture.[30] Jiang et al. (2018) find empirical evidence for all three effects in China. The joint venture firm itself as well as other external R&D intensive firms (that is, mostly other joint ventures in China) benefitted the most from positive externalities, especially if the foreign partner firm was from the USA.

Of course, FDI can also have negative spillover effects including the negative competition effect. However, these were usually outweighed by the positive effects of technology diffusion (Tang et al. 2008).

[30] In principle, these external effects can also emerge through backward and forward industrial linkages. However, this is less the case of the Chinese economy due to the FIEs' focus on export processing trade (Chen 2011).

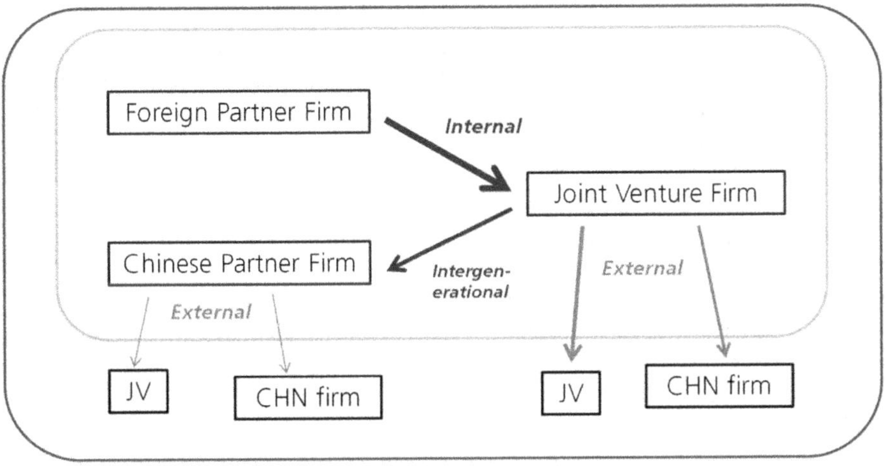

Fig. 4.18 Joint Venture spillover effects. *Source* Own representation based on Jiang et al. (2018). *Notes* "JV" stands for joint venture and "CHN" for Chinese

4.5.5 Accelerated Financial Reforms

4.5.5.1 Creation of Policy Banks and Improved Legal Framework

During the third plenary session of the fourth Central Committee of the CPC in 1993, a new financial system reform was announced (Zhang 2019a). The **Resolution On Financial System Reform** which was issued by the State Council formulated several main targets, including the establishment of policy banks, and, related to this, the conversion of the Big Four into actual commercial banks, the creation of an independent micro-regulatory system of the PBC which implemented monetary policy under the leadership of the State Council, a foreign exchange control reform, adequate guidance for the non-bank financial institution (NBFI) development, the formation of the financial-service infrastructure, and the establishment of unified, open, and competitive financial markets (cf. Okazaki 2007; Zhang 2019a).

In 1994, **three policy banks** were established, namely, the Agricultural Development Bank of China (ADBC), the China Export–Import Bank (CEIB), and the China Development Bank Corporation (CDBC). They took over the policy-based lending responsibilities of the ABC, CCB, BOC, and ICBC to protect them from political influence (Naughton 2018). The latter were converted into actual commercial banks in 1995, and in the same year, the Law of the People's Republic of China (PRC) on Commercial Banks (**Commercial Bank Law**) was promulgated with the aim of enhancing the independence of commercial banks (DaCosta and Foo 2002). Overall, the main goal of the creation of the policy banks was to separate the policy related lending from commercial lending. The reform also lifted the restrictions that the state-owned commercial banks could only operate in their specialized field (Zhang 2019a; Cheng and Degryse 2010; Rehman et al. 2016).

Various other laws promulgated in 1995 provided the **legal framework** for the financial sector's rule of law, including the **Central Bank Law** (which provided the PBC the full autonomy in applying the monetary instruments), the **Insurance Law** of the PBC, the Law of the PRC on Negotiable Instruments, and the **Guarantee Law** of the PRC (Okazaki 2007).

The 1990s also brought a relaxation of the geographical restrictions for foreign banks to set up branches: starting from 1994, foreign banks could obtain a license by the central authorities to operate in 23 cities. However, they could still only operate in businesses related to foreign investors. Even when the PBC allowed eight foreign banks to use local currency funding at the end of the 1990s, they were still not allowed to conduct consumer transactions in renminbi (RMB) with mainland residents (Li et al. 2015). An overview of the structure of China's financial system is provided in Fig. 4.19.

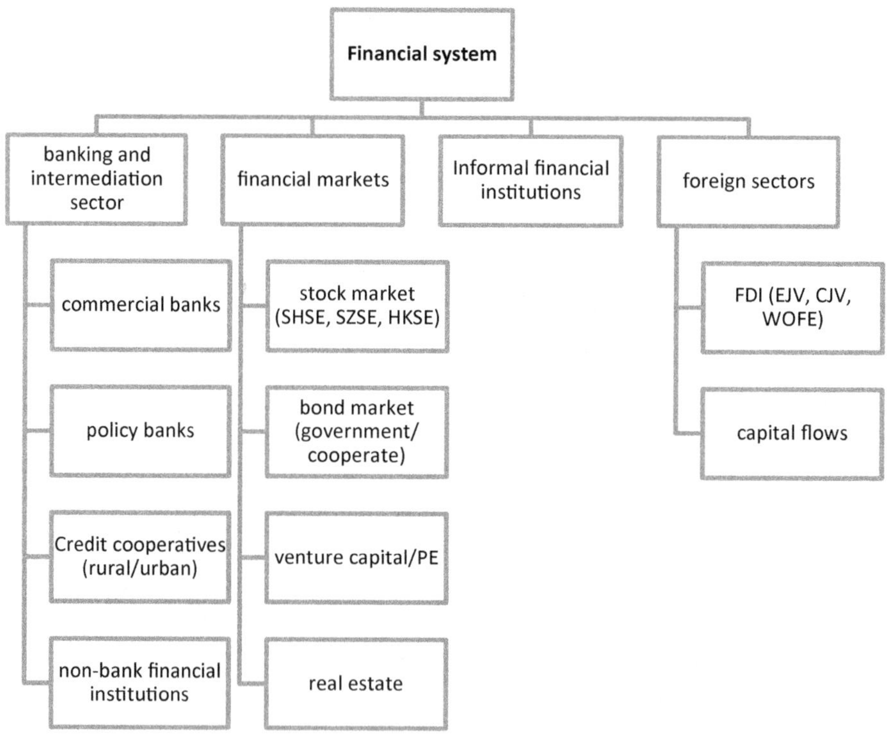

Fig. 4.19 Structure of China's financial system. *Source* Own presentation based on Allen et al. (2014) and Cousin (2011). *Notes* "SHSE" stands for Shanghai Stock Exchange, "SZSE" for Shenzhen Stock Exchange, "HKSE" for Hong Kong Stock Exchange, "FDI" for foreign direct investment, "EJV" for equity joint venture, "CJV" for corporative joint venture, "WOFE" for wholly owned foreign enterprise, and "PE" for private equity

4.5.5.2 The Increasing Non-performing Loan (NPL) Problem

During the first reform phases, the allocation of funds was still mostly managed through the credit plan of the State Planning Commission, and not through market mechanisms (even as financial markets were already established around 1992). As a consequence of the soft budget constraint and the "reform without losers" mentality between 1978 and 1993, China's banks continued to lend to unviable SOEs, resulting in an increasing number of **non-performing loans (NPLs)** (Okazaki 2007; Naughton 2018). By 2000, the share of NPLs in GDP amounted to a record high of 22.5%. Figure 4.20 depicts the development of NPLs over the period 1998–2006 (when official information became first available). However, according to Allen et al. (2014), the number of NPLs for the first 2 years is very likely underestimated. In general, estimates on the extent of NPLs at the end of the 1990s and beginning of the 2000s range from 20 to 35% of GDP and from 20 to 40% of total loans (Cousin 2011).

Additional impetus to reform the financial system was provided by the **Asian Financial Crisis** of 1997 which led the Chinese authorities to worry about the fragility of the financial sector and insufficient supervision (Okazaki 2007; Naughton 2018).

Consequently, the government implemented major reforms in order to cope with the NPLs problem starting in 1998. The most important one will be briefly discussed in the following.

NPL bailout. In August 1998, the government **injected RMB 270 billion of special government bonds** into the banking system to recapitalize state-owned banks. In addition, four **Asset-Management Companies (AMCs)** were established which purchased NPLs from the Big Four for **1.4 trillion RMB**. Each AMC paired

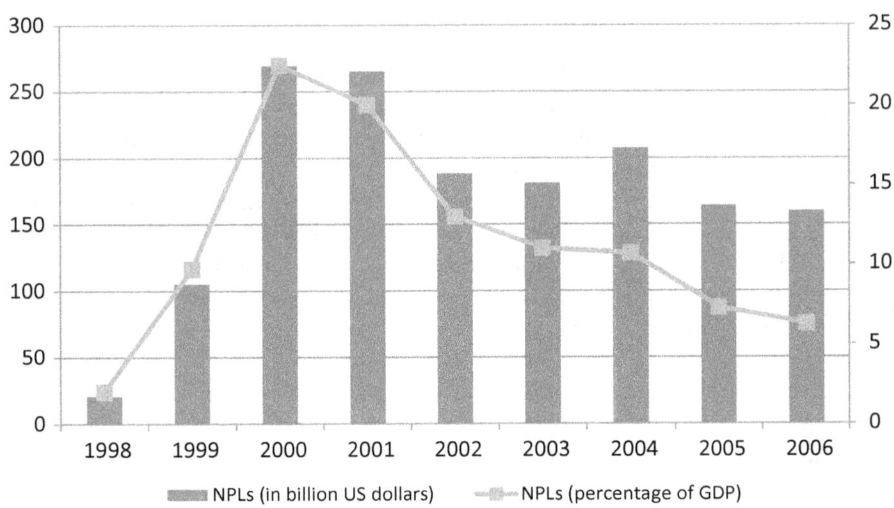

Fig. 4.20 NPLs in China, 1998–2006. *Source* Allen et al. (2014)

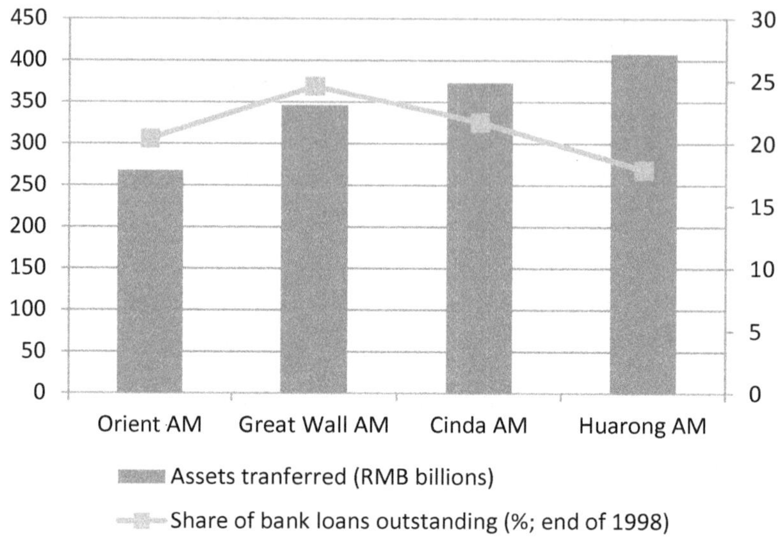

Fig. 4.21 AMCs, 1999–2000. *Source* Ma and Fung (2002)

up with one of the Big Four state-owned banks (the BOC with the Orient Asset Management, the ABC with the Great Wall Asset Management, the CCB with the Cinda Asset Management, and the ICBC with the Huarong Asset Management). For more details on the scope of NPL transfers from banks to AMCs, see Fig. 4.21. More detailed information regarding the government's capital injection and the establishment of the AMCs is provided by Okazaki (2007) as well as by Ma and Fung (2002). To prevent SOE bankruptcies, the government used the debt-for-equity swap system for 580 SOEs (Okazaki 2007).

Adoption of international NPL classification standards. Banks were required to adopt international NPL classification standards. In particular, the previous four-tier loan classification based on the status of payments was replaced by a forward-looking, risk-based five-tier loan classification system in order to increase the transparency of the banks (Okazaki 2007; Mo 1999; Cousin 2011). Also the accounting system was changed gradually. The number of days overdue after which loans could be classified as accruing interest or not was first reduced to 180 days between 1998 and 2001 and then further to 90 days under the "Accounting System for Financial Institutions" published by the Ministry of Finance (MOF) (Okazaki 2007).

Abolishment of the credit plan. Prior to 1998, the allocation of funds was still mostly managed through administrative measures, in particular through the credit plan of the State Planning Commission, and not through market mechanisms, even as financial markets were already established around 1992. The eventual abolishment of the credit plan system for the Big Four provided the state-owned commercial banks with more freedom to select projects and enterprises eligible for loans

(Okazaki 2007).[31] However, even though credit quotas were no longer assigned, the central bank still controlled the volume of loans. The influence of the PBC only became less direct.

Central bank responsibilities. In 1998, nine district branches of the PBC were established (in Tianjin, Shenyang, Shanghai, Nanjing, Jinan, Wuhan, Guangzhou, Chengdu, and Xian), replacing the previous 31 provincial level branches in order to reduce local government intervention. The central bank took over the responsibility of appointing senior bank managers which was previously controlled by local governments. The reforms stemmed the tide of local governments' overambitious and non-profitable projects (that had been responsible for a significant portion of the bad loans) by preventing them from influencing the lending decision of banks (see Zhang 2019a; Mo 1999).

After the WTO accession, further reforms of the financial system were initiated by the Chinese government in order to move toward a market-oriented banking system and also to face problems that still persisted after the reforms in the 1990s. While the government had succeeded in reducing the financial difficulties of banks by removing bad assets from their balance sheets, it did not solve the underlying structural problems. For instance, it did not change the ownership structure of the state-owned commercial banks (Okazaki 2007; Fang and Jiang 2016). In addition, in the wake of the WTO accession, China agreed to a further liberalizing of the financial sector which raised fears from Chinese financial market participants. Moreover, foreign banks were regarded as a destabilization risk. Policymakers were worried that the Chinese banking sector was not (yet) competitive enough and still lacked corporate governance capacity, leading to a potential crowding out of domestic banks (Li et al. 2015). However, these fears proved relatively groundless and the market share of foreign banks increased rather slowly. The share of foreign banks in China's banking system is still relatively low since their main business focus is still on foreign companies. In 2007, the percentage of banks with foreign capital still amounted to only 2.36% and the share even shrank over the next decade, only amounting to 1.26% in 2016 (Sun 2018).

4.5.5.3 Ownership Reform of State-Owned Commercial Banks

The ownership reform of the state-owned commercial banks (also referred to as the joint-stock reform or shareholding system reform) started in 2003 after the 16th Central Committee of the CPC.

In the same year, the **China Banking Regulatory Commission** was created in order to increase the efficiency in the regulation of the banking system. The Big Four state-owned commercial banks and the BOCOM which was a non-listed joint-stock commercial bank (JSCB) but often regarded as a state-owned commercial bank, should be transformed into listed JSCBs (Okazaki 2007). The reform followed a multiple stage procedure: first, there was a financial restructuring of the banks by capital injections, followed by the establishment of joint stock companies

[31] Credit quotas for joint-stock commercial banks and cooperative financial institutions had already been abolished in 1994.

and the introduction of strategic investors. The final step was the issuance of stocks in the capital market (via initial public offerings, IPOs). However, some details of the joint stock reform differed among the big state-owned banks due to the varying conditions (Fang and Jiang 2016; Amstad et al. 2020).

The BOC and the CCB were the pilot banks for the new ownership reform (Podpiera 2006). In December 2003, they received US$45 billion of China's foreign exchange reserve for recapitalization through the newly established Central HuJin Investment Company (Naughton 2018).[32] In 2004 and 2005, the BOCOM and the ICBC followed. Moreover, the big state-owned commercial banks were allowed to transfer a large portion of their NPLs into AMCs.[33] In August and September 2004, the BOC and the CCB were restructured into joint-stock commercial banks. The ICBC followed 1 year later. Foreign strategic investors were introduced into the banking system and the government encouraged Chinese commercial banks to make deals with foreign financial institutions—not only to get access to new capital but also to benefit from staff training, new management systems, and techniques to foster corporate governments (Okazaki 2007; Huang et al. 2013). Between 2005 and 2007, the CCB, the BOC, the ICBC, and the BOCOM conducted **initial public offerings (IPOs)**. In 2005, the CCB and the BOCOM had their stocks listed in the Hong Kong exchange. In 2006, the BOC and the ICBC were listed on both, the Shanghai stock exchange and the Hong Kong stock exchange. One year later, also the BOCOM was listed in the Shanghai stock exchange.

The ownership reform of the ABC took more time and it was not until 2009 that it turned into a joint stock limited company. This can be mostly attributed to the fact that the ABC faced a more serious NPL problem than the other state-owned commercial banks (see Fig. 4.22). Moreover, the activities of the ABC were of great strategic importance for the Chinese leadership (Cousin 2011). In 2010, the ABC was listed on the Shanghai stock exchange and the Hong Kong stock exchange. At this point, it was the biggest IPO worldwide.

It has to be noted that even though the IPOs induced a change in the ownership structure, state ownership was still dominating. Moreover, the Big Four banks still accounted for a large portion of total banking assets (Lu 2016). Overall, the central government still had considerable control over the business operations of banks. As a result, smaller private enterprises faced severe financing problems and had to turn to the shadow banking sector. However, even though this financing method appeared to work rather well in the beginning, the situation changed after the Global Financial Crisis when the economic conditions worsened. Not only did the export activity decline but also the property market boom came to a stop (Lu 2016). Consequently, there was an increasing number of lending credit crunches and corporate insolvencies, first in 2011 in Wenzhou and subsequently all over China. Eventually, the true extent of the shadow banking's systematic risk came to light

[32] Each bank received US$22.5 billion (Cousing 2011).

[33] An auction system was introduced and the NPLs of the state-owned commercial banks were sold to the AMCs with which they were not originally paired up in order to increase market mechanisms (Okazaki 2007).

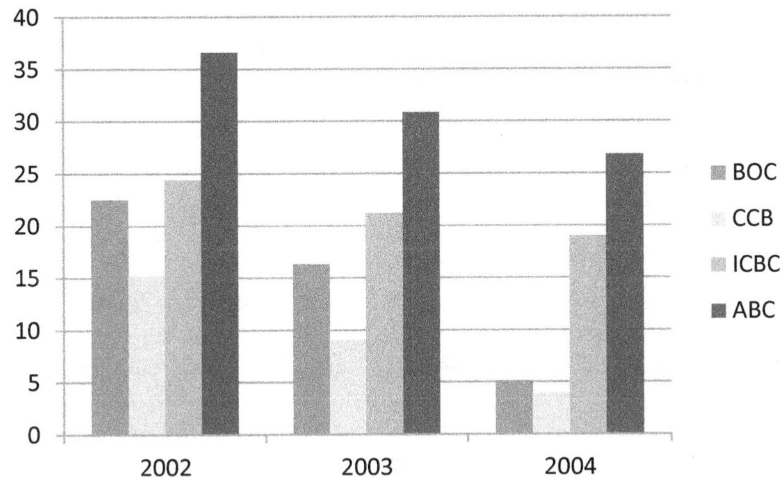

Fig. 4.22 NPLs in the Big Four, 2002–2004. *Source* Podpiera (2006)

(Lu 2016). A key priority identified in Li Keqiang's Government Work Report of 2018 was to get the systematic risks of the financial system under control (Huang and Wang 2019). Also the IMF and the World Bank raised concerns regarding the rapidly increasing credit expansion in the shadow banking sector and risky lending activities in the less well-supervised sectors of the financial system in their Financial System Stability Assessment of 2017 (IMF and World Bank 2017).

4.5.5.4 Opening of the Financial System to Foreign Firms and Bank Privatization

As already mentioned above, the opening up of China's financial system to foreign firms gained momentum after China's WTO accession. This was mainly due to the fact that China had to commit to extensive liberalization measures. One year after China joined the WTO, foreign banks could engage in businesses with Chinese firms and residents in foreign currency. Moreover, local currency services were authorized in some cities. The restrictions on the RMB business (with respect to both, geographic limitations and constraints regarding which customers foreign banks could do business with) had been lifted by 2006. Also, the number of local incorporated foreign banks which enjoyed national treatment in many areas increased significantly during the 2000s (most of them from Asia).

In 2014, a pilot program was started by the China Banking Regulatory Commission (CBRC) to allow **non-financial companies** to found new private banks in order to experiment with new schemes in which banks are responsible for their own risks. Initially, five new private banks were approved, targeting areas that were not sufficiently covered by the traditional banks (cf. Borst and Li 2016). Probably, the most prominent examples include MYbank by Ali Baba and WeBank by Tencent.[34] The focus of the private banks was on small and medium-sized private enterprises that usually had financing difficulties because of the still existing preferential treatment of SOEs regarding the provision of loans (Lu 2016).

Box 4.22 Summary: Financial Reforms (II)

Financial reforms in the early 1990s

(1) **Separation of policy related lending and commercial lending**: establishment of three policy banks (1994); conversion of the Big Four into actual commercial banks (1995); promulgation of the Commercial Bank Law
(2) **Legal framework** for the **financial sector's rule of law** (1995): Central Bank Law, Insurance Law, Guarantee Law
(3) **Relaxation of the geographical restrictions** for foreign banks to set up branches (since 1994); but still restrictions.

Reforms to cope with the NPL problems since 1998

(1) **NPL bailout**: RMB 270 billion of special government bonds injection into the bank system; establishment of four asset management companies to purchased NPLs from the Big Four for 1.4 trillion RMB
(2) **Adoption of international NPL classification standards**
(3) **Abolishment of the credit plan**
(4) **Increasing central bank responsibilities** to reduce influence of local governments.

Ownership reform of state-owned commercial banks (after 2003)

- Creation of the **China Banking Regulatory Commission** (2003)
- Stepwise **transformation** of the **Big Four** and the **BOCOM into listed JSCBs** (CCB, BOC, ICBC, and BOCOM between 2005 and 2007; ABC in 2010) → state ownership was still dominating, smaller private firms had to turn to the shadow banking sector.

Opening of the financial system to foreign firms and bank privatization (after 2001)

- Permission for foreign banks to engage in businesses with Chinese firms and residents in foreign currency (2002)
- Lifting of restrictions on the RMB business (2002)

[34] The remaining three private banks are KinCheng Bank of Tianjin, Shanghai HuaRui Bank, and Wenzhou Minshang Bank.

- **Pilot program** (CBRC): **non-financial companies** were **allowed to found new private banks** in order to experiment with new schemes in which banks are responsible for their own risks (2014).

4.5.5.5 Interest Rate Liberalization

The Chinese central bank liberalized the interest rates for money and capital markets gradually starting from the late 1990s. In 2004, the ceiling on lending rates and the floor on deposit rates were abolished, and the floor on lending rates was eventually removed in 2013, followed 2 years later by the ceiling on deposit rates.

4.6 Reform Slowdown After 2003 (and the Transition to the Xi Jinping Era)

Economic reform efforts slowed down significantly after 2003, when the Hu Jintao-Wen Jiabao administration came into office. This reform stagnation can be interpreted as resting on the previous successes and as hoping for independent growth dynamics (following the WTO accession). There was also no immediate crisis that required the implementation of market-oriented reforms (unlike during the previous two reform phases). In addition, there was uncertainty about the potential negative consequences of the WTO entry, and consequently reformers proceeded more carefully.

Even though the trajectory of economic reforms altered dramatically, the extent of this change was not immediately noticeable. The growth rate still remained very high—GDP per capita grew at an average annual rate of 10.6% between 2003 and 2010 (cf. World Bank 2021); however, this impressive growth performance can be mainly attributed to the economic and institutional reforms carried out during the 1990s under Zhu Rongji, including trade liberalization efforts (to prepare for the WTO entry) and the SOE reforms as a result of which state firms began to become more profitable (see also Sects. 4.5.3 and 4.5.1). In addition, the growth-rewarding promotion system for local government officials had generated a powerful self-reinforcing dynamic (see also Sect. 4.4.4).

Another reason for the changed course of reforms can be attributed to the fact that reformers had underestimated the negative side effects of unbridled growth. The policy measures during the 1990s had generated a group of reform losers, especially SOE workers that had lost their job in the course of the state firm restructuring process. Social economic problems intensified, including the erosion of the social safety net, rising house prices, unemployment, and increasing income inequality (especially between the urban and rural population). Reforms to combat these negative side effects had been neglected or not tackled strongly enough during the 1990s because of the fear of an economic slowdown that could have threatened the CPC's legitimacy. However, economic performance alone was gradually considered as not enough to ensure sufficient legitimacy of the party since the growing middle class could regard the rising non-economic problems as a kind of violation of the implicit social contract between the CPC and Chinese citizens. The growing discontent among population groups non-negligible in terms of size could have engendered instability.

The Chinese authorities recognized the urgency to address these problems and changed their policy priorities. In particular, they focused more on maintaining stability, among others, by tackling social problems. Even though China has already made considerable progress regarding this issue, it remains to be seen to what extent it can fully accomplish this ambitious task (see also the discussion on the "Chinese trilemma", Wagner 2021).

4.6.1 Tackling Social Problems

Why exactly did the social problems intensify and which reforms were undertaken to solve them?

Prior to the beginning of economic reforms under Deng Xiaoping, there was a collective unit-centered social security system, the unit usually being the state-owned enterprise. SOEs were responsible for the provision of public services such as education, housing, health insurance, and pension provision. Moreover, they ensured lifetime employment. However, during the reform period, state firms were forced to become more efficient since they had to increasingly compete with more profitable non-state enterprises such as TVEs. In addition, in the course of the "grasping the large, letting go of the small" policy initiative since the second half of the 1990s, especially smaller SOEs were gradually privatized which further increased their pressure to improve efficiency (see also Zhou 1998; Zhu and Walker 2017; cf. also Sect. 4.5.1). Unprofitable small state firms were often shut down. Already prior to the start of the privatization process, SOEs were granted more and more decision-making rights. For instance, they were allowed to retain part of their profits which then could be used to pay bonuses to workers in order to boost their incentives.

The permanent employment system was abolished in the mid-1980s and replaced by a labor contract system (on a 5-year basis) which was expanded gradually (Zhang 2019a). In general, labor mobility was encouraged; for instance, firms had the authority to engage and dismiss personnel and also (urban) workers had more freedom to choose their workplace (Meng 2012). Consequently, many labor contracts were terminated and the risk of unemployment increased. The abolishment of the lifetime employment also implied that more and more people were excluded from receiving social security services.

The main "losers" of this second reform period were certainly the SOE workers who previously enjoyed many benefits but now faced massive layoffs. More than 30 million workers became jobless alone between 1997 and 1998 (Wang 2007), and according to Xiao and Sui (2011), between 1998 and 2001, around 28 million workers lost their job. This resulted in a rising dissatisfaction among these people who felt left behind.[35] Even though the government undertook various efforts to improve the situation for laid-off workers, the success of these measures has been rather limited. In 1995, the government launched a "**Re-employment Project**" that should ensure the basic livelihood of the laid-off workers (Solinger 2002). It included living subsidies and payments into the laid-off workers' medical insurance and pension funds for a period of up to 3 years. The related "**Re-employment Service Centers**" (zaijiuye fuwu zhongxin) organized by state enterprises (first in Shanghai) disbursed at least theoretically the "basic livelihood allowances" (jiben shenghuofei) and provided re-training and job placement assistance (Zhang 2019a; Cai et al. 2014). However, the implementation of this program was far from satisfactory; reasons for that included scarce funds, corruption, and the sheer lack of potential jobs. Often, workers did not even know of the existence of these centers or received less than the already rather low standard payment of 280 yuan per month. Also, contributions to the insurance funds amounted to less than stipulated or were even refused (Solinger 2002). The 30,000 newly established job introduction centers failed to place unemployed people in a job (the success rate was only around 20%).

In 1999, the government standardized its unemployment insurance program which provided subsidies for a maximum of 2 years (Cai et al. 2014). At around the same time, the **Minimum Living Standard Program (MLSP)** was initiated and in the early 2000s, the central government's financing for the MLSP expanded to around ¥542 million. Around 2004, more than 20 million households received subsidies from the MLSP (Cai et al. 2014). Also, some reforms regarding other social services were undertaken, including the introduction of the Basic Medical Insurance (BMI) scheme for urban workers in 1995 and its nationwide extension 3 years later (Giles et al. 2013).

However, even though various political reforms were introduced in order to establish social insurance programs, very often, flexibly employed workers as well as self-employed and rural migrant workers were excluded from these services. The social safety was still incomplete and important parts were missing.

In addition, the administrative barriers installed in the 1950s that had resulted in a dualistic system including different types of citizenship (rural vs. urban), had been maintained until the 1990s. This was ensured via the hukou (household registration) system that prevented rural citizens from moving to cities since they there would not have received adequate social services such as education for their children, healthcare, etc. Consequently, the rural–urban gap (with respect to incomes, but also with respect to education and the provision of social services) had been widening significantly. In the 1990s, restrictions on migration into cities were relaxed, leading to large migration inflows into cities. Still, it was very difficult for

[35] The situation was still somehow better for laid-off workers in wealthier regions because of more job possibilities.

migrant workers to obtain an urban hukou so that they were highly disadvantaged (see also Sect. 4.6.1.3 below for more detailed information).

Especially due to the fear of political instability, the problems outlined above came into the focus of the Chinese authorities in the 2000s (Wen Jiabao in particular was an advocate on this topic, see Naughton 2018). Thanks to the continued and even accelerating growth, the budgetary revenues that could be spent on social services had also risen dramatically, providing a good base for this endeavor. The reform progress with respect to healthcare, the pension system, and rural–urban inequality will be discussed in the following.

4.6.1.1 Healthcare System Reform

As already briefly mentioned above, the old free healthcare system was abandoned in the course of reforms; instead, a universal healthcare system in which urban and rural residents were separately covered was set up (Zhang 2019a).

Main problems of the health system included the rather low coverage of medical insurance (only around 15% were covered by the main social health insurance schemes in 2000, cf. Li and Fu 2017), and the fact that basic health services were unaffordable for many citizens. The provision of healthcare and other social services lagged significantly behind in the countryside. A popular expression to describe the dissatisfying healthcare system situation was "kan bing nan, kan bing gui" meaning "seeing a doctor is hard, seeing a doctor is expensive" (cf. State Council 2009).

Between 2000 and 2008, the share of total health expenditures in GDP remained relatively stable around 4.5%. However, in absolute terms, the government provisions on health and social services were increased significantly in the 2000s (Naughton 2018). In 2009, the **Rural Cooperative Medical System** became the basic health insurance system in rural China. In the same year, the central government also announced an ambitious **three-phase healthcare system reform plan** with the aim of universal coverage of essential health services for all Chinese citizens by 2020. Several population groups (including students, children, and urban jobless people) were increasingly covered by the health insurance (Wills 2018).

During the first phase of the plan (between 2009 and 2012), the healthcare sector received funding amounting to more than US$125 billion (Li and Fu 2017). Between 2009 and 2017, the total health expenditure to GDP ratio increased from 5 to 6.4% (Meng et al. 2019). Top priorities included the expansion of the public health insurance, the establishment of an essential medicine program, the improvement of primary healthcare, the gradual equalization of basic public health services, and pilot reforms with respect to public hospitals (State Council 2009). The public hospitals suffered heavily from distorted incentive structures as well as inefficient governance and they eventually became the main focus during the second reform phase between 2012 and 2015. Among others, the management was improved, a tiered service delivery system that clearly defined the functions of primary, secondary, and tertiary healthcare providers was established, price policies were improved, and payment schemes changed (Meng et al. 2019). In addition, more than 80 pilot cities experimented with innovative and at the same time workable approaches to allow a nationwide implementation of the public hospital reform (Li and Fu 2017). In the final phase, reform efforts were intensified to provide an integrated health system. Measures included the strengthening of primary care, a greater generosity of the public health insurance, and the unification of the three public insurance schemes.[36] However, even though some progress has been made, low quality of primary healthcare (and thus, its low use) is a still unsolved problem. This is mainly due to the low education level of doctors in township health centers. In general, more qualified health personnel is needed in the primary care system (Meng et al. 2019).

Between 2009 and 2017, the government health expenditure increased by 100–150 billion yuan per annum (corresponding to about 14-21 US dollar); also the contribution of the social health insurance system grew rapidly, surpassing the out-of-pocket expenditures by 2010 and contributing to more than 40% of total health expenditures in 2017 (Meng et al. 2019). Still, health services are expensive, particularly for poor households (Fang et al. 2019). This is also one of the reasons for the high household savings rate in China.

Other unsolved problems of the healthcare system include the insufficient cooperation between different health institutions units, and moral hazard problems: Since government subsidies are based on rather quantitative factors such as the volume of services rather than the quality, i.e. the actual health outcome, there is an overuse of healthcare services (see Meng et al. 2019).

4.6.1.2 Pension System Reform

Prior to reforms, SOEs were responsible for the provision of pension benefits to retired workers (Dixon 1981; Liu and Sun 2016). As already outlined above, the old pension system had gradually been eroded in the course of the SOE restructuring process of the 1990s that aimed at increasing the efficiency of state firms.

The government designed a new mixed pension system for urban areas. The new **Enterprise Employee Basic Pension (EEBP)** system was established, and by 2005, retired urban workers received two pensions, one from the social pooling account (containing accumulated employee contributions) and another one from an individual account (Zhu and Walker 2017). This two-pillar system was actually a mix of different pension models and thus inherited not only the benefits but also the various different problems associated with each of these models.

Initially, only few employees were covered by the new pension scheme. During the late 1990s and 2000s, the coverage of the pension system reform was gradually extended. For instance, since 2005, also self-employed urban workers were covered. Still, large population groups were excluded, including unemployed urban residents and jobless migrants. Especially, the pension system reform for rural residents significantly lagged behind. This can be partly attributed to the fact that, in

[36] In total, there were three health insurance schemes, the Urban Employee Basic Medical Insurance plan, the Urban Residents Basic Medical Insurance (URBMI) plan, and the Rural Cooperative Medical Schemes (NCMS) plan.

line with Confucian values, children and the extended family were usually responsible for the protection and monetary support of the elders in rural areas. However, this approach became unsuitable to the changed social and economic environment which was characterized by decreasing birthrates and rural–urban migration of mostly young Chinese (Liu and Sun 2016). First pilot projects regarding the establishment of the rural pension program were conducted in the 1990s. However, these experiments turned out to be a failure and only very few people participated. This was partly due to the fact that the program was only organized as a one-pillar system and therefore lacked the social pool component (Liu and Sun 2016). It was not until the late 2000s that rural residents and urban residents not protected by the EEBP were covered by the **Urban–Rural Resident Basic Social Pension Scheme (URRSP)** (He 2020). More than 500 million people were covered by the URRSP by the end of 2016 (Zhu and Walker 2017). The URRSP has a similar structure than the EEBP; however, the basic account was financed by the central and subnational governments, and the individual account by personal contributions and subsidies from the local government. This implies that differences in the level of local economic development resulted in rising pension inequality across Chinese regions. Besides the EEBP and the URRSP, there also exists the **Government Institution Pension (GIP)** system that usually provided higher benefits. Because of non-negligible social discontent about this preferential treatment which was regarded as unfair, the GIP was eventually restructured and it now follows a similar model than the EEBP. However, until today, the pension system exacerbates inequality. One possible solution to mitigate this problem is the integration of all three main pension schemes into one. Moreover, Zhu and Walker (2017) propose that the central government (and not the subnational governments) should be responsible for the management of pension.

4.6.1.3 Decreasing the Rural–Urban Income Gap

As already argued above, the rural–urban income gap had widened significantly since the second reform phase, and especially with respect to the provision of social services, reforms lagged behind in the rural parts of China. It was not until 2003 that the Chinese authorities focused more on the problems inherited in the dualistic rural–urban institutional structure. Policy examples include significant rural tax reductions, and by the end of 2005, the main agricultural tax was even abolished. The budgetary expenditures for services such as education and health increased considerably during the 2000s. Moreover, farmers received subsidies to counteract potential negative effects of the increasingly liberalized agricultural trade since the WTO entry. Rural migration to cities was progressively encouraged. For instance, in the course of the "**Sunshine Project**" (which was actually a series of policy initiatives) that started in 2004, the surplus rural labor was trained at reduced (and even increasingly eliminated) fees in order to prepare them for urban jobs (cf. Wang and Shaw 2012). In the first year, 2.5 million potential rural migrant workers received such a vocational training; until 2005, the total number had increased to 10 million (ILO 2011; Li 2010). The Sunshine Project was part of the larger **National Migrant Worker Training Plan** from 2003 to 2010 that aimed at providing migrant laborers with introductory training in the areas of health, law, and job-seeking, as well as in vocational skills (cf. Shaohua 2005).

In 2014, the **"New-type Urbanization Plan" (NUP)** was introduced. It also included documents regarding the institutional reform of the household registration system. Among others, the restrictions with respect to the access to urban hukou should be relaxed. The administrative procedure was simplified and the conditions for getting an urban hukou were classified into four categories according to city size (namely, small, medium, large, and mega cities). In addition, social services were also expanded to migrant workers and other people without an urban hukou (cf. Chen et al. 2020). Still, the hukou system was not completely abolished.

Another important policy initiative focused on the strengthening of **farmers' property rights**. Among others, individual land contracts were significantly extended. Moreover, in the first half of the 2010s, property rights of farmers were further strengthened. At the same time, there was a much clearer distinction between different kinds of rural land. In particular, it was differentiated between "permanent agricultural land" and "nonfarm rural land" (either for rural housing or rural enterprises) in order to ensure that a certain amount of land could not be sold for non-agricultural purposes which would have threatened food security, etc. (cf. Naughton 2018).

While the above-described measures present a good start to fight the rural–urban gap, much effort still has to be made and this issue is far from being resolved. For instance, to some extent, the rural–urban divide has just been relocated to *within* the cities (due to the still varying social insurance coverage and unevenly paid jobs). In addition, while it has become easier to receive urban resident status in smaller and medium-sized cities, there are still much more restrictions for "megacities" such as Shanghai.

Box 4.23 Summary: Social Security System Reform

Prior to 1978: collective unit-centered social security system (SOEs responsible for the provision of public services and for ensuring lifetime employment).

→ competition from TVEs and gradual privatization → increasing pressure to improve efficiency → abolishment of lifetime employment → exclusion of more and more people from social services.

Labor market

Replacement of the Permanent Employment System by a Labor Contract System.

SOE workers as main losers of the second reform period due to massive layoffs.

Reforms: Re-employment Project and Re-employment Service Centers (1995); standardization of the unemployment insurance program, Minimum Living Standard Program.

Healthcare system

Abandonment of the old free healthcare system and introduction of a universal healthcare system (separation between urban and rural residents).

Reforms: Rural Cooperative Medical System (2009); three-phase healthcare system reform plan (starting in 2009).

Pension system

Gradual erosion of the old pension system in the course of the SOE restructuring process; new mixed pension system for urban areas: Enterprise Employee Basic Pension System (EEBP) (excluding unemployed urban residents and jobless migrants).

Reforms: Urban–Rural Resident Basic Social Pension Scheme (late 2000s) (covering rural residents and urban residents not protected by the EEBP); restructuring of the Government Institution Pension System.

Rural–urban inequality

Widening rural–urban income gap (reforms in rural areas lagged behind).

Reforms: rural tax reductions, abolishment of the agricultural tax (2005), increased budgetary expenditures for education and health services, subsidies to farmers, strengthening of farmers' property rights; encouragement of rural migration: National Migrant Worker Training Plan (2003–2010) including the Sunshine Project (2004); New-type Urbanization Plan (2014); hukou reform.

4.6.2 The Return of Industrial Policy

Besides the gradual expansion of the social safety net (especially the reforms of the pension and healthcare systems), another important feature of the third reform period was the return of industrial policy.

During the second reform phase under Zhu Rongji, direct government intervention in sectoral development policy was reduced significantly; instead, the national innovation system became increasingly market driven (similar as it has earlier been the case in Japan and South Korea). However, there was a significant break with this trajectory in 2003 when the "**techno-industrial policy**" returned.[37,38] As argued by Naughton (2019), the industrial policy since the 2000s

[37] However, as argued by Chen and Naughton (2016), the previous model has probably never really been abolished but only temporarily scaled back because of lacking state resources and development capacity.

[38] For an excellent discussion on this issue, see Chen and Naughton (2016). Here, we only outline the most important aspects.

differed from earlier policy initiatives regarding its scope, intensity, and volume of resources in terms of which it was substantially higher.

In 2003, the System Reform Commission (SRC) and the State Development Planning Commission were amalgamated to form the **National Development and Reform Commission (NDRC)** which became more conservative (Naughton 2018). Also the SASAC was established in that year. It enabled the state to exert a more direct role in the promotion of economic development. The SASAC was responsible for the oversight of 196[39] large Chinese state firms in strategically important industries which each had numerous subsidiaries (in total more than 23,000 in 2010) and should be transformed into national champions (Lardy 2019; Naughton 2018; Chang and Jin 2016). Together with the provincial SASAC entities, the special commission has control over 60% of all non-financial state firms (Lardy 2019). See Sect. 4.5.1 for more information.

The policy shift regarding the resumption of comprehensive industrial policies took place in two waves (Chen and Naughton 2016).

During the **first wave**, the central government created the **Medium- and Long-Term Program of Science and Technology (MLP)** in the course of which the dependence on foreign technology should be reduced and domestic R&D fostered. The MLP was initially led by the Ministry of Science and Technology. Since around 2003, domestic R&D expenditures had outpaced the expenditures on technology imports, and between 2003 and 2012, the foreign dependence declined from around 40% to only around 20% (Chen and Naughton 2016). In addition, **16 megaprojects** were launched in 2006.[40] While in 2007 the share of megaprojects in GDP was literally zero, it had increased to 0.1% by 2009 and subsequently fluctuated around this value. The central budget on science and technology rose from 61 billion RMB in 2003 to 221 billion RMB in 2012 (i.e. a 3.6-fold increase) of which the 16 megaprojects accounted to more than 20% (Chen and Naughton 2016). The number of the national industrial policy programs adopted increased considerably during the second half of the 2000s. Between 1995 and 2006, a maximum of three projects per year was adopted; on average, there was only one project. Between 2007 and 2011, the average number of approved projects increased to seven, peaking in 2011 with a total of 15 adopted programs (Heilmann and Shih 2013).

The return of industrial policy was further fostered by the **Global Financial Crisis** around 2008. In order to cope with the decreasing export demand, there was a huge stimulus program in 2009 and the state's influence on economic development expanded rapidly in the short run. The majority of bank credits were granted to state-linked companies and measures undertaken to fight the crisis mixed with industrial policy initiatives (see also Sect. 4.6.3). The implementation of the 16 megaprojects was expedited (Chen and Naughton 2016).

---

[39] This number was subsequently reduced in the course of the restructuring process and various mergers. Currently, there are slightly less than 100 SOEs controlled by the SASAC.

[40] Interestingly, among those 16 projects, there were also three that had previously been terminated by Zhu Rongji.

In 2009, the "10 Industrial Revitalization Plan" was introduced.[41] The industrial restructuring blueprints usually included (among others) tax reliefs and enhanced credit provision for technology upgrading and increasing energy efficiency measures (EIU 2009). As argued by Zheng (2010) and Chen and Naughton (2016), the "rapid-fire pragmatic intervention" in the course of the Global Financial Crisis paved the way for the strategic emerging industries that dominated industrial policies during the 2010s.

The **second wave** of (techno-) industrial policy accordingly started around 2010 and was centered around the **Strategic Emerging Industries (SEIs)** (zhanluexing xinxing chanye) program. The seven industries specified in the "Decision on Accelerating the Development of Strategic Emerging Industries" document are listed below.

1. Energy-efficient and environmental technologies
2. Next generation information technology (IT)
3. Biotechnology
4. High-end equipment manufacturing
5. New energy
6. New materials
7. New-energy vehicles (NEVs).

In addition, this document also laid out quantitative targets. In particular, the value added of these industries as a share of GDP should amount to 8% in 2015 and approximately 15% in 2020 (cf. US-China Business Council 2013). The catalogue of SEIs was revised in 2013 and 2016. Among others, "digital innovation" was included as the eighth SEI.

Even though the SEI projects were closely related to the previous megaprojects and sometimes even presented a continuation of them, there existed some important differences: First, the government rather created favorable conditions for the involved firms instead of fully funding the SEI initiatives. Second, they were immediately led by the **National Development and Reform Commission (NDRC)**. In contrast, the MLP and the megaprojects were only successively turned into industrial policies (cf. Chen and Naughton 2016).

The continued heavy reliance on industrial policy was amplified in the 13th five-year plan and the "Made in China 2025" strategy (Hofman 2019). The "**Made in China 2025**" initiative emphasized ten priority industries that to some extent built upon the earlier formulated SEIs (cf. Holz 2020):

1. Information technology
2. Robotics
3. Aerospace equipment
4. Ocean engineering equipment and high-tech ships

[41] The ten industries were automotive, steel, textiles, shipbuilding, petrochemicals, non-ferrous metals, equipment manufacturing, information technology (IT), light industry, and logistics (EIU 2009).

5. Railway equipment
6. Energy saving and new-energy vehicles
7. Power equipment
8. New materials
9. Medicines and medical devices
10. Agricultural machinery.

Similar to earlier reforms, also the "Made in China 2025" program was first implemented in pilot cities (in particular, in Ningbo). Also the industrial areas highlighted in the **13th five-year plan** (2016–2020) dovetailed to a large extent with the SEIs (see Kenderdine 2017 who also outlines overlaps between the SEIs, "Made in China 2025" key industries, and the 13th five-year plan, see especially Fig. 1, p. 328).

In general, government-run financing agencies became more prominent during the last decade. The central government invested in priority growth areas through investment funds. There were around 780 of such funds at the end of 2015 (Kennedy and Johnson 2016).

As already argued above, there were almost no major market-oriented economic reforms since 2003. The main exception was the financial sector, in particular the bank recapitalization reform starting around 2005.

Box 4.24 Summary: Resurgence of Industrial Policy

1992–2003 (under Zhu Rongji): reduction of direct government intervention in sectoral development.

2003-present: return of **techno-industrial policy** (merger of system reform commission and state development planning commission into the (more conservative) **National Development and Reform Commission,** establishment of the **SASAC**).

First wave (starting around 2003)

Creation of the Medium- and Long-Term Program of Science of Technology (aiming at less dependence on foreign technology), launch of 16 megaprojects (2006), rising number of national industrial policy programs, 2009 stimulus program mixed with industrial policy initiatives, introduction of the "10 Industrial Revitalization Plan" (2009).

Second wave (starting around 2010)

Centered around the seven Strategic Emerging Industries (SEIs), "Made in China 2025" strategy, and government-run financing agencies gained prominence.

4.6.3 Toward the "Xi-Strategy"

The Global Financial Crisis of 2008/9 was also a "warning shot". It revealed the vulnerability of the Chinese development model created by Deng Xiaoping, which relied on high export and investment rates (Wagner 2015). The subsequent severe slowdown in growth could only be absorbed for a while by an extremely expansive macroeconomic monetary and fiscal policy (see also above).

In November 2008, a 4 trillion yuan (US$586 billion) stimulus program was announced. Almost two-thirds (2.87 trillion yuan) of the stimulus package were assigned to infrastructure projects, including the reconstruction of the Sichuan earthquake area and the development of high-speed railways, each accounting for an estimated 1 trillion yuan. The areas "social measures" and "social security and health" were together assigned 0.7 trillion yuan; spending on technological advancement amounted to 0.37 trillion yuan (in addition, 0.58 trillion yuan were spent for the category "technology and environment") (cf. McKissack and Xu 2011). While the stimulus program had been successful in preventing the Great Recession—after the record low of 6.1% in the first quarter of 2009, growth again gained momentum, reaching 7.9% in the second quarter and even around 10% in the final quarter—it also caused a sharp rise in public debt.

Between 2006 and 2013, local government debt increased from 1.2 to 12.5 trillion yuan which is more than 20% of GDP (cf. Huang et al. 2017). As already mentioned earlier, new bank credits were especially granted to SOEs and not to the often more productive private companies (see e.g. Deng et al. 2015; Bai et al. 2016). Huang et al. (2020) show that this led to a crowding out of private firm investment.

As a result of the deteriorating debt situation, the reforms were tightened from 2011 onwards under Xi Jinping; regarding some aspects, this tightening is sometimes described as being rather "backward-looking".

Xi Jinping introduced the strategy of "**rebalancing**" which is, among others, characterized by recentralization and authoritarianism as well as stronger controls. Other aspects of this strategy (sometimes labelled as "**Xi strategy**") include (i) the attempt to further include the western regions of China into China's development strategy, (ii) the efforts to improve the social and ecological standards within China, and (iii) a more consumption- and service-led growth strategy (Wagner 2017). Accordingly, major slogans for the reforms under Xi Jinping are "One Belt, One Road", "Made in China 2025" (see also above), "Supply Side Economics", and "Chinese Dream" (Wagner 2017).

However, while in general, a rebalancing of the economy seems desirable and necessary to sustain long-run development, the Xi reforms also had the negative side-effect that economic growth was (again) further reduced during the 2010s, levelling off around "only" slightly above 6% in more recent years (which is still relatively high in international comparison). By making compromises, the natural growth-reducing consequences of structural change were further intensified (Wagner 2017, 2019, 2021). In particular, necessary structural reforms were postponed; instead, the government installed a very expansionary macroeconomic policy, which in turn created new imbalances such as rising government debt, etc. These topics will be discussed in more detail below in Chap. 6 "Current Challenges".

References

Acemoglu D (2009) Introduction to modern economic growth. Princeton University Press, Princeton

Allen F, Qian J, Qian M (2014) China's financial system: past, present, and future. In: Brandt L, Rawski TG (eds) China's great economic transformation. Cambridge University Press, Cambridge, pp 506–568

Allen F, Qian J, Shan SC, Zhu JL (2015) Explaining the disconnection between China's economic growth and stock market performance. Unpublished working paper

Allen RC, Bassino J-P, Moo-Murata C, van Zanden JL (2011) Wages, prices, and living standards in China, 1738–1925: in comparison with Europe, Japan, and India. Econ History Rev 64(1):8–38

Amstad M, Sun G, Xiong W (2020) The handbook of China's financial system. Princeton University Press, Princeton

Arora VB, Norregaard J (1997) Intergovernmental fiscal relations: the Chinese system in perspective. IMF working paper no 97/129, International Monetary Fund, Washington, DC

Ashton B, Hill K, Piazza A, Zeitz R (1984) Famine in China, 1958–61. Popul Dev Rev 10:613–645

Bai C-E, Hsieh C-T, Song M (2016) The long shadow of a fiscal expansion. Brook Pap Econ Activity, Fall 2016

Bell MW, Khor HE, Kochhar K (1993) China at the threshold of a market economy, IMF occasional paper 107. International Monetary Fund, Washington, DC

Bhagwati J (1978) Anatomy and consequences of exchange control regimes. Ballinger Pub. Co., Cambridge, MA

Bin S (2015) China's trade development strategy and trade policy reforms: overview and prospect. International Institute for Sustainable Development, Tianjin

Borst N, Li C (2016) Can private capital transform banking in China? Federal Reserve Bank of San Francisco. https://www.frbsf.org/banking/asia-program/pacific-exchange-blog/china-private-banks-transform/#_ftn1

Brandt L, Ma D, Rawski TG (2014) From divergence to convergence: reevaluating the history behind China's economic boom. J Econ Lit 52(1):45–123

Branstetter L, Lardy NR (2014) China's embrace of globalization. In: Brandt L, Rawski TG (eds) China's great economic transformation. Cambridge University Press, Cambridge, pp 633–682

Breslin S (2006) Foreign direct investment in the PRC: references, policies and performance. Policy Soc 25(1):9–38. https://doi.org/10.1016/S1449-4035(06)70125-4

Buck T, Liu X, Wei Y, Liu X (2007) The trade development path and export spillovers in China: a missing link? Manag Int Rev 47(5):683–706

Burns JP (1994) Strengthening central CCP control of leadership selection: the 1990 nomenklatura. China Quart 138:458–491

Byrd W (1991) The market mechanism and economic reforms in China. M. E. Sharpe, Armonk, NY, London

Byrd WA, Lin Q (eds) (1990) China's rural industry structure, development, and reform. Oxford University Press, Oxford, New York

Cai D et al (eds) (2008) Xi Zhongxun governing guangdong (Xi Zhongxun Zhuzheng Guangdong). Chinese Communist Party History Press, Beijing

Cai F, Park A, Zhao Y (2014) The Chinese labor market in the reform era. In: Brandt L, Rawski TG (eds) China's great economic transformation. Cambridge University Press, Cambridge, pp 167–214

Cai J, Harrison A (2011) The value-added tax reform puzzle. NBER working paper 17532, National Bureau of Economic Research, Cambridge, MA

Cao KH, Birchenall JA (2013) Agricultural productivity, structural change, and economic growth in post-reform China. J Dev Econ 104:165–180. https://doi.org/10.1016/j.jdeveco.2013.06.001

Chan KW (1994) Urbanization and rural-urban migration in China since 1982: a new baseline. Modern China 20(3):243–281

Chan T, Tracy N, Wenhui Z (1999) China's export miracle—origins, results and prospects. Macmillan, London

Chang C, Wang Y (1994) The nature of the township enterprises. J Comp Econ 19(3):434–452

Chang GH, Wen GJ (1998) Food availability versus consumption efficiency: causes of the Chinese famine. China Econ Rev 9(2):157–166

Chang S-J, Jin SY (2016) the performance of state owned enterprises in China: an empirical analysis of ownership control through SASACs. Centre for Governance, Institutions and Organisations (CGIO), NUS Business School National University of Singapore

Chavance B (2017) Ownership transformation system change in China. Revue de la régulation 21. https://doi.org/10.4000/regulation.12298

Che J, Qian Y (1998) Institutional environment, community government, and corporate governance: understanding sinus Township-Village Enterprises. J Law Econ Organ 14(1):1–23

Chen C (1997) The evolution and main features of China's foreign direct investment policies. Chinese Economic Research Center working papers no 97/15, Adelaide, SA

Chen C (2011) Foreign direct investment in China: location determinants, investor differences and economic impacts. Edward Elgar, Cheltenham, UK

Chen C (2017) Foreign direct investment and the Chinese economy: a critical assessment. Edward Elgar, Cheltenham, UK

Chen C (2019) The liberalization of FDI policies and the impact of FTI and China's economic development. In: Garnaut R, Song L, Fang C (eds) China's 40 years of reform and development 1978–2018. Australian National University Press, Acton, pp 595–618

Chen C, Chang L, Zhang Y (1995) The role of foreign direct investment in China's post-1978 economic development. World Dev 23(4):691–703

Chen J (2008) The revision of the constitution and the PRC: a great leap forward or symbolic gesture? China Perspectives 53, http://journals.openedition.org/chinaperspectives/2922

Chen L, Naughton B (2016) An institutionalized policy-making mechanism: China's return to techno-industrial policy. Res Policy 45:2138–2152

Chen M, Liu W, Lu D, Chen H, Ye C (2020) Progress of China's new type of urbanization construction since 2014: a preliminary assessment. Cities 103:102736

Chen Y (1981) The dawn for the rural area, the hope for China: report of the survey and the implementing of 'baochan daohu' in the rural area in Anhui province. In: Rural area, economy and society. Institutional for Development Problems in China, Beijing

Chen Z, Jiang X, Liu Z et al (2019) Tax policy and lumpy investment behavior: evidence from China's vat reform. NBER working paper 26336, National Bureau of Economic Research, Cambridge, MA. https://doi.org/10.3386/w26336

Cheng H-S (1991) Inflation and economic instability in China. FRBSF Weekly Letter March 2020, 1991, Research Department, Federal Reserve Bank of San Francisco, San Francisco CA

Cheng X, Degryse H (2010) The impact of bank and non-bank financial institutions and local economic growth in China. J Finan Ser Res 37:179–199

Chow GC (2007) China's economic transformation, 2nd edn. Blackwell Publishing, Malden, MA, Oxford

Cine WR (1995) Evaluating the Uruguay round. World Econ 181:1–23

Cousin V (2011) Banking in China, 2nd edn. Palgrave Macmillan, London

CRDR (China Reform and Development Report Expert Group) (1994) China reform and development report, 1992–1993: new breakthroughs and new challenges. China Finance and Economy Press, Beijing

DaCosta MMN, Foo JPN (2002) China's financial system: to decades of gradual reforms. Manag Finance 28(10):3–18

Dang X (2008) Foreign direct investment in China. Master of Arts thesis, Kansas State University

Dees S (1998) Foreign direct investment in China: determinants and effects. Econ Plann 31:175–194

Deng Y, Morck R, Wu J, Yeung B (2015) China's pseudo monetary policy. Rev Finance 19:53–93

Dewatripont M, Roland G (1992) The virtues of gradualism and legitimacy in the transition to a market economy. Econ J 102:291–300

Dixon JE (1981) The Chinese welfare system: 1949–1979. Praeger, New York

Eckel PE (1948) The far East since 1500. Harcourt, Brace, New York

Edwards S (1993) Openness, trade liberalization, and growth in developing countries. J Econ Lit 31(3):1358–1393

EIU (2009) China stimulus package: a 6-month report cards (a corporate network special report). Economist Intelligence Unit, London

Elvin M (1973) The pattern of the Chinese past. Stanford University Press, Stanford

Enright M, Scott E, Chung K (2005) Regional powerhouse: the greater Pearl River Delta and the rise of China. Wiley (Asia), Singapore

Fan G, Woo WT (1993) decentralized socialism and macroeconomic stability: lessons from China. UNU-WIDER working paper 112, UNU-WIDER, Helsinki

Fan S (1990) Effects of technological change and institutional reform on production growth in Chinese agriculture. Staff paper series P90-40, University of Minnesota, St. Paul, MN

Fan Z, Wan G (2016) The fiscal risk of local government revenue in the People's Republic of China. ADBI working paper 567, Asian Development Bank Institute, Tokyo

Fang H, Eggleston K, Hanson K, Wu M (2019) Enhancing financial protection under China's social health insurance to achieve universal health coverage. BMJ 365:l2378. https://doi.org/10.1136/bmj.l2378

Fang X (1992) Economic transition: government commitment and gradualism. Working paper no. 12, Stanford University

Fang X, Jiang Y (2016) Impact of the joint-stock reform of commercial banks on the effectiveness of monetary policy in China. Panoeconomicus 63(3):325–338. https://doi.org/10.2298/PAN1603325F

Finger JM (2001) Implementing the Uruguay round agreements: problems for developing countries. World Econ 24(9):1097–1108

Finger JM, Nogués JJ (2001) The unbalanced Uruguay round outcome: the new areas in future WTO negotiations. Policy research working paper 2732, World Bank, Washington, DC

Garnaut R, Song L (2012) China: twenty years of economic reform. ANU Press, Canberra, ACT

Garnaut R, Song L, Fang C (eds) (2018) China's 40 years of reform and development. ANU Press, Canberra ACT

Garnaut R, Song L, Yao Y (2006) Impact and significance of state-owned enterprise restructuring in China. China J 55:35–63

Giles J, Wang D, Park A (2013) Expanding social insurance coverage in urban China. Policy research working paper 6497. The World Bank, Washington, DC

Glawe L, Wagner H (2017) A stylized model of China's growth since 1978. SSRN working paper 2917433

Groves T, Hong Y, McMillan J et al (1994) Autonomy and incentives in Chinese state enterprises. Q J Econ 109(1):183–209

Guijun L, Schramm RM (2003) China's foreign policies since 1979: a review of developments and an assessment. China Econ Rev 14(3):246–280. https://doi.org/10.1016/j.chieco.2003.09.006

Guo R (2013) Understanding the Chinese economies. Elsevier, Oxford

He AJ (2020) Access to social protection by immigrants, emigrants and resident nationals in China. In: Lafleur J-M, Vintila D (eds) Migration and social protection in Europe and beyond (volume 3): a focus on non-EU sending states. Springer, Cham, Switzerland, pp 77–91

He G, Ong LH (2014) Chinese rural cooperative finance in the era of post-commercialized rural credit cooperatives. Chin Econ 47(4):81–98. https://doi.org/10.2753/CES1097-1475470404

Heilmann S, Shih L (2013) The rise of industrial policy in China, 1978–2012. Harvard-Yenching Institute working paper series, Cambridge, MA

Hofman B (2019) Reflections on 40 years of China's reforms. In: Garnaut R, Song L, Fang C (eds) China's 40 years of reform and development 1978–2018. Australian National University Press, Acton, Australia, pp 43–66

Holz CA (2018) The unfinished business of state-owned enterprise reform in the People's Republic of China. MPRA paper 94093, Munich Personal RePEc Archive, Munich

Holz CA (2020) PRC industrial policies postdate rather than lead economic activity. CESifo working paper 8097. Center for Economic Studies and ifo Institute, Munich

Huang J, Rozelle S, Lin JY (1998) Impacts of research and technological change in China's rice production. In: Pingali P, Hossain M (eds) Impact of rice research. Thailand Development Research Institute, International Rice Research Institute, Manila, pp 263–278

Huang Y (1993) government intervention and agricultural performance in China. PhD thesis, Australian National University. https://openresearch-repository.anu.edu.au/handle/1885/10898

Huang Y (1999) State-owned enterprise reform. In: Garnaut R, Song L (eds) China: twenty years of reform, Asia Pacific Press, Canberra

Huang Y, Pagano M, Panizza U (2017) The dark side of the Chinese fiscal stimulus: evidence from local government debt. VoxChina. http://voxchina.org/show-3-17.html

Huang Y, Pagano M, Panizza U (2020) Local crowding-out in China. J Financ 75(6):2855–2898

Huang Y, Wang X (2019) 'Strong on quantity, week on quality': China's financial reform between 1978 and 2018. In: Garnaut R, Song L, Fang C (eds) China's 40 years of reform and development 1978–2018 Australian National University Press, Acton, Australia, pp 291–312

Huang Y, Wang X, Wang B, Lin N (2013) Financial reform in China: progress and challenges. In: Patrick H, Park YC (eds) How finances shaping the economies of China, Japan, and Korea. University Press Scholarship Online. https://doi.org/10.7312/columbia/9780231165266.001.0001

ILO (2011) Promoting decent employment for rural migrant workers. International Labour Organization, Geneva

IMF (1989) Annual report on exchange arrangements and exchange restrictions. International Monetary Fund, Washington, DC

Javorcik B (2004) Does foreign direct investment increase the productivity of domestic firms? In search of spillovers through backward linkages. Am Econ Rev 94(3):605–627

Jefferson G (2016) State-owned enterprise in China: reform, performance, and prospects. Working paper no. 109, Brandeis University, Department of Economics and International Business School, Waltham, MA

Jefferson GH, Rawski TG (1994) Enterprise reform in Chinese industry. J Econ Perspect 8(2):47–70. https://doi.org/10.1257/jep.8.2.47

Jefferson GH, Singh I (1999) Enterprise reform in China: ownership, transition, and performance. World Bank Research Publication. Oxford University Press, New York, NY

Jiang K, Keller W, Qiu LD, Ridley W (2018) International joint ventures and internal vs. external technology transfer: evidence from China. NBER working paper 24455. National Bureau of Economic Research, Cambridge, MA

Jin G, Liu Q (2011) The transformation of Chinese society (1840–1956): the fate of its ultrastable structure in modern times (In Chinese). China Law Press, Beijing

Jin H, Qian Y (1998) Public versus private ownership of firms: evidence from rural China. Q J Econ 113(3):773–808

Jin H, Qian Y, Weingast B (2005) Regional decentralization and fiscal incentives: federalism, Chinese style. J Public Econ 89:1719–1742. https://doi.org/10.1016/j.jpubeco.2004.11.008

Johnson DG (1988) Economic reforms in the People's Republic of China. Econ Dev Cult Change 36:S225–S246

Johnson GE (1982) The production responsibility system in Chinese agriculture: Some examples from Guangdong. Pacific Affairs 55(3):430–451

Jones EL (1988) Growth recurring: economic change in world history. Clarendon Press, Oxford

Keller W (2010) International trade, foreign direct investment, and technology spillovers. NBER working paper 15442, National Bureau of Economic Research, Cambridge, MA

Keller W, Yeaple S (2013) The gravity of knowledge. Am Econ Rev 103(4):1414–1444

Kenderdine T (2017) China's industrial policy, strategic emerging industries and space law. Asia Pacific Policy Stud 4(2):325–342

Kennedy S, Johnson CK (2016) Perfecting China Inc.: the 13th five-year plan. Center for Strategic and International Studies, Washington, DC

Knight J, Ding S (2012) China's remarkable economic growth. Oxford University Press, Oxford

Kornai J (1986) The soft-budget constraint. Kyklos 39(1):3–30

Kroeber AR (2016) China's economy: what everyone needs to know. Oxford University Press, New York

Krueger AO (1978) Foreign trade regimes and economic development: liberalization attempts and consequences. Ballinger Pub. Co., Cambridge, MA

Krueger AO (1993) Political economy of policy reform in developing countries. MIT Press, Cambridge, MA

Kueh Y-Y (1984) China's new agricultural-policy program: major economic consequences, 1979–1983. J Comp Econ 8(4):353–375

Kung JK-S, Lin Y-M (2007) The decline of Township-and-Village Enterprises in China's economic transition. World Dev 35(4):569–584

Kwan YK, Chow GC (1997) Chow's method of optimal control: a numerical solution. J Econ Dyn Control 21(4–5):739–752

Lam WR, Schipke A (2017) state-owned enterprise frameworks. In: Lam WR, Rodlauer M, Schipke A (eds) Modernizing China: investing in soft infrastructure. International Monetary Fund, Washington, DC

Lardy N (2019) Private sector development. In: Garnaut R, Song L, Fang C (eds) China's 40 years of reform and development 1978–2018. Australian National University Press, Acton, Australia, pp 329–344

Lardy NR (1992) Foreign trade and economic reform in China 1978–1990. Cambridge University Press, Cambridge

Lardy NR (2000) Is China a "closed" economy? (24 February 2000). Brookings. https://www.brookings.edu/testimonies/is-china-a-closed-economy/

Lardy NR (2002) Integrating China into the global economy. Brookings Institution Press, Washington, DC

Lau LJ, Qian Y, Roland G (2000) Reform without losers: an interpretation of China's dual-track approach to transition. J Polit Econ 108(1):120–143. https://doi.org/10.1086/262113

Li B, van Zanden JL (2012) Before the great divergence? Comparing the Yangzi Delta and the Netherlands at the beginning of the nineteenth century. J Econ History 74(4):956–989

Li K, Jiang W (2018) China's foreign trade: reform, performance and contribution to economic growth. In: Garnaut R, Song L, Fang C (eds) China's 40 years of reform and development: 1978–2018. ANU Press, Canberra, ACT, pp 575–593

Li L, Fu H (2017) China's health care system reform: progress and prospects. Int J Health Plann Manage 32(3):240–253. https://doi.org/10.1002/hpm.2424

Li R, Li X, Lei W et al (2015) Consequences of China's opening to foreign banks. In: Song L, Garnaut R, Fang C et al (eds) China's domestic transformation in a global context. ANU Press, Canberra, ACT, pp 67–90

Li S (2010) The economic situation of rural migrant workers in China. China Perspectives 2010/4:4–15

Li W, Putterman L (2008) Reforming China's SOEs: an overview. Comp Econ Stud 50:353–380. https://doi.org/10.1057/ces.2008.31

Li W, Yang D (2005) The great leap forward: anatomy of a central planning disaster. J Polit Econ 113(4):840–877. https://doi.org/10.1086/430804

Li X (2019) Regulating China's inward FDI: changes, challenges, and the future. In: China's reform and opening: 40 years and counting. Brookings Institution Press, Washington, DC

Lin J, Cai F, Li Z (1998) Competition, policy burdens, and state-owned enterprise reform. Am Econ Rev 88(2):422–427

Lin JY (1988) The household responsibility system in China's agricultural reform: a theoretical and empirical study. Econ Dev Cult Change 36(3):S199–S224

Lin JY (1992) Rural reforms and agricultural growth in China. Am Econ Rev 82(1):34–51

Lin JY (1995) The Needham puzzle: why the industrial revolution did not originate in China. Econ Dev Cult Change 43(2):269–292

Lin JY, Liu Z (2000) Fiscal decentralization and economic growth in China. Econ Dev Cult Change 49(1):1–21

Lin JY, Tang G (1999) Policy burdens, accountability, and the soft budget constraint. Am Econ Rev 89(2):426–431

Lin KJ, Lu X, Zhang J et al (2020) State-owned enterprises in China: a review of 40 years of research and practice. China J Account Res 13:31–55. https://doi.org/10.1016/j.cjar.2019.12.001

Lipton D, Sachs J (1990a) Creating a market economy in Eastern Europe: the case of Poland. Brook Pap Econ Act 1:75–147

Lipton D, Sachs J (1990b) Privatization in Eastern Europe: the case of Poland. Brook Pap Econ Act 2:293–341

Liu T, Sun L (2016) Pension reform in China. J Aging Soc Policy 28:15–28. https://doi.org/10.1080/08959420.2016.1111725

Lou J, Wang S (2008) Public finance in China: reform and growth for a harmonious society. World Bank, Washington, DC

Lu L (2016) Private banks in China: origin, challenges and regulatory implications. Bank Finance Law Rev 31(3):585–599

Lubman S (2006) Looking for law in China. Columbia J Asian Law 20:1–92

Ma G, Fung B (2002) China's asset management corporations. BIS working papers 115, Bank for International Settlements, Basel

Ma J (2000) The Chinese economy in the 1990s. Palgrave Macmillan, London

Maddison A (2001) The world economy: a millennial perspective. Organisation for Economic Co-operation and Development, Paris and Washington, DC

Mah F-H (1968) Foreign trade. In: Eckstein A, Galenson W, Lu T-C (eds) Economic trends in communist China. Aldine Publishing Company, Chicago, pp 671–738

Martinelli C, Tommasi M (1995) Economic reforms and political constraints: on the time inconsistency of gradual sequencing. UC3M working papers, Economics 3916, Universidad Carlos III de Madrid and UCLA

Martinez-Vazquez J (2006) China's long march to decentralization. In: Smoke P, Gómez EJ, Peterson GE (eds) Decentralization in Asia and Latin America. Edward Elgar Publishing Inc., Northampton, MA, pp 88–135

McKissack A, Xu JY (2011) Chinese macroeconomic management through the crisis and beyond. Asian-Pacific Econ Lit 25(1):43–55

McMillan J, Naughton B (1992) How to reform planned economy: lessons from China. Oxf Rev Econ Policy 8(1):130–143

McMillan J, Whalley J, Zhu L (1989) The impact of China's economic reforms on agricultural productivity growth. J Polit Econ 97(4):781–807

McMillan J, Woodruff C (2002) The central role of entrepreneurs in transition economies. J Econ Perspect 16(3):153–170

Mehran H, Quintyn M, Nordman T et al (1996) Monetary and exchange system reforms in China: an experiment in gradualism. IMF occasional paper 141. International Monetary Fund, Washington, DC

Meng Q et al (2019) What can we learn from China's health system reform? BMJ (Clinical research ed.) 365:l2349. https://doi.org/10.1136/bmj.l2349

Meng X (2012) Labor market outcomes and reforms in China. J Econ Perspect 26(4):75–102. https://doi.org/10.1257/jep.26.4.75

Mo YK (1999) A review of banking reforms in China. In: BIS (ed) Strengthening the banking system in China: issues and experience, Bank of International Settlements, Basel, pp 90–109

Mokyr J (1990) The lever of riches: technological creativity and economic progress. Oxford University Press, New York

Morck R, Yeung B (2017) East Asian financial and economic development. NBER working paper 23845, National Bureau of Economic Research, Cambridge, MA

Nan Y, Gao Y, Zhou Q (2018) Rural credit cooperatives' contribution to agricultural growth: evidence from China. Agric Financ Rev 79:119–135. https://doi.org/10.1108/AFR-06-2017-0042

Naughton B (1991) Why has economic reform led to inflation? Am Econ Rev 81(2):207–211

Naughton B (1992) Implications of the state monopoly over industry and its relaxation. Modern China 18(1):14–41

Naughton B (1993) Deng Xiaoping: the economist. China Quart 135:491–514. https://doi.org/10.1017/S0305741000013886

Naughton B (1995) Growing out of the plan: Chinese economic reform, 1978–1993. Cambridge University Press, Cambridge

Naughton B (2017) The current wave of state enterprise reform in China: a preliminary appraisal. Asian Econ Policy Rev 12(2):282–298

Naughton B (2018) The Chinese economy: adaptation and growth. The MIT Press, Cambridge, MA

Naughton B (2019) State enterprise reform today. In: Garnaut R, Song L, Fang C (eds) China's 40 years of reform and development 1978–2018. Australian National University Press, Acton, pp 375–394

NBS (National Bureau of Statistics of China) (1997–2020) China statistical yearbook. China Statistic Press, National Bureau of Statistics of China, Beijing

Needham J (1969) The grand titration. Science and society in East and West. Allen and Unwin, London

OECD (2006) Recent development in China's policies towards cross-border mergers and acquisitions (M&A). OECD Investment Policy Review, Organisation for Economic Co-operation and Development, Paris

Okazaki K (2007) Banking system reform in China: the challenges of moving toward a market-oriented economy. RAND Occasional Paper, RAND Corporation, Santa Monica

Ostry S (2000) The Uruguay round north-south grand bargain: implications for future negotiations. In: Kennedy D, Southwick J (eds), The political economy of international trade law: essays in honor of Robert E. Hudecpp. Cambridge University Press, Cambridge, MA. pp 285–300. https://doi.org/10.1017/CBO9780511494512.016

Otsuka K, Banerjee AV (1998) Rural industry as a in East Asia. In: Hayami Y, Aoki M (eds) The institutional foundations of East Asian economic development. Palgrave Macmillan, New York, pp 447–481

Perkins D (1994) Completing China's move to the market. J Econ Perspect 8(2):23–46

Perkins D, Rawski TG (2014) Forecasting China's economic growth to 2025. In: Brandt L, Rawski TG (eds) China's great economic transformation. Cambridge University Press, Cambridge, pp 829–886

Perotti EC, Sun L, Zou L (1998) State-owned versus township and village enterprises in China. WIDER working paper 1998/150, The United Nations University WIDER, Helsinki

Podpiera R (2006) Progress in China's banking sector reform: has bank behavior changed? IMF working paper 06/71, International Monetary Fund, Washington, DC

Pomeranz K (2000) The great divergence: China, Europe, and the making of the modern world economy. Princeton University Press, Princeton and Oxford

Prasad ES, Rajan RG (2006) Modernizing China's growth paradigm. Am Econ Rev 96(2):331–336

Prime PB (1991) Taxation reform in China's public finance. International Business Faculty Publications, Georgia State University

Qi B (2008) China capital markets development report: China securities regulation commission. China Financial Publishing House, World Bank, Washington, DC. https://openknowledge.worldbank.org/handle/10986/12643

Rawski TG (1994) Chinese industrial reform: accomplishments, prospects, and implications. Am Econ Rev 84(2):271–275

Rehman R, Mangla IU, Zhang J (2016) Chinese banking reforms: an analysis and evaluation of non-performing loans. In: The Pakistan development review, papers and proceedings: the 32nd conference of the Pakistan Society of Development Economists, Islamabad, 13–15 December 2016, pp 563–578

Rodrik D (2008) Second-best institutions. Am Econ Rev Pap Proc 98(2):100–104

Roland G, Verdier T (1994) Privatization in Eastern Europe: irreversibility and critical mass effects. J Public Econ 54:161–183

Scott J, Wilkinson R (2013) China threat? Evidence from the WTO. J World Trade 47(4):761–782

Shambaugh D (1993) Deng Xiaoping: the Politician. China Quart 135:457–490

Shaohua Z (2005) Rural labour migration in [the People's Republic of] China: challenges for policies. Management of social transformations series. Policy papers 10, UNESCO, Paris

Shen C, Jin J, Zou H (2012) Fiscal decentralization in China: history, impact, challenges and next steps. Ann Econ Finance 13:1–51

Shujin Y, Tong Z, Sheng B (1998) China's foreign trade reform. Guizhou People's Press, Guiyang

Smith A (1776) An inquiry into the nature and causes of the wealth of nations. Printed for Strahn W, Cadell T, London

Solinger DJ (2002) Labour market reform and the plight of the laid-off proletariat. China Quart 170:304–326. https://doi.org/10.1017/S0009443902000207

Song L (2012) Trade reform and development. In: Garnaut R, Song L (eds) China: twenty years of economic reform. ANU Press, Canberra, ACT, pp 71–94

Song L (2015) State and non-state in China's economic transition In: Chow GC, Perkins D (eds) Routledge handbook of the Chinese economy, Routledge, New York

Song L (2019) State-owned enterprise reform in China: past present and prospects. In: Garnaut R, Song L, Fang C (eds) China's 40 years of reform and development: 1978–2018. ANU Press, Australia, pp 345–374

State Council (2009) Notice of the State Council on the issuance of the recent key implementation plan (2009–2011) for the reform of the medical and health system (in Chinese). http://www.gov.cn/zwgk/2009-04/07/content_1279256.htm

State Council (2015) Guideline on developing mixed ownership in SOEs. Document No. 54, 24 September. General Office of the State Council, Beijing

Strauss J (1986) Does better nutrition raise farm productivity? J Polit Econ 94(2):297–320

Sun G (2018) Banking system of China. Presentation.

Sun L (1997) Emergence of unorthodox ownership and governance structures in East Asia: an alternative transition path. WIDER research for action 38, World Institute for Development Economics Research, Helsinki

Sun S (2009) How does FDI affect domestic firms' exports? Industrial evidence. World Econ 32 (8):1203–1222

Sun S (2011) Foreign direct investment and technology spillovers in China's manufacturing sector. The Chinese Economy 44(2):25–42

Tang ASS (2005) Globalization and the development of new central business districts in Beijing, Shanghai and Guangzhou. In: Ma LJC, Wu F (eds) Restructuring the Chinese city: changing society, economy and space. Routledge, New York, NY

Tang S, Selvanathan E, Selvanathan S (2008) Foreign direct investment, domestic investment and economic growth in China: a time series analysis. World Econ 31(10):1292–1309

Tzeng F (1991) The political economy of China's coastal development strategy: a preliminary analysis. Asian Surv 31(3):270–284

UNDP (2019) What changes after China defeats poverty? United Nations Development Program, New York, 23 December 2019. https://www.cn.undp.org/content/china/en/home/ourperspective/ourperspectivearticles/2019/what-changes-after-china-defeats-poverty-.html

USC US-China Institute (1993) national People's Congress 1993 amendments to the PRC Constitution, March 29, 1993. USC US-China Institute, University of Southern California. https://china.usc.edu/national-peoples-congress-1993-amendments-prc-constitution-march-29-1993

US-China Business Council (2013) China's strategic emerging industries: Policy, implementation, challenges, and recommendations. The US-China business Council, Washington DC

Wagner H (2015) Structural change and mid-income trap—under which conditions can China succeed in moving towards higher income status? Eur J Comp Econ 12(2):165–188

Wagner H (2017) The building up of new imbalances in China: the dilemma with 'rebalancing.' Int Econ Econ Policy14(4):701–72

Wagner H (2019) On the (non-) sustainability of China's development strategies. Chin Econ 52 (1):1–23

Wagner H (2021) China's "political-economy trilemma": (how) can it be solved? Chin Econ 54 (5):311–329. https://doi.org/10.1080/10971475.2021.1875158

Wang J (2008) The evolution of China's international trade policy: development trough protection and liberalization. In: Lee YS (ed) Economic development through world trade: developing world perspective. Kluwer Law International BW, The Netherlands

Wang L, Shaw G (2012) Coping with rural transformation in the movement of workers from rural areas to cities: E People's Republic of China sometime project. In: Maclean R, Jagannathan S, Sarvi J (eds) Skills development for inclusive and sustainable growth in developing Asia-Pacific, pp 89-104, Springer, Berlin

Wang S (1997) China's 1994 fiscal reform: an initial assessment. Asian Surv 37(9):801–817

Wang X (1999) Economic growth over the past 20 years. In: Garnaut R, Song L (eds) China: 20 years of economic reform. Australian National University Press, Canberra, pp 27–50

Wang Y (2007) Inevitable "three security lines" and "two guaranties." China Soc Secur 11:22–23

Wang Z (1993) Gradualism versus big bang: an economic perspective. Mimeo, presented at the ASSA-CES joint session of ASSA meetings, Boston, 3–5 January 1994

Wang Z (2012) Corporate governance under state control: the Chinese experience. Theor Inquir Law 13(2):487–502

Wang Y (1992) East European puzzle and Chinese enigma: institutional changes as a resource allocation problem. Working paper no. 18, University of Minnesota

Wei SJ (1997) Gradualism versus big bang: speed and sustainability of reforms. Canad J Econ 30 (4b):1234–1247

Weitzman ML, Xu C (1994) Chinese township-village enterprises as vaguely defined cooperatives. J Comp Econ 18:121–145

Wen GJ (1993) Total factor productivity change in China's farming sector: 1952–1989. Econ Dev Cult Change 43:1–41

Wills K (2018) Seeking balance: China strives to adapt social protection to the needs of a market economy. Finance Dev 55(4):20–23

Wong C (1985) Material allocation and ecentralization: impact of the local sector on industrial reform. In: Perry EJ, Wong C (eds) Political economy of reform in post-Mao China, Harvard University Council on East Asian Studies, Cambridge, MA, London

Wong C, Bird R (2014) China's fiscal system: a work in progress. In: Brandt L, Rawski TG (eds) China's great economic transformation. Cambridge University Press, Cambridge, pp 676–732

Wong RB (1997) China transformed: historical change and the limits of European experience. Cornell University Press, Ithaca NY

Working Party on China Status as a Contracting Party (1988) China's foreign trade regime: note by the Secretariat. GATT, Geneva

World Bank (1988) China: external trade and capital. World Bank, Washington, DC

World Bank (1991) World development report 1991: the challenge of development. Oxford University Press, New York

World Bank (2020) The World Bank in China (overview). World Bank, Washington, DC. https://www.worldbank.org/en/country/china/overview#1

World Bank (2021) World development indicators. The World Bank, Washington, DC. https://data.worldbank.org/products/wdi

Wu Z (2008) Perspectives on the Chinese anti-monopoly law. Antitrust Law J 75:73–116

Xian-Chu Z (2009) An anti-monopoly legal regime in the making in China as a socialist market economy. Int Lawyer 43(4):1469–1493

Xiao G (1991) Managerial autonomy, fringe benefits, and ownership structure: a comparative study of Chinese state and collective enterprises. China Econ Rev 2(1):47–73

Xiao G, Sui F (2011) Economic history of the People's Republic of China. Peking University Press, Beijing

Xu C (2011) The fundamental institutions of China's reforms and development. J Econ Lit 49 (4):1076–1151. https://doi.org/10.1257/jel.49.4.1076

Xu C, Zhang X (2009) The evolution of Chinese entrepreneurial firms: Township-Village Enterprises revisited. IFPRI discussion papers 854, International Food Policy Research Institute (IFPRI)

Xu C, Zhuang (1998) Why China view: the role of decentralization. In: Boone P, Gomulka S, Layard R (eds) Emerging from communism: lessons from Russia, China, and Eastern Europe. MIT Press, Cambridge, London

Xu X, Sheng Y (2012) Are FDI spillovers regional? Firm-level evidence from China. J Asian Econ 23(3):244–258

Yang DT, Li Y (2008) Agricultural price reforms in China: experience from the past three decades. Agroalimentaria 14(27):13–23

Yao S (1999) Economic growth, income inequality and poverty in China and the economic reforms. J Dev Stud 35(6):104–130

Yao S, Wei K (2007) Economic growth in the presence of FDI: the perspective of newly industrializing economies. J Comp Econ 35(1):211–234

Yee AS (2004) Domestic support ratios in two-level bargaining: the US-China WTO negotiations. China Rev 4(2):129–163

Yeung Y, Lee J, Kee G (2009) China's special economic zones at 30. Eurasian Geogr Econ 50 (2):222–240

Yuan L, Tsai T (2000) Foreign direct investment policy in China. China Rev 2000:223–247

Yuan Y, Guo H, Xu H, Li W, Luo S, Lin H, Yuan Y (2010) China's first special economic zone: the case of Shenzhen. In: Zeng DZ (ed) Building engines for growth and competitiveness in China: experience of special economic zones and industrial clusters. World Bank, Washington, DC, pp 55–86

Zhang F (2019a) The institutional evolution of China: government vs markets. Edward Elgar Publishing, Cheltenham, Northampton, MA

Zhang T, Zou H-F (1998) Fiscal decentralization, public spending, and economic growth in China. J Public Econ 67(2):221–240

Zhang W, Yi G (1997) China's gradual reform: a historical perspective. In: Tisdell C, Chai JCH (eds) China's economic growth in transition: macroeconomic, regional, environmental and other dimensions. University of Queensland, Brisbane, pp 15–39

Zhang Z (2006) Competition or privatization: China's experience in SOE reform. J Washington Inst China Stud 1:37–59

Zhang Z, Martinez-Vazquez J (2003) The system of equalization transfers in China. International studies program working paper 03-12, Andrew Young School of Policy Studies, Georgia State University

Zhang ZY (2019b) China's SOE reforms: what the latest round of reforms mean for the market (29 May 2019). China Briefing. https://www.china-briefing.com/news/chinas-soe-reform-process/

Zhao Z (2009) Prisoner of the state: the secret journal of Zhao Ziyang. Simon & Schuster, New York, London

Zheng J, Bigsten A, Hu A (2009) Can China's growth be sustained? A productivity perspective. World Dev 37(4):874–888. https://doi.org/10.1016/j.worlddev.2008.07.008

Zheng M (2010) The beginning of strategic emerging industries (in Chinese). Caijing Magazine, 13 September 2010

Zheng P, Siler P, Giorgioni G (2004) FDI in the export performance of Chinese indigenous firms: a regional approach. J Chin Econ Bus Stud 2(1):55–71

Zhou H (2000) Fiscal decentralization and the development of the tobacco industry in China. China Econ Rev 11:114–133

Zhou KX (1996) How the farmers changed China. Westview Press, Boulder

Zhou S (1998) Review and expectation of the SOEs reform in China over the past two decades. Soc Sci China 6:44–58

Zhu H, Walker A (2017) Pension system reform in China: who gets what pensions? Soc Policy Admin 52(7):1410–1424. https://doi.org/10.1111/spol.12368

Zhu Q, Elbern S (2002) Economic institutional evolution and further need for adjustments: township village enterprises in China. ZEF discussion paper 56, Zentrum für Entwicklungsforschung, Bonn

Zhu X (2012) Understanding China's growth: past, present, and future. J Econ Perspect 26 (4):103–124

The Development Paths and Strategies of Japan, South Korea, and China—A Comparison

5

5.1 Introduction

After having extensively discussed the individual economic development trajectories of Japan, South Korea, and China, this chapter deals with the question of whether there exists an "East Asian development model". Or, more precisely: Is there a specific set and pattern of institutional and economic characteristics and development policies which is unique to these three economies (and probably also to some smaller neighbors such as Hong Kong and Taiwan) and which can explain the extraordinary economic dynamics in this area? While Western economists often answer this question in the affirmative, researchers of the East Asian region are usually less optimistic whether such a common development model really exists (cf. Klenner 2006). Consequently, Western experts rather stress the similarities of the development strategies and policies as well as the institutional foundations of these East Asian countries, whereas "domestic" economists underline more strongly the differences between the individual countries.

Against the background of the country-specific reform discussions in Chaps. 2–4, we try to answer this question by first outlining the similarities between Japan, South Korea, and China, especially regarding their development strategies and institutional-cultural characteristics. We subsequently elucidate the country-specific differences which might have influenced the development and political successes of the individual countries. In this way, we hope to provide a balanced view on this topic.

L. Glawe and H. Wagner, *The Economic Rise of East Asia*,
Contributions to Economics, https://doi.org/10.1007/978-3-030-87128-4_5

5.2 Similarities

In this section, we focus primarily on the similarities between the development paths and strategies of Japan, South Korea, and China. We first outline the general idea of an East Asian development model and subsequently compile the key characteristics of this model—first according to the existing literature and then also from our own standpoint. Finally, we investigate in how far South Korea has learned from the Japanese reform experience and China, respectively, from the South Korean and Japanese reform strategies.

5.2.1 The Idea of an East Asian Development Model

The idea of an East Asian development model was first promoted by Ezra Vogel. Originally, it was restricted to the three economies of Japan, South Korea, and Taiwan as well as the city states Hong Kong and Singapore (Vogel 1991). China was initially not included in this set of countries since at this point, it was still a low-income country whose economic transformation was yet about to start. However, since the late 1980s, China increasingly became the central point in the discussion of the East Asian development model (Hua 2015).

A popular approach for illustrating the economic development process in the East Asian region is the **flying geese (FG) model** of dynamic comparative advantage and inter-industry trade. When elaborating on the East Asian development model and the region's development dynamics, it is indispensable to also mention this model and its subsequent modifications.

The FG model was coined by Akamatsu in the 1930s; however, it was not until the early 1960s that the English-speaking academic world got in contact with this model (Akamatsu 1961, 1962). The modern version of the FG paradigm evolves around three types of economic activity sequencing, namely (1) product cycle sequencing, (2) industry-cycle sequencing, and (3) inter-economy sequencing (cf. Ozawa 1991 and Kojima 2000; see also Kasahara 2004 for a comprehensive overview on the original and modern versions of the FG model).

The product life cycle consists of four stages, namely (i) import, (ii) (import-substituting) production, (iii) export, and (iv) (again) import. The industry-cycle sequencing refers to the gradual appearance and development of industries within a country according to its factor endowments and comparative advantages. The country usually starts by producing (and exporting) labor-intensive, lower value-added (light) consumer goods and consecutively turns to higher value-added, more capital-intensive (and usually more sophisticated) goods and industries. The inter-economy sequencing refers to the continuous relocation of industries from advanced to developing countries; that is, from the "front-runner" Japan to the first-tier NIEs including South Korea, Hong Kong, and Taiwan, subsequently to the second-tier ASEAN countries (Thailand, Malaysia, and Indonesia), and then to China (and the remaining ASEAN countries). Thus, less developed Asian economies can be regarded as being "aligned successively behind the advanced industrial nations in the order of their different stages of growth in a wild-geese-flying pattern" (Ozawa 2005). In the original flying geese model, technology transfer takes place via the import of manufactured products as well as the catching up spirits of the entrepreneurs in less developed countries.[1] However, the modern FG model stresses more the importance for transnational companies.

Even though the FG model is generalizing and there surely exist deviations from this proposed sequencing in real life, it still is powerful in explaining the inter-industry trade dynamics in Asia. However, as noted by the ADB (2020) report, intra-industry trade is gaining increasingly greater importance in the Asian region, making the model far more complex. Therefore, the shape of the economic trade relations between (East) Asian countries can be best described by a ***network*** rather than a flying geese pattern (ADB 2020: 317).

5.2.2 Characteristics of the East Asian Development Model

It is noteworthy that there is no common definition of what exactly constitutes the East Asian model of development (cf. Boltho and Weber 2009). However, there is a certain set of characteristics of the East Asian model that seems to be more or less accepted among scholars (especially by Western researchers). Probably most obvious, Japan, South Korea, and China all did not only experience extraordinary GDP growth but also recorded (and partly still record) substantially high savings and investment rates (see e.g. World Bank 1993; Klenner 2006). During their development processes, all three countries gained increasing importance in the world markets for manufacturers (Boltho and Weber 2009). This was partly achieved by adopting foreign technologies from advanced countries (even though the strategies for acquiring these technologies differed significantly) and also by creating competitive market conditions (Morck and Yeung 2017; Boltho and Weber 2009). Other common factors are sensible macroeconomic policies and (partly

[1] Cf. Sect. 5.3.5 for a discussion on the different methods for acquiring foreign technologies in Japan, South Korea, and China.

related to this) a certain concern for stability which also explains the relatively late capital account liberalization (Boltho and Weber 2009).

In all three countries, there is a relatively high degree of state centralization, a critical precondition for state capacity (Acemoglu et al. 2020). In addition, governments played (and partly still play) an active and significant role for the development process of Japan, South Korea, and China; among others, by controlling the financial system and channeling resources into specific targets (cf. Klenner 2006). This helped them to develop mechanisms to coordinate the development of enterprises in multiple industries in the spirit of Rosenstein Rodan's (1943) "Big Push" (Morck and Yeung 2017).

Furthermore, Japan, South Korea, and China all have rather homogeneous populations and—at least initially—relatively equal income distributions (thanks to the early and successful implementation of agricultural reforms). In addition, all countries undertook substantial investments in human capital prior to their economic take-off, thus creating a well-educated labor force (cf. Boltho and Weber 2009; as we will see later, there were however still some differences). With respect to institutional characteristics, some scholars also argue that Japan, South Korea, and China were all institutional blank states (cf. Morck and Yeung 2017), even though this might have been even more pronounced for South Korea. In addition, they all had relatively authoritarian governments.

Below, we outline which common factors of the East Asian development model (if such a model does exist) are the most important ones in our view. They partly overlap with the set of characteristics outlined above and partly complement/augment them. It is important to note that for some aspects, it is decisive whether we adopt a global perspective (East Asia vs. the West/rest of the world) or a regional perspective (restricted to East (and South-East) Asia). If we compare the three countries to the Western world, the similarities regarding the development strategies are particularly pronounced; however, nuanced differences often become apparent when taking a closer look at the development paths of Japan, South Korea, and China.

- **First**, all three countries have experienced sustained periods of rapid economic growth which enabled them to either join the group of high-income countries (as in the case of Japan and South Korea) or reach middle-income status (as in the case of China).
- **Second**, they all followed an export-oriented development model.
- **Third**, they all share similar institutional-cultural characteristics (e.g. Confucian values).
- **Fourth**, they all gained self-confidence and independence after the Asian Financial Crisis.
- **Fifth**, there is still considerable discrimination against women (all three countries are male-dominant societies).

- **Sixth**, they all have (or had) rather authoritarian governments and/or only relatively weak democracies.

The last two similarities which will be particularly relevant for the future of the three Asian countries will also partly be addressed in Chap. 6. In the following, we will elaborate more on some of these aspects.

Regarding **Third**: In particular, there is an aversion to individualistic, egoistic actions that come at the expense of others (the group or the community). Such behavior is sanctioned by social stigmatization and discrimination/exclusion. This special cultural characteristic also helped combating the corona virus. However, it also implies that the welfare provision is usually much less in countries with strong family ties, rather collectivistic behavior, low prevalence of trust and tolerance towards unknown individuals outside the respective social group, and high acceptance of unevenly distributed power (cf. Gründler and Köllner 2020). Very often, the family provides the social safety net (and not the state).[2] However, some differences across the three East Asian countries do exist, as we will discuss in more detail in Sect. 5.3.

Regarding **Fourth**: The Asian Financial Crisis and its aftermath has been a traumatic experience for the East Asian economies, leading to an "enough is enough"-moment. It also revealed a feeling of paternalism from the West which until then had tried to impose its preferred development model and world views on East Asia—not only with regard to human rights but also concerning the economic/market system as well as the democratic system. This was achieved through loan assistance conditionality (especially by the IMF and the World Bank) which aimed to impose the guidelines of the Washington Consensus—even though these guidelines proved to be increasingly problematic starting from the mid-1990s. The economic policy prescriptions postulated by the Washington Consensus were also stipulated by the G7 which had dominated the world economy until the Global Financial Crisis (see Box 5.1 for an overview of the original Washington Consensus). Only one Asian country is represented in the G7, namely, Japan, whereas the remaining G7 member states are all located in Europe or North America.

Box 5.1 Washington Consensus

The Washington Consensus originally contained the following policy prescriptions (see also e.g. Williamson 2000 and Marangos 2009):

(1) **Budget discipline**: excessive government budget deficits are to be avoided in order to prevent an increase in the ratio of national debt to GDP and seigniorage financing (inflation tax).
(2) **Change in public spending priorities**: e.g. avoiding arbitrary subsidies, administrative and defense spending; instead investments in education and health care.

[2] However, this arrangement has been challenged more recently due to increasing rural–urban migration in China (cf. also Chap. 4).

(3) **Tax reforms** to expand the tax base, lower tax rates, and improve the tax administration.
(4) **Market-determined real exchange rate**, i.e. avoidance of undervaluation, overvaluation, and misalignment in order to promote exports.
(5) **Financial market liberalization**: lifting restrictions on the flow of international finance, removal of government intervention in financial markets.
(6) **Liberalization of foreign trade**: removal of tariff- and non-tariff trade barriers/restrictions, opening up of the market economy.
(7) **Removal of barriers to FDI**: e.g. by reducing the limit on the share of foreign ownership (e.g. in a sector or firm), relaxing administrative hurdles, etc.
(8) **Privatization** of state-owned enterprises which are often considered as relatively inefficient.
(9) **Deregulation** i.e. reducing interventions in the competition process (e.g. via state provisions, obligations, and requirements).
(10) **Securing property rights**: Property rights should be unique/unambiguous, permanent, and reliable.

The Asian countries' shift away from the West after the Asian Financial Crisis—representing a kind of structural break in international relations—was first reflected in the Japanese attempt to establish an independent Asian Monetary Fund. However, this undertaking failed at that time because of resistance from China which did not want to be dominated by Japan but was rather striving for its own supremacy in Asia (Wagner 2020). Another essential element of this shift away is the rapid building up of huge international currency reserves of many Asian countries in order to become independent of foreign speculative attacks and the subsequently necessary financial aid from the West. The latter aspect also further encouraged the rise of China as a world economic power. Ultimately, the greater self-confidence of the East Asian countries is also evident in their demand for an increasing co-determination in international organizations such as the IMF and the World Bank (this particularly applies to China and South Korea). This resulted in (still ongoing) IMF governance reforms starting from the mid-2000s.

5.2.3 Reform Strategies and Sequencing—What Has South Korea Learned from Japan? What Has China Learned from South Korea and Japan?

In this section, we try to provide a general overview on the similarities between the development strategies (and particularly reform phases and the respective sequencing) between Japan, South Korea, and China. However, we will also find

Table 5.1 Sequencing of import substitution and export promotion

	Japan	South Korea	China	Taiwan
Stage 0	Before 1870 isolation heritage	Before 1953 traditional export expansion	Before 1980 extreme form of import substitution	Before 1950 traditional export expansion
Stage I	1870–1900 traditional export expansion, coupled with mild primary import substitution	1953–64 primary import substitution	1980–1990 traditional export expansion (before 1983 marginal), coupled with mild primary import substitution	1950–62 primary import substitution
Stage II	1900–20 primary export substitution	1964–72 primary export substitution	1990–2005 primary export substitution; since 1995 more radical trade liberalization	1962–1970 primary export substitution
Stage III	After 1920 secondary import and export substitution	After 1972 secondary import and export substitution	After 2005 secondary import and export substitution (HCI already increasing since mid-1990s)	After 1970 secondary import and export substitution

Source Datta (1987), Fei et al. (1985), Fei and Ranis (1975), and own amendments

evidence for some first differences between the three countries which will be discussed more extensively in the subsequent Sect. 5.3. The focus of this section is more on the question of in how far South Korea has learned from the Japanese experience and China, respectively, from the South Korean and Japanese reform strategies. We also include Taiwan in our discussion.

Table 5.1 describes the development phases for Japan, South Korea, and Taiwan according to the Fei-Ohkawa-Ranis framework (Fei et al. 1985; Fei and Ranis 1975). Note that there appear to be some similarities to the flying geese model presented in Sect. 5.2.1 (especially regarding Stages I and II). Besides the Stage 0 which corresponds to the situation prior to the economic take-off (for Japan before 1870, for Korea and Taiwan before 1953 and 1950, respectively, and for China before 1978), the model consists of three main stages. Stage I corresponds to import substitution. During Stage II, import protection is reduced and the focus turns toward export promotion. Throughout Stage III, there is renewed pressure for certain protection during the development of the heavy industry.

We additionally include China in this Table to allow for a better comparison between the three larger East Asian countries; however, as we will see, even though some characteristics of this phase model appear to also apply to the Chinese case, there also exist some special characteristics of the Chinese reform experience that might not fit perfectly into this scheme.[3] In this context, it is suitable to quote Datta (1987: 604) who (at least to some extent) anticipated that "[...] the economic

[3] This also partly depends on the varying interpretations regarding the role of import substitution for the Chinese economy.

'miracle' of East Asia has more faces than one and the emerging visage of China will add an altogether different dimension".

In Table 5.1, Japan is our reference point. It is without much doubt that South Korea appears to have followed a very similar sequencing of development stages than Japan but with a significant time lag as well as much shorter phases usually spanning only around one decade. Also, Taiwan has followed a relatively similar pattern (fairly simultaneously with South Korea, only a few years ahead). However, some economists argue that Taiwan has always kept a certain level of import substitution (cf. Zhu 2007). We will come back to this point later. If we try to fit China into this scheme, we can find some similarities; however, also some differences become apparent. First of all, it appears difficult to divide the Chinese experience (after 1978) into clear phases as for Japan and South Korea. Prior to the beginning of the Deng Xiaoping reforms, China had pursued an extreme form of import substitution. Also, Taiwan had adopted a similar strategy in the 1950s; however, unlike China, Taiwan could rely on financial aid from the USA to finance this undertaking. In contrast, China had to mobilize all available domestic resources to import the modern technology and equipment needed for such an ambitious strategy. Consequently, domestic consumption was suppressed and people's incentives to work were relatively small (cf. Zhu 2007). After Mao's death, Hua Guofeng ended the Cultural Revolution and initiated the so-called Leap Outward (sometimes also referred to as the Leap Forward by Foreign Means) (yang yue jin) in the course of which China used its foreign exchange earnings from the export of light manufacturing consumer goods and oil to import technology from advanced countries, but soon ran out of foreign-exchange and recorded an enormous balance of payments deficit (cf. also Chap. 4). It was this crisis that showed the necessity of a strategy change and that facilitated the increasing role of export promotion in the Chinese reform strategy around 1980. However, even though China basically opened its economy most drastically among the East Asian countries, many economists including Li and Vinten (1997) argue that China did not abandon its import substitution strategy (some even describe it as a rather combined strategy, cf. Dutta 2005; Zhu 2007). This also becomes clear when looking at China's Coastal Development Strategy (and its precursor, the beneficial international cycle (BIC) framework) that was the vehicle to carry the open-door policy through China's coastal regions. In particular, in the beginning of trade decentralization/liberalization, China kept (and partly even increased) its tariff and non-tariff barriers (cf. Chap. 4). Only in anticipation of the WTO entry, these barriers were successively reduced.

Finally, it appears necessary to insert a new Stage IV to take into account the latest developments. In recent years, sustainable growth as well as the adaptation to digital change have become important goals within the development strategy of countries. At least with respect to digital change, China appears to be able to overtake Japan and South Korea. However, it is yet too early to fully evaluate this aspect. In Sect. 6.3.1.3, we offer more insights in how far South Korea, Japan, and China are coping with the digital transformation.

Besides the transition from import substitution to export promotion, there exist of course many other ways to compare the reforms (and reform phases) between the three East Asian countries. If we take a closer look at the sectoral structure, we can see that all three countries started their reforms in the agricultural sector. Land reforms are certainly one key element for the rapid economic transformation in East Asia (Evans 1998). In the case of Japan and South Korea, the land reforms after World War II were (at least partly) imposed by the US forces. (However, in the view of Grabowski 2002, land reforms in Japan and South Korea (and also in Taiwan) were the result of the unfolding of rather similar internal historical and economic forces over an extended period.) Key features of the land reforms were the disempowerment of landlords and the redistribution of land to tenant farmers. This helped to increase the incentives of farmers to work more efficiently. At the same time, the land reforms also supported the consolidation of capitalism (Cousins 2019). The initial situation in China prior to the economic reforms under Deng Xiaoping looked somewhat different. The land was collectively owned by production teams which were supposed to be self-sufficient and had to fulfil production targets set by upper government levels. The production teams' overall income was distributed among its members; however, due to the difficulty of monitoring the individual efforts of each worker, every production team member in fact received a fixed amount of money. Accordingly, incentives to work were relatively low (cf. Sect. 4.4.1). Under the new household responsibility system (HRS) reform, collectively owned land was assigned to the individual households with contracts over 15 years; after fulfilling the quota, the households were allowed to sell any extra grain at market prices. Thus, we can see similarities to the reforms in South Korea, Japan, and Taiwan since the HRS reform significantly improved the incentives of the farmers, which in turn increased agricultural productivity. Even though China faced somewhat different starting conditions compared to Japan and South Korea, it still could have learned from their experiences. One counterargument against this "learning from South Korea/Japan" interpretation would be the bottom-up character of agricultural reforms in China. Initially, production teams in Anhui province secretly divided up their collective farmland into individual family plots since the country was plagued by floods and droughts. It is questionable in how far these peasants in Anhui province were inspired by the Japanese and South Korean experience.

After the reform of agricultural sector (and according to the Kuznets facts[4] not surprisingly), all countries subsequently turned to manufacturing.[5] As argued in Chap. 2, Japan first tried to support industrialization through a state-led big push and the establishment of state-owned enterprises (SOEs). However, the SOEs faced a soft budget constraint and the imported Western technologies were not suitable

[4] The Kuznets facts state that during a country's development process, there is first a massive reallocation of labor from agriculture to manufacturing and services, and in later development stages then from manufacturing to services (cf. van Neuss 2019).

[5] It is noteworthy in this context that China initially started to build up the heavy industry during the 1950s whereas Japan and South Korea focused on light manufacturing from the beginning (cf. Boltho and Weber 2009).

for the Japanese economic conditions since they were highly capital-intensive. The idea of a state-led big push had to be abolished in favor of a (much more successful) private sector big push. Technology transfer was mainly accomplished through reverse engineering. Another key element of the Japanese strategy were the zaibatsu conglomerates which, at least according to some researchers, enabled Japan to overcome the problem of lacking coordinated big investment that usually prevents developing countries from establishing a complex network of interdependent firms necessary for the economic catching-up process. South Korea appears to have learned from the Japanese experience, in so far as chaebol conglomerates were crucial in securing scale economies inherent in HCI. The South Korean government also used targeted industrial policy to support the chaebols. In fact, the chaebols are very similar to the zaibatsus in Meiji Japan. (For a more detailed comparison between zaibatsu, keiretsu, and chaebol cf. Sect. 3.6.4.) South Korea engaged more in FDI than Japan; however, it still relied on the concept of reverse engineering and the import of foreign technology. Overall, the zaibatsu driven big push in Meiji Japan appears to have played a non-negligible role for South Korea's HCI drive.

The situation looks a bit different in China. The Chinese economy so far still appears to not give up completely the idea of a state-led big push since SOEs are still dominant in the most decisive sectors of the economy.[6] In China, privatization started much later and more cautiously than in Japan and South Korea. This is probably due to the historical legacy of the planned economic structures and socialism (prior to the reforms under Deng Xiaoping). Even though the disaster of the Cultural Revolution and the Great Leap Forward enabled a certain pragmatism with respect to economic/market reforms, it was regarded as not feasible to immediately start privatizing the state firms. These special social-economic conditions also enabled the rise of very specific forms of companies such as the Township and Village Enterprises (TVEs). However, as we will see in Sect. 5.3.10, the TVEs later enabled the establishment of networks of small firms controlled (at least to some extent) by the township government. These networks surprisingly exhibit rather similar structures/characteristics than the conglomerates in Japan and South Korea; that is, a closer look reveals more similarities than probably initially surmised. Still, it is questionable whether these similarities were intentional or rather developed accidentally as a consequence of China's second-best institutions mentality. The experimental nature of reforms is another aspect that distinguishes the Chinese experience from Japan and South Korea.

Overall, we can say that China certainly also learned from the Japanese and South Korean experience, but has adapted reform elements to its own country-specific characteristics that were coined by the past; probably most importantly, especially in the beginning, the reforms had to be politically and

[6] Similarly to Japan, also China's SOEs faced a soft-budget problem that led to a relatively low efficiency of the state sector. However, China tried to solve this problem stepwise, first by granting SOE managers greater autonomy and exposing SOEs to greater competition with the newly flourishing non-state sector. That is, the Chinese government was aware of the soft-budget problem, but could not proceed in the same way as it was accomplished in Japan due to ideological constraints (see also below). Only in the late 1990s, more comprehensive reforms were undertaken (through the adoption of the "grasping the large, letting go of the small" reform).

ideologically acceptable. We will elaborate in more detail on some of the aspects mentioned above (such as FDI vs. reverse engineering and the industrial structure) in the following subchapters.

5.3 Differences

As already mentioned in Sect. 5.1, economists of the East Asian region usually emphasize more strongly the differences than the similarities between Japan, South Korea, and China. However, also some Western experts point to the fact that there exist discrepancies between the development strategies of these countries. For instance, Klenner (2006: 102) finds "rather weak evidence" for an East Asian development model. Baeck (2005: 494) comes to the conclusion that China resembles more of Taiwan than Japan and South Korea. Zhu (2007) comes to a similar conclusion with respect to the import substitution/export promotion reform sequencing (cf. also the previous section). In contrast, Boltho and Weber (2009: 267, 273–5) differentiate between the development strategies of Japan, Taiwan, and South Korea on the one hand, and China on the other hand.

In the following, we emphasize 12 differences, namely (1) the different starting levels at the beginning of reforms after the World War II, (2) the varying driving forces of development, (3) different political systems (and the rise of democracy), (4) different economic systems, (5) different development strategies (especially with respect to the adoption of foreign technologies), as well as differences in (6) culture, (7) size, (8) geography, (9) institutions, (10) economic/industrial policies, (11) breaks in the development processes, and (12) inequality. Section 5.3.13 summarizes the main differences and elaborates on the implications.

5.3.1 The Varying Initial Levels of Development (After World War II)

We start by investigating the different initial conditions that each country faced at the beginning of its high growth period (after the World War II). In Japan, the period of rapid growth started in the early 1950s, in South Korea in the early 1960s, and in China around 1980 (cf. Chaps. 2–4). Table 5.2 summarizes information on selected development indicators such as the GDP per capita income, the human capital endowment, and the industrial structure. The last column also provides information on the historical (and social-political) background.

Among the three countries, Japan particularly stands out since it has the "best" values for all indicators, suggesting that Japan had a much higher development level than the other two countries. For instance, Japan's initial level of per capita income was almost twice of that of China and even almost thrice of that of South Korea. Also with respect to education, Japan clearly trumps South Korea and China. The average years of schooling of the population aged above 15 was about

Table 5.2 Initial development levels (after WWII) in Japan, South Korea, and China

	Take-off	GDP p.c	Avg. school years	% of the pop. without schooling	Size agric. sector [manuf.; industry]	Background
Japan	Early 1950s	3515	6.96	4.07	36.1% [18.5%; 25.8%]	"First Industrialization" during the Meiji period; increasing militarism during the 1930s and elements of planned economy, defeat in WWII and American occupation; top-down democratization (imposed by American occupational forces)
South Korea	Early 1960s	1221	4.76	37.13	63% [7.9%; 11.2%]	Japanese colonial rule (1919–45); destruction during the Korean War (1950–53); dependence on US foreign aid; not yet democratized (first experiments)
China	Early 1980s	1622	5.31	24.75	70.5% [–; 17.3%]	Totalitarian regime under Mao Zedong, socialism, planned economy; Cultural Revolution and Great Leap Forward have left the country impoverished

Notes GDP p.c. is calculated using data from the PWT, Version 10 (Feenstra et al. 2015) (expenditure-side real GDP at chained PPPs in 2017US$ divided by the population). Starting years (selected according to the take-off points discussed in Sects. 2–4): 1952 for Japan, 1963 for South Korea, and 1978 for China. Data on the average years of schooling and percentage of the population with no schooling is obtained from the Barro and Lee (2013) dataset. This data is only available on a 5-year basis. For China, we take data from 1980, for South Korea the mean between 1960 and 1965, and for Japan the mean between 1950 and 1955. Employment per sector data comes from the ILO (2020) for South Korea (for the year 1963) and China (for the year 1978) and from the Statistics Bureau of Japan for Japan (2020) (for the year 1955). The information regarding the historical background is compiled from the previous Chaps. 2–4

6.9 years in Japan, compared to only 5.3 years in China and 4.8 years in South Korea. Correspondingly, with only 4.1%, the share of the population with no schooling was significantly smaller in Japan (compared to around 25% in China and even the 37% in South Korea). Also a closer look at the economic activity across sectors reveals very different initial conditions. In the early 1950s, the share of people employed in the agricultural sector in Japan had already sunk to only 36%, whereas the industrial sector accounted for around 25.8%. The agricultural employment shares were much higher for South Korea (about 63%) and China (about 70.5%).

Regarding the historical background of the three countries, we can ascertain that Japan was the only country that experienced democratization (imposed by American occupational forces) prior to its catching-up process. Before the country's defeat in World War II, the Japanese society had experienced increasing militarism during the 1930s. The picture looks different in South Korea and China. In South Korea, democracy had not yet developed (despite some first experiments which, however, proved to be not very successful and long-lasting) but only later consolidated from within the country. China particularly stands out for having an authoritarian regime until today. Regarding South Korea, one noteworthy feature is that after the Japanese colonial rule and the subsequent Korean War, the country was probably the blankest institutional state of all three countries. The country was highly dependent on US foreign aid. A specificity of the Chinese historical background is that prior to the reforms in 1978, the country had experienced the totalitarian regime under Mao Zedong which was characterized by socialism and a planned economy system. The Communist Party of China (CPC) basically controlled almost all aspects of everyday life. Even though also Japan experienced elements of planned economy during the increasing militarism in the 1930s, the Japanese case is by no extent comparable to the situation in China prior to the Deng Xiaoping reforms. In addition, the Cultural Revolution and the Great Leap Forward had left China impoverished; these experiences had a long lasting impression on the population and facilitated the pragmatism of the subsequent reforms.

Box 5.2 Special Case Japan? Similarities with the German Experience

Japan had not only been democratized before South Korea and China, it also had already been a highly developed industrial country during the Meiji period. However, Japan was partially destroyed after the World War II (similar to Germany). Consequently, Japan fell behind with respect to GDP per capita and infrastructure; however, it did not fall behind in terms of human capital (except for losses due to war deaths), which enabled Japan to quickly rebuild the country. In this respect, Germany was probably even more successful than Japan because of the greater destruction and the necessary renewal of infrastructure as well as a stronger focus on the market economy (in Japan, conglomerates and other interest groups had greater power). In addition, Germany also had support from the driving forces of the European integration process (cf. Glawe and Wagner 2021a, b).

In 1975, Japan belonged to the top group of industrialized countries and was accepted into the founding club of the G5 (later G7).[7] For the next 35 years, the G7 dominated the world economy (and also the IMF, World Bank, and other organizations). At this time, South Korea and China were still very underdeveloped and poor countries.

[7] Originally, only Germany, France, Great Britain, the USA, and Japan were included.

5.3.2 The Varying Driving Forces of Development

Japan and South Korea were initially externally controlled or—to put it less strongly—"guided" by the USA, whereas China developed more independently; however, with Japan, South Korea, and Singapore as role models (in this context, cf. also Sect. 5.2.1 on the flying geese hypothesis). It has to be noted that China also learned selectively from the liberal Western development models, however, the communist regime maintained control regarding "when, where and how to adopt Western ideas" (Zhao 2010). For instance, China embraced international trade and entrepreneurship, whereas it rejected or adapted other aspects of the Washington Consensus (see also Box 5.1), especially when they threatened the power of the state (and the CPC). However, the ADB (2020) report argues that many Asian countries followed a rather pragmatic approach to implement policies suggested by the Washington Consensus. This is also visible in South Korea's and Japan's industrial policies during their economic catching-up processes. Interestingly, Zhao (2010) compares China's development approach with that of South Korea during the 1970s and 1980s because of the coexistence of political authoritarianism and neo-liberal economic policy, combined with good external conditions for an export-led growth strategy.

Overall, it is difficult to come to a conclusion on whether the similarities or discrepancies between the three East Asian countries prevail with respect to the driving forces of development. The truth probably lies somewhere in the middle.

Some researchers have argued that there exists a so-called Beijing Consensus (even though this concept is not supported by all economists). Box 5.3 provides some background information on this Beijing Consensus.

Box 5.3 Is There a Beijing Consensus?

In the 1990s, the Washington Consensus was increasingly criticized since it proved ineffective/counterproductive during the East Asian crisis (see also Box 5.1). This led to the rise of the post Washington Consensus. It added further points to the original Washington Consensus and also moderated some of the previously rather strictly formulated requirements. In this context, the so-called Beijing Consensus also gained prominence. It consisted of three key features, namely (cf. Ramo 2004):

(1) a commitment to innovation and constant experimentation in reforms;
(2) an emphasis on sustainability and equality instead of per capita GDP as the only measure of progress;
(3) a commitment to self-determination.

However, this view is also questioned/criticized (cf. Kennedy 2010).

Especially, the constant experimentation in reforms can easily be validated since it was a special key feature of the Chinese development process (also compared to South Korea and Japan). Innovation appeared to be an important element in the growth strategy of all three Asian countries (even though China more strongly used imitation opportunities through FDI). However, from our standpoint, the second aspect is probably the least realized (even though sustainability has noticeably become an important goal since around 2011 under Xi Jinping).

Many aspects also appear to be influenced by the experience of Japan and South Korea, or at least they are features of all three countries, especially regarding the commitment to self-determination (see also Sect. 5.2.2) and the focus on innovation.

5.3.3 Varying Political Systems and the Rise of Democracy

The three East Asian countries had and have very different political systems. Probably most obviously, Japan and South Korea are democracies whereas China has an authoritarian political system controlled by the CPC. However, also the political systems of Japan and South Korea exhibit certain differences, particularly regarding the origin of democracy and the timing of the democratic transition as well as the political culture and the role of the opposition. We will elaborate on these aspects in this section.

China as an authoritarian system

Since the beginning of reforms under Deng Xiaoping, China can be best described as a **bureaucratic-authoritarian system** (in contrast to the rather totalitarian regime under Mao Zedong). That is, China is not a democracy, but also no dictatorship since authority lies with the Communist Party and not with an individual leader. However, also compared to other authoritarian systems China somehow stands out since the country has accomplished relatively **smooth leadership transitions** and, partly as a result of that, evinces a very high degree of **political stability** (Kroeber 2016; for an overview on the evolution of authoritarian rule in Southeast Asia see Morgenbesser 2020).[8] Another important feature is the fact that China has a **single-party system**. The CPC is an enormous organization with more than 90 million members in 2018. According to Kroeber (2016), one success factor of the CPC's resilience—despite the rapidly changing economic and social conditions—is the fact that it exercises **control over** every aspect of **organized activity in a flexible** rather than dogmatic **way**. In contrast, during the rather totalitarian Mao era, the party had almost absolute control over every aspect of citizens' life; some argue that there is an increasingly totalitarian tendency in recent years under Xi Jinping, also partly thanks to the advances in artificial intelligence (AI), see also Sect. 6.3.1.3. As described in Chap. 2, another specificity of China is the complex

[8] In this respect, China and Vietnam share some similarities.

relationship between the central government and local governments (even though, there have been increasing centralization tendencies more recently).

Starting in the 1980s, electoral reforms had been adopted that enabled citizen participation with respect to the selection of local officials (however, at a restricted level) (Minzner 2011). The experiments with **rural democracy** however were not intended to be a starting point for democracy spreading to higher government levels but rather to fight corruption among rural party leaders (Economist 2021). In particular, there exist two parallel structures in Chinese villages, the elected village committees on the one hand and the policy committees on the other hand. However more recently, the CPC wants to extend its control by promoting the system of *yijiantiao* with the aim that the memberships of both committees are the same (Economist 2021).[9]

Overall, China is far away from adopting democratic elements comparable to that in Japan and South Korea. However, as already mentioned above, this big difference between the authoritarian regime in China and the democracies in Japan and South Korea does not mean that there does not exist any differences between the latter two. We will focus more on these aspects in the next paragraphs before turning to the discussion of vertical, horizontal, and social accountability in all three countries.

Democracy in Japan and South Korea—Are there differences?

Japan is the oldest democracy in Asia. Each of Japan's democratic transitions was driven by the country's relationship with its external environment (Kennon 2012). First experiments with democracy were already conducted during the Meiji period and the Taisho era (see also Sects. 2.2 and 2.3). During the 1930s, Japan then turned into a de facto military dictatorship (cf. also Sect. 2.3). After Japan's defeat in World War II in 1945, it was occupied by the allied powers which introduced various reform measures in order to democratize Japan (cf. Sect. 2.4). Importantly, many of the American "Japan experts" somehow ignored that Japan had already prior experience with democracy (cf. Kennon 2012). In 1947, Japan eventually made the transition to a full democracy ("at least on paper", cf. Kennon 2012) by adopting a new constitution.

South Korea's first democratic experiments took place under the Rhee Singman administration and subsequently under the Chang Myon administration; however, they did not succeed to establish a true democracy. Under Park Chung-hee, the government then became increasingly authoritarian and the 1972-proclaimed Yushin Constitution granted President Park de facto dictatorial powers. Since the South Korean economy experienced extraordinarily high growth rates during these years, the South Korean middle-class tolerated the rather authoritarian turn. However, after the shooting of the Yonsei University student Lee Han Jol in 1987, a nationwide so-called "June democracy movement" started and eventually forced the

[9] On rural democracy in China, see also He (2007), Shi (2000), and Xi and Wen (2019).

government to amend the Constitution, leading to the establishment of the Sixth Republic.

That is, South Korea has seen a rather **bottom-up democratization process** driven by the civil society, that is, from within the country. Moreover, due to the authoritarian governments/regimes, the society was rather critical towards political institutions and had more trust in civil society organizations (Fukuyama 2012).[10] In contrast, the democratization process in Japan was rather **top-down and imposed by the American occupational forces**. Thus, the driving forces for the transition to democracy were different in these two countries.

There is another important difference between Japan and South Korea regarding **political party power shifts**. Since its foundation in 1955, the conservative Liberal Democratic Party of Japan has been almost continuously in power (the only exception being the years 1993–1994 and 2009–2012)—either on its own or as the dominating coalition party. In the short period during which the Democratic Party of Japan was in power, it was heavily criticized because of its inexperience. Until today, Japan did not manage to accomplish the transition towards a stable two-party system (Fukuyama 2012). While lacking alternations between government and opposition can mitigate the inappropriate use of economic policy instruments aiming at the short-term goal of re-election (cf. also the public choice theory) and can be positive with respect to long-term planning, it may give rise to corruption and complacency (cf. also Stockwin 2018). In contrast, South Korea (but also Taiwan and Thailand) have experienced more pronounced **government-opposition power shifts** (Fukuyama 2012). In addition, these countries also have developed much more **adversarial political cultures**, whereas in Japan such a culture has never flourished. In fact, very often, discontent of the society does not turn into political mobilization (Fukuyama 2012). Thus, South Korea's democracy might be somehow "more Western" than the Japanese.

Finally, Japan was also democratized prior to its economic take-off in the 1950s–1970s whereas South Korea only moved to democracy after the high growth period had already taken place in the 1960s and 1970s. Box 5.4 summarizes the key differences of the political systems in Japan, South Korea, and China described above.

Box 5.4 Summary: Key Differences in Japan, South Korea, and China (with Respect to Democracy)

(I) China versus Japan and South Korea

(1) China has been an **authoritarian state** since the beginning of the 1978 reforms (it was a totalitarian state during Mao era).
(2) Japan and South Korea have already completed the transition from an authoritarian system to **democracy**.

[10] However, more recently, there is evidence that generalized social trust in South Korea is positively associated with political trust (Lee and Yi 2018).

(II) **Japan versus South Korea**

(1) Japan is the oldest democracy in Asia and has seen the earliest democratic experiments.
(2) The democratization process in Japan was rather top-down and imposed from the American occupational forces whereas in South Korea, there was a rather bottom-up democratization process.
(3) South Korea has experienced more pronounced government-opposition power shifts and has a more adversarial political culture than Japan.
(4) Unlike South Korea, Japan was already democratized prior to its economic take-off.

Differences in accountability

One important aspect of democratization is the development of various types of accountability. ***Vertical*** accountability is understood as principal-agent relationships such as elections through which the governments (i.e. the "agents") are held accountable by the voters (i.e. the "principals") (cf. Ocampo and Arteaga 2014). In contrast, ***horizontal*** accountability is usually understood as the checks and balances exercised by specific oversight institutions (cf. Ocampo and Arteaga 2014). Usually, vertical accountability develops first, followed by horizontal accountability.

In the following, we analyze the varying sequencing of these types of accountabilities in Japan, South Korea, and China. As we will see, the most pronounced differences (again) emerge between China on the one hand, and Japan and South Korea on the other hand; however, there are also some subtle differences between the latter two countries, partly stemming from the distinctive characteristics of their democratic transition outlined above.

According to Zhu (2011), the Chinese regime is experiencing a ***reversed* sequencing** of democratization with horizontal accountability preceding vertical accountability (cf. Fig. 5.1). According to Ma (2012), horizontal accountability had already started to emerge in China; examples include the strengthening of the supervision of the National People's Congress and also the audit oversight (cf. Yang 2004; Ma 2009). In this respect, China differs not only from Western countries but also from South Korea and Japan.

To illustrate this, we employ data from the "V-Dem dataset Version 11.1" of the "Varieties of Democracy Project" (Pemstein et al. 2021). This dataset offers one "total", that is, overall accountability indicator as well as three individual accountability indicators, namely, vertical, diagonal, and horizontal accountability. ***Diagonal*** accountability refers to the range of actions and mechanisms that the civil society and media can use (indirectly and directly) to hold the government accountable (see Mechkova et al. 2019; Goetz and Jenkins 2005). It is sometimes

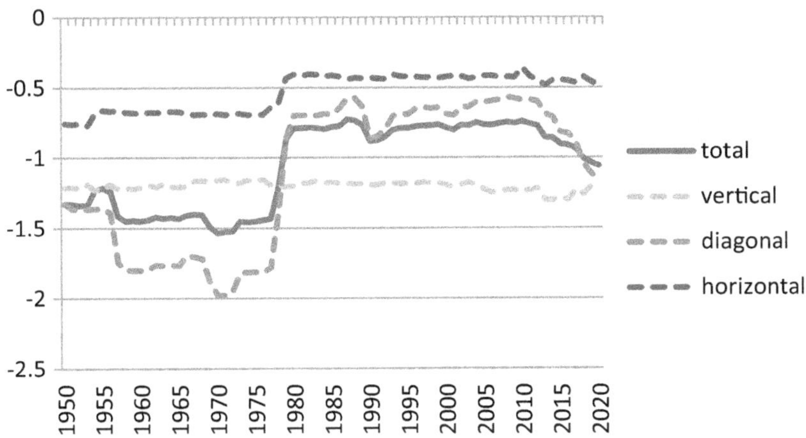

Fig. 5.1 Accountability in China, 1950–2019. *Source* V-Dem dataset Version 11.1, Varieties of Democracy Project, Pemstein et al. (2021)

also referred to as social accountability (cf. Mechkova et al. 2019). A more detailed description of each index is provided in Table 5.3 in the Appendix of this chapter.

As depicted in Fig. 5.1, vertical accountability lies significantly below horizontal accountability and this gap even widens at the beginning of reforms under Deng Xiaoping. How does the picture look in South Korea and Japan?

With respect to Japan, we see significant increase in all types of accountability in the second half of the 1940s (cf. Fig. 5.2a). This time corresponds with the American occupation that brought democratization. Since then, the scores have been relatively stable except some minor changes in the most recent years. Particularly prior to the rise in accountability, vertical and horizontal accountability were relatively equal, fluctuating around 0.5.

South Korea also experienced a sharp increase in accountability at the end of the 1940s; however, the scores were still significantly lower than that of Japan (cf. Fig. 5.2b). Starting from the 1980s, accountability gradually increased to a similar level than in Japan; however, at a somewhat lower speed. This might also depict the fact that in South Korea, democracy rather evolved within the country rather than being "enforced" by external forces. Horizontal accountability significantly lagged behind; especially during the 1960s and 1970s, it plummeted sharply and only gained momentum during the 1980s. In the Japanese case, both types of accountability have developed rather simultaneously (the horizontal accountability being somewhat higher than the vertical).

Overall, we can say that the vertical accountability either preceded horizontal accountability (in the case of South Korea) or at least both developed rather simultaneously (as in Japan). In contrast, horizontal accountability is considerably higher than vertical accountability in China and the data does not suggest a major trend reversal in the near future.

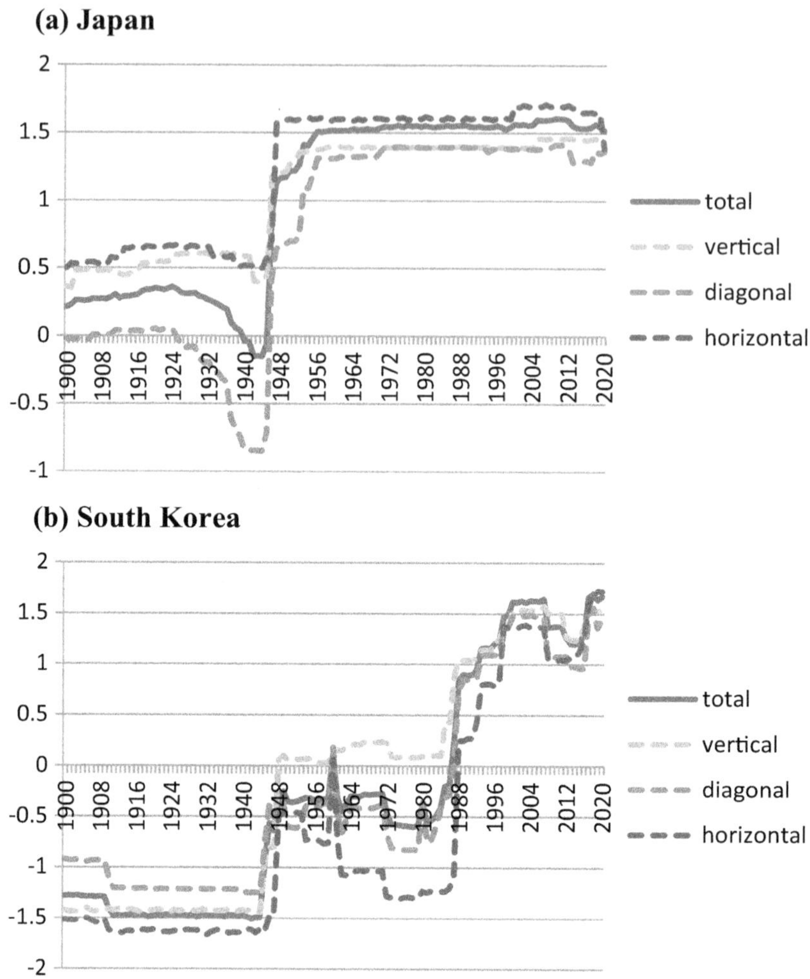

Fig. 5.2 Accountability in Japan and South Korea, 1900–2019. **a** Japan, **b** South Korea. *Source* V-Dem dataset Version 11.1, Varieties of Democracy Project, Pemstein et al. (2021)

With respect to diagonal accountability, Japan and South Korea have considerably higher values compared to China. However, according to Ma (2012), signs of increasing diagonal (or social) accountability were visible in China before 2012, e.g. Chinese individuals gradually formed a sense of citizenship. Also the operation of independent NGOs was listed as an example, as well as more autonomous (new) media.[11] However, in how far all these three points still apply in today's China is questionable.

[11] This development was probably partly supported by improved higher education.

Of course, such data has to be interpreted with caution. It is always important to take into account country specificities that cannot be adequately depicted by a single number/index. However, in essence, the figures seem to correspond with the main democratic events described previously.

5.3.4 Varying Economic Systems/Industrial Structure

In this section, we will discuss the various economic systems in China, South Korea, and Japan. In particular, we will cover the coordinated development in multiple industries, the so-called (state-led or private-led) "big push", special types of companies such as TVEs and business conglomerates, as well as the role of SMEs.

Coordinated development in multiple industries

South Korea, Japan, and China all developed mechanisms for coordinating the development of firms in diverse industries (Morck and Yeung 2017). In Meiji Japan and South Korea, this was achieved via highly diversified business groups (the zaibatsus and chaebols, respectively; for a comparison between zaibatsus, kereitsus, and chaebols see Sect. 3.6.4). China seems to still follow a state-led big push strategy as the state maintains control over certain key industries including construction, communications, and banking. Japan and South Korea had to abandon this approach and it is currently difficult to evaluate whether China will be able to successfully continue its strategy (Morck and Yeung 2017).[12]

TVEs and conglomerates

Another special feature of the Chinese economy are the Township and Village Enterprises (TVEs) which are neither public enterprises nor state firms and which presented a kind of "second-best" solution in the presence of weak private property rights. The TVEs' institutional legacy is still present in today's China, especially in the form of institutional arrangements such as relational contracting which positively affected the fast growth of clusters of abundant small private firms managed by township governments in the coastal regions of China. Xu (2011) argues that the township governments have a similar function than conglomerate headquarters.

[12] According to Klenner (2006), another difference exists between the employment system in China and Japan. For instance, the Japanese employment system exhibits rather "community-like" features; the betterment of the firm is more important than increasing personal wealth. In contrast, newly established private Chinese firms were influenced by the business cultures of foreign investors—not only from Japan, but also from the EU, USA, and Hong Kong. Therefore, they are different from the Japanese community-like enterprises. Cultural differences most likely also played a non-negligible role for these differences (see also Sect. 5.3.6), so did the different historical experiences (especially the SOEs centered social security system, see Sect. 4.6.1).

A similar argumentation is put forward by Oi (1999) with respect to regional SOEs that were owned by regional governments. Thus, even though the TVEs are unique to China, they enabled structures with a similar effect than conglomerates. Also, Klenner (2006: 96) states that "local governments behave like small business conglomerates and promote their enterprises".[13]

The role of SMEs

In all three countries, small and medium-sized enterprises (SMEs) account for the lion's share of all enterprises, ranging from around 97.3% for China to 99.7% and 99.9% for Japan and South Korea (all in the early 2010s), respectively (Yoshino and Taghizadeh-Hesary 2018). In China, starting from the late 1990s, many small and medium-sized SOEs were restructured into private companies (or went bankrupt) and the private sector absorbed the laid-off workers. In China, SMEs account for a relatively larger share of exports (41.5% vs. 18.8% in South Korea; no data available for Japan). In this respect, China in fact more closely resembles India which has a very similar share (42.4%). Also the SMEs' share in total output is higher in China compared to that in Japan and South Korea (60% vs. 43.7% and 47.6%, cf. Yoshino and Taghizadeh-Hesary 2018).[14] In the early 2010s, China's SMEs accounted for 80% of urban employment (in 2013), whereas in South Korea, 50% of the total workforce was employed in SMEs (however, there had been a 11 percentage point increase between 2000 and 2011) (cf. OECD 2016); in Japan, SMEs accounted for about 70% of national employment which is relatively high compared to their relatively low value added (cf. OECD 2017).

The OECD (2016) "Financing SMEs and Entrepreneurs 2016" also reveals another interesting difference between the three countries regarding the share of micro enterprises in the total number of SMEs (micro enterprises are usually defined as enterprises having up to nine employees even though classifications can slightly differ across countries). While in Japan and South Korea, the share of micro enterprises is relatively high (86.8% and 93.2%, respectively), they only account for 44.2% of all SMEs in China. In contrast, the share of Chinese small enterprises (with a firm size of 10–49 employees) is relatively high (43.53% vs. 5.8% for South Korea; only aggregate data for small enterprises and medium enterprises are available for Japan).

All three countries also appear to face different challenges. In more recent years, the SME development in Japan appears to loose dynamism with the total number of SMEs decreasing between 1999 and 2014 by slightly more than 20% (partly as a consequence of the Global Financial Crisis and the 2011 earthquake). Moreover,

[13] Nowadays, there are also various large Chinese companies that, like the South Korean chaebol conglomerates, have subsidiaries in different sectors. However, some argue that the motivation of these Chinese conglomerates is at least in some cases rather global dominance (e.g. in the semiconductor industry) than making profits (see https://www.bloomberg.com/graphics/2021-opinion-china-jituan-conglomerates-differences-south-korea-chaebols/).

[14] It has to be noted, however, that the indicators for output vary across countries (for China output is measured by GDP, for Japan by sales, and for South Korea by manufacturing value added; for more details see Yoshino and Taghizadeh-Hesary 2018).

they only have a relatively low productivity compared to bigger companies (especially in comparison to other OECD countries). While in South Korea, entrepreneurship and the efficiency of SMEs has been stimulated by reforms installed by South Korean policymakers in recent years (even though the access to finance could be further improved), entrepreneurial dynamics are still largely driven by micro firms concentrated in low productivity sectors that do not scale up. In addition, there is an underrepresentation of young and of female employees in SMEs. In China, the lack of access to finance is still a main hindrance—even though reforms have already brought some improvement in this respect (especially since 2014).

5.3.5 Varying Development Strategies—Learning from Foreign Technology

As argued in Sect. 5.2, the adoption of foreign technologies from advanced economies enabled all three countries to move up the value chain and produce increasingly more complex (and also more capital-intensive) manufacturing goods. However, they used fairly different strategies to acquire these technologies.

In general, development countries can profit from technology and knowledge transfers/spillovers (arising from globalization) through two major channels, namely (1) the *trade channel* (more precisely, the import of high-end products) (see among others Coe and Helpman 1995; Falvey et al. 2002) and (2) the *FDI channel* (see Keller 2010 for an overview on FDI spillover effects).

Japan and South Korea relied on the first strategy. Both countries primarily utilized *reverse engineering* to absorb the knowledge and technology incorporated in imported high-end products to be able to imitate and subsequently improve the respective products (cf. Glawe and Wagner 2020c). Essential preconditions for successfully adopting such a rather ambitious strategy are (i) a well-developed infrastructure and (ii) experienced engineers who possess the necessary skills to implement this "blueprint detection method" (cf. Wagner 2019). That is, without a certain level of absorptive capacity (and also technological entrepreneurship), the success of this strategy is relatively limited (cf. Kumar 1996).

Japan and South Korea both were able to upgrade their industrial structures by following the trade channel strategy; however, it was especially comprehensive in Japan. One major reason for Japan's success can be attributed to the fact that the Japanese economy had already undergone a first industrialization wave in the nineteenth century. Even though the physical capital was mostly destroyed during the subsequent wars, a non-negligible part of the human capital and general knowledge "survived".

With respect to inward FDI, South Korea and Japan both followed a rather restrictive policy (cf. Fu et al. 2016 for South Korea, and Goto and Odagiri 2003 for Japan). In Japan, net inflows of FDI as a percentage of GDP were close to zero between 1970 and the middle of the 1990s (even though FDI was gradually liberalized in the mid-/late-1970s) (Goto and Odagiri 2003). Since the turn of the century, the FDI-to-GDP ratio slightly increased, but until today it remains very low in international comparison and highly fluctuates. More recently, Japan again tightened its restrictions on FDI. South Korea removed its (political) barriers to FDI in the mid-1990s and early 2000s. Subsequently, FDI increased considerably (at least temporarily), peaking at 2.2% in 1999 and again at 1.7% in 2004 (cf. World Bank 2021). However, this rise in FDI occurred after the main (economic) catching-up process had been accomplished (Park and Lee 2020). Moreover, since the middle of the 2000s, FDI as a share of GDP had again decreased slightly, fluctuating around 0.7%.

In contrast to the Japanese and South Korean experience, China relied on the second, FDI-driven strategy. This can be partly explained by the fact that the country lacked the required abilities to implement the first strategy. Especially since the early 1990s, China attracted enormous amounts of FDI in order to benefit from the associated know-how transfer.[15] Moreover, on-the-job-training enabled Chinese workers to upskill and learn more about the technology from the multinational firms which could be subsequently transferred to domestic Chinese firms at a rather low cost (Glawe and Wagner 2020c). By becoming the world's work bench and being increasingly incorporated into the global production chain, China established the basis for successfully pursuing an imitation (and later even innovation) based growth strategy. China's large (and thus attractive) domestic market enabled it to force foreign companies into joint ventures and (at least to a large extent) to dictate the conditions of these collaborations. According to Mu and Lee (2005) and Lee et al. (2009), this knowledge transfer was particularly critical for the mobile telecommunication and automotive industries.

China's bargaining strength implied that the foreign partner often had to impart more technologies and intellectual property than it actually would have liked to (however, in order to enter the huge market and therefore to make the joint venture successful, the foreign partner firm also had an interest to transfer a certain amount of know-how, cf. Jiang et al. 2018 and Sect. 5.5.4.3).

5.3.6 Cultural Aspects

As already outlined in Sect. 5.2, in all three countries, there is an aversion to individualistic, egoistic actions that come at the expense of others (the group or the community). It is important to note that the cultural similarities between Japan, South Korea, and China stand particularly out if we compare them to the group of Western countries including the USA, Germany, and the UK. However, there are some country-specificities that need further investigation.

In general, Confucianism appears to play a less important role in Japan. While in China and South Korea, Confucianism is a key element of classical morality and

[15] However, also before its nationwide implementation after Deng's Southern Tour, FDI was promoted (but at a smaller scale and rather in an experimental manner) through the establishment of the special economic zones (SEZs) (see also Sect. 5.4.6).

strongly interrelated with the everyday life (even though under Mao there were attempts to push it back), in Japan it rather presents a system of knowledge and thought for studying (Wang 2012). In addition, while in South Korea the focus of Confucianism is primarily on blood-related family ties, in Japan these relations extend to larger groups with no blood relations and the emphasis is stronger on respect and consideration for others ("loyalty over filial piety") (Levi 2013; Wang 2012). This is also reflected in the fact that the Japanese society is more individualistic (and firm-centered) than that of China and South Korea (see also below).

It is very difficult to adequately measure the culture of societies, and respective indicators should always be interpreted with caution. However, they might also deliver us with some important general insights in which aspects the three countries differ most (and regarding which they share the most similarities).

We here rely among others on Hofstede's cultural dimensions that depict differences in national cultures with respect to power distance, individualism, uncertainty avoidance, long-term orientation, masculinity, and indulgence.

Figure 5.3 depicts China's, South Korea's, and Japan's positions regarding the six Hofstede cultural dimensions. Regarding some aspects, China and South Korea have relatively similar values while for others, Japan and South Korea are much closer. Our discussion is based on the Hofstede Country Comparison (accessible via https://www.hofstede-insights.com/). The interested reader might there also find further

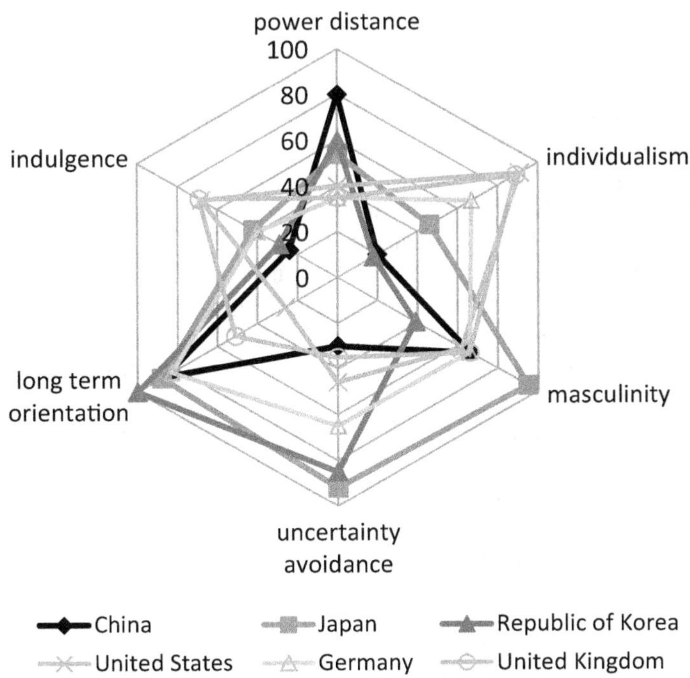

Fig. 5.3 Hofstede's cultural dimensions. *Source* Hofstede Dataset

interpretations and examples. In Fig. 5.3, we also depict the scores of the USA, the UK, and Germany in order to allow for comparison with Western countries.

The dimension **power distance** measures to which extent rather powerless members of institutions and organizations within a country accept an unequal distribution of power. China's score (80) is extremely high, indicating that inequalities among people are rather acceptable. In addition, individuals tend to be strongly influenced by formal authority and sanctions. Japan and South Korea have relatively similar values (54 for the former and 60 for the latter). This makes Japan a borderline "hierarchical" society which is in fact much less hierarchical than most other Asian countries. Still, advanced Western countries such as the USA, Germany, and the UK report much lower values of power distance.[16] South Korea is slightly more hierarchical than Japan. People usually accept their place in the hierarchy in an organization and a "benevolent autocrat" is regarded as the ideal superior.

The dimension **individualism** measures the extent of interdependence that a society preserves among its members. More precisely, it can be distinguished between

- relatively *individualistic societies* in which individuals take care of themselves (and very close relatives) and regard the achievement of personal goals as important, and
- relatively *collectivistic society* in which the goals of the group are more important than individual successes and group members take care of each other.

China's and South Korea's very low rankings (with scores of 20 and 18, respectively) indicate that both countries are highly collectivistic. In contrast, Japan's score of 46 reveals that the Japanese society is much more individualistic. While also in Japan, within-group harmony is considered as more important than the expression of individual opinions and there also exists a kind of fear of losing one's face, a striking difference is that in Japan, loyalty to one's company, independent of blood relations, is extremely important. However, this can eventually also be seen as an individualistic characteristic. Still, Japan is not as individualistic as most Western countries. One could also say that it is perceived as a collectivistic society from a Western standpoint and a relatively individualistic society from an Asian perspective.

The dimension **masculinity** depicts whether a society is rather competitive and people have a preference for achievement and success (=a masculine society) or whether the focus is more on cooperation, caring for others, and life quality (=a feminine society).

Japan has one of the highest masculinity scores worldwide (95). This realizes itself mostly with respect to the highly competitive team (!) spirit—not only at the

[16] Slow decision-making processes, sometimes perceived as a sign of hierarchy, are in fact an indication that there does not exist one decision maker at the top of the hierarchy (at least according to the Hofstede Country Comparison).

workplace but already in school and preschool. Another manifestation of the Japanese masculine society is in the perfectionism in many aspects of life. One example is the spirit of monozukuri (cf. also Sect. 2.2) which describes the pride, dedication, and excellence claim towards production.

Also, the Chinese society can be characterized as masculine, even though its score (66) is not as high as that of Japan. In China, this masculinity manifests for instance in the fact that work is considered more important than leisure time. The rural–urban migration presents another example for masculinity. Very often, farmers had (and have) to leave their families behind in the rural areas to get a better paid job in a city. Also, the highly competitive high school entrance exams (gaokao) are a characteristic of masculinity in the Hofstede interpretation.

In contrast to China and Japan, South Korea is considered as a feminine society with a masculinity score of only 39. This is even significantly less than in the USA, UK, and Germany. Especially at the workplace, there is a preference for consensus, and compromises are important for resolving conflicts. However, in our view, this score does not adequately depict the highly competitive school system which is rather comparable to that of China.

The dimension **uncertainty avoidance** reflects in how far members of a society feel uneasy about ambiguity. As shown in Fig. 5.3, Japan and South Korea have relatively similar levels of uncertainty avoidance ("risk aversion"), while China is kind of an outsider. In particular, China has an extremely low uncertainty avoidance score (30), implying that the Chinese are especially adaptable and follow a rather flexible approach which suits the actual situation. This is very well reflected in the overall Chinese reform strategy which is often described as pragmatic (cf. also Sect. 4.1). As the slogan "crossing the river by feeling the stones" aptly describes, Chinese reforms did not follow a blueprint but rather resembled a "trial and error" process. The focus of reformers was on making a first step and once this was successfully accomplished, the situation was re-evaluated and the next reform step was adapted to the changed environment. Also institutions were adapted when needed (but also maintained if possible). It was probably this cultural feature that was (among others) responsible for why China established so successfully its own second-best institutions instead of adopting the standard reform packages postulated by the IMF and others (following the then standard theory).

In contrast, Japan has one of the highest uncertainty avoiding scores worldwide (92). One reason for this can be probably attributed to the factor geography: Japan has always been subject to disastrous earthquakes and other natural disasters which made it indispensable to be prepared for all possible scenarios. However, even if this high uncertainty avoidance tendency has its origin in geographic circumstances, it can be seen in many aspects of everyday life (e.g. the reliance on rather uniform ceremonies and rituals for many events). It also manifests itself in often time-consuming business procedures which are necessary in order to adequately assess the potential risks and eliminate all uncertainties (Katz 2005). In general, the high level of uncertainty avoidance also means that changes are difficult to realize and it might also be detrimental to innovation (Jones and Davis 2000; Efrat 2014; Sekizawa 2017). Also, South Korea has a relatively high score of 85 (even though it is somewhat smaller than for Japan). Similar to Japan, there is also a rather emotional need for rules and a valuing of punctuality. Uncertainty avoidance might also partly explain why Japan and South Korea were much more restrictive with respect to FDI than it was the case in China (even though other factors, e.g. historical experience, might also have played a role).

Interestingly, all three countries have a similar level of **long-term orientation**, even though South Korea has a specifically high score. This long-term orientation might also partly explain the high savings rates in the three East Asian economies. Long-term orientation is also reflected by the fact that the long-term development of enterprises is regarded as more important than the short-term performance (which was one of the success factors of the business conglomerates and the related private sector big push). This could also be interpreted as a preference for sustainable growth. However, this development only recently began in China which had previously followed an unsustainable growth strategy at the expense of environmental pollution and the building up of imbalances during the first decades of the reform period. However, there has been a dramatic shift in this policy starting in the mid-2000s and particularly since the early 2010s.

The Hofstede dimension **indulgence** reflects how far members of the society have a problem to restrain themselves, that is, control their desires and impulses. China, South Korea, and Japan all have relatively low scores of 24, 29, and 42, respectively (that is, they can control their desires and impulses rather well). Even though Japan's score is somewhat higher, all three countries are interpreted as having a very low indulgence. Also, this can be an explanatory factor for the high savings rate in these countries.

Overall, we can summarize that people in all three East Asian countries have a rather long-term orientation and are relatively restrained (i.e., they have a low score). The most striking differences are reported for the dimensions uncertainty avoidance (where China stands out by having very low score) and masculinity (where Japan has an extremely high value). Regarding the dimensions power distance and individualism, China, South Korea, and Japan appear to be relatively similar if compared to Western economies. However, when focusing solely on the East Asian region, the picture is more nuanced and there appears to be always one "outlier": For instance, the power distance is greatest in China, even though also South Korea and Japan have relatively high scores in international comparison. All three countries are also rather collectivistic societies from a Western standpoint; however, Japan is one of the most individualistic societies in Asia.

5.3.7 Country Size

The next two sections discuss the geographical characteristics of the three Asian countries. In particular, this section focuses on the country (and also population) sizes, whereas the next Sect. 5.3.8 is dedicated (among others) to the discussion of the climate, topography, and coastlines.

Probably most obviously, in comparison to China, Japan and especially South Korea are both relatively small countries. Japan is approximately 378,000 km^2, making it around 3.8 times larger than South Korea (being approximately 100,000 km^2).[17] In contrast, China has an area of over 9.5 million km^2. That is, Japan is less than 4% of the size of China (South Korea constitutes even only slightly above 1% of the Chinese country size). In addition, China accounts for more than 30% of Asia's total population with about 1.4 billion inhabitants, whereas Japan contributes to around 2.8% and South Korea even only to around 1.1% with populations of approximately 127 million and 51 million, respectively.

The relatively small country sizes of Japan and South Korea imply that their markets are much smaller compared to that of China. This is an important advantage for the Chinese economy since its enormous (and thus, for foreign investors highly attractive) domestic market enhances the country's bargaining power vis-à-vis foreign companies. In particular, it enabled China to force foreign firms into joint ventures and by dictating the conditions of these collaborations, China tried to exploit the technological progress embodied in FDI as much as possible in order to generate knowledge spillovers to domestic companies. For a more in-depth discussion see also Sect. 5.3.5.

China's large domestic market (and the impossibility to precisely govern such a huge country with many heterogeneous provinces) might however also explain why its industrial planning was formulated less concretely compared to Japan and South Korea which both had more detailed plans for specific industries. In fact, China's five-year plans resembled a little bit "wish lists for almost everything", as formulated by Boltho and Weber (2009: 274). However, China's domestic market also allowed the country to pursue a broader strategy since scale economies were much easier to achieve. Thus, in this respect, China had probably better preconditions for a (state-led?) big push strategy, even though the above mentioned size and relative "independence" of the provinces may have complicated such an undertaking.

It is also because of China's large size, that it could in the future potentially challenge the US hegemony's position. While the question of whether such a change in leadership will actually occur or not cannot be answered at this point in time, it is certainly clear that significantly smaller countries such as Japan and South Korea could most likely not strive for such a path in the present time.

[17] Still, Japan is roughly the size of Italy and thus not that small from a European standpoint.

5.3.8 Geographical Differences

Even though all three countries are obviously located in East Asia, there are striking differences regarding the geographical characteristics of South Korea, Japan, and China.[18] In addition to the considerable size differences discussed in the previous section, China is a continental country, South Korea a peninsula, and Japan an archipelago (see also below). Moreover, Japan and especially South Korea both have less big coastal cities than China. In Japan, there is a centralization on Tokyo, Nagoya, and Osaka[19] and in South Korea on Seoul. In contrast, China has a huge coastal area with many large cities, various megacities (e.g. Tianjin, Shanghai, Shenzhen, and Guangzhou), and several free trade zones. Eleven of the 31 provinces of mainland China are located at the coastline which covers approximately 14,500 km.[20] Due to the fact that Japan is an island, its coastline (with a total length of almost 30,000 km) is naturally longer (about twice as long as that of China and 12 times as that of South Korea); however, the dispersion of Japan's coastline significantly differs from that of continental China, and, maybe even more importantly, the Japanese coastline is extremely narrow (see also below). Other geographic specificities of mainland China include the country's proximity to Hong Kong and Taiwan which played an important role for the success of the special economic zones (cf. Sect. 5.4.5 and also below). Since China is such a huge country (see also Sect. 5.3.7), it also has a great variety of topography as well as of climate and vegetation zones, ranging from (sub-)tropic zones in the south-eastern parts of China, over deserts and steppes in western China to even subarctic areas in the most northern parts. China's size also had important implications for the country's development strategy since it is almost impossible to develop such a vast country at once. Therefore, geographically advantageously located coastal provinces received preferential policies and benefited from FDI inflows in the newly established special economic zones. Interestingly, Démurger et al. (2002) find that the coast location itself was as important as the preferential policies installed to foster economic growth. Moreover, even after the nationwide implementation of FDI-enhancing policies, the differences in the level of deregulation between 1996 and 1998 remained substantial and caused a one percentage point gap in growth between coastal provinces on the one hand and central, north-western, and south-western provinces on the other hand. Figure 5.4 depicts the average preferential policy index constructed by Démurger et al. (2002) between 1978 and 1998. Box 5.5 provides more detailed information regarding in how far geography and institutional quality are related to each other in the Chinese case.

[18] Some of these (like multiple climate zones) are of course related to or a consequence of the size differences.

[19] However, more recently, Fukuoka has gained more prominence for being "Japan's most innovative city" (cf. Gent 2019).

[20] These provinces are: Liaoning, Hebei, Tianjin, Shandong, Jiangsu, Shanghai, Zhejiang, Fujian, Guangdong, Guangxi, and Hainan (from north to south).

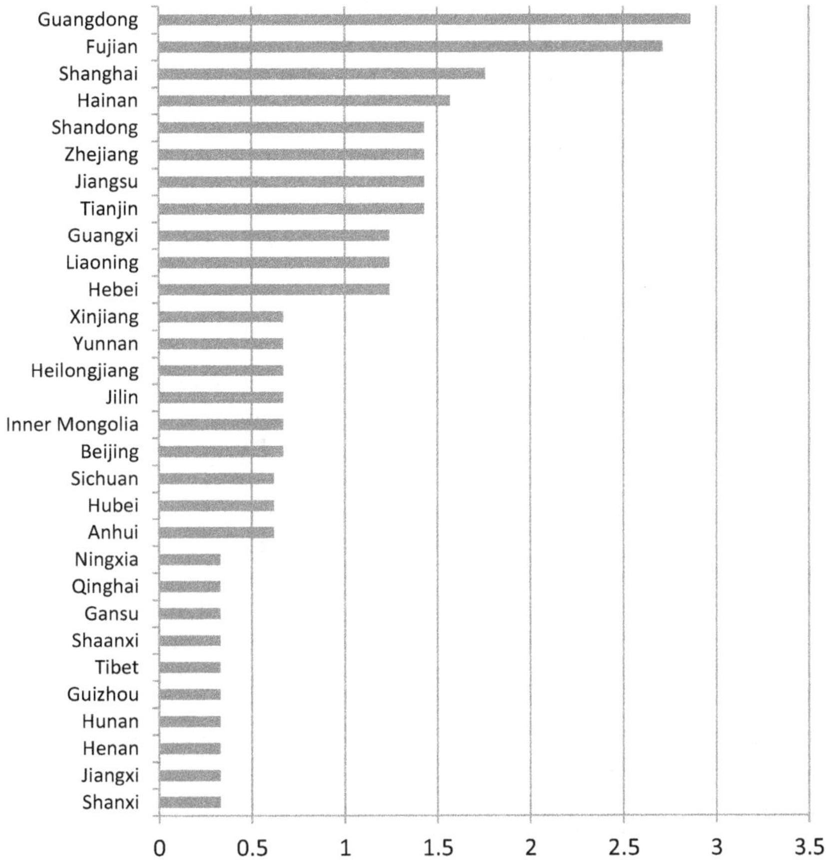

Fig. 5.4 Preferential policy index, Chinese provinces (1978–1998). *Source* Démurger et al. (2002)

Box 5.5 Geography and Provincial Institutional Quality in China

Geography also played a role for the development of institutions in China. In this context, Glawe and Wagner (2019, 2022) analyze the role of geography, institutions, and trade (the so-called "deep determinants") for China's economic development at the provincial level. Even though geography appears to play only a minor direct role, it has a positive effect on provincial development by influencing institutional quality. In a subsequent paper, Glawe and Wagner (2020b) show that institutional quality improvements only unfold their positive effect on growth in coastal provinces but not in inland regions. Due to the preferential policies during the first two reform phases, coastal provinces were on average much earlier exposed to international trade than the interior provinces. Consequently, the coastal provinces much earlier developed market economy characteristics. Because of their stronger orientation towards a free market, there was a greater necessity to provide an adequate institutional environment in coastal provinces, including property rights protection and a well-functioning competition on the different markets. Consequently, provincial levels of institutional quality differ significantly. Improving the institutional framework can be costly in the beginning (and even growth-reducing) and the benefits will usually only start to translate into economic gains when a certain institutional environment has already been developed.

While at the first glance, the differences between South Korea and Japan on the one hand and China on the one hand appear to be predominant (especially regarding the size and the importance of the coastline for the development strategy), also Japan has a very unique geography: It is an archipelago consisting of four main islands (Hokkaido, Honshu, Kyushu, and Shikoku) and various thousand small islands. The terrain is rugged and mountainous with many non-navigable rivers, making only a small percentage of the country's landmass suitable for agriculture and living and representing a challenge for internal transportation.[21] The coastline is fertile (partly due to the volcanic activity) but usually very narrow. Even though South Korea has many hills and mountains as well, there is a coastline plain in the west and south as well as mountain valleys and river flats in the interior.[22] The high volcanic activity and the fact that the Japanese islands are separated several hundred kilometers from the Asian mainland engendered a sense of security that also shaped the Japanese culture (e.g. the dimension uncertainty avoidance; cf. also Sect. 5.6). Even though South Korea is relatively close to Japan, it does not suffer from such a volatile volcanic activity.

The final geographical (or rather geo-political) specificity we are going to present is the fact that prior to Japan's defeat in World War II, South Korea and North Korea formed a single country. They had a rather complementary economic structure based on their respective geographical characteristics, resulting in a focus on agriculture in South Korea and on electricity production in North Korea. This affected South Korea's development in the early reform stages (see also Sect. 3.3). In the following years to come, a potential reunification of South and North Korea would have important political implications.

[21] In addition, Japan has almost no natural resources which made it very dependent on imports. See also Sect. 6.3.3.1.F.

[22] Also China is mountainous; however, the highest mountain ranges are located in (South) Western China.

5.3.9 Institutional Quality

We have already briefly touched upon the role of institutional factors in the course of the discussion on the political systems and geographical factors (see Sects. 5.3.7 and 5.3.8). In this section, we will take a closer look on the marginalization of extractive elites in the three countries. We subsequently take a closer look at specific institutional indicators over the period 1996–2019 by using data from the Kaufmann et al. (2010) Worldwide Governance Indicators (WGI) dataset.

Marginalization of extractive elites

As already briefly mentioned in Sect. 5.2, Japan, South Korea, and China all have been institutional blank states prior to the phase of rapid economic development; the traditional extractive elites have been significantly weakened or abolished (see Morck and Yeung 2017 for an in-depth discussion; cf. also Acemoglu et al. 2001).[23] In the case of Japan, this happened during the Meiji restoration. The South Korean "traditional elite" was marginalized during the Japanese colonial rule. The subsequent "colonial era elite" was then destroyed after Japan's defeat in World War II, and the Korean War was more or less the final blow (cf. Morck and Yeung 2017). Due to this rather rapid succession of elite wiping out events, in our view, South Korea was probably the institutionally "blankest" of all three East Asian states at the beginning of the post-World War II development process. This could also have been the reason why democracy only involved in a bottom-up manner (that is, from within the country) in South Korea. In China, the inefficient policies imposed by the traditional elite led to a legitimacy loss, and during the 1960s the Cultural Revolution did the rest (Morck and Yeung 2017). However, in the case of China, even though the traditional elites were marginalized (at least in the short-run),[24] the planned economy gave rise to other institutional structures that very likely also have played a role for China's second-best institutions strategy followed after 1978 (see also below).

More recent institutional quality developments

In the following, we will take a closer look at specific institutional indicators using data from the Worldwide Governance Indicators (WGI) dataset. Table 5.4 in the Appendix briefly describes the six WGI dimensions.

Most importantly, China's institutional quality is still lagging behind that of South Korea and Japan, with respect to both, the *political* institutions measured by

[23] The devastation of the traditional elites does not necessarily imply that all institutional achievements including the building up of state capacity were lost and did not play a role at all (see also Gray 2014 on this issue). See Alesina et al. (2020) on the persistence of elites and the related re-emergence of pre-revolution inequality patterns in China (see also the following footnote).

[24] Alesina et al. (2020) find that even though the Chinese Communist Revolution and the Cultural Revolution effectively homogenized the population in the short run, the pre-revolution inequality pattern re-emerges today. In particular, individuals whose grandparents belonged to the pre-revolution elites earn more and have higher levels of education. Thus, the former elites probably have persisted through the intergenerational transmission of values.

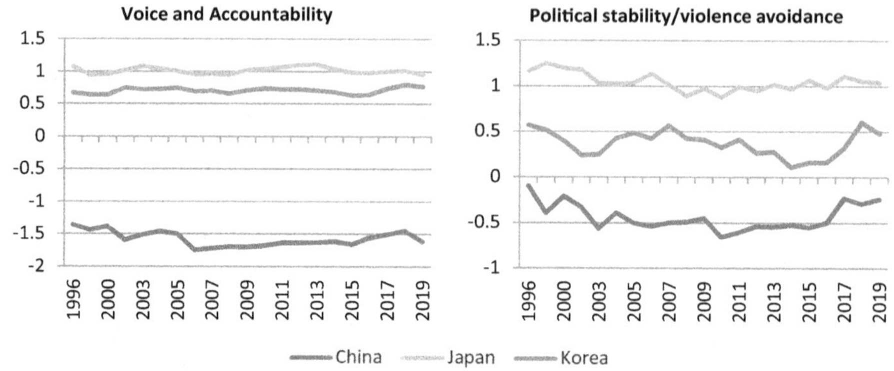

Fig. 5.5 Worldwide governance indicators, political institutions, 1996–2019. *Source* Kaufmann et al. (2010)

the WGI dimensions "voice and accountability" and "political stability and violence avoidance" (see Fig. 5.5) as well as the *economic* institutions measured by the WGI dimensions "government effectiveness", "regulatory quality", "rule of law", and "control of corruption" (see Fig. 5.6). For all indicators, South Korea is also lagging behind Japan, especially with respect to "political stability and violence avoidance" and "control of corruption".

For most indicators, China has not seen any improvement since the mid-1990s, the only exception being "government effectiveness" for which China managed to reach a value above zero (the WGIs range between −2.5 and 2.5). The lowest values are reported for the indicator "voice and accountability". Due to its historical, social, and ideological background, China has focused predominantly on improving its economic institutions; this strategy has proven rather successful so far. However, as noted by Acemoglu and Robinson (2006), economic institutions do not exist in a vacuum but need to be supported by certain political institutions. According to the authors, sustainable growth can only be sustained by a combination of inclusive economic and political institutions. Accordingly, Zhang (2019: 243) argues that "China's most serious problems in the long run are institutional, not economic". It is very interesting to see whether the Chinese case will eventually turn out to be an exception; in particular, the political stability implied by China's authoritarian system could also be beneficial for sustainable development to some extent (cf. Wagner 2019). Another important aspect in this respect is the importance of second-best institutions in China (see also Rodrik 2008; Xu 2011, as well as Glawe and Wagner 2020a, b, d on this issue).

The idea of second-best institutions was developed by Rodrik (2008) who argued that because of potential interactions with institutional features in the system, institutional improvements can also have adverse effects on economic development. Even though a strong system of contract enforcement and low entry regulations present desirable so-called "first-best" institutions, strengthening the

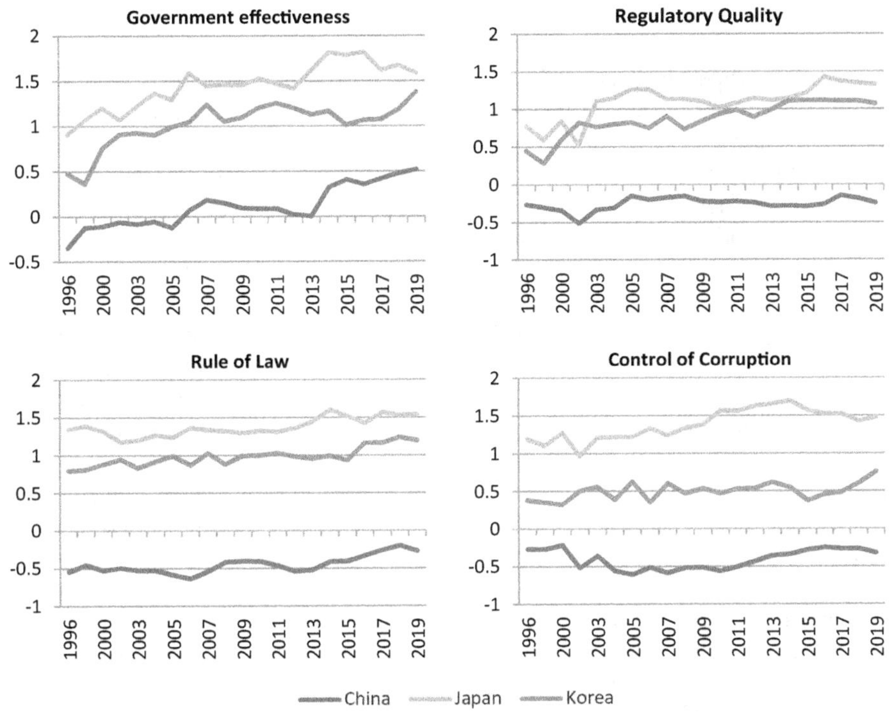

Fig. 5.6 Worldwide governance indicators, economic institutions, 1996–2019. *Source* Kaufmann et al. (2010)

judicial enforcement can do more harm than good in the presence of well-functioning relational contracting which is a kind of informal substitute; this phenomenon is also relevant for the transformation process of the Chinese economy, as shown by Wang and Ming (2009). Second-best institutions can be identified in various aspects of the Chinese economy, for instance, with respect to Township and Village Enterprises.

Finally, it is important to note that (economic) institutional quality differs substantially across Chinese provinces, as discussed in Glawe and Wagner (2019, 2020a, b). As shown in Glawe and Wagner (2020d), there even appear to exist multiple institutional clubs within China with only some provinces following an above-average, high-institutional trajectory. Taking into account region-specific institutional dynamics is crucial for further reforms (probably much more than it is the case in Japan and South Korea).

5.3.10 Economic/Industrial Policies

As already outlined in Sects. 2.5 and 3.6.4, industrial policy played an important role for the development strategies of Japan and South Korea, even though the impact of these policies is still subject to controversy among researchers (see e.g. Klenner 2006 for a discussion). Even though also China's development strategy involves industrial planning, it is usually formulated less concretely compared to that of Japan and South Korea (probably also because of the large domestic market and size, see Sect. 5.3.7). In contrast, the Japanese and South Korean plans for specific industries were much more detailed.

Another important point is that in all three countries, government intervention was accompanied by competition. In the case of Japan, there was competition between the different keiretsu conglomerates (in order to get access to foreign technologies by the MITI, cf. Boltho and Weber 2009). Usually, a keiretsu conglomerate is active in the most sectors of the economy. In South Korea, chaebols had to fulfil performance criteria (e.g. meeting export targets) in order to get subsidies (Morck and Yeung 2017). According to Boltho and Weber (2009), competition was rather domestic in Japan and Taiwan, whereas there was a rather foreign competition in South Korea. In China, competition first took place rather internally (e.g. between TVEs and SOEs) and subsequently also globally when China opened to the world economy during the 1990s. Interestingly, in China, there is also the dimension of interregional competition which was fostered by the (economic) growth-oriented incentive scheme for local government officials (see also Sect. 4.1).

Since the mid-2000s, industrial policy appears to have played (again) a bigger role in China, especially with projects related to science and technology. In Sect. 4.6.2, we have discussed more extensively this return of "techno-industrial policy". Contrary to earlier policy initiatives, the scope, intensity, and volume of resources/subsidies is substantially higher for this new wave of industrial policies. It is difficult to judge whether China has sought inspiration from the Japanese and South Korean experience in this respect.

5.3.11 Breaks in the Development Process

All three countries have experienced a break in their development. For Japan, this breaking point occurred in the 1970s with two oil crises hitting the country in 1973 and 1979, respectively. Japan managed the crisis by following market-oriented policies (as a part of the G7). At around 1980 at the latest, Japan eventually managed to economically and technologically catch up to the group of advanced countries, a goal that China intends to reach from 2035 on with the help of the "Made in China 2025" initiative. In South Korea, the Asian Financial Crisis can be regarded as a breaking point. Similar to Japan, market-oriented reforms and strengthening of democracy helped to overcome the crisis (it has to be mentioned, however, that the transition to democracy had started already during late 1980s). For China, 2010 may be regarded as a similar turning point. After the Global Financial Crisis and the following global economic downturn, China used expansive monetary and fiscal policy to cope with the crisis. However, China was not as hard hit as Western countries by this crisis. If compared to the crisis coping strategies of Japan and South Korea, one striking feature is that China did not try to manage the crisis with market and democracy strengthening reform measures but rather with centralization, authoritarianism, nationalism, and monitoring citizens with the help of AI.

5.3.12 Inequality

In Sect. 5.2, we have highlighted that all three East Asian countries had relatively equal income distributions at the beginning of reforms. Figure 5.7 confirms this view, even though data for Japan and South Korea is only available starting from 1961 and 1965, respectively.

We can see that China's net Gini index at the beginning of economic reforms was 28.1, South Korea's Gini index was around 30.3 (in 1966), and Japan's Gini index was still around 25.6 even after more than a decade after the (post-World War II) reforms had started. However, subsequently the three countries showed rather different inequality trajectories. Probably most strikingly, the Chinese economy has seen a soaring Gini index, especially during the late 1980s and 1990s. Only after the turn of the century, inequality stabilized at a level of around 43 and then decreased slightly to around 41 in the early 2010s where it stayed since then. This levelling off in the 2000s corresponds to the initiating of various reforms of the social system in China, for instance, health care sector and pension system reforms (cf. also Sects. 4.6.1.1 and 4.6.1.2). Contrary to China, Japan and South Korea have managed to keep comparatively low levels of inequality. Since the 1990s, Japan and South Korea have recorded relatively similar levels of inequality. Prior to the

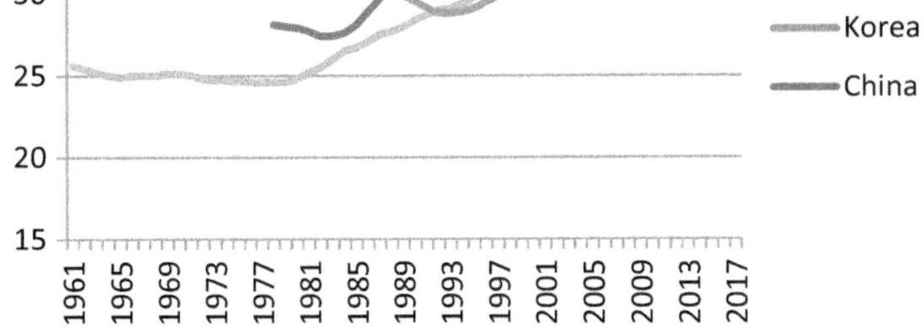

Fig. 5.7 Net Gini index in Japan, South Korea, and China, 1961–2017. *Data* Solt (2020)

Fig. 5.8 Kuznets curve (hypothetical)

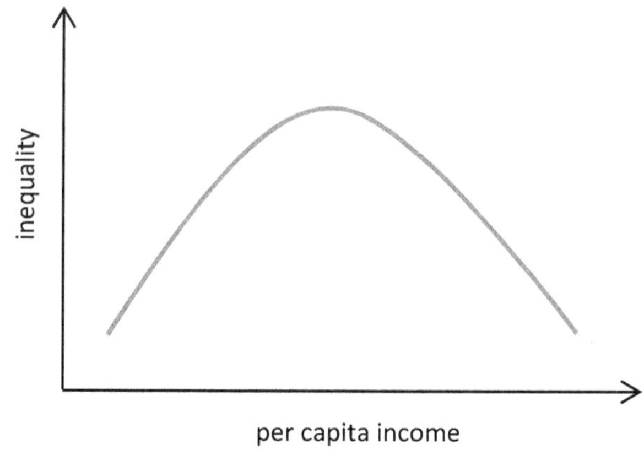

1980s, Japan even managed to keep its Gini index fluctuating around 25. It almost appears as if Japan and South Korea did not have experienced the so-called Kuznets curve (cf. Kuznets 1955; Islam 2015; see Fig. 5.8 for a stylized (!) visualization of the Kuznets curve).

In China, **regional inequality** is a major problem. The inland provinces are on average still lagging behind the coastal provinces with respect to per capita income, but also regarding other development indicators. This is partly due to the preferential treatment of coastal provinces during the early reform phase, especially with respect to the formation of special economic zones, etc. However, **rural–urban inequality** is also a considerable problem in China (cf. Kanbur and Zhang 1999; Sicular et al. 2007; Zhang and Zou 2012; Rozelle and Hell 2020). The ratio of urban-to-rural disposable income has increased from 1.9 in 1985 to above 3 during the 2000s; only after around 2010, the ratio started to decline again, stabilizing at around 2.7 in 2018 (Fig. 5.9).

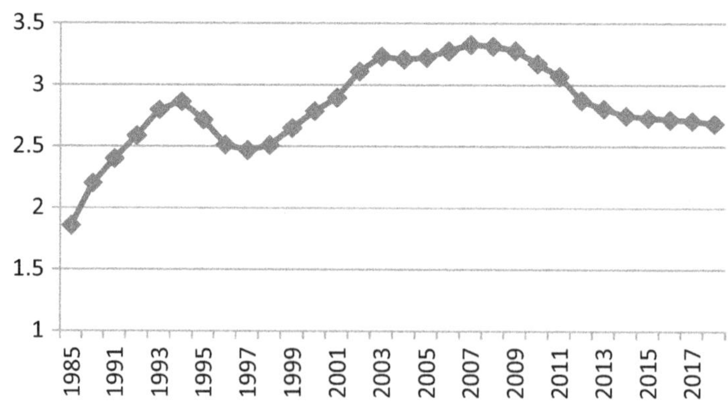

Fig. 5.9 Ratio of urban-to-rural disposable income within China, 1985–2018. *Source* OECD (2019)

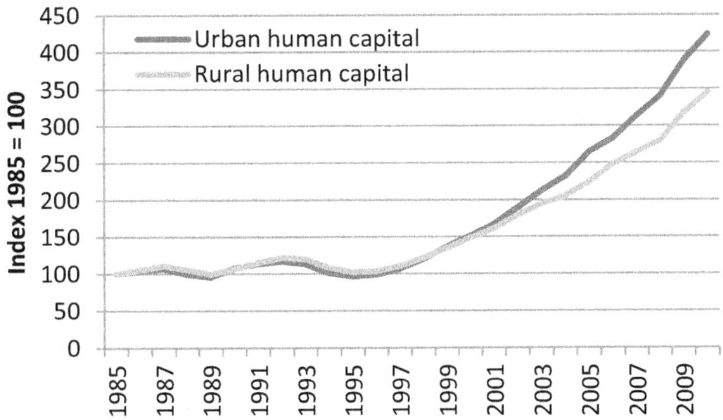

Fig. 5.10 Urban and rural human capital in China, 1985–2010. *Source* OECD (2015)

The rural–urban divide is not restricted to income, but also concerns education, as depicted in Fig. 5.10. Especially after the WTO entry, urban human capital increased faster than rural human capital and this gap had widened over the subsequent decade (see also Glawe and Wagner 2020a for further discussion). China's sheer size that made it impossible to develop the entire country at once and the respective policy measures are responsible for the much more pronounced regional and rural–urban inequality compared to South Korea and Japan.

Still, the problem of inequality is also of relevance for the latter two countries. For instance, in Japan, the rapidly aging society as well as the rising number of non-regular workers could continue to widen inequalities in the future. Also the polarization of the labor market due to the increased use of industrial robots and AI is a challenge that all countries will have to cope with (see also Sect. 6.3.1.3 for a more detailed discussion on the challenges of digital change).

5.3.13 Implications and Summary

The development paths of the three countries show remarkable similarities regarding individual aspects; however, there also exist differences, especially with respect to China. This is not surprising since China has always operated a different political system and has faced different development-relevant framework conditions than Japan or South Korea. Here, it has to be distinguished between exogenous framework conditions (geography, size, etc.) and endogenous framework conditions. The latter naturally have to change permanently, since global structural change is constantly developing. China carried out the structural change process (and consequently also the development process) a few decades later than Japan and South Korea, just as South Korea lagged behind Japan for two decades in this regard. Both countries could learn from Japan (and China additionally from South

Korea), and could study and learn from the strengths and weaknesses of the other's (others') development path(s). As already mentioned above, at the same time, the framework conditions have changed over time. For example, globalization flourished in the 1990s and 2000s, which meant, for example, that the hitherto valid Washington Consensus as a guide (of the West) for the development of the East (and for developing and emerging countries in general) produced less and less good results and had to be replaced by newer concepts, e.g. recommendations of the New Financial Architecture after the Asian Financial Crisis. In this respect, the East Asian development model, if one comes to the conclusion that such a model exists, cannot simply be regarded as recommendations for action for other continents/developing countries. The influence/importance of spatial effects (country- and region-specific) and also of time-dependent differences plays a central role in whether the East Asian development model works similarly well in other countries and regions.

5.4 Conclusions

Overall, our analysis has shown that there are similarities but also differences between the development strategies of Japan, South Korea, and China. The question of which of the three countries was more successful (the most successful one) is very difficult to answer. It depends on the distinct goals of the countries but also on the external restrictions to which the individual countries were exposed and which —as we have shown—were not the same.

Which of the countries have already managed to avoid a growth slowdown at the middle-income range, so-called middle-income trap? These were Japan and South Korea which already managed to join the club of high-income countries quite a while ago (Japan passed the high-income threshold in 1977 and South Korea in 1995).[25] For China, it is very likely, that it will accomplish the successful transition in the near future.[26] The open question is if this success will be sustainable.

All in all, it remains controversial whether there is a uniform East Asian development model. In any case, there are significant differences (particularities) between the development policy approach in East Asia and that in other continents/regions of the world. In addition, what is characteristic and ultimately most relevant for the economies in East Asia is that they were one of the very few

[25] Using data from the Maddison Porject Database, Version 2013 data (cf. Bolt and van Zanden 2014) and income thresholds proposed by Felipe et al. (2012, 2017). Notice that the high-income threshold is 11,750 US$ (in Geary-Khamis (GK, international) dollar).

[26] In fact, China has already overcome the high-income threshold proposed by Felipe et al. (2012) in 2016 when using Maddison data and growth rates of the IMF World Economic Outlook from October 2020 (of constant GDP p.c. in national currency). However, when Japan surpassed the high-income threshold, its GDP p.c. was around 68% of that of the USA; for South Korea, it was around 50% (in 1995); and for China only around 37% (in 2016). Therefore, it is questionable in how far the "absolute" 11,750 US$ threshold is meaningful over time. For an extensive discussion on the middle-income trap probability of the Chinese economy, see Glawe and Wagner (2020a).

(larger) countries that have managed (or will very likely do so in the future) to avoid a (lower) middle-income trap. More precisely, South Korea moved very quickly from a very poor country with an underdeveloped starting level to a rich country. Similarly, China has transformed from a very poor into a relatively prosperous upper middle-income country. Also Japan accomplished a very fast recovery from the devastating destruction after World War II (however, the starting level, especially with respect to human capital was not as low as in China and South Korea).

Maybe one distinctive feature of the East Asian development model is that it allows for a certain flexibility and adaptation of reforms. This makes the East Asian development model a dynamic concept that evolves over time, attuning to the country-specific characteristics and the changed external environment. Probably, the most important lesson for other developing countries is that there is no unique way for a development country to succeed in the catching-up process; a one-size-fits-all solution does not exist. However, learning from others (from their mistakes in particular) and carefully picking individual reform elements and adapting them to the local needs might be a very fruitful even though ambitious undertaking.

Appendix

See Tables 5.3 and 5.4.

Table 5.3 Types of accountability V-Dem Dataset

Vertical accountability	"[…] extent to which citizens have the power to hold the government accountable". Mechanisms "include formal political participation on part of the citizens—such as being able to freely organize in political parties—and participate in free and fair elections, including for the chief executive"
Diagonal accountability	"[…] range of actions and mechanisms that citizens, civil society organizations CSOs, and an independent media can use to hold the government accountable". Mechanisms "include informal tools such as social mobilization and investigative journalism to enhance vertical and horizontal accountability"
Horizontal accountability	"[…] power of state institutions to oversee the government by demanding information, questioning officials and punishing improper behaviour. This form of accountability ensures checks between institutions and prevents the abuse of power. The key agents in horizontal government accountability are: the legislature; the judiciary; and specific oversight agencies such as ombudsmen, prosecutor and comptroller generals"

Source Description of the V-Dem Varieties of Democracy Codebook, slightly shortened

Table 5.4 WGI dimensions, short description

Dimension	Description
Voice and accountability	Capturing perceptions of the extent to which a country's citizens are able to participate in selecting their government, as well as freedom of expression, freedom of association, and a free media
Political stability and violence avoidance	Capturing perceptions of the likelihood that the government will be destabilized or overthrown by unconstitutional or violent means, including politically motivated violence and terrorism
Government effectiveness	Capturing perceptions of the quality of public services, the quality of the civil service and the degree of its independence from political pressures, the quality of policy formulation and implementation, and the credibility of the government's commitment to such policies
Regulatory quality	Capturing perceptions of the ability of the government to formulate and implement sound policies and regulations that permit and promote private sector development
Rule of law	Capturing perceptions of the extent to which agents have confidence in and abide by the rules of society, and in particular, the quality of contract enforcement, property rights, the police, and the courts, as well as the likelihood of crime and violence
Control of corruption	Capturing perceptions of the extent to which public power is exercised for private gain, including both petty and grand forms of corruption, as well as "capture" of the state by elites and private interests

Source Kaufmann et al. (2010: 22)

References

Acemoglu D, Johnson S, Robinson JA (2001) The colonial origins of comparative development: an empirical investigation. Am Econ Rev 91(5):1369–2141

Acemoglu D, Robinson JA (2006) De facto political power and institutional persistence. American Economic Review 96: 325–330

Acemoglu D, Robinson JA, Torvik R (2020) The political agenda effect and state centralization. J Comp Econ 48:749–778

Akamatsu K (1961) A theory of unbalanced growth in the world economy. Weltwirtschaftliches Archiv Rev World Econ 86:3–25

Akamatsu K (1962) A historical pattern of economic growth in developing countries. J Dev Econ 1 (1):3–25

Alesina AF, Seror M, Yang DY, You Y, Zeng W (2020) Resistance despite revolutions. NBER Working Paper 27053, National Bureau of Economic Research, Cambridge, MA

Asian Development Bank (ADB) (2020) Asia's journey to prosperity: policy, market, and technology over 50 years. Asian Development Bank, Manila

Baeck SW (2005) Does China follow "the East Asian development model"? J Contemp Asia 35 (4):485–498

Barro R, Lee J-W (2013) A new data set of educational attainment in the world, 1950–2010. J Dev Econ 104:184–198

Bolt J, van Zanden (2014) The Maddison Project: collaborative research on historical national accounts. Econ Hist Rev 67(3):627–651

Boltho A, Weber M (2009) Did China follow the East Asian development model? Eur J Comp Econ 6(2):267–286

Coe DT, Helpman E (1995) International R&D spillovers. Eur Econ Rev 39(5):859–887

Cousins B (2019) Global and historical lessons on how land reforms have unfolded. The Conversation (8 Dec 2019). https://theconversation.com/global-and-historical-lessons-on-how-land-reforms-have-unfolded-127627

Datta A (1987) Understanding East Asian economic development. Econ Polit Wkly 22(14):602–606

Démurger S, Sachs JD, Woo WT, Bao S, Chang G, Mellinger A (2002) Geography, economic policy, and regional development in China. NBER Working Paper 8897. National Bureau of Economic Research, Cambridge, MA

Dutta M (2005) China's industrial revolution: challenges for a macroeconomic agenda. J Asian Econ 15:1169–1202

Economist (2021) The West once dreamed of democracy taking root in rural China (16 Jan 2021). https://www.economist.com/china/2021/01/14/the-west-once-dreamed-of-democracy-taking-root-in-rural-china

Efrat K (2014) The direct and indirect impact of culture and innovation. Technovation 34(1):12–20

Evans P (1998) Transferable lessons?: Re-examining the institutional prerequisites of the East Asian economic policies. J Dev Stud 34(6):66–86

Falvey R, Foser N, Greenaway D (2002) North-South trade, knowledge spillovers and growth. J Econ Integr 17(4):617–650

Feenstra RC, Inklaar R, Timmer MP (2015) The next generation of the Penn World Table. Am Econ Rev 105(10):3150–3182. www.ggdc.net/pwt

Fei JCH, Ranis G (1975) Agriculture into types of open economies. In: Reynolds LG (ed) Agriculture and development theory. Yale University Press, New Haven

Fei JCH, Ohkawa K, Ranis G (1985) Economic development in historical perspective: Japan, Korea, and Taiwan. In: Ohkawa K, Ranis G (eds) Japan and the developing countries. Basil Blackwell, New York

Felipe J, Abdon A, Kumar U (2012) Tracking the middle-income trap: What is it, who is in it, and why? Levy Economics Institute of Bard College, Working Paper No. 715. Levy Economics Institute, Annandale-on-Hudson, NY

Felipe J, Kumar U, Galope R (2017) Middle-income transitions: trap or myth? J Asia Pac Econ 22 (3):429–453

Fu X, Woo WT, Hou J (2016) Technological innovation policy in China: the lessons, and the necessary changes ahead. Econ Change Restruct 49(2):139–157

Fukuyama F (2012) China and East Asian democracy: the patterns of history. J Democr 23(1):14–26

Gent E (2019) Fukuoka is being positioned as Japan's answer to Silicon Valley—a breeding ground of new start-ups. BBC (9 May 2019). https://www.bbc.com/future/article/20190508-why-fukuoka-is-japans-most-innovative-city

Glawe L, Wagner H (2019) The deep determinants of economic development in China—a provincial perspective. J Asia Pac Econ 24(4):484–514

Glawe L, Wagner H (2020a) China in the middle-income trap? China Econ Rev 60(101264):1–25

Glawe L, Wagner H (2020b) The role of institutional quality and human capital for economic growth across Chinese provinces—a dynamic panel data approach. J Chin Econ Bus Stud 18 (3):209–227

Glawe L, Wagner H (2020c) The middle-income trap 2.0: the increasing role of human capital in the age of automation and implications for developing Asia. Asian Econ Papers 19(3):40–58

Glawe L, Wagner H (2020d) The 'double trap' in China—multiple equilibria in institutions and income and their causal relationship. SSRN Working Paper No. 3719951

Glawe L, Wagner H (2021a) Divergence tendencies in the European integration process: a danger for the sustainability of the E(M)U? J Risk Financ Manag 14(3), 104:1–22

Glawe L, Wagner H (2021b) Convergence, divergence, or multiple steady states? New evidence on the institutional development within the European Union. J Comp Econ 49(3):860–884
Glawe L, Wagner H (2022) New evidence on the impact of institutions on economic development in China. In: Parent A, Le Riche A (eds) Institutional change and China capitalism: frontier of cliometrics and its application to China. World Scientific Publishing, London (forthcoming)
Goetz AM, Jenkins R (2005) Reinventing accountability: making democracy work for human development. Palgrave Macmillan, London
Goto A, Odagiri H (2003) Building technological capabilities with or without inward direct investment: the case of Japan. In: Lall S, Urata S (eds) Competitiveness, FDI and technological activity in East Asia. Edward Elgar Publishing, Northampton MA
Grabowski R (2002) East Asia, the land reform and economic development. Can J Dev Stud 23 (1):105–126
Gray K (2014) U.S. aid and uneven development in East Asia. Ann Am Acad Polit Soc Sci 656 (1):41–58
Gründler K, Köllner S (2020) Culture, diversity, and the welfare state. J Comp Econ 48(4):913–932
He B (2007) Rural democracy in China: the world of village election. Palgrave Macmillan, New York
Hua S (2015) Introduction: the East Asian development model. In: Hua S, Hu R (eds) East Asian development model: twenty-first century perspectives. Routledge, London, New York
International Labor Organization (ILO) (2020) ILOSTAT Database. International Labor Organization, Geneva
Islam SN (2015) Will inequality lead China to the middle income trap? DESA Working Paper No. 142
Jones GK, Davis H (2000) National culture and innovation: implications for locating global R&D operations. Manag Int Rev 40(1):11–39
Jiang K, Keller W, Qiu LD, Ridley W (2018) International joint ventures and internal vs. external technology transfer: evidence from China. NBER Working Paper 24455. National Bureau of Economic Research, Cambridge, MA
Jones GK, Davis H (2000) National culture and innovation: implications for locating global R&D operations. Manag Int Rev 40(1):11–39
Kanbur R, Zhang X (1999) Which regional inequality? The evolution of rural–urban and inland-coastal inequality in China from 1983 to 1995. J Comp Econ 27:686–701
Kasahara S (2004) The flying geese paradigm: a critical study of its application to East Asian regional development. MPRA Working Paper 21881
Katz L (2005) On avoiding uncertainty. Leadership crossroads. http://www.leadershipcrossroads.com/arti_oua.asp
Kaufmann D, Kraay A, Mastruzzi M (2010) The worldwide governance indicators: a summary of methodology, data and analytical issues. World Bank Policy Research Working Paper No. 5430. The World Bank, Washington, DC. https://info.worldbank.org/governance/wgi
Keller W (2010) International trade, foreign direct investment, and technology spillovers. In: Hall B, Rosenberg N (eds) Handbook of the economics of innovation. Elsevier
Kennedy S (2010) The myth of the Beijing consensus. J Contemp China 19(65):461–477
Kennon J (2012) Democracy in Japan: from Meiji to MacArthur. Lehigh Rev 20:17–25
Klenner W (2006) The East Asian development model. In: Kidd JB, Richter F-J (eds) Development models, globalization and economies. Palgrave Macmillan, New York
Kojima K (2000) The "flying geese" model of Asian economic development: origin, theoretical extensions, and regional policy implication. J Asian Econ 11(4):375–401
Kroeber AR (2016) China's economy: what everyone needs to know. Oxford University Press, New York
Kumar N (1996) Foreign direct investments and technology transfers and development: a perspective on recent literature. United Nations University Working Paper 9606, United Nations University, Institute for New Technologies, Maastricht

Kuznets S (1955) Economic growth and income inequality. Am Econ Rev 65:1–28
Lee J, Yi D (2018) Still a new democracy? Individual-level effects of social trust on political trust in South Korea. Asian Journal of Political Science 26(2):201–220
Lee K, Cho S-J, Jin J (2009) Dynamics of catch-up in mobile phones and automobiles in China: sectoral systems of innovation perspective. China Econ J 2(1):25–53
Levi N (2013) The impact of Confucianism in South Korea and Japan. Acta Asiatica Varsoviensia 26:7–16
Li L, Vinten G (1997) An overview of the experiences of Chinese industrialization strategies and development. Managerial Audit J 12(4/5):183–191
Ma J (2009) The dilemma of developing financial accountability without election. Aust J Public Adm 68(S1):62–72
Ma J (2012) The rise of social accountability in China. Aust J Public Adm 71(2):111–121
Marangos J (2009) The evolution of the term 'Washington Consensus.' J Econ Surv 23(2):350–384
Mechkova V, Lührmann A, Lindberg SI (2019) The accountability sequence: from de-jure to de-facto constraints on governments. Stud Comp Int Dev 54:40–70
Minzner C (2011) Countries at the crossroads 2011: China. Freedom House. https://www.refworld.org/docid/4ecba65032.html
Morck R, Yeung B (2017) East Asian financial and economic development. NBER Working Paper 23845, National Bureau of Economic Research, Cambridge, MA
Morgenbesser L (2020) The rise of sophisticated authoritarianism and South East Asia. Cambridge University Press, Cambridge
Mu Q, Lee K (2005) Knowledge diffusion, market segmentation and technological catchup: the case of the telecommunication industry in China. Res Policy 34(6):759–783
Ocampo JA, Arteaga NG (2014) Accountable and effective development cooperation in a post-2015 era. United Nations Department of Economic and Social Affairs, New York
OECD (2015) OECD economic surveys: China 2015. Organization for Economic Co-operation and Development, Paris
OECD (2016) Financing SMEs and entrepreneurs 2016: an OECD scoreboard. OECD, Paris. https://doi.org/10.1787/fin_sme_ent-2016-en
OECD (2017) Japan policy brief (April 2017): economy-improving the performance of Japan's SME sector. OECD, Paris
OECD (2019) OECD economic surveys: China 2019. Organization for Economic Co-operation and Development, Paris
Oi JC (1999) Rural China takes off: institutional foundations of economic reform. University of California Press, Berkeley, London
Ozawa T (1991) The dynamics of Pacific Rim industrialization: how Mexico can join the Asian flock of "flying geese". In: Roett R (ed) Mexico's external relations in the 1990s. Lynne Rienner Publications, Boulder, London
Ozawa T (2005) Institutions, industrial upgrading, and economic performance in Japan. Edward Elgar Publishing, Northampton MA
Park E, Lee A (2020) Neighbors with different innovation patterns: the implications of industrial and FDI policy for the openness of local knowledge production. Transnatl Corp 27(1):3–33
Pemstein D, Marquardt KL, Tzelgov E, Wang Y, Medzihorsky J, Krusell J, Miri F, von Römer J (2021) The V-dem measurement model: latent variable analysis for cross-national and cross-temporal expert-coded data. V-Dem Working Paper Series 2021(21). https://ssrn.com/abstract=3395892
Ramo JC (2004) Beijing Consensus: notes on the new physics of Chinese power. Foreign Policy Center, London
Rodrik D (2008) Second-best institutions. Am Econ Rev: Papers Proc 98(2):100–104
Rosenstein-Rodan PN (1943) Problems of industrialisation of Eastern and South-Eastern Europe. Econ J 53(210/211):202–211

Rozelle S, Hell N (2020) Invisible China: how the urban-rural divide threatens China's rise. University of Chicago Press, Chicago
Sekizawa Y (2017) Is uncertainty really a problem? Research Institute of economy, trade and industry. https://www.rieti.go.jp/en/columns/s17_0007.html
Shi T (2000) Rural democracy in China. Singapore University Press, Singapore
Sicular T, Ximing Y, Gustafsson B, Li S (2007) The urban-rural income gap and inequality in China. Rev Income Wealth 53(1):93–126
Solt F (2020) Measuring income inequality across countries and over time: the standardized world income inequality database. Soc Sci Q 101(3):1183–1199. SWIID Version 9.0, October 2020
Statistics Bureau of Japan (2020) Historical data 5: (3) Employed person by industry. https://www.stat.go.jp/english/
Stockwin A (2018) Explaining one-party dominance in Japanese politics. East Asia Forum (19 Jan 2018). https://www.eastasiaforum.org/2018/01/19/explaining-one-party-dominance-in-japanese-politics/
van Neuss L (2019) The drivers of structural change. J Econ Surv 33(1):309–349
Vogel EP (1991) The four little dragons. The spread of industrialization in East Asia. Harvard University Press, Cambridge, MA
Wagner H (2019) On the (non-) sustainability of China's development strategies. Chin Econ 52 (1):1–23
Wagner H (2020) Comments on toward an Asian monetary fund: ideas for transition. Asian Econ Papers 19(2):78–80
Wang Y, Ming L (2009) Costs and benefits of relational contracting in China's transition. Transition Studies Review 16(3):693–709
Wang Z (2012) Corporate governance under state control: the Chinese experience. Theor Inq Law 13:487–502
Williamson J (2000) What should the World Bank think about the Washington Consensus? World Bank Res Obs 15:251–264
World Bank (1993) The East Asian miracle: economic growth and public policy. World Bank, Washington DC
World Bank (2021) World development indicators. World Bank, Washington, DC. https://data.worldbank.org/products/wdi
Xu C (2011) The fundamental institutions of China's reforms and development. J Econ Lit 49 (4):1076–1151. https://doi.org/10.1257/jel.49.4.1076
Xi J, Wen F (2019) Sustainable rural governance: how rural elections in China lead to long-term social stability? Sustainability 11, 6196; https://doi.org/10.3390/su11226196
Yang DL (2004) Remaking the Chinese Leviathan: market transition and the politics of governance in China. Stanford University Press
Yoshino N, Taghizadeh-Hesary F (2018) The role of SMEs in Asia and the difficulties in accessing finance. ADBI Working Paper 911, Asian Development Bank Institute, Tokyo
Zhang F (2019) The institutional evolution of China: government vs markets. Edward Elgar Publishing, Cheltenham, Northampton MA
Zhang Q, Zou H (2012) Regional inequality in contemporary China. Ann Econ Finance 13 (1):113–137
Zhao S (2010) The China model: can it replace the Western model of modernization? J Contemp China 19(65):419–436
Zhu T (2007) Rethinking import-substituting industrialization: development strategies and institutions in Taiwan and China. In: Chang H-J (ed) Institutional change in economic development. United Nations University Press, New York, pp 261–279
Zhu Y (2011) "Performance legitimacy" in China's political adaptation strategy. J Chin Polit Sci 16(2):123–140

Current Challenges 6

In this chapter, we discuss the current challenges East Asia is facing. After a brief overview of the current state of the catching-up process, we outline the recent policy course in Japan, South Korea, and China. We then elaborate in detail on various selected challenges for this and the next decade(s). Finally, we discuss who may be the next East Asian miracle (success model) country. Box 6.1 again summarizes the outline of this chapter.

Box 6.1 Outline of This Chapter

6.1 **Introduction: Where does East Asia stand today?**
6.2 **Recent policy course in Japan, South Korea, and China.**
6.3 **Challenges (for this and the next decade/s).**
6.4 **Who will be the next China (successful model country) in Asia?**

6.1 Introduction: Where Does East Asia Stand Today?

In the preceding Chaps. 1, 2, 3 and 4, we have seen that and how East Asian countries have developed and caught up rapidly with Western countries. The latter, i.e. the catching-up process, and how East Asia stands today, can well be seen in the following Tables 6.1 and 6.3. Table 6.1 shows the catching-up process using the

L. Glawe and H. Wagner, *The Economic Rise of East Asia*,
Contributions to Economics, https://doi.org/10.1007/978-3-030-87128-4_6

most prominent economic wealth indicator, GDP per capita (here in 2010 US$ as well as in PPP). Table 6.3 will then illustrate the catching-up process using other indicators that are at least as important for a country's development (such as education/years of schooling, infant mortality, and life expectancy).

Tables 6.1 and 6.3 show that all East Asian countries have steadily improved in all prosperity indicators over the last 70 years. The only exception is Japan in terms of GDP per capita, where it has fallen back since the 1990s (after having overtaken the USA (in 2010 US$) for a shorter period of time before).

Table 6.1 The catching-up process in East Asian countries (measured by GDP p.c.)

	Japan	South Korea	China	Taiwan	Hong Kong	Singapore	USA	UK
	Relative to USA [UK]	Relative to USA [UK]	Relative to USA [UK]	Relative to USA [UK]	Relative to USA [UK]	Relative to USA [UK]	Relative to UK	Relative to USA
Panel A: GDP p.c. (2010 US$)								
1960	49.01 [61.77]	5.31 [6.69]	1.09 [1.38]	–	–	19.95 [25.14]	126.04	79.33
1980	90.43 [118.25]	12.87 [16.83]	1.21 [1.59]	–	37.52 [49.06]	47.34 [61.90]	130.76	76.48
1990	105.59 [132.68]	23.56 [29.61]	2.02 [2.54]	–	50.61 [63.60]	62.60 [78.66]	125.66	79.58
2000	94.28 [118.21]	34.46 [43.21]	3.95 [4.96]	–	51.46 [64.52]	75.68 [94.18 9]	125.38	79.76
2010	91.83 [112.86]	47.63 [58.54]	9.39 [11.53]	–	67.16 [82.54]	97.46 [119.78]	125.38	81.37
2019	88.22 [112.53]	51.43 [65.60]	14.78 [18.86]	–	68.03 [86.77]	105.52 [134.59]	127.55	78.40
Panel B: GDP p.c. (PPP)								
1950	18.30 [28.89]	–	–	–	–	–	157.86	63.35
1960	30.80 [45.26]	6.48 [9.52]	5.27 [7.75]	13.51 [19.86]	21.94 [32.25]	14.57 [21.41]	156.57	68.05
1980	68.21 [98.23]	16.56 [23.84]	5.46 [7.86]	37.17 [53.52]	53.72 [77.36]	41.69 [60.04]	155.52	69.44
1990	73.05 [113.24]	33.71 [52.26]	6.34 [9.83]	54.40 [84.33]	67.51 [104.65]	55.11 [85.43]	155.01	64.51
2000	73.53 [103.28]	48.47 [68.08]	8.53 [11.98]	71.05 [99.80]	77.58 [108.98]	82.39 [115.73]	144.01	71.19
2019	62.53 [85.82]	64.39 [88.38]	22.07 [30.29]	77.13 [105.87]	93.46 [128.27]	139.79 [191.87]	137.25	72.86

Source Panel A: World Bank (2021); Panel B: Penn World Tables Version 10, Feenstra et al. (2015)
Notes "–" indicates missing data. Values are expressed relative to the US [UK] in percentages. GDP p.c. (PPP) is calculated using data from the PWT, Version 10 (expenditure-side real GDP at chained PPPs in 2017 US$ divided by the population)

In Table 6.1, we choose GDP per capita as the most common, significant economic measure of wealth, which measures the average economic wealth of a country. (In contrast, the Gini coefficient tells us something about the unequal distribution of wealth.) In Panel B of Table 6.1, we use the GDP data of the PWT database since it provides us with data for all East Asian countries (in PPP). For a discussion of discrepancies across (different versions of) databases, see below (and in the Appendix).

Table 6.1 shows how the development gaps in the East Asian countries vis-à-vis the USA and the UK (representing the "West") have narrowed more and more since 1950.[1]

Only Singapore has already overtaken the USA in GDP p.c. in both variants, i.e. also when weighted by PPP (i.e. also in Panel B of Table 6.1). Japan had overtaken the USA only in 2010 US$ and only for a short amount of time from 1988 (see Panel A of the table).

As far as **Japan** is concerned, already by 1980 at the latest, its development process (evolution from a developing to an advanced economy measured in GDP p. c. and other indicators as well, see Table 6.3) was largely complete: on all indicators, it had largely caught up. In contrast, as argued by Hsu (2016: 189), the 1980s took a turn for the worse, though for a while Japan still continued to grow and converge with the aim of catching up with the USA economically and technologically. However, an asset price bubble began to build up in the second half of the 1980s, which then burst in the early 1990s. By 1973, Japan's per capita GDP (in 2010 US dollars) already had surpassed that of the UK and approached nearly 90% that of the USA (ADB 2020: 45). According to our own calculations based on World Bank data on GDP p.c. in constant 2010 US dollars, Japan surpassed 100% of UK in 1968; in 1973, it had around 108% of UK and around 86% of USA; eventually in 1988, Japan had overtaken the USA for a while. However, after 1990, when the financial crisis hit Japan (and the asset price bubble burst), the dream of overtaking the USA ended abruptly. Japan fell back below 100% of USA in 1998 (98%). From then on, it was more about not falling back further, which, however, could not be prevented.

With respect to GDP p.c. in PPP (Panel B of Table 6.1), Japan has in the meantime (in 2019) reached a low 63% (South Korea even reached a higher level, namely 64%) of the US level and 86% (88%) of the UK level, respectively.[2] The city-states of Hong Kong and Singapore have already surpassed the USA with respect to GDP per capita, even in PPP (in the case of Singapore in 2004) or have come at least very close (in the case of Hong Kong).[3] In addition, both countries report a much higher GDP per capita (in PPP) than the UK. Also, Taiwan managed

[1] We choose the USA and UK as representatives of the "West" because these two countries were the dominant hegemonic powers of the last centuries.

[2] Japan had surpassed 100% of the UK's GDP p.c. (in PPP) briefly in 1977/78 and subsequently for a somewhat longer period between 1989 and 2002. However, it then fell back below 100% and starting from 2015 below 90%.

[3] In fact, Hong Kong had already surpassed the USA between 2011 and 2013, but fell back since then with the sharpest drop occurring between 2018 and 2019 (a more than 4% point decrease

to surpass the UK since the early 1990s (with a longer interruption in the 2000s during which it fluctuated between 96 and 99%; only partly displayed in the table). In PPP, its GDP per capita is still "only" 77% of that of the USA (see Table 6.1 Panel B). Even though China still accounted (in PPP) "only" 22% of the US per capita income (and 30% of that of the UK) in 2019, it only had (in PPP) about 5% in 1980 and 9% in 2000 (8–12% when using the UK as benchmark). That is, China accomplished a considerable catching-up process in a very short amount of time, however, is still far behind.

It is important to note that the per capita income gap between each of the East Asian countries and the USA or the UK varies depending on which database we use. Above and in the following, we always try to clarify which database is used in order to obtain the relative per capita income information, since the results reported can differ significantly across studies. In addition, Table 6.7 in the Appendix provides an overview regarding in which years Japan, South Korea, and China surpassed the 50, 90, and 100% threshold (if applicable to the respective country) depending on different databases. We focus especially on the World Bank database, the Maddison Project Database Version 2013 (Bolt and van Zanden 2014) (extended with IMF growth rates), and Penn World Table Version 10 database since these three are frequently used when discussing the per capita income development. However, there, of course, also exist many other databases that could provide other values (also depending on the version of the database).

A final remark on Japan: The drastic decline of Japan after 1990 is striking and seems unreal at first glance. However, one can easily explain this development. The growth rate in Japan was on average 2.6% points per annum HIGHER than that in the USA in the 30 years from 1960 to 1989, which enabled Japan to catch up from 49 to 102%. In contrast, Japan's growth rate was LOWER than that of the USA by an average of 0.62% points annually over the subsequent 30 years from 1990 to 2019, causing a rebound from 105 to 88% (for a general, fictitious example see Box 6.2). The other East Asian countries have so far been spared this fate of falling back. See also Chap. 2 for a discussion of the underlying reasons for Japan's backslide. One of the (deeper) reasons was certainly the demographic structural change (with a shrinking working-age population) and the hesitant, far too late reaction of the Japanese government(s) to this with necessary structural reforms; see Sect. 6.3.1.1 "Demographic Change (Population Aging)" below.[4]

from 97.7% to only 93.5%). This might, at least to some extent, be due to the increasing (political) instability within Hong Kong in recent years.

[4] When adjusting for demography (population aging), the Japanese and American economies would have grown at about the same rate over the past 30 years, as Krugman emphasizes (Krugman 2021). However, this does not automatically mean that Japan's economy would have grown as fast as that of the USA without population aging, as other developments might then have taken a different course (cf. Sect. 6.3.1.7 "Structural (System) Interdependencies").

Table 6.2 Convergence process (fictitious) example

Year	GDP p.c. country A	GDP p.c. country B	Relative GDP p.c. (%)
1	25,000	50,000	50.00
25	$25{,}000 \cdot (1.05)^{24}$ $= 80{,}627.5$	$50{,}000 \cdot (1.02)^{24}$ $= 80{,}422.9$	100.26
50	$80{,}627.5 \cdot (1.015)^{25}$ $= 116{,}986.1$	$80{,}422.9 \cdot (1.02)^{25}$ $= 131{,}941.5$	88.67

Box 6.2 Convergence and Catching Up: A Numerical (Fictitious) Example
In year 1, country A has a GDP per capita of US$25,000 and country B has a GDP per capita of US$50,000. Assuming that country A grows at a rate of 5% per annum and country B grows at a rate of 2% per annum, country A will overpass country B in the year 25. However, when the growth rate of country A subsequently decreases to only 1.5% per annum (for instance, after a major shock) and country B remains at 2% per annum, then in year 50, its GDP per capita will only account for around 89% of that of country B (see also Table 6.2).

In Table 6.3, we look into the catching-up process using other important wealth indicators.

The average years of schooling can be interpreted as a proxy for the level of human capital of a country; infant mortality and life expectancy are proxies for the quality of the health sector. Both, the level of human capital and the quality of the health sector are important areas of a country's institutional quality, which, in turn, has a decisive influence on a country's economic prosperity (in terms of GDP per capita or economic growth).

With respect to life expectancy, all East Asian countries have either already surpassed the UK and USA or report levels very close to them. Infant mortality is even significantly lower in most East Asian countries, the main exception being China. Regarding schooling/human capital, the gap between the East Asian countries and our two Western countries has already closed significantly (even though the Barro and Lee dataset only provides data up to 2010). With respect to qualitative human capital data (e.g. PISA or TIMMS results), most Asian countries have already surpassed the USA (see Glawe and Wagner 2019).

Today, most of the East Asian countries (China is still lagging behind somewhat due to the later start of reforms) have become technologically and economically advanced countries whose companies are now serious competitors of (on par with) the corresponding European and American companies on many fields of the world market.

Table 6.3 The catching-up process in East Asian countries (measured by education/years of schooling, infant mortality, and life expectancy)

	Japan	South Korea	China	Taiwan	Hong Kong	Singapore	USA	UK
	Relative to USA [UK]	Relative to USA [UK]	Relative to USA [UK]	Relative to USA [UK]	Relative to USA [UK]	Relative to USA [UK]	Relative to UK	Relative to USA
Panel A: Average years of schooling								
1950	80.12 [105.4]	53.54 [70.43]	19.19 [25.25]	36.09 [47.48]	51.87 [68.24]	32.21 [42.38]	131.56	75.61
1960	84.61 [113.06]	45.85 [61.27]	27.33 [36.52]	40.46 [54 0.06]	53.38 [71.33]	40.36 [53.93]	133.62	74.84
1980	75.70 [108.25]	67.59 [96.65]	44.11 [63.08]	56.00 [80.09]	66.23 [94.71]	43.72 [62.53]	143.00	69.93
2000	86.58 [110.35]	87.55 [111.57]	58.38 [74.39]	75.82 [96.63]	73.65 [93.87]	72.42 [92.29]	133.35	78.47
2010	87.97 [94.73]	91.42 [98.45]	60.29 [64.93]	84.12 [90.59]	86.31 [92.94]	81.99 [88.29]	107.69	92.86
Panel B: Infant mortality								
1960	131.89 [149.45]	370.10 [418.80]	–	–	–	158.80 [179.70]	113.16	88.37
1980	66 [70.21]	240 [255.32]	415.33 [441.84]	–	–	98.67 [104.96]	106.38	94
2000	53.57 [69.23]	89.29 [115.38]	438.10* [566.15]	–	–	46.43 [60]	129.23	77.38
2017	39.39 [60.47]	50 [76.74]	140.91 [216.28]	–	–	42.42 [65.12]	153.49	65.15
Panel C: Life expectancy								
1950	89.66 [89.00]	52.16 [51.77]	63.00 [62.54]	81.46 [80.86]	91.11 [90.43]	85.61 [84.98]	99.26	100.74
1960	97.06 [95.79]	78.91 [77.87]	62.52 [61.70]	91.78 [90.57]	96.37 [95.10]	93.62 [92.38]	99.26	101.33
1980	103.17 [103.62]	89.45 [89.84]	90.44 [90.83]	96.71 [97.13]	101.04 [101.48]	97.36 [97.78]	100.43	99.57
2000	105.67 [104.39]	99.00 [97.80]	92.95 [91.82]	99.00 [97.78]	105.14 [103.86]	101.541 [100.27]	98.78	101.24
2019	107.31 [104.07]	105.29 [102.11]	97.53 [94.58]	102.02 [98.94]	107.60 [104.35]	106.03 [102.83]	96.98	103.12

Notes Data on the "average years of schooling" are obtained from the Barro and Lee (2013) dataset. Data on infant mortality are obtained from the World Bank (child mortality rate is expressed as the probability per 1,000 that a newborn baby will die before reaching age 5, if subject to age-specific mortality rates of the specified year). Data on life expectancy are obtained from Riley (2005), Zijdeman et al. (2015), and the UN Population Division (2019). *The above data are in relative terms. However, in absolute terms, infant mortality in China almost halved between 1980 and 2000

As explained in Chap. 5, Japan has led the catching-up process and the reform process behind it within East Asia (albeit also from a favored, because higher, starting position[5] than the other East Asian countries). Japan initiated the Asian model of export-led-growth; followed by Singapore, Taiwan, and South Korea in the 1960s/70s,[6] later also (from the 1990s on) by China.[7] Today, their path to success serves as a model for countries such as Vietnam, Malaysia, and others in their efforts to catch up (Hsu 2016: 187).

6.2 Recent Policy Course in Japan, South Korea, and China (in Period 2010–2020, After Global Financial Crisis)

Japan

Japan's policies over the past decade have been shaped by the policies of Shinzo Abe (also known as "Abenomics").

Shinzo Abe is a Japanese politician who served as Prime Minister of Japan and President of the Liberal Democratic Party (LDP) from 2006 to 2007 and again from 2012 to 2020. He is the longest-serving prime minister in Japanese history. His economic strategy (in his second term), called Abenomics, consisted of the so-called "three arrows" (a reference to an old Japanese story) of policy. The first arrow was monetary expansion (with the introduction of "quantitative and qualitative easing", and—from 2016 on—"Yield Curve Control"), which aimed to achieve a 2% inflation target. The second arrow was flexible fiscal policy, which was intended to act as an economic stimulus in the short term and then achieve a budget surplus. (These two arrows should be best coordinated (IMF 2017: 23).) The third arrow was a growth strategy that should focus on structural reforms and private sector investment to attain long-term growth.

As mentioned above (in Chap. 2), after long years of political instability with very frequent changes of government (14 changes within 20 years), a long and unprecedented period of political stability returned with the rule of Shinzo Abe in the period 2012–2020. Abe also brought about a strategic stability that had not been seen for a long time. Unlike his predecessors, Abe tried to develop a coherent concept and had 8 years to implement it (as far as possible). As a deeper motivation for Abe's reform zeal, it can be considered that he also wanted to forget the disgrace of the prior two decades, which consisted, on the one hand, of Japan's failure in the

[5] Having already become a major global industrial power in the early 1900s, Japan's success was subsequently interrupted by imperial and expansionist ambitions and by military disaster, due to which (after the defeat in World War II) the economy was devastated (ADB 2020: 43). See Chap. 2 above.

[6] Hong Kong had already adopted the export-led growth model in the 1950s (cf. Koo 1986).

[7] According to this "flying geese" model (Akamatsu 1962), economies that were in earlier development stages, aligned behind industrial nations (particularly neighboring ones such as Japan in East Asia).

early 1990s in its attempt to further catch up with the USA technologically and economically and to overtake it in perspective. A second ignominy for Japan was and is that it failed in overcoming the subsequent "stagdeflation", which was characterized by two "lost decades" of persistent stagnation and deflation. Japan under Abe was trying to overcome the protracted crisis of the past two decades and return to the dynamic growth path of earlier times, thus emerging from the "High-Income Trap" (HIT), into which it had fallen in the meantime. At the same time, Japan was and is concerned with emancipating itself from the West/USA (what had begun at the latest after the Asian Financial Crisis).

So far Abe's political reform course has only partially been successful. In the year after he started his second term in office (2013), nominal GDP in Japan was at the same level as 1991 while the Nikkei 225 stock market index was at a third of its peak ("Economist" 18.5.2013). In other words, Japan was stuck in an HIT for two decades. Since then until 2019 (the year before Abe's resignation), nominal GDP in Japan had even decreased by 1.4% (World Bank current US$) while the Nikkei index had increased by 112%. In addition, employment had increased by 6.4% (WDI/ILO) and inflation only risen to 0.48% in 2019 (starting from 0.35% since 2013; CPI; World Bank). However, one cannot deny Abe's policy some (slight) success during his term in office. The question is how consistent this (partial) success will be. This depends above all on the structural reforms that have been initiated but have not yet made sufficient progress.

China

China's policy in the last decade has been shaped by the development strategy and derived from it, policy course of Xi Jinping ("Xinomics").

Xi Jinping came into office about the same time as Shinzo Abe in Japan (late 2012), since 2012 as General Secretary of the Communist Party of China (CPC) and Chairman of the Central Military Commission (CMC), and since 2013 as President of the People's Republic of China (PRC). Under his rule, the main goal of Chinese policy changed further away from unrestrained economic growth to social stability in order to stabilize the economic and social system and consolidate the rule of the Communist Party (see Wagner 2021 for more details). In other words, he has essentially been concerned with stabilizing the country, with preventing/reducing the imbalances (such as environmental pollution, income inequality, indebtedness/financial instability, dependence on the West/on Western demand and suppliers) that built up more and more in the late (or post-)"Deng era" (especially after 2000).

Ultimately, however, he is also concerned with erasing the ignominy of the West's paternalism and oppression, which began two centuries ago and led to the impoverishment of the once rich and highly developed country through conquest, plunder, and colonial dependencies. The country is to regain its former greatness and world importance (leaving behind the dark past of the last two centuries). These can be regarded, so to speak, the "deep determinants" (driving forces) that determine the current policy in China.

Again, it is not yet possible to say with certainty whether this path will succeed (Wagner 2021). One problem with Xi's policy is the following: Despite a shift away from the previous strategy of unrestrained economic growth, the Xi government has been unwilling to refrain from repeatedly launching large expansionary macroeconomic stimulus programs to limit the slowdown in growth triggered by external shocks and by ongoing structural change. This has been at the cost of new imbalances (especially rising debt). Moreover, and more importantly, by focusing on expansionary macroeconomic policy, necessary structural reforms[8] have been slowed down (see, in more detail, Wagner 2017).

South Korea

South Korea, in recent years, has been characterized by less political stability than Japan and China. This was mainly related to the corruption scandals surrounding President **Park Geun-hye**, who served as South Korea's president from February 2013 to March 2017 and who was impeached and later convicted on related corruption charges and sentenced to 24 years in prison (later increased to 25 years) for corruption and abuse of power by South Korean courts.

In 2017, **Moon Jae-in** took office as president of South Korea and has started implementing a comprehensive economic program to address low growth and worsening income inequality. Among else, he launched a series of minimum wage hikes, a reduction of the maximum hour work week, and promised a permanent expansion in welfare spending (IMF 2018: 7). However, during the past 2 years, he or his government has primarily been preoccupied with combating the COVID-19 ("Corona") crisis and its aftermath, and before that had to deal with deteriorating relations with Japan. Relations with Japan, a fellow American ally, continued to be disrupted by a simmering argument over Japan's obligations to elderly Koreans forced to work in factories and brothels by the Japanese army during World War II, and at times escalated into a minor trade war. Even if the IMF still in 2019 certified the country "strong fundamentals", important further reform steps have failed to materialize or had to be postponed during the past 2 crisis years. To promote long-term growth and job creation, the IMF recently suggested:

- Fiscal policy should remain expansionary in the medium term, focusing on increasing social protection, boosting female labor force participation, and supporting growth-enhancing structural reforms.
- Flexicurity should be adopted as a basis for labor market policies.
- Public sector job creation should be linked to developing services that cannot be provided by the private sector.
- Barriers to entry and the protection of incumbents in the product market need to be reduced further (IMF 2019a: 1).

[8] The IMF emphasizes as the most pressing structural reform needs (those reform needs with "limited progress" so far): SOEs and finance sector reform (IMF 2020: 42).

Summing Up

The fundamental challenge in all three countries is to address necessary/appropriate structural reforms swiftly, as structural change continues permanently in all three countries—albeit with perhaps different challenges for the individual countries (see next section for more on this). If this does not succeed, there is a risk of regression in development (toward a middle- or high-income trap (MIT or HIT)).

Japan made the typical mistake in 1991ff. of reacting to a crisis triggered by structural problems[9] primarily with expansive macroeconomic policy (and neglecting/postponing necessary structural reforms). This has led to the so-called two "lost decades" there, in which Japan has again fallen somewhat/further behind the West/USA in terms of development (see at the end of Chap. 2; and in Table 6.1). Government debt rose and rose (from 67% in 1990 to 266% at the end of 2020); and the central bank's balance sheet extension grew larger and larger without really bringing stagnation and deflationary tendencies under control. This may have prevented worse things from happening, but at a high (growth) cost; in any case, it can be assumed that the recovery would have been more rapid and at lower growth cost if structural reforms had been tackled sooner and in a more determined manner. This is what Abe's policy (Abenomics) with the three pillars was aimed from 2012 onward, although structural reforms also fell short under Abe, were repeatedly pushed out or watered down.

The question is whether South Korea and China will make the same mistakes as Japan after 1990 or learn from Japan's mistakes, according to an old Chinese proverb (attributed to Confucius) which reads: "The wise man learns from the mistakes of others. The fool from his own." (quoted, for example, in the book by Bernhard Moestl "Shaolin", cf. Moestl 2012).

6.3 Challenges (for This and the Next Decade/s)

This subsection deals only with the "Current" Challenges, i.e. challenges foreseeable from today's perspective (as of 2021) for the next few decades and already recognized as such and discussed (and started to be addressed) to a greater or lesser extent. We do not see any point in speculating about "Future" Challenges, i.e. about new challenges that might emerge in the future. This would be highly speculative/uncertain/ambiguous, as it would depend on all kinds of future economic, political, socio-cultural, and ecological circumstances/imponderables, which we do not yet know today. For this reason, we will limit ourselves here to the "current" challenges for East Asia.

We first ask: what are the ***common*** challenges facing Japan, South Korea, and China in the coming decades? In doing so, we will see that some of these common challenges (which are mostly structural) are more likely to occur in time and/or to a

[9] These structural problems at the time included aging, weak corporate governance, and policy uncertainty, which contributed to depressed investment and production offshoring (IMF 2017: 4).

greater extent in one or the other country than in the other(s). Subsequently, we will also address some challenges that are largely ***unique*** to one or two of the East Asian countries. What all these challenges have in common is that the development process in the East Asian countries under consideration will only be able to continue (i.e. these countries will only be able to avoid slipping into an MIT or HIT) if they respond to these challenges swiftly and adequately.

In Sect. 6.3.1, we will first look into the "General (Common) Challenges" that affect all or many countries worldwide, thus also the East Asian countries (although the latter will be affected to different degrees and over different periods of time, as mentioned). Then, in Sect. 6.3.2, we will look into "Specific East Asian Challenges", i.e. challenges in all or some of the East Asian countries that, however, also indirectly affect the other Asian and non-Asian countries to a greater or lesser extent. Finally, in Sect. 6.3.3, we will briefly look into some "Specific Challenges in individual East Asian countries" that affect only individual East Asian countries and affect others only indirectly, if at all.

In the following Box 6.3, all these challenges are listed.

Finally, we could also address issues of sequencing/temporal prioritization (against the backdrop of scarce resources) and general/basic prioritization (what is more important to which country). However, due to the speculative character of such an attempt, and in order not to let the chapter expand too much in scope, we will refrain from doing so here.

Box 6.3 Challenges Facing East Asia (Japan, South Korea, and China)

6.3.1 ***General (Common) Challenges*** *(Structural Change in a wider sense)*
6.3.1.1 Demographic Change (Population Aging)
6.3.1.2 Climate Change (Environmental Problems)
6.3.1.3 Digital Change
6.3.1.4 Cultural Change
6.3.1.5 Contact Change ((De-)Globalization) and Pandemics
6.3.1.6 (Sectoral) Structural Change and Welfare System
6.3.1.7 Structural (System) Interdependencies.

The challenges listed in 6.3.1 are external conditions that cannot (or only to a very limited extent) be prevented/changed by a country (especially a smaller one) in an open, global world; they are, so to speak, global public goods or bads (with global spillovers), which basically can only be altered in the long run in a globally coordinated effort of (as far as possible) all countries; as an individual country, one can only react to them in the best possible way (crisis management) or take appropriate precautions in time (risk management)). The latter also applies to 6.3.1.1 (aging), however, aging in China has greatly accelerated through the imposed one-child policy from 1979 to 2015.

6.3.2 ***Specific Current East Asian Challenges***
6.3.2.1 Risk of Financial Crises.
6.3.2.2 System Competition (*China–USA*).
6.3.2.3 Strained International Relations.
6.3.2.4 Avoiding the Disappointment of Expectations (raised by project announcements).
6.3.2.5 Reducing Inequalities/Ensuring Social Stability.

The challenges listed in 6.3.2 are conditions or circumstances that can be partly or largely influenced by the respective country itself.

6.3.3 ***Specific Challenges in Individual East Asian Countries***
6.3.3.1 Overcoming Risks of Stagnation.

In the following remarks, a certain emphasis will be placed on China. This is partly because China still has the arduous path ahead of it that the other two countries have already successfully completed, namely overcoming the MIT in a sustainable manner. Second, China is aiming for higher goals (also of a global political nature) that the other two did not have on their development agenda at the time (when they were at the same stage of development as China is now). Third, China is much larger than Japan and South Korea, and thus much more relevant for the rest of the world. And last but not least, China is going its own way, i.e. it is not following the USA and its development model/policy recommendations as Japan and South Korea have done, but is pursuing a different economic and social model that represents a counter or competing model to the Western development path, so to speak, and is thus challenging the USA as a system competitor in perspective. Because of all this, China is generally seen by the USA and the West as a threat and a challenge to them (especially to the USA), which means that China has to reckon with more headwinds (compared with Japan and South Korea at the time). The challenges for China in the coming decades will, therefore, be greater and more demanding. This justifies a kind of overweighting of China in the following presentations.

6.3.1 General (Common) Challenges (Structural Change in a Wider Sense): Demographic, Climate, Digital, and Cultural Change

Box 6.4 General (Common) Challenges (Structural Change in a Wider Sense)

6.3.1.1 Demographic Change (Population Aging).
6.3.1.2 Climate Change (Environmental Problems).

6.3.1.1 Demographic Change (Population Aging)

Population aging is a major problem or challenge for the East Asian countries (particularly for Japan, South Korea, and China)[10] as these countries are aging rapidly, even more so than many of the other industrialized and emerging countries.[11] This brings with it the danger that Japan and South Korea may get stuck in a high-income trap (HIT) and China in a middle-income trap (MIT), at least that they will at some point not be able to catch up further with the USA and some other of the less rapidly aging industrialized countries, but rather fall further behind. For China, in particular, it could mean that the country will grow old before it gets rich.

Why? Because there is then a danger that long-term growth (the growth potential) in these countries will weaken due to slowing productivity gains (see on this Nagarajan et al. 2015, and for other effects of population aging, e.g., Denton and Spencer 2000). The primary concern is the further decline in the labor force participation rate (a shrinking working-age population). But more importantly, under some circumstances, due to aging, the reduction in labor, especially the reduction in the number of younger workers, will lead to lower average labor productivity in these countries (especially when aging is accompanied by a reduction of creative talent and thus innovation,[12] see Jones 2020; see also in this context Acemoglu and Restrepo 2017).

Moreover, the phenomenon of a so-called "silver democracy" looms, in which an ever-increasing number (ultimately a majority) of older voters, will push for rising health care and pension spending (see, e.g., Sota 2018; Harney 2013). If governments give into this pressure out of (re)electoral interests, it will tend to lead

---

[10] See, e.g. Yeung and Lee (2021).

[11] The global proportion of older people (60 years and older) in the whole of Asia was 57.1% in 2017 and is projected to be 61.2% in 2050 (see United Nations 2017; an older study is OECD 1996).

[12] However, artificial intelligence and automation could improve our ability to produce ideas to the extent that growth in living standards continues even with a shrinking population (see the section "Digital Change" below).

to increasing government debt and growing debt service payments. A simultaneous curtailment of other public investments and of public funding for education, research, and development would push down the country's growth potential. With lower potential output, the goal of a rapid increase in GDP per capita or living standard growth (and thus further convergence/catching up) would be more difficult to achieve.

In addition, the expansion of the welfare state (in the form of more services for older citizens) expected in such a "silver democracy" will drive tertiarization in the economy (sectoral structural change), especially the part of tertiarization that (keyword "Baumol's cost disease") is responsible for a declining average productivity of the economy (see, in more detail, below in Sect. 6.3.1.6 "(Sectoral) Structural Change and Welfare System").

Among the most important **countermeasures** an aging country (facing a shrinking labor force and a rapidly increasing dependency ratio) can take to avoid the risk of reversion to growth and convergence are the following: (i) getting today's workers to work longer (if necessary, by raising the compulsory retirement age), (ii) getting more women into the workforce, (iii) allowing more immigration, (iv) implementing labor market reforms in order to increase mobility in the labor market, (v) bringing about technical change in production toward increasing the use of capital in production (increase in capital coefficient), particularly investing in robots and artificial intelligence (AI) to boost productivity.

As always, for development/growth success (a lasting MIT/HIT overcoming), it is crucial to make the necessary institutional adjustments to the challenges of structural change (here population aging) in time. In doing so, it is important to learn from countries that have faced this challenge and the adjustments—due to the fact that they had developed earlier—to learn from their mistakes and insights. In East Asia, this was Japan, the first to develop in the last century, and the first to age. That is, for South Korea and China, Japan is an example of learning how best to respond (or not respond) to aging.

JAPAN is often seen as a country that has done too little, too late, to effectively address the aging problem. This was acknowledged by Prime Minister Abe early last decade and consequently led to the third pillar of his Abenomics program, the emphasis on structural reforms, in particular, reforms to respond effectively to the aging problem (see in more detail in Chap. 2).

Abe's government has opened up more to free trade against massive opposition (see below in Sect. 6.3.2.3 "Strained International Relations"). There are now 10 special economic zones. And the employment rate for women now exceeds that of France or the USA. The country is even recruiting more foreign workers today. More digitalization is being promoted, especially in small and medium-sized enterprises. Japan is one of the world's leaders in the use of robots. A further positive factor for the country is that around 90% of the national debt is held domestically (a larger share of which is held by older citizens). This contributes to financial stability. In addition, it must be taken into account that even in a stagnating economy (with national income not rising or rising only slightly), growth rates *per capita* and also per capita income can be significantly higher than before because of the shrinking population.

Box 6.5 Demographic Change in East Asia

The figure below depicts the working-age population as a percentage of the total population in Japan, South Korea, and China, respectively. Between 1950 and the mid-1960s, the share of the working-age population has increased significantly in **Japan** and then stayed at this level until the early 1990s (there was, however, a slight dip in the 1970s/early 1980s). The share of the working-age population peaked in 1992; from that point onwards, Japan has experienced a declining share of the working-age population. **South Korea** has seen a particularly strong increase in the working-age population in the 1970s and 1980s. However, starting from the 1990s, the working-age population grew at a somehow lower speed, leveling off in the early 2010s. In recent years, there appears to be even a slightly declining tendency, indicating that also South Korea might already have reached or is reaching its demographic turning point; however, at a slightly higher level than Japan (with currently a working-age share of 73% compared to Japan's peak value of around 70%). Interestingly, in **China**, there has been a steady declining trend already since 2010—even though the country still records a much lower GDP per capita compared with the other two East Asian countries. This is an indication that China's demographic dividend is coming to an end with the danger that China will get old before it gets rich.

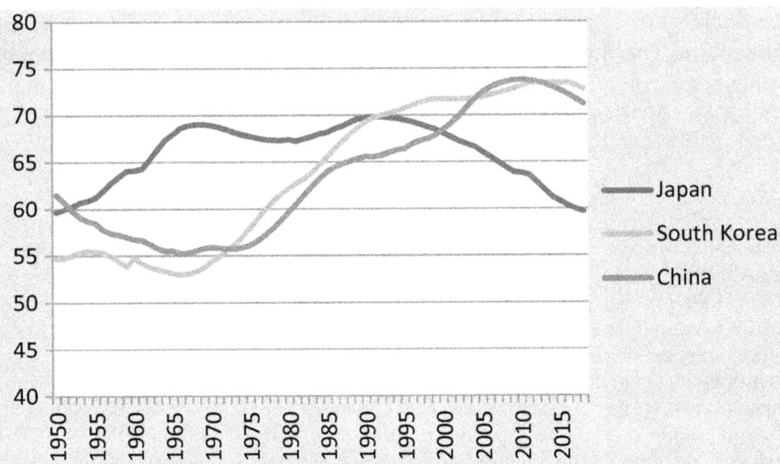

Working-age population (% of total population). *Source* OECD (2021). https://www.oecd-ilibrary.org/social-issues-migration-health/working-age-population/indicator/english_d339918b-en

CHINA's government or Communist party has also recognized the problem and reacted to it in the 14th five-year plan (among other things by announcing a gradual increase in the retirement age, which is currently still a low 60 years for men and 55 (50) years for women).[13] However, the forecasts of the United Nations (UN) and other organizations sound very gloomy. For example, the UN expects the population to decline by a total of 10% by 2040.[14] Unlike countries like South Korea, Japan, or Italy (all of which are currently aging rapidly), China is aging at an earlier stage of economic development, according to a recent study by the Chinese central bank. Since, according to the IMF, the productivity of China's economy is currently only about 30% of that of the world's best economies, such as the USA, Japan, or Germany, China is in danger of not being able to make up the productivity gap to these countries in time (IMF 2021). Only swift countermeasures (see above), both institutional and technological (e.g. automation), could avoid or mitigate this danger.

China's Seventh National Population Census (conducted in 2020 and published in May 2021) provides new insights regarding China's demographic trends. In 2020, the number of persons aged 60 and above climbed to 264 million which is 80 million more than in 2010. In addition, the number of birth dropped significantly—by almost 20% between 2019 and 2020 (with only 12 million births being recorded in 2020). The expected baby boom after the abolishment of the one-child policy did not occur; in fact, many women decide not to get married, in particular, because of the rising costs of education and housing. With 1.3 children per woman, China's fertility rate is very similar to that of Japan and considerably below the 2.1 necessary to keep the population stable. Chinese officials state that China will experience the population growth peak within the next couple of years, which is in fact one decade earlier than previously assumed (the working-age population, however, is already declining as we show in Box 6.5). The question in this context is if "China will grow old before it gets rich". Population aging is usually associated with an increasing spending share attributed to health and social services and pension system. These sectors typically exhibit a lower productivity compared with industrial sectors or ICT or financial services. However, other developments give hope: between 2010 and 2020, the number of university graduates had almost

[13] For blue-collar women, the retirement age is 50. In addition, increasing China's fertility rate is relevant. Already in 2016, the Chinese leadership had abolished the one-child policy (in force since 1979 at the provincial level and 1980 at the national level) and allowed two children per couple, with the aim of reaching a birth rate of 1.8 children per couple in 2020, which, however, has by far not yet been achieved even today.

[14] In the process, the number of the working-age population will fall disproportionately. The fact is that China's working-age population has been declining since 2011. At the same time, the proportion of people over 60 has risen from 10.4% in 2000 to 17.9% in 2018. By 2050, it is estimated that one third of the Chinese will be 60 or older. In a report published in 2019, the Chinese Academy of Social Sciences warned that China's main pension fund could run out of money by 2035. Further indebtedness of the state (see subsection "Indebtedness" below) may then become necessary. Data are from the "Economist" of 30 April 2021 "Is China's population shrinking?" (see also Zheng et al. 2019).

doubled (to 280 million). In addition, rural–urban migration has increased by 14% points between 2010 and 2020 (to almost 64%).

6.3.1.2 Climate Change (Environmental Problems)

The ecological transformation of society is often seen as the greatest challenge of the coming decades. It is about mitigating (the consequences of) man-made climate change.

All East Asian countries face this major challenge equally. However, each country realizes that no country alone can significantly affect climate change. Only through concerted action by as many countries as possible around the world is there any chance of effectively addressing climate change (even if some claim it is already too late). Combating climate change is THE central task of this century, and it is a global public task.

JAPAN started to address environmental problems already in the 1970s (see Chap. 2). Moreover, Japan—as a founding member of the G7—was among the first to take countermeasures or, as a G7 member, to work on a common strategy to combat it. Definitely, Japan was the first of the East Asian countries to take precautions against climate change (in consultation with the other G7 countries). However, Japan's efforts have slowed down considerably, especially in the last three decades. While the European Union reduced its greenhouse gas emissions by 22.5% between 1990 and 2018, Japan only managed 2.5%. One problem, as the global Climate Action Tracker criticizes, is that the country relied heavily on coal-fired power generation.

Also, in order to do its part in combating climate change, Japan unwaveringly clings to nuclear power to this day (and is not alone in this; many other countries, such as France, also cling to nuclear power, while Germany, after the Fukushima disaster, took the decision to phase out nuclear power as soon as possible). Only in September 2020, after taking office, the new Prime Minister Yoshihide Suga promised that Japan would aim for a climate-neutral economy in 2050, just like the EU. But nuclear power and fossil fuels shall then still supply 30–40% of Japan's electricity.

SOUTH KOREA's current Prime Minister Moon Jae-in also set completely new accents in climate and energy policy at the beginning of his term in office (in 2017).

Until then, South Korea met 70% of its electricity needs with coal and nuclear power plants. According to Moon Jae-in's plans, the share of coal should be halved from the current 40% by 2030. Instead of tax breaks, taxes should now be introduced on coal and nuclear power. Old coal-fired power plants are to be decommissioned and, in return, renewable energies and gas-fired power plants are to be promoted.

CHINA is the East Asian country the world is most likely to look to today. Indeed, due to its size and high economic growth (and high industrial share), China emits 27.9% of global CO_2 emissions, with the USA following at 14.5% (early 2021; source: European Environment Agency). Per capita, of course, China consumes much less than the USA (7.1 t compared to 16.0 t). China is still dependent on coal for about 60% of its electricity generation. In addition, China finances 70% of coal-fired power plants as part of the New Silk Road. On the other hand, in solar and wind energy, Chinese companies have already outstripped their German competitors, thanks to lavish support from the Chinese government. In the field of electromobility, China is preparing to achieve something similar. China promises to achieve carbon neutrality by 2060, 10 years later than leading industrialized countries.

The environmental problem has been on China's mind for some time. Even in the years before Xi Jinping took office, the problem of environmental pollution was recognized in China as a major threat to further development. Pollution had increased rapidly in China in the wake of unrestrained economic growth during the Deng- and post-Deng period (especially in the 1990s and the 2000s) when China prioritized economic growth over environmental concerns so that by the end of the 2000s, combating this problem was proclaimed an important task for the future. It had gradually been realized that it could not make sense for China to keep building more and more airports, roads, railways, and buildings at the expense of the environment just to keep stimulating growth. However, it was only under Xi Jinping that this was effectively attempted. In March 2014, at the opening of the annual meeting of the People's Congress, Premier Li Keqiang denounced smog as "nature's warning against inefficient and blind developments" and declared a "war on pollution" (see Greenstone et al. 2021), and China has then also made significant progress in improving air quality since 2014. The government has launched a large-scale clean energy program, replacing coal with natural gas as a heating fuel (Atmospheric Pollution Prevention and Control Law (2018 Amendment)). Nevertheless, air pollution in China remains high, so further efforts are needed.

But there is a well-known practical problem with implementing the Xi government's new green economy-based strategy. This is that counties and provinces in China that are heavily dependent on coal mining and utilization or have a particularly polluting production structure have a natural tendency to be as reluctant as possible to implement the center's environmental targets. In most cases, it is also regions with below-average incomes where those in charge fear the displeasure of the local population. This is the familiar, constant tug-of-war in China between central policy targets and regional implementation, which is occasionally reflected in the form of "alternative facts" in regional statistics.

On the other hand, there are conflicting goals even at the general government level: the implicit 15-year targets included in the latest five-year plan include economic growth averaging about 5% per year until 2035 (see Sect. 6.3.2.4 "Avoiding the Disappointment of Expectations (raised by project announcements)" below). This quantitatively ambitious target places enormous pressure on many responsible parties to succeed. A targeted doubling of the gross national product by 2035 with a simultaneous sharp reduction in the (domestic) share of coal would further increase the required import volume of oil and gas, i.e. of primary energies whose path to China is not entirely certain. China's economic development would be more vulnerable; the only way out of this strategic problem is a much faster pace of expansion of renewable energies. In this situation of conflicting interests, the huge Chinese state apparatus has many possibilities to slow down or even avert changes without showing open resistance. The local interests described above play a role, as does the resistance of sectors that expect environmental and climate policy measures to worsen their international competitive situation. (On this topic, see also Greenstone et al. 2021.)

In summary, even though party and state leaders are on the side of the environment and climate, China's political leadership is struggling against a reluctant administration amid weak popular support. Last but not least, given the current tense political situation between the USA and China, difficult negotiations between the two most important partners in the fight over climate change on climate policy are also to be expected.

6.3.1.3 Digital Change

Adapting to digital transformation is likely to be among the greatest challenges facing governments (with respect to adopting digital public services) and companies[15] worldwide in order to remain or become competitive in global markets. This also applies to the (East) Asian countries, and the success of this task is likely to contribute substantially to whether these countries succeed in avoiding middle-income or high-income traps. Digital transformation can have a very positive impact on development not only in industrialized countries but also in developing countries and emerging economies. For example, digital transformation can benefit human capital formation in developing countries through new opportunities for virtual participation in global education and health/medical advice (telemedicine) in rural and educationally and medically deprived areas of these countries. However, the emergence of digital change is not only associated with hopes but also with major fears.

There are fears that digital transformation, especially artificial intelligence (AI), will lead to job losses and rising inequality. Developing countries in particular could emerge as losers. Their previous comparative advantage was based on an abundance of labor and natural resources. Since AI (the digital transformation) will lead to diminishing returns on labor and natural resources (due to the labor-saving and resource-saving properties of the new digital technologies)—and furthermore is likely to lead to a concentration of economic power in a few superstar companies mostly based in a few highly developed countries—developing countries and most of the emerging market countries could become the losers of the digital transformation. Thus, even all the positive developments of the last 50 years of a reduction of poverty and inequality and thus the convergence progress of the last half century could be reversed (so the fear of Korinek and Stiglitz 2021). And overcoming MIT is likely to be made even more difficult, if not impossible (see Glawe and Wagner 2020b). Only emerging-market countries that have already undergone a deep economic and technological transformation—such as China—are likely to escape this vicious circle. China might even be among the winners of the digital transformation due to its size and dynamism, as are many technologically and

[15] On digital transformation regarding companies, see, e.g. Westerman et al. (2014).

institutionally highly developed countries (such as Japan and South Korea). For these, Nordhaus' optimistic view might apply rather, according to which: "rapid growth in computation and artificial intelligence will cross some boundary or singularity, after which economic growth will accelerate sharply as an ever-increasing pace of improvements cascades through the economy" (Nordhaus 2015). By contrast, most developing and emerging economies (among them, many Southeast Asian countries) are likely to be on the losing side (their terms of trade and international competitiveness are likely to deteriorate in the wake of the digital transformation). The manufacturing-based export-led growth model, on which the East Asian "miracle" (East Asia's development success) was essentially based, is also likely to lose much of its appeal or impact (based on the decline of traditional manufacturing). This means that the upward (convergence) opportunities for developing countries will deteriorate. In the worst case, developing countries are on a path back to Malthusian stagnation "dynamics".

Whether this can be stopped by global governance reforms, as envisioned by Korinek and Stiglitz (2021), can be doubted, especially against the background of an emerging bipolarity in world economic governance (two competing systems, East (China/Russia+) and West (US/Europe+)). At most, regional governance convergence clubs are conceivable (as in the EU). In contrast, viable transatlantic reform results are difficult to achieve if an agreement on a joint vaccine supply program has already failed in the current pandemic due to the (vaccination) nationalism of individual states.

Whether, as suspected above, South Korea and Japan will be winners in the digital transformation alongside China depends not least on the infrastructural inputs/investments of the public sector in education, training, continuing education but also on the quality of digital public services. As far as the latter is concerned, Japan is in a worse position than China and South Korea. Japan, like Germany, is a laggard in the rich world in adopting digital public services. Few reforms would benefit Japan (like Germany)[16] as much as bringing government services online. The potential productivity gains associated with this would be enormous. Japan could follow South Korea's example here by making more of its public data, processes, and services "open by default" and transparent.

However, a particular challenge here, not only for the East Asian aging societies, is to reconcile digitalization with aging. This means familiarizing the growing number of older people with digital devices and procedures, reducing fear of contact, and providing counseling services (senior-friendly services) and applications (such as online medical consultations via telemedicine) for this age group.

6.3.1.4 Cultural Change

Cultural frameworks, like geographic and environmental frameworks, are often viewed as a kind of constant in development. That is, they change very slowly[17];

[16] In some countries such as Germany, the main obstacle is the rigid data protection laws there, which has also severely hampered pandemic control.

[17] On cultural change, see, e.g. Persson and Tabellini (2020).

they can act as exogenous constraints on institutional and policy change or reform over centuries; and they constitute an important legitimacy standard or sensor for (the sustainability of) political, economic, and social systems. However, cultural frameworks/perceptions can also change over time; and they are changing much faster worldwide in recent decades than in the past due to the dynamic process of globalization and the new information technologies. This can also be seen in the East Asian countries[18]; and there not only in the rapid change of cityscapes in the East Asian metropolises. Especially after the turn of the millennium, this becomes more and more visible.

For example, since the 1950s, Japan and (with a delay also) South Korea, as close allies of the USA, have come into contact with "Western", or rather American, culture earlier than China, which has also left its mark there. This influence was first seen in the cities, and after the new information technologies that have been spreading worldwide for two decades, gradually in rural areas as well. This is reflected above all in the changing patterns of thought and action of the younger generations.

Such a slow ("creeping") process of cultural change is often triggered or accelerated by deeper, prolonged economic crises.

Example Japan

For example, Jeff Kingston reports in his 2004 book "Japan's Quiet Transformation" that the shock of Japan's 1990 financial crisis and the subsequent prolonged economic crisis triggered a process that drove cultural transformation in Japan ("Japan's civil society is under construction", see Kingston 2004: 310). As a result, "the ways and means of the old system have been so thoroughly discredited that there is no turning back; the problems of the present, and those anticipated, are forcing a reinvention of Japan" (311).

However, it is also evident here that cultural change is proceeding only very, very slowly and does not affect all areas equally.

For example, Juro Teranishi shows in his book "Culture and Institutions in the Economic Growth of Japan" (2020) that "the internalized culture nurtured historically is still living deeply in the mindset of the Japanese" (Teranishi 2020 p. x). That is, not all old traditions and behaviors die out immediately but have a long-lasting effect (on this, see also the recent literature in economics on the influence of culture and old institutional structures, such as the existence of colonies; on the latter, see e.g. Acemoglu et al. 2001).

The mentality of "inward-looking" also seems to be reluctant to change in Japan, despite globalization. A recent study (reported in the "Economist", February 6, 2021: 38) shows that, despite globalization, only a few Japanese still want to work or study abroad. An "inward-looking youth" still dominates, with little interest in

[18] It is not entirely clear whether there is a common "East Asian culture" or exactly which countries belong to this cultural community. American *sinologist* and historian *Edwin O. Reischauer* grouped China, Korea, and Japan into a cultural sphere that he called the *Sinic world*, a group of centralized states that share a Confucian ethical philosophy (see Reischauer 1974).

moving outside Japan. This 2019 government survey found that only one-third of young Japanese want to study abroad, compared with 66% of South Koreans and 51% of Germans. Japanese are equally reluctant to work abroad. A 2017 study by Sanno University found that 60% of young workers do not want to work in other countries, up from 36% a decade earlier. This may prove to be a detriment to Japan's economic dynamism.

As just mentioned, (young) people in South Korea have a very different mindset. There, the old behaviors in this regard (of an outward orientation) are changing much faster. In other areas, however, very little is moving in South Korea as well. For example, there is still a strong prevalence of patriarchy in South Korea. In addition, South Korea has the largest wage gap in the world between men and women. This is somewhat reminiscent of Germany in the 1950s (until the mid-1960s). The question is what will be in South Korea in 30 years: will it be like Germany today (or already in the 1990s), here much has/d changed. Or will it be like Japan today, where not so much has changed yet (is there perhaps something like a persistence of "East Asian character"?).

The question is how a country/system/government deals with such "quiet" and not so "quiet" transformations as the push or call for democratization, for more environmental protection (currently "Fridays for Future" movement), for more women's rights/equality, diversity demands, among others. There are attempts to embed these democratically (by assimilation, integration, participatory involvement in the democratic process, as observable in Western European countries in recent decades), or more authoritarian responses, which are currently gaining a foothold even in parts of the European Union (Hungary, Poland) and rely on restrictions on the rule of law, or even—as in Russia and China, for example—on repression or ideological re-education (see in more detail in the Sect. 6.3.2.2 "System Competition" below).

An alternative option is to re-promote old "home-grown" conservative values as a counter-model. This is currently being practiced in China where Confucianism is being rediscovered and promoted as a basic moral tool in education, also by the Chinese government under Xi Jinping, in the hope that it will strengthen patriotism and fill a moral vacuum. During the Cultural Revolution under Mao Zedong, Confucianism was still attempted to be branded as old-fashioned ideological and eradicated (or at least marginalized). Only 10 years after Mao's death was this ban gradually loosened again, and under Xi Jinping a U-turn is being made and the system-stabilizing role of a home-grown Confucianist worldview positively emphasized.

6.3.1.5 Contact Change ((De-)Globalization) and Pandemics

Contact change occurs through strengthening or weakening of economic, political, social, and cultural interdependencies (integration). Transnationally, this is also referred to as globalization or, respectively, deglobalization.

A. Globalization: Exploiting the Advantages

All East Asian countries have benefited greatly from globalization (opening up). Without it, the convergence process would have been nowhere near as fast. China, in particular, is a major beneficiary of globalization. The challenge for the East Asian countries to continue to benefit from globalization is, on the one hand, to create favorable conditions for promoting the benefits of globalization, which are primarily the following: more efficient allocation of production factors, enabling specialization (division of labor); greater competition, resulting in improved product quality, price reductions and a greater variety of products; exchange of ideas and dissemination of technologies, resulting in technology transfers and increases in human capital quality; economies of scale and scope; possibility of smoothing consumer spending through (cross-border) borrowing; disciplining economic policy; and last but not least a greater convergence, reducing the poverty gap between rich and poor countries.

B. Globalization: Preventing and Combating the Disadvantages

A second challenge for the East Asian countries to continue to benefit from globalization is to minimize the negative side effects of globalization (through appropriate risk management) or to combat them efficiently (through good crisis management). These negative side effects of globalization include a tendency toward rising income and distribution inequality, global spillovers during crises, an increased danger of erratic price fluctuations, asset price bubbles, and financial crises. In addition, there is currently an increased danger of pandemics triggered by increasing transnational (private and corporate) contacts—tourist and business travel—in the course of globalization. Given the topicality of the latter danger, we will deal with this aspect in more detail in the next subsection as an example.

C. Example: Pandemics

The world is currently being hit by a severe pandemic. Pandemic describes the spread of an infectious disease without local restriction across continents and national borders. If the statements of many virologists and experts in the insurance industry are to be believed, such pandemics could become more frequent in the coming decades against the backdrop of advancing globalization and our modern lifestyle.[19] Preparing for this in good time is an important task and challenge for all countries, including those in East Asia. The question is: how will the countries deal with it? What distinguishes the East Asian countries in particular?

[19] The October 2020 report "Era of Pandemics" by the United Nations Intergovernmental Science-Policy Platform on Biodiversity and Ecosystem Services, authored by 22 experts from a variety of fields, says anthropogenic destruction of biodiversity is paving the way to the era of pandemics and could lead to as many as 850,000 viruses being transmitted from animals—particularly birds and mammals—to humans.

After the first year of the "Corona pandemic", one had the impression that the East Asian countries have handled the current pandemic better than the West (in terms of death toll as well as economic damage). Does this also apply to pandemics yet to come?

On the one hand, the experience with SARS, MERS, avian flu, and other previous disease outbreaks in Asian countries has meant that health systems were better prepared, and the population was more receptive to protective measures. Japan and South Korea have also been much more successful in protecting nursing homes and other facilities for the elderly. More important, however, have probably been characteristics, sometimes referred to as "East Asian virtues" found in East Asian countries, namely cultural-institutional factors such as (compared with the West) a greater patience, a greater (self-)discipline; greater acceptance of rules; lower time preferences (for companies, a longer planning horizon; in China, also for the government); a prioritization of the community of solidarity over individual well-being.[20] These prevailed in authoritarian systems as well as in democracies such as Taiwan, Japan, and South Korea. One commonality was also greater stamina in anti-corona measures until the virus is gone.[21]

Future pandemics will show whether this continues to be so positive in East Asian countries. This depends among others on what we discussed above under "Cultural Change".

The consensus view today is that countries that are better digitized will tend to be more able to control pandemics in the future. China and South Korea currently seem to have an advantage here, while Japan is more of a laggard in this area, especially in public digitization (see above in the section "Digital Change").

It currently appears that China will emerge stronger from the pandemic, while "the West" is weakened by identity crises and increasing state interventionism that could cripple the economy. This would mean that the Corona pandemic could possibly accelerate China's catching up (since China has come through the crisis better than the West so far).

But even China (and the other East Asian nations) will not emerge from the current and future pandemics without negative consequences.[22] The following threatens to occur during/after pandemics: (1) Firms may first be less profitable in a pandemic and respond by cutting fixed investment; (2) income distribution is likely

[20] This is also indicated by the fact that East Asian countries were not uniform in their pandemic control policies. For example, unlike most other East Asian nations, Japan did not adopt a "zero tolerance" policy (in the first year of the pandemic). Instead, the Japanese government focused on keeping the economy running as undisturbed as possible. Thus, there were never any harsh curfews or closures in Japan. What seems to have been more important there, as in other East Asian countries, was that citizens complied with government requests, such as wearing masks.

[21] In the absence of the above virtues of the East Asian countries, the Western countries had to rely to a greater extent on expansive financial compensation aid and stimulus programs, which, however, brought with it the problem of massively increased national debt.

[22] Here, one should also consider that the great caution/risk aversion shown during the pandemic up to now (with respect to contacts, restriction to international travel) that so far has been beneficial for the corona pandemic management might in the future constrain growth opportunities.

to worsen; (3) government intervention in the economy with excessive expansionary financial assistance will lead to a much larger share of zombie firms (and thus additional financial stability risks); and there could be (4) a prolonged loss of human capital due to educational gaps/lacks during the pandemic (response). Bold economic reforms are needed, but so are social reforms to offset this. One good(?) thing, on the other hand, will be that pandemic control will lead to faster digitalization of all areas of life and faster innovations.

D. **Preparing for Possible Deglobalization**

Contact change can also mean a *reduction* in contacts, in this case (in the transnational sphere) deglobalization. Deglobalization goes hand in hand with the danger of a resurgence of (more) protectionism, punitive sanctions, associated political destabilization, a decrease in convergence (reduction of the poverty gap between rich and poor countries) as well as a retraction of the benefits of globalization listed under A above. We have seen hints of such a deglobalization process in recent years under the US presidency of Donald Trump, which also has to do with the system competition described in Sect. 6.3.2.2 below. Currently, countries like China and Russia are reacting to this with the new strategy of "dual circulation", see Sects. 6.3.2.2 and 6.3.2.4.

Pandemics can also lead to calls for a reversal of globalization (contact change), especially a restriction of the global supply chain. However, this (and the associated disadvantages) can be partly offset by digital change (see Sect. 6.3.1.3), which enables economic interdependence (international trade, especially of services) even with reduced physical contacts (business travel) by means of new information and communication technologies. This could also help to limit climate change.

6.3.1.6 (Sectoral) Structural Change and Welfare System

The development into an upper-middle-income country and beyond (even more so if supported by globalization) is usually accompanied by increasing inequality of distribution. Therefore, the need to build/expand the welfare system arises (with a time lag) in order not to endanger social stability in the country. At present/in the near future, this applies above all to China, but earlier still to South Korea.[23] Even Japan has some catching up to do. This can lead to financial bottlenecks there, as the sectoral structural change toward tertiarization is generally associated with a decline in productivity growth and economic growth, and a country's financial leeway, therefore, becomes smaller.

The latter can be explained as follows:

(Sectoral) Structural change means the change in the dominance of sectors. Over time, the economy transitions from an agriculture-dominated economy to a manufacturing-dominated economy to a services-dominated economy (see van Neuss 2018). The transition from agriculture as the leading sector to manufacturing as the dominant sector is called "industrialization". The second transition from manufacturing as the dominant sector toward services as the leading sector is

[23] See the description of the Policy Initiatives of the Moon Jae-in Government in Sect. 6.2 above.

usually called "tertiarization" or deindustrialization. China still lags somewhat behind Japan and South Korea in this process of structural change (see Box 6.6 below).

There are at least three major explanations for this process for this structural change[24]:

- *High-income elasticity of services demand* that increases private demand for services in countries with rising income levels (see Kongsamut et al. 2001);
- *Sectoral differences* in total factor productivity (TFP) growth, factor intensity, and the elasticity of substitution between factors (see e.g. Baumol 1967; Ngai and Pissarides 2007; Acemoglu and Guerrieri 2008); and
- *Significant negative side-effects of industrialization* such as increasing income disequilibria and other undesired distortionary effects that cause governments to take countermeasures that favor tertiarization (see Wagner 2013, 2015 for details).

Regarding the second explanation, theoretical and empirical studies suggest that productivity growth in the service sector is lower than productivity growth in the manufacturing sector (Wagner 2013, 2015). One reason for this is "Baumol's cost disease", a phenomenon identified in the seminal studies of Baumol and Bowen (1965, 1966) and Baumol (1967). These studies, which show that wage increases generally outpace corresponding productivity increases in the service sector, conclude that overall productivity growth and overall economic growth eventually slow in a society with a growing service sector (tertiarization). China is currently experiencing such a structural change toward tertiarization and an implied growth slowdown associated with it.[25]

Regarding the third explanation:

There are costs of industrialization that, after a while, tend to induce governments to take measures favoring tertiarization[26]:

(1) In many emerging economies, the process of industrialization has tended to create increasing inequalities in income distribution, together with high macroeconomic imbalances and volatilities.[27]

[24] The following section closely builds upon Wagner (2019).

[25] In the current era of digital transformation and the "Industry 4.0" phase, tertiarization (compared to the past) need not (anymore) necessarily lead to a decline in productivity growth if a large part of tertiarization is based on B2B services (i.e. a combination of industrial and service elements). But the construction of a welfare system is more likely to be characterized by the expansion of services with traditional Baumol's cost disease, which are associated with below-average productivity gains (see also Murach and Wagner 2017).

[26] The following section closely builds upon Wagner (2013).

[27] See, e.g. Brenner et al. (1991, eds.). See also Steckel and Floud (1997), Szreter (1997), Kniivilä (2007), Rosenbloom and Stutes (2008) ZOECD (2021) Working age population (indicator), https://doi.org/10.1787/d339918b-en, and OECD (2012). Imbalances and volatilities here refer mainly to current account imbalances and "price imbalances and volatilities" incorporated in inflation episodes and asset-price booms and busts.

(2) These inequalities, imbalances, and volatilities have regularly led to complaints and revolts in the poorer part of the population, so endangering the legitimacy or acceptance of the economic and political systems (depending upon the conflict culture or mentality of a country or society). Therefore, to prevent further revolts and to stabilize their systems, governments eventually aim for a fairer distribution of income by introducing institutional reforms such as higher minimum wages, investment in a healthcare system and in social security, unemployment insurance, etc.
(3) These institutional reforms in the welfare system and social policy have strengthened the tertiary sector, in particular consumer services, in terms of catching up with corporate services because of rising incomes.

Although these measures to reduce the risk of social discontent (due to increasing distributional inequalities) apply not only to China but also to South Korea and are likely to increase the financial bottlenecks (increase in public debt) there as well, China is particularly affected in view of the still strongly underdeveloped welfare system in China. In other words, financing a welfare state in the face of declining growth is likely to further aggravate the debt problem (see subsection "Indebtedness" below) in China.

Last but not least, regarding China, it could be argued that the industrial sector may become less important (relative to the service sector) soon, since manufacturing offshoring (workbench) may not be attractive anymore for the industrial countries when wage—and other—costs continue to rise so much in China. At any rate, there is currently a tendency toward significant rise in wage costs in China, which reduces its attractiveness as an offshoring location. Against the backdrop of fierce locational competition in the context of globalization, this should reduce offshoring investments in China and thus the share of the industrial sector there.

The question is how fast the structural change process happens. At this point, one has to consider that a specific characteristic of today's world appears to be that, driven by intensified competition in the context of the globalization process, the stepwise transition from the dominance of one sector to the other occurs or has occurred faster than in earlier times. That is to say, the structural change tends to develop faster (toward tertiarization) in times of globalization.

Box 6.6 Sectoral Employment Shares

Table 6.4 depicts the sectoral employment shares in Japan (Panel A), South Korea (Panel B), and China (Panel C) for different time periods. In 1980, the service sector already accounted for the largest share of employment in **Japan** (53%), and until 2019, it further increased to above 70%. At the same time, the agricultural and industrial sectors have seen a declining trend, reaching 3% and 24% in 2019, respectively. In 2019, Japan and **South Korea** had a very similar employment structure with respect to the three broad sectors: Like in Japan, the service sector dominated the South Korean economy (with

Table 6.4 Sectoral employment shares, Japan, South Korea, and China (1980–2019)

	Agriculture	Industry	Services
Panel A: Japan			
1980	13.01	34.40	52.59
1990	8.79	33.79	57.42
2000	6.35	29.96	63.69
2010	4.91	23.80	71.29
2019	3.38	24.22	72.4
Panel B: South Korea			
1980	34.12	29.16	36.72
1990	18.06	35.73	46.21
2000	10.78	28.62	60.60
2010	6.90	26.52	66.58
2019	5.14	24.58	70.28
Panel C: China			
1980	68.75	18.19	13.06
1990	60.10	21.40	18.50
2000	50.00	22.50	27.50
2010	36.70	28.70	34.60
2019	25.33	27.42	47.25

Source ILO (2021) and World Bank (2021)

respect to employment). However, South Korea had accomplished this structural transformation in a shorter time span; in 1980, the service sector share was still 16% points lower than that of Japan, and the agricultural sector still accounted for around 34% of total employment. South Korea's industrial sector peaked at around 36% in 1990, a similar value that Japan had reached in the early 1970s.

China was still a predominantly agricultural society in the 1980s, with the share of the population employed in agriculture standing at almost 70%. Since then, both, the industrial and the service sector have recorded significant increases regarding the employment shares. In 2019, the service sector was the dominating one with 47% employment share (it had in fact already overtaken the industrial sector in the mid-1990s); however, with 25% and 27%, respectively, also the agricultural and industrial sectors still accounted for non-negligible employment shares in China. Especially from 2000 onwards, the industrial sector had seen strong increases. However, after reaching its peak at slightly above 30% in 2012, it reported, in general, a declining tendency while service sector growth accelerated.

6.3.1.7 Structural (System) Interdependencies

We have considered above:

(a) economic challenges (demographic change (6.3.1.1), globalization (6.3.1.5))
(b) environmental challenges (climate change (6.3.1.2))
(c) technological challenges (digital change (6.3.1.3))
(d) cultural challenges (cultural change (6.3.1.4), also by contact change (globalization, 6.3.1.5))
 Furthermore, in Sect. 6.3.2 we will still look at
(e) political challenges (system change (6.3.2.2)).

Now there are interrelationships (interdependencies) that need to be considered when dealing with/managing these challenges (see Stijepic and Wagner 2019; Wagner 2021).

It is important to recognize that the effects of policy responses to some of the challenges are interdependent. For example, progress in 6.3.1.3 digitization (in care; robotics) also determines success in dealing with (and the costs of) 6.3.1.1 population aging (which is a particular form of structural change). 6.3.1.2 climate change is itself a form of structural change in the ecological system. Mutual influences are for example: 6.3.1.1 population aging influences 6.3.1.2 climate change; 6.3.1.3 digital change influences 6.3.1.1 population aging. 6.3.1.3 digital change influences 6.3.1.2 climate change. 6.3.1.2 climate change is accelerating the breakthrough of 6.3.1.3 digitalization. 6.3.1.3 digital change is itself a type of structural change in the technological system (specifically, e.g. enforcement of digital currencies). This suggests that Structural Change is a kind of umbrella category.

The better 6.3.1.1 population aging is mastered (i.e. the less growth is lost as a result), the sooner/better the challenge of debt (6.3.2.1A) can be mastered (kept within bounds ("sustainable")).

The better 6.3.1.3 digitization is mastered, the lower the extent/costs of 6.3.1.2 climate change.

We leave it here with these short hints/comments.

6.3.2 Specific Current East Asian Challenges: Financial Crises, System Competition, and Strained International Relations

Box 6.7 Specific Current East Asian Challenges

6.3.2.1 Risk of Financial Crises

A. Indebtedness
B. Shadow Banking (Fintech Activities) and House Price Boom.

6.3.2.2 System Competition (*China–USA*)
6.3.2.3 Strained International Relations

A. Relations between the East Asian (EA) Countries
B. Relations between EA and other Countries
C. Relations South Korea–North Korea.

6.3.2.4 Avoiding the Disappointment of Expectations (raised by project announcements)
6.3.2.5 Reducing Inequalities/Ensuring Social Stability.

A. Rising Income and Wealth Inequality/Unequal Development
B. Rising Unemployment.

6.3.2.1 Risk of Financial Crises

A. **Indebtedness**

Even though the measures to combat the pandemic, as well as the aid measures for the economy and population, have increased government and private debt worldwide, the East Asian countries have currently escaped somewhat more lightly than others (Western countries) in this respect. However, the debt situation in the East Asian countries currently varies (see Box 6.8). While that in Japan has been extremely high for a long time, it has only risen rapidly in China in the last 12 years (after the Global Financial Crisis). By contrast, debt in South Korea is still comparatively low. Nevertheless, there is a concern in all East Asian countries, especially China, that they could suffer Japan's fate. After a furious growth and catch-up process, Japan suffered the bursting of an asset price bubble in 1990, as a result of which the country fell into two decades of stagnation and deflation, a situation from which it was unable to extricate itself even through ever greater expansionary debt-financed stimulus programs. Only in the course of the Abenomics, reform policy has there been some improvements, The high debt level (particularly government debt), the highest in the world among industrialized countries, has remained and threatend to grow even further as a result of the pandemic. At the same time, Japan started from a much lower level in the mid-1990s, which is comparable to that in China today (see the first figure in Box 6.8) or to that in South

Korea in a few years. This is a warning to the other East Asian countries that the debt situation can change very quickly if an asset price bubble or general financial instability is not counteracted in time.[28] The latter also explains the recent financial reform processes in South Korea and China discussed in Chaps. 3 and 4. Learning from Japan's mistakes is the motto there, especially with regard to avoiding a (burst of) bubble (as in Japan in the late 1980s).

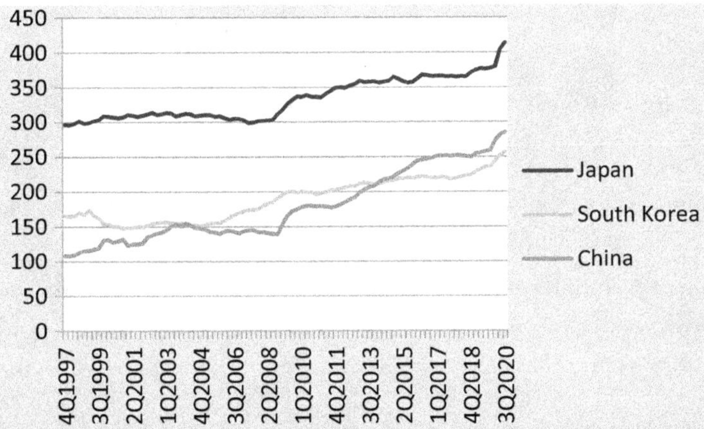

Credit to the non-financial sector (% of GDP). *Source* Bank of International Settlement (BIS) (2021). *Notes* All numbers are expressed as percentage of GDP (adjusted for breaks). Credit to the non-financial sector from all sectors at market value

Box 6.8 Debt in Japan, South Korea, and China

The top figure depicts the credit to the non-financial sector as a percentage of GDP. This indicator is often used to measure the country's debt. Japan has the largest credit-to-GDP ratio among the three East Asian countries. Between 1997 and 2007, the credit to the non-financial sector was relatively stable (fluctuating around 300% of GDP); however, after the Global Financial Crisis, it increased considerably, surpassing 400% in 2020. China has seen the sharpest surge/rise in the credit-to-GDP ratio between 1997 and 2020 (by more than 170% points), overtaking South Korea in 2013. The overall increase in South Korea has been relatively modest ("only" 87% points) compared with Japan and China.

Interestingly, the composition of the credit to the non-financial sector differs considerably across countries. The bottom figure illustrates Japan's,

[28] Debt will also rise (especially in China and South Korea) due to the need (there) to build up a welfare system or expand the existing one, which has been explained in the previous section "(Sectoral) Structural Change and Welfare System".

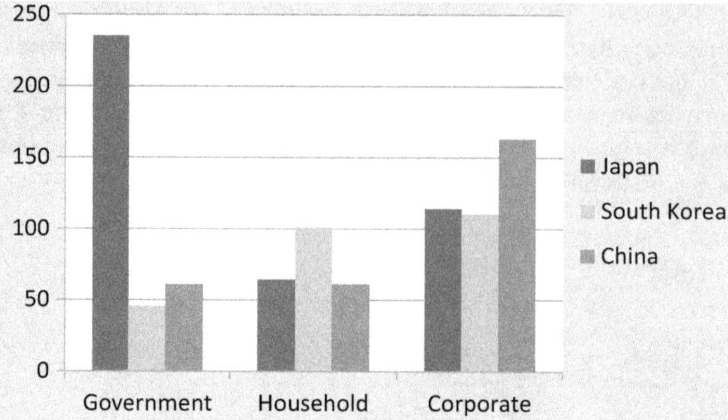

Credit to government, households, and non-financial corporations in 3Q2020 (% of GDP). *Source* Bank of International Settlement (BIS) (2021). *Notes* All numbers are expressed as percentage of GDP (adjusted for breaks). Credit to general government/households and non-profit institutions serving households (NPISHs)/non-financial corporations from all sectors at market value

Table 6.5 Credit to the general government, households, and corporations (% of GDP)

	Japan	South Korea	China
Panel A: Credit to general government			
31.12.1997	90.1	5.7	20.6
31.12.2005	147.3	18.8	26.4
31.12.2010	174.5	27.3	33.7
31.12.2015	205.4	38.0	41.7
30.09.2020	235.1	45.6	60.9
Panel B: Credit to households			
31.12.1997	69.3	49.9	
31.12.2005	60.5	63.5	11.5*
31.12.2010	61.3	73.2	27.3
31.12.2015	57.1	83.1	38.9
30.09.2020	64.3	101.1	61.1
Panel C: Credit to non-financial corporations			
31.12.1997	136.9	107.2	
31.12.2005	101.2	73.3	105.3*
31.12.2010	100.7	93.2	117.8
31.12.2015	94.9	97.8	158.5
30.09.2020	114.2	110.5	163.1

Source Bank of International Settlement (BIS) (2021)

Notes All numbers are expressed as percentage of GDP (adjusted for breaks). Credit to general government/households and non-profit institutions serving households (NPISHs)/non-financial corporations from all sectors at market value

South Korea's, and China's credit to the general government, to households, and to non-financial corporations (always as a share of GDP) in the third quarter of 2020. In addition, Table 6.5 provides an overview of the development of the different credit categories over time for all three countries. Most strikingly, the bottom figure reveals that Japan has a significantly higher government debt than South Korea and China (235% of GDP compared with 45.6% and 60.9%, respectively). South Korea records the highest household debt, and China has the highest corporate debt (all measured as credit-to-GDP ratios).

Now the financial markets seem to have become accustomed to the high "over-indebtedness" figures in Japan. In February 2019, for example, interest rates on 10-year Japanese government bonds fell below 0% and have been well below that since then, but this is no guarantee that this will remain the case. For example, there is currently a lively debate in monetary macroeconomics and monetary policy about whether interest rates might not rise sharply again in the medium term (see a new heavily discussed book by Goodhart and Pradhan (2020), which argues that inflation rates of 5–10% can be expected soon due to higher wages as a result of demographics (labor shortages occur in aging economies), deglobalization, and higher government spending. Consequently, the debt burden for many states would increase to an unbearable level, and they would then have to pay much higher interest rates on their debts again. This book is arguably very controversial at the moment. However, a new narrative seems to be gaining ground at the moment, which focuses on higher inflation and higher debt in the medium term. Counter-arguments include: Increasing precautionary saving (due to the pandemic as well as aging) should limit the risk of inflation. In addition, it is possible to grow out of debt: The debt only has to grow more slowly than the economy and (as a pre-condition) the interest rates (on debt) have to be lower than the growth rate of the economy. As for China, it can be argued that it is not very likely that, given China's high saving rate and current account surplus, the high debt ratio in China will end in a debt crisis there in the near future. However, with debt ratios currently above 270% (and rising)—in China and Japan—there is a risk of **zombification** of the economy (with more and more companies actually kept afloat only by state aid), which limits the performance of an economy and thus its growth opportunities, and thus makes it more difficult to grow out of debt as mentioned above.[29]

Moreover, as for Japan, it must be taken into account that Japan has so far benefited very much from the fact that a high share of its government debt is held in the form of low-yielding government bonds by the elderly population, who,

[29] According to calculations by the Bank of International Settlements (BIS), the proportion of zombie firms worldwide rose to 18% in the first year of the pandemic, the highest figure ever measured. (Before the crisis, it was 12%.) According to the authors of the BIS study, around 70% of the current zombies will remain so permanently, which the BIS attributes in part to low-interest rates. On this topic see also Banerjee and Hofmann (2020).

however, may have to sell more of their government bonds for consumption purposes in old age in order to supplement their meager pensions. On the other hand, the Japanese central bank has been holding more and more of these government bonds in its balance sheets in recent years, as well as more and more private debt securities.

B. Shadow Banking (Fintech Activities) and House Price Boom

Over the past years, East Asian countries, and China in particular, have been experimenting with market financing and private innovation, most notably in the fintech sector. Fintech companies have pioneered digital products that are used by large swathes of the population. However, the rapid growth, particularly in **shadow banking** (including fintechs) far outstripped regulatory capacity so the result of this was increased stock market volatility, fraud, massive profits, and colossal losses. According to figures from the Central Bank of China, as of December 2020, there were a total of 889 billion yuan (about 115 billion euros) in outstanding loans with microcredit firms. The fintechs cooperate with banks in granting these loans and secure only a fraction of the receivables themselves. This is making the government increasingly nervous, because there are risks lying dormant here that are almost impossible to control. New rules (stricter regulations) are therefore to apply soon.

The new stricter rules are to bring more stability back into the financial sector. The Chinese government has set several goals in this regard. First, it wants the shadow banks (fintechs etc.) to "return to its roots" (to focus on their core businesses). The state's second aim is to control data. China's digital companies have built some of the largest and most advanced databases in the world (mining everything from users' loan repayments to their friend networks, travel patterns, and spending habits).[30] The state's third objective is to play a more active role in fintechs. In this context, the central bank is testing a digital currency.

The second challenge in this context is the **booming housing sector** in China (see Rogoff and Yang 2020). The market value of the housing stock in China is more than double that of the USA, and more than triple that of Europe. This reminds of the Japanese housing bubble of the late 1980s and early 1990s, when the market value of real estate in Japan was also more than twice that of the USA compared with less than one-third the value today. The question arises: is there an oversupply in housing in China today?

Here, one has to take into account that house prices in China are high in large cities and low in small towns. The property sector makes up a quarter of China's GDP. In 2021, Chinese developers are on the hook for more than $100bn in bond

[30] So far, the state has refrained from explicitly ordering companies to share data (China's law states that personal data belongs to the individual). Changing this, however, should not be a major hurdle.

repayments, according to Moody. Moreover, one-third of Chinese homes are vacant.[31] As the "Economist" recently wrote (30 January 2021), housing investment equates to about a 10th of GDP annually, higher than the prodigious levels reached in Japan before its bubble popped three decades ago. Therefore, the Chinese government has pledged to develop what it calls "a long-term mechanism" for stabilizing prices and investment. Specifically, more and more rules are being imposed, lotteries are being held, and people are being barred from buying second homes resulting in obtaining fake divorces in order to buy another house. In the end, the key question is just how much scope there still is for China's housing stock to grow.

6.3.2.2 System Competition (China–USA)

China and the USA currently have a very special, tense relationship. China is in the process of challenging the USA as a hegemonic leader (the only dominant nation). Since 1945, the USA has been the undisputed number 1 in the world (militarily, politically, and economically).[32] China is now trying to become a second superpower. Propaganda speeches talking about the decline of the West and the rise of the East (China) and the "Great Rejuvenation of the Chinese nation" (Xi Jinping) currently dominate the Chinese political landscape. (Successive crises, from the financial crash of 2008 to the COVID-19 pandemic, have left Chinese leaders increasingly confident that their model of techno-authoritarian state capitalism is superior to the partisan squabbling, short-termism, and selfish individualism they see in the democratic West.) The USA is arming itself with defensive (boycott and sanctions) measures to prevent China from rising. China's response culminates in the announced strategy of "dual circulation" (see in more detail below).

This means, these sanctions and exclusions by the challenged nation(s) usually require the emerging country (the challenger) to try to become less technologically and economically dependent on the still leading country. This requires the challenger to build up its own technological know-how and to "breed" its own allies (allies, with whom a sufficiently large sales market is created together; in China's case, something like a "new Eastern bloc" together with Russia and the states along the Silk Road(s)—under China's leadership, of course).[33] This is also behind the newer Chinese projects like "New Silk Road"/"Belt and Road Initiative" (BRI), "Made in China 2025", "dual circulation strategy", "China Standards 2035".

The strategy of making oneself less dependent (of becoming independent) is known in China under the new term "dual circulation". **Dual Circulation** refers to the fact that China wants to strengthen its domestic market and its domestic companies. Instead of imported goods, China's consumers are to buy more domestic products, and supplies are to come from domestic companies instead of

[31] Nevertheless, according to official figures, real-estate loans still accounted for 26% of total new loans in China at the end of 2020. The number of unreported cases is estimated to be even higher.
[32] Only the USSR was at times a serious competitor in the military field.
[33] Russia, too, is currently going down the path of "decoupling" in order to better protect itself from the threat of sanctions by the USA (the West) for human rights violations and other things and is allying itself with China in the process.

foreign firms.[34] This implies domestic market and self-sufficiency in several important fields (especially the high-technology ones) to buffer uncertain global shocks.

The "Dual Circulation" plan puts pressure on Chinese companies and authorities to create conditions for faster implementation of innovations and for technological upgrades of manufactured products (to enable China to become technologically more independent as soon as possible).[35]

One should distinguish here between (a) struggle for supremacy between the USA and China and (b) clash of two value systems (liberal democracy versus authoritarian regime; where for the West it is also about fair competition, transparent conditions, (adherence to) international standards and legal security for private investors). For US allies, (b) is more likely to be the driving force for engaging in sanctions against the US challenger (China in this case).

A key challenge here is operating in a global system where national systems differ so much (as between China/Russia/ + and the USA/West/EU).

The **greatest danger** from the struggle for supremacy between the USA and China arises from (unintended) slipping into a war, as so often in history, when dominant powers/states felt challenged by "upstarts". This is explained in the historical literature under the term "**Thucydides Trap**".[36] The key difference between the past and the present is the type of weapons used (today more trade war and cyber war; although traditional military confrontations up to nuclear war are not excluded) and the more developed art of diplomacy in times of globalization.

Although meeting this challenge directly affects only a few (two) states, the impact (negative externalities) on other states is immense. (This also affects non-military disputes: Example: impact of the trade war between the USA (under President Trump) and China in recent years).

6.3.2.3 Strained International Relations

A. Relations between the East Asian (EA) Countries

The economic ties between Japan, South Korea, Taiwan, on the one hand, and China, on the other hand, have become very close; see the trade links: China's share of Japan's trade (export) volume is around 20% (in 2018), slightly more than America's 19% (in 2018); that of South Korea's trade (export) volume is 26% (in 2018), that of Taiwan's trade volume is 24% (in 2020). In this respect, Japan, South Korea as well as Taiwan are very interested in stable relations with China, which

[34] The latter somehow resembles the import substitution strategy in the earlier industrialization process.

[35] Not only China but also basically all highly developed countries—the USA, the EU countries, Great Britain, Japan, South Korea, and others—are currently trying to become more technologically independent by reforming the global supply chains, partly due to the observed problems in pandemic control.

[36] See Allison (2017).

does not exclude the possibility of recurrent tensions between the countries, based on past events (colonization experiences, China's claim to Taiwan as part of China; but also tensions in the context of the BRI project (accusations of overreaching by China)). But there are also tensions between Japan and South Korea due to acts of war committed in South Korea on the part of Japan (although the trade relationship between Japan and South Korea is also very close so that both would have much to lose by a reduction in political relations). These tensions have recently boiled up again from Japan's lingering anger over a South Korean court ruling that Japanese companies must compensate South Korean workers for forced labor during the war.[37] Japan rejects the ruling, arguing that the issue of reparations was resolved in 1965 when the two countries normalized relations.

On the tensions between Mainland China (PRC) and TAIWAN: Since the days of Deng Xiaoping, Chinese leaders have been binding Taiwan to the mainland economically. They have also tried to woo the Taiwanese public with promises of autonomy should they accept rule from Beijing, under the rubric of "one country, two systems". The latter, however, is for Taiwan no longer credible after the 2019/20 experience with Hong Kong. Moreover, China is apparently losing patience with "peaceful reunification". To that extent, this relationship is being watched closely by world opinion. There is fear of a violent annexation of Taiwan. Especially after the experience of the PRC's treatment of Hong Kong in 2020/21 and after relevant statements/threats by the Chinese government toward Taiwan, this fear has increased. This could lead to armed conflict, ultimately also between China and the USA, at least to an intensification of the "Cold War". A belligerent unification, i.e. a military incorporation of Taiwan, is currently only prevented by the threat of military protection/defense by the USA. A violent conquest of Taiwan by the PRC would destabilize the entire East Asian region and possibly even lead to armed conflicts between China and the USA. How Japan and South Korea would (or should) obsolesce in such a case is the question. China is quick to take punitive action against countries that criticize or even sanction it for human rights violations, for example, as recent years have shown. So Japan and South Korea have a lot to lose if they were to be dragged into such a conflict (pushed into it by the USA).

B. Relations between EA and other Countries

As described in the section "System Competition" above, **China** will have a very tense relationship with the USA in the coming years because China is the US's system rival and challenger (and thus potential adversary).

Japan and South Korea, on the other hand, are close US allies. This makes the situation in East Asia very special. Japan and South Korea might prefer to remain neutral, but this will be anything but easy in the coming years and decades. In this

[37] Historical background is Japan's occupation of the Korean Peninsula in the run-up to World War II. During that time, thousands of so-called comfort women were forced into sexual slavery and thousands more were forced to work without pay.

respect, great tensions and upheavals could come to Japan and South Korea in the economic relations/interdependencies with China.

Currently, dark clouds are already looming in the sky due to Japan's involvement in the revival of the US "quad" alliance with Japan, India, and Australia. This is part of the strategy of the new Biden administration in the USA to form democratic alliances (with Europe and Asian allies) to build pressure on China.

Countries in **Southeast Asia** are also concerned about China's rapid rise and power expansion ambitions (including in this area).[38] People throughout Southeast Asia already see America and China as two poles pulling their countries in opposite directions. This tug-of-war will only get sharper. First, Southeast Asia is of enormous strategic importance to China. While China is encircled to the east by Japan, South Korea, and Taiwan, all staunch US allies, Southeast Asia is less hostile terrain. Southeast Asia is home to 700 million people and growing rapidly. In this respect, it is an interesting market for China and its companies. However, Chinese companies in this area are often accused of corruption or environmental destruction. China is also accused of alienating its neighbors by throwing its weight around militarily. This kind of warmongering makes China unpopular in large parts of Southeast Asia. By contrast, Southeast Asians are more likely to trust Japan than any other foreign power, according to a survey by the Asean Studies Centre, a think-tank in Singapore (Seah et al. 2021). Japan also seems willing to take a stronger (leading or at least mediating) role in the region.

C. **Relations South Korea—North Korea**

The relationship between South and North Korea is also being closely followed by world opinion. Reunification along the lines of West–East Germany in 1990 (with a rebuilding of North Korea) would initially impose great financial burdens on South Korea and greatly increase financial instability (especially debt) there. In the medium to long term, however, such reunification could lead to a win–win situation for both Koreas and trigger an economic recovery process in South Korea as well. In addition, the politico-military situation would be greatly improved as tensions would be reduced.

6.3.2.4 Avoiding the Disappointment of Expectations (Raised by Project Announcements)

In all countries, politicians make great promises that cannot always all be kept and thus lead to disappointments in the expectations of citizens (and in democracies, voters). However, there is hardly a country that is currently setting up such eminently ambitious plans and projects as China. This has already been mentioned above in the section "System Competition". There are projects such as "Made in China 2025", the "New Silk Road" project, and the global claim to power (the

[38] But Australia, almost 40% of whose exports go to China, has also had increasing tensions with China recently (in the context of Huawei's exclusion from supplies for the 5G network, as well as Australia's withdrawal from the BRI project).

claim to economic and technological supremacy) that President Xi Jinping has repeatedly raised in recent years, with the time perspective extending to 2049. Therefore, the danger of disappointing expectations is very great, especially in China. The latter (a failure to deliver on promises and the resulting disappointment of expectations) would probably cost the Chinese Communist Party its supremacy if it cannot find/implement other substitute legitimations through new ideological and technological methods (see Wagner 2021).[39] Political purges of disloyal party cadres are also among the measures of stabilizing party supremacy.[40]

President Xi Jinping stated that China has entered a "new development stage", having achieved a first centennial goal of building a "moderately prosperous society". China's new goal is to be a "great modern socialist country" by 2049,[41] when the People's Republic turns 100. In plainer language, China wants to be a superpower of unchallenged strength and influence.

This is also expressed in the **14th five-year plan** (in 2021):

There it is promised that China will be a "mid-tier developed country" by 2035. The 14th five-year plan also includes numerous other goals such as:

- Increase in spending on research and development of at least 7% annually over the next 5 years.
- 65% of the population shall be urban by 2025, up from nearly 61% at the end of 2019.
- "Dual circulation strategy": requires China to remain part of the "international circulation" of global trade—the plan says it must defend its share of export markets. But it emphasizes improving of "domestic circulation"—that is, building of a vibrant economy at home while reducing dependence on others.
- Recognition of the need to relax *hukou* system (this shall be paired with a point-based arrangement that could make domestic migration easier, especially for young, educated workers).
- Calls for China to keep critical parts of supply chains (of manufacturing) in the country.
- Plans to nearly double the length of China's high-speed rail network to 70,000 km within 15 years.

[39] "The government under Xi Jinping presidency is trying to rely on additional, in part new, instruments for system stabilization. These include (i) the emphasis on nationalism (national sentiment), (ii) the One Belt One Road project with the aim of making China great again, and (iii) the widespread use of digital surveillance. If (as long as) the population accepts this, the government can maintain its course." (see Wagner 2021: 12; see there for more details).

[40] For example, on 27 February 2021, the Communist Party announced the start of a long-expected purge of its ranks. It will involve, say officials, "turning the knife-blade inwards" to gouge out those deemed corrupt or insufficiently loyal to the party and its leader, Xi Jinping. State-controlled media have described it as the biggest such campaign since the late 1990s within the domestic security system, which includes the police, the secret police, the judiciary, and prisons. It is due to last for about a year. The aim is to ensure that these agencies are "absolutely loyal, absolutely pure and absolutely reliable" ("Economist" March 2021).

[41] Official rhetoric still describes China's economy as "socialist" even though private business generates 80% of urban employment and 60% of GDP.

- Commitment to stabilizing or reducing the ratio of China's debt to GDP.
- Vows that the country will be carbon neutral by 2060. But the plan gives little indication of how this goal will be achieved, other than increasing nuclear power generation from 52 gigawatts today to 70 gigawatts by 2025. It promises to promote the "clean use of coal" and to reduce the amount of carbon dioxide emitted for each unit of GDP by 18% between 2021 and 2025.

China's goal/interest is apparently not to reach a top position in terms of average GDP/capita by 2049 (at least the government/party is cleverly holding back here, since otherwise expectations are built up that may later have to be disappointed; whereby disappointments in expectations are among the worst for the legitimacy of a political, social and economic system). The proclaimed goal is to be technologically and economically at the top in 2049, which is possible without a top place in GDP/capita due to the sheer dominance in the size of China (Xi Jinping often speaks only of the goal of making China a "moderately wealthy country" by 2049). This implies that one is also willing to accept that not all regions will become rich at the same time (which was already Deng's concession at the beginning of the reform in 1978).

However, fear of disappointing the population's expectations is not only present in China and poses a problem/challenge for the country but also in the other East Asian countries, especially for Japan. There, the issue is the promised/announced end of the two-decade "stagdeflation" period. This was arguably interrupted temporarily during Abe's second term; the only question is whether this is ongoing (now under Abe's successor/s).[42]

The danger of deflation has still not been completely averted in Japan (2% target not yet reached). Most importantly, the third pillar of Abenomics has not yet been (sufficiently) implemented, namely structural reforms.

However, the overarching goal common to all East Asian countries can be seen as the lasting overcoming of an MIT (in China) or an HIT (in Japan and South Korea); see in more detail below in Sect. 6.3.3.1 "Overcoming Risks of Stagnation".

6.3.2.5 Reducing Inequalities/Ensuring Social Stability

A. **Rising Income and Wealth Inequality/Unequal Development**

In the following, we address (in a more compact form) a few more challenges that affect many, also individual East Asian, countries (here, in particular, **China**).

From Table 6.6, one can observe a strong **discrepancy between East China and West/Central China** in terms of income growth in recent decades. The increased overall economic inequality in China is reflected in the so-called Gini index (see also Table 6.6). In addition, a North–South imbalance has also emerged

[42] Further appropriate structural remedies are listed in Yoshino and Taghizadeh-Hesary (2017).

Table 6.6 Economic inequality in China, various indicators

	Urban-to-rural income ratio	Net Gini Index	GDP p.c		
			East	Central	West
1985	1.86	28.1	1394	752	671
2000	2.79	38.6	13,548	6074	5411
2010	3.17	42.7	44,607	23,734	21,949
2018	2.69	40.9*	87,411	49,703	50,797

Source Urban-to-rural income ratio and Net Gini Index: OECD. (2019); GDP p.c.: NBS, own calculations
Notes GDP p.c. in constant 2010 yuan. * The Net Gini Index is for 2017 (due to data availability)

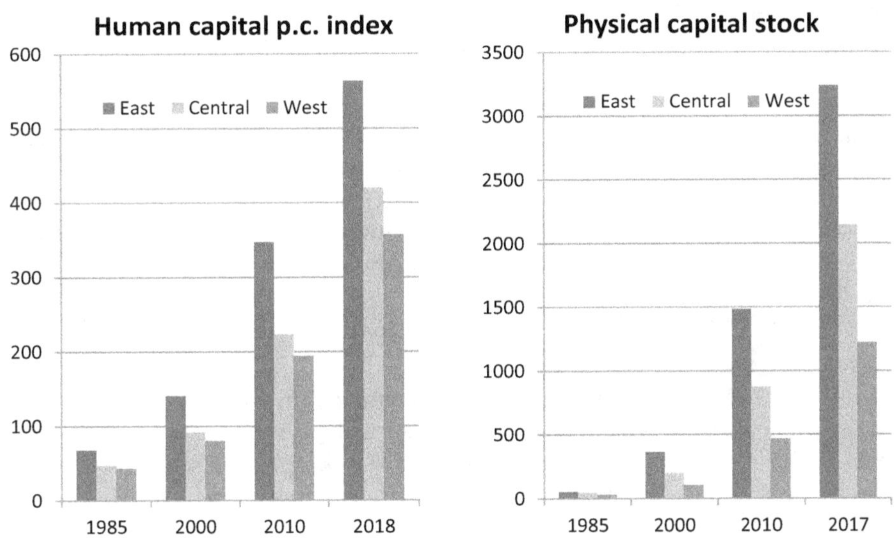

Fig. 6.1 "Wealth" inequality in China by region, 1985–2018. *Sources* Human capital index (per capita): CHRL Human Capital Project; Physical capital stock: Holz and Sun (2018). *Notes* Human capital (per capita) in constant 1985 yuan. Physical capital stock (in billion) in constant 1985 yuan

in recent years. On this **North–South imbalance**: The south's share of GDP has risen to a peak of 65%, from 59% in 2015. Some of it is down to luck. The north, home to China's largest coal mines and oil reserves, was caught out by falls in commodity prices after 2013. It also has large industrial firms; China's shift from construction-fueled growth toward consumption and services has hurt.[43] China's

[43] Nonetheless, China's share of global manufacturing is still close to 30% (27.74% in 2018)—about the same as the combined shares of Japan, South Korea, the USA, the UK, and Hong Kong (29.12% in 2018; without UK 27.31%; own calculations based on manufacturing value added in current US$; constant 2010 US$ data not available for China). However, China's focus on this sector, particularly on production of apparel, footwear, furniture, and related products, which peaked in the early 2010s, and its share in their global exports is now in decline.

two most dynamic regions are in the south, anchored by Shanghai and Shenzhen. The north has also been disrupted more by sporadic COVID-19 outbreaks. Geography is part of the problem: a harsh winter makes the virus more transmissible.

Last but not least, there is also a **discrepancy between urban and rural areas** in terms of living standard development (see Table 6.6). This is not least due to the fact that infrastructure provision is very unevenly distributed between urban and rural areas in China: this concerns the quality of institutions in general, as well as that of human capital and medical care in particular (the quality of health care is still poor in rural areas).

As depicted in Fig. 6.1, there is also a pronounced regional divergence with respect to wealth (here defined as physical and human capital). Eastern provinces that are usually more urban record on average a much higher per capita human capital and also have a considerably higher stock of physical capital.

One of the ways the Chinese government is currently responding to these inequalities is by moving labor-intensive factories from the densely populated and expensive coastal cities to the interior. (This mirrors the decentralization of manufacturing production in the USA and Europe that occurred after World War II, Hanson 2021.) However, this alone will not be enough unless the provision of infrastructure (including human capital and health care) in rural areas (especially in the central and western parts of China) is greatly improved.

B. **Rising Unemployment**

During the COVID-19 crisis, hundreds of thousands of small and medium-sized private companies in Japan, South Korea, and China went bankrupt. All three countries have experienced a pandemic-related shrinkage of the labor force, which may become permanent. Youth unemployment is a particular concern. Massive investments in digital infrastructure and "green" technologies are made with the aim of creating more well-paid jobs. However, the latter will not be realized so quickly given the skills mismatch between the workers who have been cut and the new workers needed.[44]

In China, the unemployment rate in July 2020 was arguably officially only 5.7%, which at first glance seems low and unproblematic. But the statistics are incomplete, as about 300 million migrant workers were not even included in the figure. More realistic estimates put the unemployment rate at 10% (Economist Intelligence Unit). This jeopardizes the silent agreement that China's population will largely

[44] In South Korea, the overall employment has started to recover from the pandemic and by March 2021, the country had again reached pre-pandemic unemployment levels. However, this recovery did not take place evenly across sectors. In particular, employment in many service occupations is still lagging behind (compared with the 2020 levels). Thus, the pandemic has, in general, aggravated the division between high-technology manufacturing, on the one hand, and low productivity services, on the other hand. In addition, even as overall employment has started to recuperate, youth unemployment has kept rising (reaching 10% in March 2021; cf. also the 1 May 2021 "Economist" article entitled "The pandemic has accentuated South Korea's two-speed economy").

endure the regime's repression as long as their wealth grows (this is a hallmark of modern autocracies, according to Guriev and Treisman 2019). The Chinese government is now trying to counteract this. Both university students and migrants are high-risk groups, but policy responses prioritize the former (Yue Sue of Economist Intelligence Unit). The government has recently proclaimed combating unemployment as the most important goal. Local governments created new opportunities for training, among other things. "Flexible employment" is what the government calls these measures. In contrast to many developed European countries, however, the unemployed in China receive virtually no financial assistance from the state. Migrant workers usually return to their villages and cultivate land there to make ends meet.

6.3.3 Specific Challenges in Individual East Asian Countries

Box 6.9 Specic Challenges in Individual East Asian Countries

6.3.3.1 Overcoming Risks of Stagnation

A. Overcoming an MIT (*China*)
B. Overcoming an HIT (*Japan*; *South Korea*)
C. Human Capital Weakness (*China*)
D. Resource scarcity.

6.3.3.1 Overcoming Risks of Stagnation

A. **Overcoming an MIT** *(China)*

The term middle-income trap (MIT)—introduced by Gill and Kharas (2007)—commonly refers to countries that have experienced rapid growth and thus quickly reached middle-income status; however, they then fail to overcome that income range to further catch up with the developed countries (Glawe and Wagner 2016). A distinction can be made here between absolute and relative MIT definitions. The former interprets the MIT as a prolonged growth slowdown, whereas the latter understands the MIT as a failed catching-up process. In many ways, the MIT concept can be regarded as an application of the convergence concept to a particular income group, the middle-income countries (Glawe and Wagner 2016). The MIT concept deals with the specific challenges and policy implications for this middle-income group: Today, many countries are confronted with the challenging middle-income transition, especially many (South-)East Asian and Latin American countries. Overall, more than 5.7 of the world's 7.7 billion people live in middle-income countries (in 2019, cf. World Bank 2021), and this country group is home to more than 60% of the world's poor population (World Bank 2020).[45]

China is a candidate for an MIT. The relevant literature studies on this come to a mixed picture as to China's chances of avoiding (overcoming) an MIT. Remaining trapped in an MIT is one of the greatest fears of the current government in China. Concepts such as "Made in China 2025" (see in Sects. 6.3.2.2 and 6.3.2.4) are strategies the government is using to try to avoid such an MIT. Glawe and Wagner (2020a) analyze under which conditions China could be caught in a middle-income trap by focusing on the empirical MIT definitions, and the MIT triggering factors identified in Glawe and Wagner (2016). Their analysis reveals that in most scenarios China enters the MIT only if the Chinese growth rate drops to the levels (3–4% p.a.) predicted by the most pessimistic growth projections in the literature. Regarding the MIT triggering factors, their main findings can be summarized as follows: China performs quite well with respect to its export performance; further improvements with respect to human capital accumulation and education as well as a mitigation of the widening (rural–urban) income inequality seem to be adequate measures for preventing an MIT in China. The picture is less clear regarding productivity because TFP data vary widely across studies.[46]

Furthermore, one can say: Only and above all by steadily creating both, new technological innovations (at the highest level) *and* institutional reforms, can an emerging country avoid getting stuck on an MIT path and become a high-income country (without the risk of backsliding).

B. **Overcoming an HIT** *(Japan; South Korea)*

A high-income trap (HIT) is when the convergence process in a country that has already overcome the MIT hurdle and has risen to become a rich country is interrupted and the country thus stagnates in its convergence efforts and does not continue to catch up, possibly even falling back somewhat compared to the richest (benchmark) country. A primary example of this is Japan in the 1990s and 2000s (when Japan stagnated for two decades ("two lost decades"); see Chap. 2 as well as in Sect. 6.1 of this chapter).

[45] Simultaneously, they are the major engines for global growth and constituted more than half of the global gross domestic product (GDP) in 2017. China—a potential future MIT candidate—alone produces 18% of the world GDP (WTO 2015). Thus, a slowdown in the emerging market economies will also have strong implications for the low-income and high-income countries. Therefore, the danger of the MIT is of great relevance for the future welfare of many people.

[46] China produces one in every five college graduates in the world. College admission in China is governed by a single exam—the national college entrance exam, and the government sets admission cutoff scores for elite colleges (see Jia and Li 2021).

South Korea could suffer a similar fate if it does not respond adequately to the challenges of the near future. Only and above all through the timely implementation of constantly necessary structural reforms (in line with the above types of structural change) can a country avoid an HIT in the long run.

Population aging and the corresponding rising share of the (unproductive part of the) service sector not only present increasing financial burdens for advanced countries but can also be unfavorable to the innovation mentality of a country (Wang 2018). In addition, emerging market economies can also become serious competitors to more advanced countries once they start moving up the value chain.

C. **Human Capital Weakness** *(China)*

China has invested huge amounts in physical infrastructure but somewhat neglected its human capital. The good-looking Chinese numbers/ratings in rankings such as PISA are not for the whole country. The children of rural migrants are barred from good schools (a main cause being the hukou system, see Chap. 4). Many of them are so-called "'left-behind' children" (children who have left behind in their home towns or villages by their parents working elsewhere).[47] Rozelle and Hell (2020) gave an IQ-like test and found that more than 50% of rural Chinese toddlers were cognitively delayed and unlikely to reach an IQ of 90. Half of rural babies are undernourished. Currently, 70% of the Chinese workforce is unskilled. To escape from "middle-income trap", China needs rapidly to improve its people's skills. Yet its workers are far less educated than those in other middle-income countries, such as Mexico, Turkey, and South Africa. Much of the blame for all this rests not only with Mao's Cultural Revolution[48] but also with an almost unbelievable oversight on the part of China's more recent leaders. Advice from Rozelle and Hell is: Spend a bit less on bridges and a bit more on its people's brains; improve rural schools, end discrimination against rural children, teach rural parents to read to their babies and so on. If not, predict mass unemployment, social unrest, and perhaps a crash (Rozelle and Hell 2020).

To overcome the human capital weakness, however, it is also necessary to improve the still underdeveloped health care system, especially in the rural regions of China.[49] Currently, fully 36% of spending on health care in China comes from patients, compared with 14% in the OECD. Moreover, medical scandals further undermine confidence; and China's doctors have long worried about violence (Chinese have a word for this: *yinao*, meaning "medical disturbance").[50]

[47] In a 2015 UNICEF report, the UN Children's Fund estimated that more than one in three children in China (or nearly 100 million) have experienced the prolonged absence of at least one parent.

[48] On Mao's original policy ideals, see e.g. Graham Hutching's book "China 1949" (Hutching 2021).

[49] China still has only two doctors per 1,000 people, compared with 3.5 on average across the OECD countries, and most are poorly paid.

[50] Much of the trouble originated in the 1980s, when the reform of the free, state-funded health care system began. Hospitals, lacking state funding, began to charge patients for treatment and often prescribed too many drugs. Many ordinary people were unable to pay. This created a "general feeling of distrust" towards the medical profession.

There is also a risk that China's distorted demographics will limit the size of the market and talent pool, hindering human capital accumulation (see Sect. 6.3.1.1).

D. **Resource Scarcity**

Resource scarcity is a serious constraint for all East Asian countries. As for **China**, which is already the world's largest energy consumer, its appetite for energy will only grow, and its energy imports are rising. In 2005, China's energy imports accounted for around 6% of the country's energy use; in 2014, this number had increased already to 15% (cf. World Bank 2021). **South Korea** has relatively few mineral resources within its borders, and the most important mineral reserves in the country include graphite, iron ore, coal, silver, gold, zinc, lead, and tungsten. All these minerals constitute approximately two-thirds of the total value of mineral resources in the country. In **Japan**, the amount of land suitable for agriculture is insufficient to produce enough food for Japan's large population (in 2018, the share of arable land in the total land area was only around 11%).[51] As a result, Japan imports most of its food from other countries. Moreover, Japan lacks many raw materials needed for industry and energy, such as oil, coal, iron ore, copper, aluminum, and wood.

For the next few years, commodity shortages are currently more likely (rising demand due to expansionary global demand policies meets supply shortages due to production cuts during the first phase of the pandemic and various other supply shocks). This is likely to be reflected in a rise in commodity prices and the cost of living index in general. (This is likely to be particularly problematic for some emerging and developing countries. For example, rising fuel and food prices could drive inflation there and also trigger social unrest in countries that rely on commodity imports, such as India.)

Currently, there is also a shortage of chips or semiconductors worldwide. On the one hand, this is due to temporary factors, such as reduced production capacities during the first COVID-19 wave and subsequent restart of demand/production as well as an increase related to the spread of telecommuting (working from home), which has fueled sales of consumer electronics. On the other hand, the chip shortage may not be a temporary phenomenon, but a longer-term one, as semiconductors play a more central role than ever in supply chains, e.g. cars/electric vehicles, consumer goods, information technology, and 5G-related sectors, as well as other megatrends that are changing consumer behavior. Incidentally, Asia is now the largest market for semiconductors in this regard, with China being the largest consumer.[52]

[51] In contrast, Germany reported a share of 36% and the UK of 25%. China's and South Korea's shares are slightly above Japan's 11% (13% and 14%, respectively) (cf. World Bank 2021).

[52] The level of self-sufficiency in semiconductors is currently 100% in Taiwan, 80% in Japan and South Korea respectively, and 60% in China (compared with only 50% in the USA), according to McKinsey (Handelsblatt 14.06.2021, p 20).

In the future, however, these resource scarcities may not be so important if, as a new study by McKinsey predicts, a large part of the economy's raw materials can be produced in the laboratory in the future (keyword in this context: an expected revolution in synthetic biology).

6.4 Who Will Be the Next China (Success Model Country) in Asia?

Here we can only speculate. We pick out two countries here from several promising candidates.

6.4.1 India

If we go by sheer size alone, the next China (success model) would have to be India, which will replace China as the world's largest country by population in the next few years.[53] And indeed, in view of rising tensions with China, the West is focusing on diversifying supply chains and production locations in Asia and sees India, which is roughly the same size as China in terms of population, as a promising alternative. However, India currently still suffers from the unpredictability of its economic policy. Although the Modi government has pushed ahead with important reforms to modernize and open up the Indian economy in recent years, potential investors often see India as an unstable and unpredictable market. A lack of reliability stands in the way of one of the main goals of Europe's and America's Asia policy. India's dealings with international partners, therefore, unsettle foreign investors. Five years ago, for example, India terminated bilateral investment protection agreements with 50 countries, including 23 EU states, with no replacements yet in place. The focus of Indian policy currently seems to be more on national politics and little willingness to compromise with international partners.[54]

Nonetheless, India is obviously being attractive for foreign investors, if only because of its market size, which requires early positioning to conquer. India is also rich in IT specialists; and its legal system is considered more reliable than China's. In addition, India's positive demographic trend (which offers a young and rapidly-growing labor force in the next decades) is one of its major advantages over the East Asian countries. Therefore, it is not surprising that while foreign direct

[53] In terms of economic size, India is projected by Bank of America to have the third largest GDP in the world as of 2030. However, this depends on how much India will still be affected by the current pandemic and its aftermath in the coming years.

[54] In its 2019 Country Report, in addition to a credible fiscal consolidation path (and other), the IMF furthermore urged "continued labor, product market, land, and other reforms aimed at increasing labor market flexibility, enhancing competition, and reducing the scope for corruption" (IMF 2019b: Executive Board Assessment).

investment plunged 42% worldwide last year (2020), it grew 13% in India despite the Corona crisis—more than in any other major economy, according to the UN Conference on Trade and Development (UNCTAD). By comparison, foreign investment in China grew by 4%.

As far as India is concerned, the question arises, which we do not want to and cannot answer conclusively here, whether the mixture of democracy, federalism, and cultural fragmentation (caste system) at such an early stage of development, in which India still finds itself, does not have a destabilizing effect and hinders/slows down the catching-up process (compared with China). On the other hand, there is some evidence to suggest that at a later stage of development, it might have a positive effect on creativity, innovative capacity, and thus on India's development/catching-up process.

6.4.2 Vietnam

When it comes to a country's growth momentum and political stability, other Asian countries have the edge over India. Vietnam, for example, has developed into a middle-income manufacturing powerhouse in recent years. The authorities have staked their legitimacy on rising incomes while also accepting that the upswing/convergence in Vietnam comes at the cost of rising inequality.

A recent Economist Intelligence Unit study lists the following strengths and weaknesses of Vietnam (excerpted from the "Economist", February 6, 2021):

- Low-skilled manufacturing wages will continue to be competitive for the following years, while scarcity of specialized labor (lack of skilled labor) will persist as a disadvantage of business environment.
- Regarding investment incentives, Vietnam will go on to offer generous arrangements for international firms. Following China's example, it has incentivized FDI into specific sectors through industrial zones (which include industrial parks and export-processing zones), special economic zones, and technology parks. Eligible FDIs can profit from corporate and personal income tax exemption and rate reduction. So far only a few manufacturing industries have developed into large clusters and some are yet to profit from increasing economies of scale (Vietnam lags behind the domestic capabilities of middle-income economies such as Malaysia and Thailand until at least later this decade; a big concern for business will be increasing land prices).
- Vietnam's proliferating membership of free trade agreements confers an advantage for its trade relations, lowering export costs.
- Among other aspects, the country's internal political stability in recent decades is appealing to investors. This is in contrast with many of Vietnam's regional neighbors, which have suffered policymaking instability and intermittent breakdowns in relations with major countries. This does not mean that Vietnam is without major hindrances to doing business—among others, corruption among public officials is still a major problem.

– The economy moves up rapidly the value chain. In fact, the economy is at an initial stage in its industrial development (with only a small amount of skilled labor).

The communist party of Vietnam has tended to disapprove of the kind of personal power that Xi Jinping has gathered next door in China. Rather, authority is spread among the four "pillars" of the government: the general secretary of the party, the prime minister, the president, and the speaker of the national assembly. In any case, Vietnam's leadership is very authoritarian so that the communist party's intolerance of dissent will continue (seen as necessary to keep the country on course). That this need not be an obstacle for foreign investors has been shown by China's history over the last 40 years.

Last but not least, Vietnam's age structure is also very important for its future growth prospects. Vietnam is a country of 96 million, more than half of whom are under the age of 35. This highlights a key difference with Japan, South Korea, and China and is an advantage of Vietnam for the future.

Appendix

See Table 6.7.

Table 6.7 GDP per capita relative to the USA and UK, various databases

	Relative to the USA	Relative to the UK
	>50% (>90%) [>100%]	>50% (>90%) [>100%]
Panel A: World Bank WDI constant 2010 US$		
Japan	1961 (1980) [1988]	<1960 (1967) [1968]
South Korea	2016 (-) [-] 2019: 51%	2007 (-) [-] 2019: 66%
China	- (-) [-] 2019: 15%	- (-) [-] 2019: 19%
Panel B: PWT Version 10 expenditure side at chained PPPs 2017 US$		
Japan	1969 (-) [-] 2019: 63%	1962 (1972) [1977–78; 1989–2002] *since 2015 <90% 2019: 86%
South Korea	1995 (-) [-] 2019: 64%	1990 (-) [-] 2019: 88%
China	- (-) [-] 2019: 22%	- (-) [-] 2019: 30%
Panel C: Maddison (2013) (GK$) extended by IMF growth rates (as in Felipe et al.) 2012		
Japan	1968 (-) [-] 2019: 69%	1962 (1970) [1980–1998] *GFC < 90% 2019: 95%
South Korea	1996 (-) [-] 2019: 77%	1990 (2010) [2018]
China	- (-) [-] 2019: 41%	- (-) [-] 2019: 55%

Notes GK$ stands for Geary-Khamis-Dollar (international Dollar). GFC stands for Global Financial Crisis

References

Acemoglu D, Guerrieri V (2008) Capital deepening and nonbalanced economic growth. J Polit Econ 116(3):467–498

Acemoglu D, Johnson S, Robinson JA (2001) The colonial origins of comparative advantage. Am Econ Rev 91:1369–1401

Acemoglu D, Restrepo P (2017) Secular stagnation? The effect of aging on economic growth in the age of automation. Am Econ Rev 107(5):174–179

ADB (2020) Asia's journey to prosperity: policy, market, and technology over 50 years. Asian Development Bank (ADB), Manila

Akamatsu K (1962) A historical pattern of economic growth in developing countries. Dev Econ 1:3–25

Allison G (2017) Destined for war: can America and China escape Thucydides's trap? Houghton Mifflin Harcourt, New York

Banerjee R, Hofmann B (2020) Corporate zombies: anatomy and life cycle. BIS working papers no 882. Bank for International Settlements, Basel

Bank of International Settlements (BIS) (2021) Credit to the non-financial sector dataset, Update 1 March 2021. https://www.bis.org/statistics/totcredit.htm

Barro R, Lee J-W (2013) A new data set of educational attainment in the world, 1950-2010. Journal of Development Economics 104:184–198

Baumol WJ (1967) Macroeconomics and unbalanced growth: the anatomy of urban cities. Am Econ Rev 57(3):415–426

Baumol WJ, Bowen WG (1965) On the performing arts: the anatomy of their economic problems. Am Econ Rev 55(1/2):495–502

Baumol WJ, Bowen WG (1966) On the performing arts, the economic dilemma: a study of problems common to theater, opera, music, and dance. Twentieth Century Fund, New York

Bolt J, van Zanden JL (2014) The Maddison Project: collaborative research on historical national accounts. The Economic History Review 67(3):627–651

Brenner YS, Kaelble H, Thomas M (eds) (1991) Income distribution in historical perspective. Cambridge University Press, Cambridge

Denton FT, Spencer BG (2000) Population aging and its economic costs: a survey of the issues and evidence. Canad J Aging 19(S1):1–31

Feenstra RC, Inklaar R, Timmer MP (2015) The next generation of the Penn World table. Am Econ Rev 105(10):3150–3182. Available for download at https://www.ggdc.net/pwt

Felipe J, Abdon A, Kumar U (2012) Tracking the middle-income trap: what is it, who is in it,and why? Levy Economics Institute of Bard College, Working Paper No. 715.

Gill I, Kharas H (2007) An East Asian renaissance—ideas for economic growth. World Bank, Washington, DC

Glawe L, Wagner H (2016) The middle-income trap—definitions, theories and countries concerned: a literature survey. Comp Econ Stud 58:507–538

Glawe, L, Wagner H (2019) Schooling is not learning—the impact of the learning-adjusted years of schooling on growth in a dynamic panel data framework. SSRN working paper no 3640242, forthcoming 2022 in World Development

Glawe L, Wagner H (2020a) China in the middle-income trap? China Econ Rev 60:101264 (2020). https://doi.org/10.1016/j.chieco.2019.01.003

Glawe L, Wagner H (2020b) The middle-income trap 2.0: the increasing role of human capital in the age of automation and implications for developing Asia. Asian Econ Pap 19(3):40–58

Goodhart C, Pradhan M (2020) The great demographic reversal—ageing societies, waning inequality, and an inflation revival. Palgrave Macmillan, Cham

Greenstone M, He G, Li S, Zou E (2021) China's war on pollution: evidence from the first five years. NBER WP 28467

Guriev S, Treisman D (2019) Informational autocrats. J Econ Perspect 33(4):100–127
Hanson GH (2021) Who will fill China's shoes? The global evolution of labor-intensive manufacturing. East Asian Econ Rev 24(4):313–336
Holz CA, Sun Y (2018) Physical capital estimates for China's provinces, 1952–2015 and beyond. China Economic 51(C):342–357
Hutching G (2021) China 1949: year of revolution. Bloomsbury Academic
Harney A (2013) Japan's Silver Democracy: the costs of letting the elderly rule politics. Foreign Affairs, July 18, 2013
Hsu S (2016) Economic reform in Asia—China, India, and Japan. Edward Elgar, Cheltenham, UK
IMF (2017) Japan: selected issues. IMF country report no. 17/243. July 2017. International Monetary Fund, Washington, DC
IMF (2018) Republic of Korea: 2017 Article IV Consultation. February 2018. International Monetary Fund, Washington, DC
IMF (2019a) Republic of Korea: staff report for the 2019 Article IV Consultation. April 22, 2019. International Monetary Fund, Washington, DC
IMF (2019b) India: 2019 Article IV Consultation. December 2019. International Monetary Fund, Washington, DC
IMF (2020) People's Republic of China: staff report for the 2020 Article IV Consultation. December 2, 2020. International Monetary Fund, Washington, DC
IMF (2021) People's Republic of China: 2020 Article IV Consultation-press release; staff report; and statement by the executive director for the People's Republic of China. January 8, 2021. International Monetary Fund, Washington, DC
Jia R, Li H (2021) Just above the exam cutoff score: elite college admission and wages in China. NBER working paper no. 28450, February
Jones CI (2020) The end of economic growth? Unintended consequences of a declining population. NBER working paper no. 26651
Kingston J (2004) Japan's quiet transformation: social change and civil society in the twenty-first century. RoutledgeCurzon, New York
Kniivilä M (2007) Industrial development and economic growth: Implications for poverty reduction and income inequality. In: Industrial development for the 21st century: sustainable development perspectives. United Nations, Department of Economic and Social Affairs, New York
Kongsamut P, Rebelo S, Xie D (2001) Beyond balanced growth. Rev Econ Stud 68(4):869–882
Korinek A, Stiglitz JE (2021) Artificial intelligence, globalization, and strategies for economic development. NBER working paper 28453
Krugman P (2021) Wonking out: economic nationalism, Biden-style. New York Times, 11 June 2021. https://www.nytimes.com/2021/06/11/opinion/economic-nationalism-biden-trump-trade.html.
Moestl B (2012) Shaolin. Knaur-Verlag, München
Murach M, Wagner H (2017) How severe will the growth slowdown in China caused by the structural change be? An evaluation based on experiences from Japan and South Korea. J Chin Econ Busin Stud 15(3):269–287
Nagarajan R, Teixxeira AAC, Silva S (2015) The impact of population ageing on economic growth: a bibliometric survey. Singapore Econ Rev 62(02):1550068
Ngai LR, Pissarides CA (2007) Structural change in a multisector model of growth. Am Econ Rev 97(1):429–443
Nordhaus W (2015) Are we approaching an economic singularity? Information technology and the future of economic growth. NBER working paper no. 21547
OECD (1996) Aging in OECD countries: a critical policy challenge. Social policy studies no. 20
OECD (2012) The product space and the middle-income trap: comparing Asian and Latin American experiences (by Jankowska A et al). OECD Development Centre working paper no. 311. OECD, Paris

OECD (2021) Working age population (indicator), https://doi.org/10.1787/d339918b-en
OECD (2019) Economic surveys: China 2019. OECD, Paris
Persson T, Tabellini G (2020) Culture, institutions and policy. CEPR discussion paper no. DP15233. Forthcoming in: Bisin A, Federico G (eds) The handbook of historical economics
Reischauer EO (1974) The Sinic world in perspective. Fore Affairs 52.2 (January): 341–348.
Riley JC (2005) Estimates of regional and global life expectancy, 1800–2001. Population and Development Review 31(3):537–543
Rogoff KS, Yang (2020) Peak China housing. NBER WP 27697
Rosenbloom JL, Stutes GW (2008) Reexamining the distribution of wealth in 1870. In: Rosenbloom J (ed) Quantitative economic history (Routledge explorations in economic history). Routledge
Rozelle S, Hell N (2020) Invisible China: how the urban-rural divide threatens China's rise. University of Chicago Press, Chicago
Seah S et al (2021) The state of Southeast Asia: 2021. ISEAS-Yusof Ishak Institute, Singapore
Sota K (2018) The demographic issue and silver democracy. In: Funabashi Y (ed) Japan's population implosion. Palgrave Macmillan, Singapore, pp 131–153
Steckel RH, Floud R (1997) Health and welfare during industrialization. University of Chicago Press, Chicago and London
Stijepic D, Wagner H (2019) A system-theoretical discussion of the (non-) sustainability of development strategies. SSRN-paper 3317576. https://doi.org/10.2139/ssrn.3317576
Szreter S (1997) Economic growth, disruption, deprivation, disease, and death: on the importance of the politics of public health for development. Popul Dev Rev 23(4):693–728
Teranishi J (2020) Culture and institutions in the economic growth of Japan. Studies in economic history. Tokyo, Springer Japan
United Nations (2017) World population ageing 2017—highlights (ST/ESA/SER.A/397). Department of Economic and Social Affairs, Population Division
UN Population Division (2019) World Population Prospects 2019. https://population.un.org/wpp/DataQuery/
Van Neuss L (2018) The drivers of structural change. J Econ Surveys 33(1):309–349
Wagner H (2013) Challenges to China's policy: structural change. Comp Econ Stud 55:721–736
Wagner H (2017) The building up of new imbalances in China: the dilemma with 'rebalancing'. Int Econ Econ Policy 14(4):701–722
Wagner H (2019) Structural change, rebalancing, and the danger of a middle income trap in China. Int J China Stud 10(1):1–25 (2019)
Wagner H (2021) China's "political-economy trilemma": (how) can it be solved? Chin Econ 54 (5):311–329. https://doi.org/10.1080/10971475.2021.1875158
Wang M (2018) Causes of "high income trap" in developed countries and coping strategies. Asian Agric Res 10(5):10–14
Wagner H (2019) Structural change, rebalancing, and the danger of a middle income trap in China. International Journal of China Studies 10(1):1–25
Westerman G, Bonnet D, McAfee A (2014) Leading digital: turning technology into business transformation. Harvard Business Review Press, Boston, MA
World Bank (2020) The World Bank in middle-income countries: overview. The World Bank, Washington, DC. https://www.worldbank.org/en/country/mic/overview
World Bank (2021) World development indicators. The World Bank, Washington, DC. https://data.worldbank.org/products/wdi
World Trade Organization (WTO) (2015) International trade statistics 2015. World Trade Organization, Geneva
Yeung W-JJ, Lee Y (2021) Aging in East Asia: new findings on retirement, health, and well-being. J Gerontol Series B. https://doi.org/10.1093/geronb/gbab055
Yoshino N, Taghizadeh-Hesary F (2017) Japan's lost decade: lessons for Asian economies. Tokyo, Springer Japan

Zheng B et al (2019) China pension actuarial report 2019–2050 (中国养老金精算报告 2019–2050. China Social Security Press, Beijing (中国劳动社会保障出版社)

ZOECD (2021)Working age population (indicator), https://doi.org/10.1787/d339918b-en

Zijdeman R, Ribeira da Silva F (2015) Life expectancy at birth (total). https://hdl.handle.net/10622/LKYT53, IISH Data Collection, V1

Conclusions

7

East Asia's fabulous economic catch-up process since the middle of the last century is still a mystery or even a miracle for many. This book attempted to shed more light on this and the background of this development.

As late as the 1950s, Asia (together with Africa) was the poorhouse of the world (see Table 7.1). An exception was Japan, which had already developed into a major economic and military power since the end of the nineteenth century but had fallen behind in its level of development for a longer period of time due to the participation and defeat in World War II.

Accordingly, since the 1950s, the world has been dominated by the West (led by the USA), especially economically, and also in international organizations (such as the IMF, the World Bank, the UN). At least until the 1980s, the USSR still formed a military and political counterweight as the leader of the so-called "Eastern Bloc" (characterized by the institutions of the planned economy and communist rule), but from the end of the 1980s, this Eastern Bloc crumbled and with it the counter-model to the West (i.e. to market economy and democracy).

The East Asian countries were not all part of the same bloc: Japan, South Korea, Taiwan, and Hong Kong were allies of the West, while China, Vietnam, and others (to some extent also India)[1] had turned more toward the Eastern bloc.

With the help of the West/USA, first Japan, then (besides Singapore) Hong Kong and Taiwan, and finally South Korea developed into a developed (rich) country. China began its catching-up process later, through partial and gradual disengagement from the so-called former Eastern bloc model. At present, China is

[1] At least, during the Cold War, India and the Soviet Union (USSR) had a strong strategic, military, economic, and diplomatic relationship.

L. Glawe and H. Wagner, *The Economic Rise of East Asia*,
Contributions to Economics, https://doi.org/10.1007/978-3-030-87128-4_7

Table 7.1 GDP p.c. across regions (unweighted averages)

	Western Europe	Eastern Europe	Latin America	East Asia*	East Asia (excl. JPN)	South and South East Asia	Sub-Saharan Africa
1820	2307	818	953	1023	949	929	800
1900	4724	2700	1751	1527	1378	994	850
1950	7263	4082	3713	2080	**1835**	**1070**	**1323**
1970	16,161	8241	6286	6630	4417	1546	1958
1980	20,950	9933	8728	10,974	8366	1897	2026
1990	25,440	10,344	8132	18,121	15,164	2574	1801
2000	32,536	8986	10,225	24,146	21,880	3437	1981
2010	37,318	17,021	13,453	31,353	30,438	5367	3156
2017	39,257	20,116	14,087	36,333	35,812	7306	3524

Source Maddison Database 2020, Bolt and van Zanden (2020)
Notes GDP per capita adjusted for price changes over time (inflation) and price differences between countries (measured in international-$ in 2011 prices). "*" Japan, South Korea, China, Hong Kong, and Taiwan. East Asia (excluding JPN): South Korea, China, Hong Kong, and Taiwan

still on its way to becoming a developed, rich country. That is, strictly speaking, China is still in transition with an uncertain outcome.

The most significant aspect of the East Asian success story has been the economic recovery or catching-up process, especially of the larger East Asian countries. We have analyzed this process in more detail here in the book in the three larger (and therefore most important in global economic terms) countries—Japan, South Korea, and China. Their combined share of world (merchandise) trade was still 2.4% in 1950 (5.3% in 1960), and then rose to 19.5% by 2020 (WTO 2021).

China (the largest country in the world in terms of population) has a special position among the three: it developed last, is still a non-democratic (authoritarian) country with a one-party rule of the CPC and with strong interventions in the economy; and it is striving and on its way to become the challenger of the USA as the leading world power (leader of a "new Eastern bloc"). Last but not least, the East Asian countries (except Japan) are also claiming ever greater rights of co-determination and influence in international organizations.

Now, almost all emerging countries have grown more strongly than the already developed industrialized countries in the last 30 years, in the course of globalization and the dismantling of trade barriers that became possible after the collapse of the Eastern bloc. Only the East Asian countries (without Japan) have been particularly successful here. They grew earlier and on average more than comparable countries in other regions/continents (see Fig. 7.1 and Table 7.1); Japan stagnated for a longer period of time during the past 30 years but had developed more dynamically than the others in the 40 years before that.

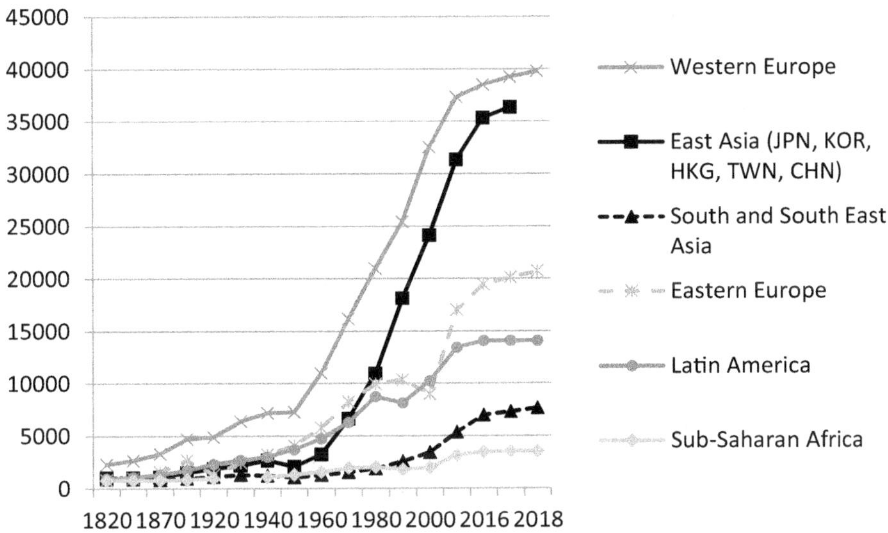

Fig. 7.1 GDP p.c. across regions. *Source* Maddison Database 2020, Bolt and van Zanden (2020). *Notes* GDP per capita adjusted for price changes over time (inflation) and price differences between countries (measured in international-$ in 2011 prices). East Asia here includes Japan, South Korea, Hong Kong, Taiwan, and China

In the book, we also looked into commonalities among East Asian countries in terms of the causes and drivers of their successes. In doing so, we asked whether there was something like a unified "East Asian development model", a kind of "East Asian secret of success" that developing and emerging countries elsewhere could also use today to overcome the low and middle-income traps and rise to become a rich industrialized country. To this end, in Chaps. 2, 3 and 4, we examined in detail the development paths and strategies of the three major East Asian countries (Japan, South Korea, and China), and in Chap. 5, we identified not only similarities but also differences. We discovered significant commonalities in that all three countries experienced astonishing GDP growth, which enabled them to join the group of advanced countries (in the case of Japan and South Korea) or respectively to attain middle-income status (in the case of China) in a considerably short amount of time. This was among others achieved through an export-oriented development model as well as high savings and investment rates. Moreover, Japan, South Korea, and China all shared similar institutional-cultural characteristics (at least compared with Western countries) and had relatively homogeneous populations. In addition, they all had (and partly still have) rather authoritarian governments.

The commonalities also include: often strong state intervention in the economic process (along the lines of Keynesian stimulus policies) and in structural conditions (through industrial policy in a general sense, but also through rigid socio-cultural integration of individuals through group norms). Both may be conducive to the first stages of development in the development process (to overcome the middle-income trap: MIT), but they tend to hinder the last stage of development (avoidance of a high-income trap: HIT; due to a lack of flexibility and creativity).

Nevertheless, it is not easy to speak of an East Asian model of development, as there have also been significant differences between the countries, especially the three countries examined in more detail here. These include, in particular, the following ones: Their initial development levels after World War II (with respect to GDP per capita but also regarding the human capital endowment and structural transformation) differed considerably. In particular, Japan was much more developed than South Korea and China, partly because it had already undergone a first wave of industrialization during the Meiji period. Another apparent difference concerns the country size. While South Korea is a relatively small state (in terms of population and area), China is one of the largest countries (the largest by population) in the world. This implies that China also has a much larger domestic market and consequently more bargaining power vis-à-vis foreign investors. The varying political systems present another striking difference: While Japan and South Korea are both democracies, China still has an authoritarian political system controlled by the CPC. However, we can also identify differences between Japan and South Korea (even though they are of course less pronounced than those between Japan/South Korea and China). Examples include the democratization process (top-down versus bottom-up), government-opposition power shifts, and the timing of democratization (prior versus after the economic take-off). Also regarding cultural aspects, some differences do exist between the three countries, even though the latter appears to be culturally rather homogenous when compared with Western countries. With respect to the economic/industrial structures, South Korea and Japan both relied on conglomerates to achieve the coordinated development of firms in diverse industries (also with the help of industrial policy), while no such business groups existed in China.[2] Moreover, industrial policy in China was usually formulated less concretely compared with that of Japan and South Korea. Finally, Japan, South Korea, and China also had different strategies with regard to the adoption of foreign technologies. While the former two countries relied primarily on reverse engineering, China focused predominantly on fostering FDI in order to generate knowledge spillovers.

Overall, there indeed exist considerable differences between the three countries. On average, the differences between Japan and South Korea, on the one hand, and China, on the other hand, appear to have been more pronounced than that between Japan and South Korea; however, this has not necessarily always been the case (e.g. with respect to the initial conditions).

China here can be regarded as an example of how state-enforced structures (such as the imposed one-child policy; through authoritarian steering structures and

[2] However, the institutional legacy of the township and village enterprises (TVEs) enabled clusters of abundant small private firms managed by Township governments, which somehow resemble the conglomerate structures.

sanctions for non-compliance) can promote development for a long time (in the first stages of development), and thus possibly overcome MIT first or at least more quickly; at the cost, however, of possibly getting stuck in a HIT in the last stage of development (lack of flexibility and creativity).

In Chap. 6, we then asked ourselves where the East Asian countries stand today (compared with Western benchmark countries like the USA and Great Britain), how much they have caught up in which areas. Furthermore, we looked there at the particular challenges facing the three countries this decade and in the next two decades, distinguishing between common ones and different/country-specific ones. The common ones include: dealing with (managing) the demographic, climate, digital and cultural changes, as well as future pandemics and (de-)globalization. The country-specific challenges, on the other hand, include: dealing with rising indebtedness, financial instability (shadow banking), the system competition (between China and the USA/West), the arousal of excessive expectations and attitudes of entitlement, and a necessary expansion of the welfare system. Here, a further distinction can be made between challenges, the overcoming of which also strongly affects the other countries and those challenges that are likely to remain more limited to the individual countries.

Finally, at the end of Chap. 6, we asked who could become the next China (success story) in Asia (perhaps Vietnam as an authoritarian regime, or India as a democratically constituted, yet diverse, huge empire in terms of population).

JAPAN, as explained in more detail in the book, was the first East Asian country to succeed in catching up, thanks to a better starting position. That is, compared with the others, Japan was the first and most advanced in development. On the other hand, Japan was the first East Asian country to have long passed its zenith and to have fallen back into something like a “high-income trap” for three decades. Japan had been stagnant for 20 years and was meanwhile overtaken by China as the world’s second-largest economy in 2010. By contrast, the other two countries are still in the process of catching up (particularly China), and as latecomers they can learn from Japan’s mistakes and try to avoid a similar HIT.

In 1991 onwards, Japan made the typical mistake of reacting to a crisis triggered by structural problems primarily with expansive macroeconomic policy (and neglecting/postponing necessary structural reforms). This led to the so-called two “lost decades” in which Japan fell behind the West/USA in terms of development (see end of Chap. 2). Public debt rose and rose; and the central bank’s balance sheet extension became larger and larger without really bringing the stagnation and deflationary tendencies under control. Perhaps worse was prevented, but at what a high cost; the recovery would probably have been quicker and at less cost if the structural reforms had been tackled sooner and in a more determined manner. This was the aim of Abe’s policy (Abenomics) with the three pillars (“arrows”) from 2012/3 onwards, although structural reforms also fell short under Abe, i.e. were repeatedly postponed or watered down.

Only after the Global Financial Crisis did this new policy emerge under Abe, in which monetary policy was to be supported by fiscal policy and structural reforms (the three pillars).[3] Knowing that structural reforms are the most important pillar, but that, on the other hand, the implementation of structural reforms takes time, the expansionary monetary and fiscal policies of the previous two decades were continued and even strengthened. However, the longer the structural reforms were/are delayed, the greater the negative side effects of an unrestrained expansionary macro policy, with which the Abe government actually only wanted to buy itself time until the structural reforms take effect.

Japan's development over the last three decades should be a warning for the other East Asian countries (and not only for them). If there is no timely proactive response to the challenges of structural change with appropriate measures (above all with structural reforms), the other countries will also be in danger of having to accept the Japanese path of a slide into an HIT and a relapse in the catching-up process. In this respect, it is important for the other countries to learn from Japan and not make the same mistakes.

As far as CHINA is concerned, China is a special case among the three countries considered. China is still the least advanced in the development process (still has to overcome MIT in a sustainable way). Moreover, China follows its own development path (supported by an authoritarian political system and a special mix of market and planned economy). For China, too, the structural side (and thus structural reforms) will be more important than the cyclical side (which has dominated the last 10 years) in the following years.

We have shown that many factors have simultaneously influenced or determined East Asia's development. These include not only the classic factors such as capital supply, labor supply and sectoral labor migration, and technical progress (through imitation or innovations) but also more fundamental, predominantly non-economic factors (so-called "deep determinants") such as institutions, culture, geography, environment and resources, openness (to trade, FDIs, offshoring and labor immigration from abroad). It would be too simplistic to say: institutions alone or in particular mattered, or culture was the all-dominant determinant of East Asian countries' success. Depending on the country and the time period, some of the factors/determinants have temporarily been more important than others as drivers of change/progress. However, it is generally true that only the interaction of the various direct and indirect (deeper) determinants determines a development process. In other words: the dynamic interdependence of individual factors and subsystems (economic, political, socio-cultural, technological, and ecological) matters.

The literature on this (on this interaction and dynamic interdependence) is still in its infancy. There is still a great need for research and discovery. Addressing this is one of the central future tasks of development and growth research. Just as the challenges described in Sect. 6.3 in Chap. 6 cannot be addressed and overcome unilaterally, the success of the East Asian countries cannot be explained

[3] The question was, which of the two macropillars, monetary policy or fiscal policy, should be the leading force, and how should the coordination problem between the two be solved.

one-dimensionally (only attributable to economic, only attributable to cultural or only to politico- or socio-institutional factors). It is the interaction that does it. This means that a lot of research is still waiting for the social sciences to (jointly) adequately explain the puzzle of the different development of countries and regions in different eras. So far, we have only scratched the surface, so to speak. But it is important to start on the right path.

We should keep in mind that this book was about practical convergence research. Why has East Asia mastered the convergence or catching-up process better and faster than most other regions (with the exception perhaps of Europe) in the last 50–70 years? Convergence research has developed rapidly (only) since the 1990s, but it is far from having reached its goal. While in the 1950s and 1960s, the Solow model (Solow 1956) dominated growth and development theory, with the implication that poor countries (assuming free access to technologies) must grow faster than (i.e. converge to) rich ones because they have a smaller capital stock and thus a higher marginal productivity of capital, a new (the one we know today) development research—with the possibility of explaining divergence as well—only began in the early 1990s with Barro's seminal paper (Barro 1991). This so-called New Growth Theory then also established what is standard today, the knowledge of conditional convergence and the explanation of the possibility of (development) divergence, and also broadened its perspective beyond purely economic factors. In the 2000s, a literature emerged that searched for "deeper determinants" and focused first on institutional determinants (driven mainly by the work of Acemoglu et al.) and later on cultural determinants (driven by the work of Guiso et al. 2006; Tabellini 2008; Alesina and Giuliano 2015 and others) and declared them to be the most important determinant(s).

As already mentioned, the interaction between all these determinants — the "deep determinants" (such as historical determination, institutional, cultural and other determinants such as geographical, environmental/resource bottlenecks) and proximate "classic" determinants (such as captial and labor) — is still not sufficiently explored. Depending on the country and the time period, all these factors interact differently (and to varying degrees), with one or the other factor dominating more strongly at times. It would be nice if we could map these interactions in a general theoretical model. However, it is difficult to set up such a comprehensive (dynamic) theory as an abstract/formal and at the same time manageable model, and to empirically test the correlations found there in a theory-based manner. Such a theory will have to remain very abstract and very complex. Nevertheless, the search for such a comprehensive theory (such a theoretical framework), in which the above-mentioned dynamic interdependence is taken into account, is eminently important for further development and growth research. Whether it will succeed is still uncertain. However, small-scale empirical work will continue to be decisive, but it needs an (abstract) theoretical foundation. All research, whether it likes it or not, is theory- and/or ideology-driven in terms of the choice of model, parameters, data, as well as the structure of the empirical research. It is important to make this open/transparent every time, that is what matters. A search for commonalities in the convergence process (convergence dynamics) of individual countries and regions, which was our starting point in this book, is important and useful. This also requires trying out new methods, such as club convergence at present, which seem promising (see e.g. Glawe and Wagner 2019, 2021). This applies to the application not only to East Asia but also to other regions.

References

Alesina A, Giuliano P (2015) Culture and institutions. J Econ Lit 53(4):898–944

Barro RJ (1991) Economic growth in a cross section of countries. Quart J Econ 106:407–444

Bolt J, van Zanden JL (2020) Maddison style estimates of the evolution of the world economy. A new 2020 update. https://www.rug.nl/ggdc/historicaldevelopment/maddison/releases/maddison-project-database-2020?lang=en

Glawe L, Wagner H (2019) The 'double trap' in China—multiple equilibria in institutions and income and their causal relationship. SSRN working paper 3719951. https://ssrn.com/abstract=3719951

Glawe L, Wagner H (2021) Convergence, divergence, or multiple steady states? New evidence on the institutional development within the European Union. J Comp Econ 49(3): 860–844. https://doi.org/10.1016/j.jce.2021.01.006

Guiso L, Sapienza P, Zingales L (2006) Does culture affect economic outcomes? J Econ Perspect 20(2):23–48

Solow R (1956) A contribution to the theory of economic growth. Quart J Econ 70:65–94

Tabellini G (2008) Institutions and culture. J Eur Econ Assoc 6(2–3):255–294

WTO (2021) International trade statistics. World Trade Organization, Geneva. https://data.wto.org/

CPSIA information can be obtained
at www.ICGtesting.com
Printed in the USA
LVHW081142070322
712805LV00003B/199

9 783030 871277